NATIONAL POST

Smart Funds 2000

A Fund Family Approach to Mutual Funds

JONATHAN CHEVREAU AND STEPHEN KANGAS, CFA
WITH SUSAN HEINRICH

KEY PORTER BOOKS

Canadian Cataloguing in Publication Data

Chevreau, Jonathan
Smart Funds 2000

6th ed.
Previous eds. Published under title: The Financial post smart funds.
ISBN: 1-55263-088-9

1. Mutual funds—Canada—Handbooks, manuals, etc. I. Kangas, Stephen. II. Heinrich, Susan. III. Title. IV. Title: Financial post smart funds.

HG5154.5.C46 1999 332.63'27 C99-931933-7

The Canada Council for the Arts since 1957 | Le Conseil des Arts du Canada depuis 1957

The publisher gratefully acknowledges the support of the Canada Council for the Arts and the Ontario Arts Council for its publishing program.

We acknowledge the financial support of the Government of Canada through the Book Publishing Industry Development Program (BPIDP) for our publishing activities.

Key Porter Books Limited
70 The Esplanade
Toronto, Ontario
Canada M5E 1R2

www.keyporter.com

Electronic formatting: Alissa Lee Communications Design Inc.

Printed and bound in Canada

99 00 01 02 03 04 6 5 4 3 2 1

Disclaimer: *Smart Funds 2000* contains the opinions and ideas of its authors. It is sold with the understanding that the authors and publisher are not engaged in rendering legal, accounting, investment or other professional services. If the reader requires expert financial or other assistance or legal advice, a competent professional should be consulted.

Many "Smart Funds" are equity funds investing in publicly traded stocks. Past performance is no guarantee of future results and neither the fund companies nor the authors can promise that a Smart Fund or Noteworthy Fund will not lose money under certain circumstances.

The authors and publisher therefore disclaim any responsibility for any liability, loss or risk incurred as a consequence of the use or application of any of the contents of this book.

Acknowledgements

The authors wish to thank all the talented people in the Canadian mutual fund industry, who were both prompt and patient in providing the detailed information that makes *Smart Funds* possible.

Jonathan Chevreau thanks his wife, Ruth, and daughter, Helen, for their loving support.

Stephen Kangas would like to thank his mother and father, for their encouragement throughout the years, and Catherine, Taylor and Nolan Ryan for their love and their unlimited patience with this project. Special thanks to Dom Rando, mutual fund analyst at CT Securities, for all his technical support.

Susan Heinrich would like to thank her family for their encouragement.

Contents

Preface to the Sixth Edition

This sixth edition of the annual *National Post* mutual fund guide—*Smart Funds 2000*—is a completely revised version of *Smart Funds 1999*. We again profile the 50 top fund families and provide in-depth snapshots of 100 Smart Funds. But because of the unique historical circumstance of the Year 2000 computer problem, or Y2K, we have departed in certain ways from the previous format.

Naturally, we asked all fund families for their views on Y2K, on how they believe it may affect asset allocation for individual investors, and on how stock pickers will use Y2K screens to assess risks in equity funds. Their responses appear under the heading Year 2000 Stance, immediately following the normal Fund Family overview.

Our introduction has been revised from previous years to summarize the Y2K climate as it relates to mutual funds.

Because of these concerns, we have retained and expanded the coverage begun in *Smart Funds 1999* of several major life insurance "segregated funds," which provide investors who are nervous about a possible stock market correction with some guarantees against loss. Thus, we have added coverage of firms such as London Life to a list that previously included Canada Life, Great-West Life, Standard Life, and the firm that ignited the trend to mutual fund/insurance alliances—Manulife Financial.

Y2K-concerned investors should also consider the many mutual fund companies that have seg fund versions, a list that now includes Investors Group, TD GreenLine, AIC, and Talvest, in addition to those mentioned in last year's edition: Trimark, Templeton, BPI, and C.I. We also look at the new Protected Funds from firms such as CIBC Securities Inc. and Dundee Mutual Funds, and related innovations in the high-net-worth market. Thus, we have added certain high-net-worth families that have "market-neutral" funds that can gain on both the long and short side, such as Montreal's @rgentum, and noted the introduction of new high-net-worth "protection" products at places such as CIBC Trust.

A radical revision of the structure for this year's edition was to divide the 100 Smart Funds into three, though not necessarily equal, camps. Lead author Jonathan Chevreau has long been bearish on Y2K, as reflected in a recent book he co-wrote with Stephen Gadsden: *Krash! Why Y2K Could Sink the Stock Market and What Canadians Can Do About It* (McGraw Hill, July 1999). We refer readers to that book for an explanation of how Y2K could be the pinprick that punctures the overvalued stock balloon.

But with three authors on *Smart Funds 2000*, we felt it important to reflect the only three possible views on Y2K investing:

1) It may be a trivial problem with no investment ramifications. This "Y2K OK" stance is the prevailing one on both Wall Street and Bay Street.
2) It may be an investing catastrophe for the stock market and equity mutual funds, as argued in *Krash!*
3) The truth may be somewhere between these two extremes.

Accordingly, we have divided the 100 Smart Funds and Noteworthy Funds into three camps:

1) **Y2K OK.**

Funds for those who believe that Y2K poses no great threat to capital markets. These we call our Y2K OK Funds. These funds are closest to our traditional equity-based Smart Funds and generally would benefit by ongoing prosperity and the continuance of the bull market. Note: Do not be confused and inadvertently believe that these funds are Y2K OK in the event of serious Y2K problems. They are OK only if Y2K turns out to be OK. See Y2K KO funds below for funds that we believe can withstand a true Y2K meltdown.

2) **Y2K KO.**

Funds for those who believe Y2K is a disaster, as in a "Knock Out" for the stock market. At their simplest, these would be money market or bond funds, gold funds, or balanced funds with seg fund guarantees. Special funds such as the @rgentum Market Neutral Portfolio are also included in this category.

3) **Y2K Agnostic.**
Funds for balanced investors who hold the middle ground. While not convinced that Y2K is as serious as some alarmists portray, they nevertheless want to hedge their bets in case the optimists have presented too rosy a picture. These would be classic balanced or asset-allocation funds, or conservative, value-oriented equity or dividend funds with a seg fund guarantee to preserve initial capital.

As in previous editions, Smart Funds are indicated with a blue star, plus the designation OK, KO, or AG, for Agnostic. Noteworthy funds are indicated with a black pyramid, followed by an OK, KO, or AG. All other funds that are offered in a family appear in black. Look then for a sea of blue stars and black pyramids in the matrices as indicators of the relative strength of fund families.

If the fund you're interested in is shown with a blue star, you'll find a full one-page analysis of that fund in the second half of the book. Use the index at the end to locate the particular fund. If the fund you're considering is shown with a black triangle, then a short comment on the fund is contained in the pages immediately following the matrix.

Generally, a "Noteworthy" fund is either potentially a future candidate for Smart Fund status, or a former Smart Fund whose circumstances have changed. Generally, they are other strong funds in a family we'd consider using to round out a portfolio. If you've selected a particular fund family and three of its Smart Funds as core funds, for example, the Noteworthy funds allow you to stay within that fund family and fill in niches such as small-cap, precious metals, and so on.

The co-authors are the same as last year: *Financial Post* mutual funds reporter Susan Heinrich, personal finance columnist Jonathan Chevreau, now in his sixth year on the project, and Stephen Kangas, who returns for his fifth year as co-author. Kangas is vice president of third-party mutual funds for Canada Trust.

Anyone contemplating purchase of a Smart Fund, or any other mutual fund, must be fully acquainted with the nature of risk. Ultimately, for investors, Y2K must be regarded as the joker in the investment pack that introduces an unknown level of risk. Many Smart Funds are load funds sold through brokers, dealers, or financial planners: obtain the advice and service that you are already paying for from these individuals. Discuss with them how some of these funds or fund families may meet your investment objectives; be clear about what volatility and risk mean and how any particular fund selection can lead to losing money.

Above all, understand that any given fund is unlikely to be a panacea for all that ails you financially. Some funds should not take up more than 5% or 10% of a total investment portfolio, although conservative balanced or dividend growth funds can account for a far larger portion of your wealth. That's why it's critical that the choice of any fund be placed in a broader context of asset allocation, preferably conducted with a professional financial advisor.

In the segment on asset allocation, we've retained the authors' philosophy of choosing two or three core fund families, an approach that—as it turns out—can also be used to reposition or protect portfolios against Y2K threats, either real or imagined. We continue to emphasize our belief that diversification across asset classes, geographical areas, and management styles is the best protection against market volatility—Y2K-induced or otherwise.

To repeat: equity mutual funds—and even bond funds—can decrease in value and should be bought with an understanding of the associated risks. Accordingly, the full page devoted to each Smart Fund includes important measures of associated risks. If you do not feel comfortable with the risk level of a particular fund, do not invest in it. Find a more conservative fund that is more suited to your investment personality, or be willing to pay the insurance premium for seg funds or their equivalents.

Whether or not markets correct in a *fin de siècle* sell-off, remember that in the longer term, most projections are for stock markets that are higher than today's (Dow 11,000; TSE 7,000 as we write in mid-summer 1999). The demographic wave of baby boomers saving frantically for retirement, in the opinion of authors such as Harry Dent Jr. (*The Roaring 2000s*), means the Dow will hit 41,000 by 2008. If so, then any short-term Y2K-related sell-off will mean the proverbial buying opportunity of the century. A glance through the "Year 2000 stance" entries in each fund family reveals the intention by money managers to scoop up stocks at bargains should a merely psychological sell-off materialize. For example, @rgentum expects a "relief rally" early in 2000, one that investors will be able to enjoy only if they are partly or fully invested in stocks and/or equity mutual funds.

Therefore, the underlying premise in earlier editions of *Smart Funds* still holds true: own equities or equity funds for the long term, diversify your holdings, and choose your holdings from the best fund companies and managers available.

Many *Smart Funds* readers who have been with us from the outset may find that they have done so well in the bull market that they now have a significant amount of money in mutual funds. As part of the fund family overviews, we have tried to identify so-called "high-net-worth" products and services that complement the group's mutual fund products. A glance at the revised section on CIBC Securities Inc. reveals how more and more fund companies or their sister firms (CIBC Trust in the above case) are targeting affluent baby boomers who are just on the cusp of achieving real wealth (defined as $100,000 in investable financial assets).

Many of these products are mutual fund–like products, such as pooled funds ($150,000 minimum, sold without a prospectus), or "wrap programs," which include portfolios of mutual funds. While open-end retail mutual funds are appropriate for many investors, both young and old, they are not necessarily the only investment alternative available. Fee-conscious high-net-worth investors and those who are prepared to do more legwork may wish to investigate a companion volume also published by the *National Post* and Key Porter Books in 1998: *The Wealthy Boomer: Life After Mutual Funds.*

How to Use This Book

Smart Funds 2000 is organized into three parts.

The first part, extensively revised from previous editions, features an overview of the Y2K situation and various views on how it may affect mutual fund investors.

The largest part of this book is devoted to the major mutual fund families in Canada and the best individual funds, which we call Smart Funds, most of which are sold by the families profiled.

You'll find profiles of the top 50 fund families, arranged alphabetically. A fund matrix at the beginning of each fund family shows at a glance which core and specialty funds it offers. It's arranged so that all Canadian funds are in the top half of the matrix; all international funds are in the bottom half.

BLUE STAR ★ = Smart Fund. Refer to index at end to find the page the Smart Fund is on. Think of it as a Buy recommendation.

BLACK TRIANGLE ▲ = Noteworthy Fund. This indicates a fund that may one day be a Smart Fund but we have certain reservations about it. Depending on your other fund selections, it may still be an appropriate investment. A short comment on the fund follows immediately after the matrix. Think of it as a Hold recommendation.

BLACK SQUARE ■ = Available. This indicates only that the fund family has a fund in a particular category, such as Far East or Precious Metals. It may be an average or below-average fund, and occasionally even above average in performance, but the authors did not feel the fund possesses the investment characteristics to merit a Smart Fund or Noteworthy designation.

Following those three symbols are three Y2K ratings: OK, KO, or AG.

OK = Fund should perform well if Y2K is a non-event and the bull market continues.

KO = Fund may preserve capital if Y2K is serious and causes the stock market to fall significantly.

AG = Middle-of-the-road, "agnostic" stance on Y2K and the markets.

Examples:

★ OK = A Smart Fund that will do fine if Y2K passes uneventfully.

▲ KO = A Noteworthy Fund that should preserve capital if Y2K turns out to be more serious than expected.

★ AG = A Smart Fund for cautious bulls who are unsure about Y2K's impact.

Finally, we list the 100 Smart Funds in the third part of the book. These are mutual funds selected by the authors from the almost 2,000 funds available in Canada. Each listing contains comments on the fund and its manager, measures of the fund's risk, the portfolio's asset allocation as well as cumulative and year-over-year performance data going back 10 years. The graph illustrates the growth of a $1,000 investment in the fund, the appropriate benchmark, and Canada Savings Bonds. You will also find the fund's quartile ranking, which shows how well the fund has performed relative to other funds in the same category, both on a CAGR basis and on a calendar-year basis.

Clearly, choosing fund families with several Smart Funds should increase the odds of creating a high-performance portfolio. We expect that readers, using this guide as a reference, will flip back and forth between the fund families and the Smart Funds, narrowing down first their choice of major fund families and then choosing the most appropriate Smart Funds within each.

INTRODUCTION

A Fund Family Approach to the Y2K Problem

Since the second edition (in 1996), these annual mutual fund guides have been entitled *Smart Funds: A Fund Family Approach to Mutual Funds.* This annual section has been extensively revised for this edition in favour of an analysis of the Y2K problem.

Interestingly, the same fund family approach also holds up for Y2K, regardless of whether you believe the Year 2000 computer crisis is trivial, apocalyptic, or somewhere in between. Just as different fund families have markedly different views of capital markets, so too is there a wide range of opinion on the possible severity of Y2K. The bear's case is presented in *Krash!*, as above (see page viii), or by Deutsche Bank's Edward Yardeni on his web site (www.yardeni.com), and by Y2K web sites like Y2Knewswire (www.y2knewswire.com) and Westergaard (www.westergaard.com). Because much could change in Y2K developments between the time this book was submitted for publication and the actual century change, we suggest that readers bookmark and monitor these sites. For an overview of technological problems and progress, refer to Y2K gurus who have been computer programmers—notably Peter de Jager (www.year2000.com), Karl Feilder (www.gmt-uta.com), and Edward Yourdon (www.yourdon.com).

For the Y2K OK argument, most brokerage reports on Bay Street and Wall Street tend to view Y2K lightly. Putting aside the fact that brokerage "buy" recommendations now outnumber "sells" by something like ten to one, and that such investment disasters as Bre-X Minerals Ltd. escaped their fraud-detectors, we will present some of their views. For example, J.P. Morgan Securities Inc. issued a Y2K Update, *January 1, 2000: Ready or Not!* in February 1999. It concluded:

i) In our judgement, significant investment by industry and government makes major Y2K-caused disruption in the United States unlikely.
ii) The results of our survey paint a modestly positive picture for the United States critical infrastructure sectors (energy, telecommunications, financial services, transportation, and health care).
iii) J.P. Morgan's economists do not envision Y2K as a truly important economic theme in the next 24 months.
iv) Our market forecast envisions no major shift in demand for stocks caused by Y2K.

On the other hand, a Canadian brokerage report published in 1998 by C.M. Oliver—*Year 2000: Are You Ready?*—was more sober and suggested that investors review their stock portfolios and mutual funds to determine whether they are Year 2000 compliant.

In soliciting material for *Smart Funds 2000*, we specifically requested each fund family's views on how the century end will affect global stock markets and their view of how investors might recast their asset allocation to reflect their concerns.

Some Canadian fund families seem to take Y2K seriously: for example, CIBC Securities Inc., its sister firm Talvest Fund Management, and C.I. Mutual Funds. In our fund family treatments we have appended each family's Year 2000 stance after our normal overview section, immediately prior to the Noteworthy sections.

We find the following statement from the world's largest mutual fund company, Fidelity Investments, instructive in its brevity and dismissal of the problem. It is so succinct that we reproduce it here in its entirety:

> Fidelity knows that the Year 2000 is an issue not only for financial services companies, but also for the portfolio companies in which mutual funds invest. As a mutual fund company, Fidelity's overriding obligation is to maximize shareholder value for its investors, consistent with the investment objectives of the funds. Fidelity continues to use a bottom-up approach in its research. Our portfolio managers and research analysts seek to identify and evaluate all facts about a company that may have an impact on the value of a company. Our analysts and fund managers have been briefed on the Year 2000 issue and equipped with appropri-

ate questions to ask senior management of these companies. The information on Year 2000 that we receive is only one piece in the mosaic of information we consider in making investment decisions.

One should not be surprised by such bafflegab. As the world's largest mutual fund company, any substantive negative statement about Y2K by Fidelity would be enough to crash an already overvalued stock market.

But several Canadian money managers are surprisingly frank about the issue. Contrast the Fidelity statement with CIBC/TAL's far longer statement, only some of which is reproduced here (for more details, see the respective fund families). Right up front, TAL acknowledges what it calls the "gravity of the situation." Like Fidelity, it says that it views Y2K as only "one of many issues that will drive capital market returns over the course of the next 12 to 18 months." But unlike many fund companies that are publicly ducking the issue, TAL went public in May 1999 with the announcement that it was withdrawing from emerging markets investments because of its poor record on Y2K fixes.

Further, in a road tour in June and July conducted by TAL and CIBC Trust's Wealth Management arm, TAL revealed that it viewed the chances of a stock market correction at 50% in part because of Y2K, adding that it assigned only a 2% chance of a depression and a 5% chance of a bear market. TAL did say that it disagrees with Ed Yardeni's estimate of a 70% chance of a Y2K-induced global recession. On the other hand, it recognizes that many investors will seek some comfort just in case. Thus, in August 1999, CIBC Trust announced that a "segregated fund"–style "protection" program would be available for its Professional Investment Management Services (PIMS) clients. Clients with at least $100,000 in either the actively managed Professional Portfolio Services or the passively managed Index Portfolio Services could purchase a 10-year guarantee that could be turned on and later switched off. They could, it suggested, do so in the run-up to 2000 in order to secure some peace of mind, then dispense with it later if the fuss turned out to be unjustified. This program was later suspended, which suggests the reinsurance costs in advance of Y2K may have grown prohibitive.

Glance through the "Year 2000 stance" statements throughout this book and you'll see a combination of happy talk and more cautious disclaimers, some of them virtually written in code. AGF, for example, warns that "in part because of the uncertainty surrounding third-party Year 2000 readiness and notwithstanding the steps taken by AGF, there can be no assurance that AGF's business operations will not be materially and adversely impacted." What you see here are lawyers at work, trying to cover their backsides with "we told you so" just in case Y2K turns out to be a bigger problem after all.

Many fund companies quite appropriately counsel that investors seek balance and the traditional diversification of asset classes and geographies. While various financial planners, such as The Equion Group's Wayne Lang and Stephen Gadsden and Peer Financial's Ralph Burgess in Calgary, have advocated a retrenchment from pure equity funds to balanced, bond, or money market funds, it's rare to get such suggestions from the fund companies themselves. Here again, TAL was the most refreshingly candid when it suggested that any investor truly concerned about the problem emphasize cash or bonds over stocks.

What seems to be missing in the general discussion is a comprehensive analysis of the risk inherent in the stock market and equity mutual funds, which have been the rocket fuel of the mutual fund industry's phenomenal growth.

As Y2K expert Karl Feilder (chairman of UK-based Greenwich Meantime) writes in the foreword to *Krash!*, Y2K is about risk assessment, *not* compliance. Earlier editions of *Smart Funds* have always favoured equity funds. As we have written, "Although investing in equities can increase your return over time, it does mean taking on more risk." We discussed how most people still define investment risk as losing principal, but that an equally concerning risk was of not having enough money in the future to support themselves as their capital is eroded by inflation and taxes.

Over the long run, equity—or common—stocks may indeed be the only asset that will keep up with inflation and provide the kind of returns necessary to meet the retirement goals of Canadian investors. We will write those words again in future editions but for the balance of 1999 and throughout the Year 2000—what Edward Yourdon (author of *Time Bomb 2000*) terms the "year of living dangerously"—we return to the traditional Main Street view of risk: that of losing principal.

We are concerned that too many investors have automatically placed themselves in the super-aggressive 100% equity camp in the belief that there is no longer stock market risk, or worse, leveraged themselves to the hilt in the belief that markets will only rise. If nothing else, Y2K should give such investors pause to seriously consider how they would truly feel and behave if there were a market decline of 15%, 30%, or even 45%. Y2K is about risk assessment, including an assessment of your own true personal tolerance for risk. That much-cited "tummy test" of financial planners should be your guide here.

Anyone who views themselves as a Y2K Agnostic and is at least willing to consider the Y2K KO argument, must ask themselves how much principal they are willing to risk in return for a few more months of gains in late 1999 and early 2000. Given the historic highs reached when the Dow Jones Industrial Average touched 11,000 in the first half of 1999, one could argue that the combination of such overvalued markets and the risk of the certain century change does not add up to a favourable risk/reward ratio.

As *Krash!* explains in detail, the true risks that Y2K poses are to equity funds in emerging markets, including Asian and Latin American funds. North America is considered by TAL to be a "Y2K-safe" zone, which would bode well for equity funds in the United States and Canada if Y2K turns out to be benign. Because Canadian markets never became as overvalued as the American markets, there is perhaps slightly less downside to Canadian equities. Also, Canadian equity funds would benefit from a rise in gold, as occurred in late September.

In previous years, we have portrayed European equity funds as the next best thing to North American markets. But they pose a little more risk in a Y2K environment because so much of Europe focused its computer maintenance attention on the Euro conversion project rather than Y2K. In fact, Karl Feilder says he is amazed by the complacency that much of Europe demonstrates over Y2K.

If you accept the premise that North America is Y2K OK, then by definition EAFE (Europe/Australia, Far East) funds carry a somewhat greater level of risk. Generally, fund companies call their non–North American equity funds "international" funds, and reserve the term "global" for truly all-global equity funds, which include North America. Given this, we would favour global funds over international funds.

If you glance at our Y2K KO and Y2K Agnostic picks, you will see many alternatives to pure equity funds: global and Canadian balanced funds, tactical asset allocation funds, global bond and Canadian bond funds, even the humble money market funds.

For those who wish to remain partially or fully invested, we see two main hedges: using segregated funds for pure equity funds, or balanced funds of the non-segregated variety. For double peace of mind, balanced segregated funds would provide both asset diversification as well as a market guarantee of initial principal.

The ultimate Y2K KO fund is, of course, a money market fund. We will encounter criticism here because switches to money market funds amount to nothing less than market timing. As we note in our treatment of asset allocation, below, we generally counsel long-term strategic asset allocation rather than the market-timing-oriented tactical asset allocation approach. Clearly, some readers may decide that Y2K is enough of a potential spanner in the works of the markets to justify some degree of market timing.

The subtitle of *Smart Funds 2000* is a variant on previous years: *A Fund Family Approach to the Y2K Problem.* It turns out that our previous philosophy of holding two or three fund families—a strong Canadian family, a strong international family, and a specialty family—is also valid within the Y2K context.

You could, for example, decide that because Canada is well positioned for Y2K and that its markets are less overvalued, you will choose a Canadian-oriented fund family with no seg fund guarantees but which emphasizes low MERs, possibly through strong index offerings. You could then take the view that seg or other guarantees are necessary for the Y2K-riskier global markets and for the overvalued U.S. stock market, and choose a second fund family on that basis. And the third fund family might be a specialty group, such as @rgentum and its market neutral approach, or the many families that provide 100% RRSP-eligible foreign funds.

Let's recap the five main steps on deciding on core fund families, but with a Y2K perspective in mind.

1. Determine your optimum asset allocation.

Still the critical step. You must decide what percentage of your portfolio should be in each of the major asset classes—equity (funds invested in the stock market, both domestic and foreign), fixed income (bond and mortgage funds), and cash (money market funds). With Y2K, you spend a little more thought contemplating how much volatility you can really stomach and then choose your stock exposure accordingly.

If your goal is long-term growth, for instance, and you can stand a little volatility along the way, then equity funds should comprise the largest portion of your portfolio, particularly if you think Y2K will be a non-event. You may even keep some cash handy to snap up bargains if the psychological sell-off occurs.

If, on the other hand, you're nearing retirement age and/or want your investments to generate income, you may choose to put most of your portfolio into fixed-income funds. The traditional range for the equity portion of a portfolio is 25% to 75%, as established by Benjamin Graham, author of the classic investment text *The Intelligent Investor* (Harper & Row, New York, 1973, 4th ed.). To decide where you fall within that range, you can use a rule of thumb suggested by many advisors, which is to make the fixed-income allotment equal to your age. That is, a typical 40-year-old would have 40% fixed income and

60% equities. If you are a little more aggressive, equities might rise to 65% or 70%; if you are on the cautious side, fixed income might rise to 45% or 50%. You may also have a small cash component, either because you need some money in the short term for another purpose, or because you haven't yet committed it to a specific investment. It's usually more convenient if you use a money market fund or funds from your core families to hold any cash.

If you're uncertain how to divide your portfolio, you can use balanced funds, asset allocation funds, or asset allocation services—in which case one or more fund managers will make this decision for you. Asset allocation services, such as Mackenzie's STAR, Bank of Montreal's MatchMaker, or Canada Trust's Investment Planner Plus, each of which has over $2 billion of investors assets in them, and many others, provide questionnaires that assess your personal financial situation and suggest the best asset mix. Many investors may find the convenience of the new fund of funds products such as TD Bank's Managed Asset Program (MAP) or Canada Trust's Investment Portfolios attractive. Or, you can rely on a professional investment advisor to make this recommendation.

2. Pick a core Canadian fund family.

Once you've got your asset allocation sorted out, you're ready to choose your first core fund family—your core Canadian-content fund family.

Why? About half of all mutual fund dollars are invested in RRSPs. Since equity funds offer the best chance of growth and protection against inflation, and the federal government requires pensions and RRSPs to be 80% Canadian content, Canadian equity funds are naturally more popular than foreign equity funds. The top half of the fund matrices that begin each fund family profile show at a glance the Canadian funds available in each family.

Your core Canadian family should also be strong in fixed-income products, since they'll also be an important part of your overall portfolio (and are subject to the same Canadian content rules).

Note: If you have investments outside your RRSP, be sure to arrange your holdings so fixed-income funds—which are 100% taxable–are held inside your RRSP, and equity funds—which generate capital gains that are taxed at a more favourable rate—are held outside your RRSP in order to make use of the dividend tax credit, which reduces the tax payable on dividends from Canadian companies.

While there is much talk about eliminating the 20% foreign-content rule, and more and more fund companies are introducing products that allow investors to skirt the guidelines, the authors believe that Canada is among the best-positioned countries for Y2K. Our banks had an early start on remediation and the rest of the financial services industry appears to have the problem well in hand. In addition, the Canadian market never became as overvalued as the U.S. market, so in the event of a correction, there is less distance to fall. Finally, while gold has been a terrible investment in recent years, there is a school of thought that at its current 20-year lows, bullion has bottomed and could rise if a Y2K economic crisis is sparked. Such an event would help the gold portion of the TSE and investors holding gold or precious-metals mutual funds. We saw an apparent rebirth of gold in September.

3. Choose a core international fund family.

As the fund matrices show, many fund families are strong domestically, many are strong internationally, but only a handful are strong in both.

If your core Canadian fund family is not also a strong international player, ensure that your second core family has a strong global emphasis. That way, you can select funds for the 20% foreign-content portion of your RRSP as well as for your taxable (open or outside RRSP) portfolio. The bottom half of the fund matrices list the international funds offered by a family.

Outside your RRSP, of course, you can invest as much as you want in global equities or bonds. Inside your RRSP, you or your advisor will have to decide whether maximizing foreign content is your main goal. If 20% is enough, almost any fund family will do, provided that it qualifies on other criteria. But you can have as much as 36% of your RRSP in foreign content if you include Canadian funds that invest the permitted 20% of their portfolios in foreign equity.

And, finally, if your belief in Canada is so shaky that you want to fill your RRSP with 100% non-Canadian product, look for internationally oriented fund families that offer 100% RRSP-eligible bond funds, equity funds, or balanced funds that are invested in foreign products through derivative-based strategies.

In the fund matrices, under the heading "RRSP/Foreign," "RRSP" indicates that a fund can be held in an RRSP without using any of the 20% foreign-content limit, even if it appears to be a foreign fund. The entry "Foreign" indicates that a fund must be counted as part of that valuable foreign-content portion.

From a Y2K point of view, remember TAL's decision to avoid emerging markets, which could include much of Asia and Latin

America. If you believe that North America is Y2K OK, then you could argue that EAFE (Europe/Australia/Far East) funds that are not invested in North American securities may be at greater risk to Y2K.

Investors will need to examine "all-global" equity funds for their relative exposure to Y2K OK and Y2K-risky geographical areas. If they are Y2K Agnostics, they may decide that the extra insurance protection of seg funds and similar products are worth it for global equity funds and regional funds in Europe and the Far East.

4. Diversify your management styles with complementary families or funds.

Step 1 diversifies your portfolio among asset classes. Steps 2 and 3 diversify your holdings by geographical area. The next step is to diversify by management style.

No single fund family is perfect. One may have most fund types, for instance, but perhaps not all those funds are winners. But there's no point choosing similar funds from more than one family—for instance, more than one Canadian equity fund—unless they're complementary, or, to use the fund industry's jargon, "non-correlated"; that is, their performance fluctuates in different directions at the same time. The idea is to find pairs of funds in which one zigs when the other zags, so that overall performance is less volatile.

This is why it may make sense to choose a third fund family to supplement your core Canadian and core international families. Then pick from these three families at least two funds for each of your Canadian and international allotment: one a value investment style, the other a more aggressive growth style. Generally, growth funds are invested in large-cap growth companies that perform best when the economy is growing rapidly or tending toward inflation, while value funds tend to emphasize out-of-favour blue chips that will outperform at the end of a recession and during an economic recovery. We would view value funds as somewhat more resilient to a Y2K-triggered correction.

5. Round out your portfolio with some specialty funds.

Once you've chosen your core fund families, consider specialty funds. These higher-risk, higher-reward funds are usually volatile and should be restricted to no more than 5% or 10% of your portfolio. They include precious metals (particularly if you're a Y2K KO investor) and the new technology or e-commerce funds (if you're in the Y2K OK camp).

HOW TO USE THE FUND FAMILY SECTION AND THE FUND MATRICES

Applying the fund family approach will be easier once you've studied the fund families. Representing more than half of the content of this book, it presents 50 major Canadian fund families, arranged alphabetically.

Once you have selected, say, three core fund families, the next step is choosing individual funds from these families. Leading off each fund family profile entry is a "fund matrix" that shows at a glance all the Canadian and international funds available from any given fund group.

If one of the matrix entries shows a Smart Fund (indicated by a blue star), you'll find an analysis of that fund in the Smart Funds section in the second half of the book, and an index at the very end to direct you to the appropriate page. It presents 100 funds ranked as the best in their class, with consideration given to the potential Y2K problem.

A second category is Noteworthy funds, indicated with a black triangle, which are commented upon in text immediately following the fund family Overview. Because there are so few Smart Funds compared with the almost 2,000 funds that are available, and because some fund families have relatively few Smart Funds, we've decided to include a few hundred other funds worthy of investor consideration. We call this secondary list the "B team." We believe that if you have narrowed your choice to two fund families, each having several Smart Funds, this "B team" provides other good funds, many of them first quartile (that is, among the top 25% in investment performance), that weren't selected as Smart Funds but can nevertheless be used to round out a fund portfolio.

MARKET TIMING VS. STRATEGIC ASSET ALLOCATION

Many of our Smart Funds are equity funds, because we believe they offer the best prospects for long-term growth. But that doesn't mean we think an investor should be invested in equities only, particularly in these turbulent times of record high North American stock markets, volatile gold prices, and of course the Y2K problem. Equities go up and down. And while nobody complains about the ups, the downs sometimes test even the most dedicated investor.

The answer—in late 1999 and early 2000—is more than ever to diversify your fund portfolio among the major asset classes: stocks, bonds, and cash and, in some portfolios, gold or precious metals, real estate, and perhaps even futures or derivatives. This diversification should be achieved through the use of a strategy called asset allocation, which is simply the process of choosing a combination of investments that will achieve your financial goals with an accepted level of risk.

The power of asset allocation is that it establishes a framework within which all your investments are made. An appropriate mix of cash, bonds, and equities in an investment portfolio will increase your return and decrease risk. This simple strategy can be enhanced by adding international bonds and stocks to the portfolio and by seeking out alternative money management styles—options made available through mutual funds to even the most modest investor.

Not only can you diversify into different asset classes, but now asset allocation services are available that try to identify the most optimal or efficient (in terms of risk versus reward) combination for each individual investor.

Asset allocation protects investors from their two worst enemies: themselves and media hype. It's not the same as market timing, which so many investors think is a "magic bullet" against risk and loss. The plaintive cry of those naive individuals typically goes like this: "I need to find somebody or something to tell me which funds will go up, which ones will go down, and when it's best to simply be in cash!"

For some professionals, market timing is a practised science but most are lazy about it. Without bothering to learn or practise a disciplined approach to investing, they try to convince themselves that they can "make the perfect calls."

The authors of this book are skeptical about market timing. Even moving out of the market because of Y2K could prove to be a mistake. The reality is that, for most people, investing and following the markets are immensely challenging chores. It's difficult and time-consuming to learn and to keep up with the professionals. Finding the time to plan an investment strategy, to achieve short-, medium-, and long-term goals, determine the best way to execute a plan, and regularly monitor its success is a daunting task. Most people are just too busy. As a result, too many put off the need to plan, execute, and maintain an appropriate investment strategy.

Asset allocation, on the other hand, is not a fad. There is a strong foundation for the principles of asset allocation. The most often-cited research in this area is "Determinants of Portfolio Performance" (*Financial Analysts Journal*, July–August 1986, pp. 39–44), a study conducted in 1986 by three investment practitioners: Gary P. Brinson, L. Randolph Hood, and Gilbert Beebower. The authors examined the returns of 91 large U.S. pension plans for the period 1974–1983. They examined the variation in quarterly returns over that 10-year period and determined the following:

- On average, 93.6% of the total variation in the actual plans' return was explained by the investment policy (asset mix) alone.
- Market timing, when combined with investment policy, "added modestly to the explained variance." It raised it to 95.3%. Adding the selection of individual stocks accounted for 97.8% of the variance.

This study, which was updated in 1991, shows that the emphasis must be on selecting the right asset mix and sticking with it. Clearly, asset allocation is important; in fact, it's more important than choosing the right stocks.

MODERN PORTFOLIO THEORY AND THE NOBEL PRIZE

Behind the concept of asset allocation is years of work by two prominent professors: Harry Markowitz and William Sharpe. Beginning in the mid-1950s, they developed the hypothesis that became known as Modern Portfolio Theory, which examines the correlation of assets. Their work was recognized with the Nobel Memorial Prize for Economics in 1990.

When the values of two assets fluctuate in the same direction at the same time, they are said to be "correlated." The degree to which they are "correlated" can be measured mathematically. If two assets have a correlation measure equal to one, the values will fluctuate by exactly the same amount at exactly the same time. If you own these two assets, you have not helped your portfolio. You would do just as well or poorly by owning either one.

If you combine assets that are non-correlated (those that have a correlation measure of less than one), you have diversified your portfolio. More importantly, by using this approach, you can add riskier (and potentially more rewarding) assets to your portfolio and still lower the overall risk of your combined assets. In theory you can do this until your portfolio is "optimized"—that is, it combines the highest potential reward with the lowest potential risk.

Computer programs analyze past returns of asset classes (using benchmarks, such as the TSE 300 composite index for Canadian equities) and calculate correlation measures in order to combine assets into an "optimal" or "efficient" portfolio. Given the almost infinite number of possible combinations of risk and return preferences, an almost infinite number of portfolios can be generated. Plotting all these portfolios on a graph of risk and return produces a line known as the efficient frontier.

ILLUSTRATION OF AN EFFICIENT FRONTIER

On this graph, point A is usually representative of a portfolio consisting entirely of T-Bills and point B, a portfolio entirely of equities. People who have never seen this graph are often surprised by its shape. It clearly shows that if their portfolio is at point A, they can move all the way up to point C (increase their return) without taking any more risk. This movement would be accomplished by the addition of a combination of bonds and stocks. Even more significant is the fact they can move to any point on the frontier between A and C and both increase their return and decrease their risk.

While the concept of the efficient frontier is appealing, the question remains, "How do I get on the curve?" And, more importantly, "Where on the curve is the best place for me?"

Determining the exact answers to these questions is a difficult task. The efficient frontier is, after all, a theory. Computers generate efficient frontiers using historical data (that is, past performance), and expected returns based on forecast data. In practice, the efficient frontier is a moving target wholly dependent on the data fed into a computer. Indeed: "The sensitivity analysis we performed with optimizations… should convince anyone that the output is indeed very sensitive to minor changes in the input variables," wrote Roger C. Gibson in *Asset Allocation—Balancing Financial Risk* (Irwin Professional Publishing, 1990, p. 176).

The more appropriate task for individual investors should be to try to get as close to the optimal portfolio. There are two ways to do that: strategic and tactical asset allocation. Strategic asset allocation defines the appropriate limits of each asset class for a type of portfolio

An Efficient Frontier

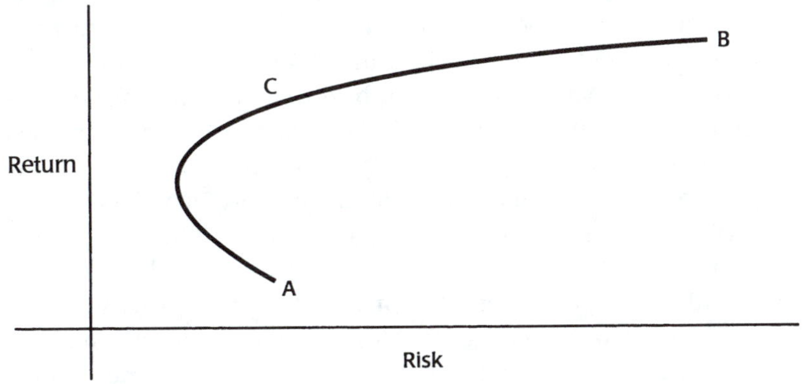

and sticks with those limits regardless of market conditions. Tactical asset allocation focuses more on market conditions and varies the proportions of each asset class in an effort to have more of the portfolio in any class that appears ready to outperform the others. In other words, TAA is a form of market timing.

STRATEGIC ASSET ALLOCATION (SAA)

The simplest form of strategic asset allocation is a fixed balanced fund. Such funds have restricted limits on how much can be invested in equities and fixed income. A neutral stance is 50% of each asset class, with limits for each typically 40% to 60%. That means that even if a fund manager believes that equities will outperform bonds, she could never invest more than 60% of the portfolio in equities or, vice versa, less than 40% even if she believes the market is due for a correction. (A variation of this is a "fund of funds" in which a fund company pools two or more of its funds, say one equity fund and one bond fund, to create a balanced portfolio with stringent allocation allowances.)

Examples of fixed balanced funds are:

- Altamira Balanced
- Royal Balanced
- Saxon Balanced
- Trimark Income Growth
- Universal Balanced Fund

Recently, the mutual fund industry began recommending personalized portfolios of mutual funds with different investment objectives, with the mix of funds based on investor responses to questionnaires. The idea behind these questionnaire-driven services is that personal asset allocation depends on four factors: objectives, time horizon, ability to tolerate risk, and financial situation.

A number of SAA services exist, based on a similar process. A questionnaire is given to assess these factors, and the resulting score identifies the investor as a particular type (income, balanced, growth, and so on). An investor with a maximum income profile will be matched with a portfolio that is heavily, if not entirely, invested in fixed income. The maximum growth investor, on the other hand, will be shown a portfolio with a substantial equity portion. And there are any number of variations in between—for example, emerging market funds have a place in a growth portfolio, but not in a maximum income portfolio.

The mix, once allocated, does not change unless the investor's profile changes (for example, through job loss, approaching retirement, or inheritance). The portfolio is rebalanced periodically, however, to maintain the initial allocation if one asset group does particularly well relative to the rest.

TACTICAL ASSET ALLOCATION (TAA)

Tactical asset allocation is a form of market timing. These types of services or mutual funds offer the small investor a one-stop investment vehicle that:

1) Tries to overweight whichever asset class is deemed by the manager to be undervalued and likely to outperform over the near term; and

2) Avoids market downturns by moving to safer assets before one occurs.

The following are the more prominent TAA funds available in Canada:

- Dynamic Partners Fund
- Fidelity Canadian Asset Allocation Fund
- First Canadian Asset Allocation Fund
- AGF Canadian Tactical Asset Allocation Fund
- Investors Asset Allocation Fund
- Universal World Asset Allocation Fund

The performance of most of these funds is, so far, merely average. That's because even the most sophisticated models, coupled with highly experienced managers, are up against big odds of not getting it right. And, as we saw earlier, missed opportunities can have a significant effect on portfolio return.

The other problem with tactical asset allocation funds is they are not tailored to the individual investor. The manager's market calls might be too aggressive for some investors, at other times not aggressive enough. For most investors, the alternative—strategic asset allocation—is more appropriate.

Money Manager Profiles

CATHERINE (KIKI) DELANEY—TRIMARK INVESTMENT MANAGEMENT INC.

Kiki Delaney is the first to admit that the behaviour of stock markets in recent years has challenged the convictions of value-style money managers. She has always believed that picking stocks with a value style—buying stocks that are cheap relative to their potential worth—is the best way to manage money. And she is adamant that good stock pickers will beat market indices over the long term. But both of those philosophies have been put to the test.

"Value investing has been difficult for a couple of years," she explains. "You can see that both in the U.S. and Canada. In the U.S., the more expensive stocks just got more and more expensive and it didn't seem to matter."

And because the rise in stock markets was narrowly focused among a handful of hot stocks, few professional managers could keep pace with markets in Canada or the U.S. "Last year you could have just bought BCE and Nortel and gone to the beach," Delaney jokes.

Value investing seemed almost naive in markets where novice investors could watch their fortune rise in a couple of Internet stocks and beat the pros. In fact, it was enough to cause some managers to change their strategy mid-stream; however, Delaney stuck to the approach she has used for more than 20 years as a money manager. "For starters I believe that value rules long-term," she says, because historically stocks picked that way perform better than growth-type stocks. And logically she cannot see how buying high-flying stocks makes sense as a long-term strategy. "How can you do well when you buy something that sells at 50 times (earnings) and it has a 10% growth rate. Ultimately how can you keep winning year after year?"

As confident as she is in her money management style, she admits that her decision in early 1999 to end the relationship between her Toronto firm, C.A. Delaney Capital Management Ltd., and Spectrum United Mutual Funds Inc., was a tough one. Having held only three jobs throughout her career as a money manager, she wasn't anxious to make a change. "It wasn't an easy thing to make that move. I lost a lot of sleep over it," she admits. When she finally made the decision to work instead with Trimark Investment Management Inc. to manage two new funds, she was sure it was the right one. Ultimately the opportunity to work with Trimark chairman Robert Krembil and the other portfolio managers was "compelling," she says. And she was not concerned about the performance troubles that Trimark had in some of its funds. "Every manager has a bad year," she says.

Delaney founded C.A. Delaney Capital Management Ltd. in 1992. Prior to that she was a partner and executive vice president of Gluskin Sheff & Associates. She began her career in 1972 as an analyst with Guardian Capital Investment Counsel.

She says her years of experience give her needed perspective in the kind of unusual markets we've seen. Take Y2K, for example. Delaney falls into the "not too concerned" camp. "What really de-stabilizes a market is something that comes out of left field," she says. "It [Y2K] has been so well telegraphed for such a period of time and there's been so much money spent on it that I can't believe it is going to alter the world as we know it."

That is not to say there won't be some Y2K bumps. "I think that there are going to be problems. There are going to be companies that have problems, there are going to be countries that have problems." She adds, "I think economically it could have an effect, you could see a boost in the GDP in the fourth quarter [of 1999] and a taking away from the GDP in the first quarter [of 2000]."

But as a money manager investing in Canada, she is confident that most companies are Y2K ready. "If I were sitting in Asia, I'd probably be quite a bit more alarmed. But I think North America—and particularly the large companies—has given it the time and attention."

Delaney acknowledges high valuations in some areas of the market continue to present a challenge for the value manager. "You've always got lists of stocks that you think are terrific but they're too expensive, that's the value buyer's dilemma. I've said to a couple of people: 'In my next life I'm coming back as a growth investor'."

As for the U.S. she believes that some parts of that market are trading at levels that defy logic. "I would say we are dealing in a multi-tiered market—at least a two-tiered market—and that the top tier is scary. [But] beyond that top tier you've got some reasonable value," she adds.

With the new Trimark funds, launched in June 1999, she and partner Lynn Miller are taking advantage of the chance to manage the portfolios the way they like to while they are still small enough. They will hold about 45 to 50 stocks, making them very concentrated. That concentration will distinguish Trimark Enterprise from the $1.4-billion Spectrum United Canadian Equity fund she managed previously. "I think there will be differences. Because the fund is smaller you don't have as many names. In a perfect world I prefer fewer names. In a perfect world I like more concentration. But that perfect world involves a lot of value, a lot of cheap stocks, where the risk return is skewed to the return. And when you've had as good a market as we've had for as long as we've had, you're not quite in that perfect world."

Delaney is using the same management style she always has, which includes using themes to choose stocks. In the summer of 1999 she was focusing on the rebound of Asia and how it plays out in Canadian companies in areas such as commodities and in companies that have exposure to that part of the world.

When asked whether aging investors and their penchant for stocks have pushed stock markets into a new era, Delaney is quick to respond: "We're clearly in a new era. We're in a new era of valuations, we're in a new era in terms of technology and productivity." But that cannot entirely explain and justify the rise of stocks markets, she notes. "I think demographics are having a big influence on a lot of companies and a lot of industries. But does that make me think the Dow is going to go up, up, up, and then we're going to blink and the markets are going to be trading at 40, 50, or 60 times earnings? No." Other factors have had a hand in lifting markets—such as interest rates that came off tremendously—so people have been prepared to pay much higher valuations. And profits were improving dramatically, she says. Delaney also notes that nothing ever happens in isolation. "I don't think it's baby boomers in a vacuum pushing markets up and nor do I think in a vacuum they'll push markets up forever."

STEVE ROGERS—AGF MANAGEMENT LIMITED

In a highly competitive corporate world, being number two is viewed by most companies as a lofty goal and noble achievement. But for Steve Rogers, manager of a top-performing U.S. equity fund, second best is not quite good enough. The manager of AGF American Growth Class, a blue-chip fund that invests in the biggest American companies, buys market leaders, a strategy that has served him well.

"One dominant theme of the fund is focusing just on the market leaders," says Mr. Rogers in an interview at the Toronto offices of AGF Management Limited. His rationale is simple. The leaders have the best financial resources to dedicate to research and development, a crucial ingredient to success in so many industries today that are in some way dependent on fast-changing technology.

"When I look at what has made the real winners in technology... the primary characteristic is market share," he says. "The cost of R&D is far greater than the back-end cost of production and distribution and so the economies of scale [required] are tremendous. That's why an Intel or Microsoft just took over once their market share was considerably greater than everybody else." With companies like these, "short of an incredible management blunder or a complete revolution in the technology that your industry is based on, it's very hard to displace the leader."

That same dynamic is at play, although to a lesser degree, in pharmaceuticals and industrials. And he must be comfortable in the long-term prospects for a company, a strategy he likes to call the "Rip Van Winkle test."

"To me you can't call it a blue-chip stock unless you're willing to put it in your back pocket and not allow yourself to sell it for five years. If you can't do that it has no business being in a blue-chip portfolio."

That attitude has resulted in a low turnover for the fund of little more than about 18% a year. As of late summer 1999, the fund has a heavy weighting in technology companies, totalling about 34%. He is not betting on the high-flying Internet companies, but rather blue-chip names that are positioned to benefit from the Internet, such as Cisco Systems Inc., Microsoft Corp., and Intel Corp.

Other key ingredients that Rogers looks for include a management team with a strong vision that he sees as crucial and a solid balance sheet. Less important in his view is share price and the price-to-earnings ratios that some managers live by.

"I've never bought anything because of valuations and I've never sold anything because of valuations," Mr. Rogers says. However, he has reduced positions—adjustments that he refers to as "haircuts."

In these highly valued times a disregard for valuations may send shudders through more cautious investors. But Rogers will argue there is still much room in the U.S. market for growth, based in large part on the fact that he believes the world is in a deflationary environment.

"Inflation is for all intents and purposes, dead," he says. "And there's no reason to expect it to come back."

The cold war, which went on for decades, was the biggest barrier to trade and therefore barrier to disinflation that the world has ever experienced, he explains.

In the late 1980s and early 1990s after the fall of the Iron Curtain, trade liberalization began to spread around the globe and that wrung inflation out of the system because goods could be purchased in an open system that encouraged price competitiveness.

The Internet is taking that phenomenon a step further, he says.

"The Internet is a vast disinflationary force by allowing consumers to price compare," he says. "If someone in Northern Siberia is offering it cheaper and willing to send it to you for 25¢ postage, you click and here it comes." And the power of that goes beyond individual consumers. "It's also Taiwan Airlines that wants to buy spare parts for its engines," he says as an example. "And the Internet is still in its infancy."

He believes that once investors have accepted this disinflation, they will become comfortable with paying higher price multiples for the future earnings of stocks.

"There is an inverse relationship between P/E's and inflation: lower discount rates equal higher present values," he explains.

Could Y2K dampen enthusiasm for such a blatant bull as Mr. Rogers? Not likely.

"My whole take on Y2K was that it was way, way overblown," he says. He believes the market became alarmed early on because companies that were in the process of fixing and testing glitches could not yet say definitively that they were Y2K ready. That was worrisome. But as of late summer he is comfortable that most large companies in North America, and the other crucial elements, are as prepared as they could be.

"All the critical infrastructure is fixed as far as I'm concerned." There could be sporadic failures "but it is not going to be everybody and everything at the same time. Every major institution has had systems problems and an information technology failure. Should it happen is not something any company that owns a computer has not dealt with before."

He believes that North American markets are unlikely to be hurt by any short-term problems elsewhere in the world. Just look at the Asian crisis, he says. "You had the biggest growth engine in the world essentially stop dead in its tracks last year. And did the U.S. economy slow down? No. It kept speeding up."

Granted, emerging markets are further behind in dealing with it, but "those economies are far less technology dependent." And besides, he says, worst-case scenario, investors start fleeing Asia: "Hey guess what, when they flee Asia where do they go? They go to the U.S."

The 50 Major Fund Families

1. ACUITY FUNDS LTD. (CLEAN ENVIRONMENT)

FRONT OR REAR

Strengths	Profits in the environment business Ethical/socially conscious investing
Weaknesses	Limited family of funds
RESPs?	Yes
Web Site	www.cleanenvironment.com **Toll Free** 1-800-461-4570

CANADIAN	Category	Rating	Fund Name	MER%	RRSP/Foreign
		▲ KO	Acuity Money Market Fund	New	RRSP
		■	Acuity Bond Fund	New	RRSP
		■	Acuity High Income Fund	1.97	RRSP
Equity:	Mid-Large Cap	▲ OK	Clean Environment Equity Fund	2.47	RRSP
		■	Acuity Canadian Equity Fund	New	RRSP
Multi-Asset:	Balanced	▲ AG	Clean Environment Balanced Fund	2.47	RRSP
		■	Acuity Canadian Balanced Fund	New	RRSP

FOREIGN	Category	Rating	Fund Name	MER%	RRSP/Foreign
Global Equity:	All-global	■	Clean Environment International Equity Fund	2.47	Foreign

Acuity Funds Ltd. is the new name for Clean Environment Mutual Funds Ltd. The name change and introduction of a separate new family of funds under the Acuity label took place on November 30, 1998.

The Clean Environment Income Fund was renamed Acuity High Income Fund and is therefore the only one of the Acuity funds shown in the matrix with an MER. As we have noted in previous editions, MERs of this family have been at the high end of the range, but have been reduced considerably since the last edition.

The original Clean Environment family will continue to appeal to the specialized segment of the mutual-fund buying public who wants a clean environment and who believes that a welcome by-product of such a concern is strong investment returns. So far this has been the case. The Clean Environment Equity Fund was a Smart Fund even with a 2.75% MER and dropped to Noteworthy this year.

The Clean Environment Funds are run just like any other mutual fund, except that certain "screens" are used to eliminate choosing certain stocks judged to be destructive to the environment. But Clean Environment is a little broader than that and objects to being categorized as "ethical" funds; rather, it seeks companies that can grow and profit from the environment business itself. It finds companies that redesign processes, use alternative techniques, preserve, recycle, and reduce pollution—since, in theory at least, damaging, "unethical" stocks should ultimately underperform.

Both the Clean Environment as well as the five new Acuity Mutual Funds are managed by Acuity Investment Management Inc., which has also been running institutional and private client portfolios since 1991.

Founder and president Ian Ihnatowycz continues to be the main stock picker. In addition to being a specialist in environmental technology, he approaches investments in the sector in the classic value style. Other principals at Acuity Investment Management are portfolio manager Hugh McCauley, investment analyst David Stonehouse, and VP Steven Smith, who handles the wealth management division and the Acuity pooled funds sold to high-net-worth investors.

Smart Funds 2000

None

Noteworthy Funds

Y2K OK

Clean Environment Equity Fund. Dropped as Smart Fund. MER is lower but still a stiff 2.47%. The fund has underperformed over the past two years.

Acuity Money Market Fund. Strictly a parking spot if the storms rage. The MER will clock in at slightly more than 1%—no bargain for the asset class. The alternative, Acuity High Income Fund (formerly the Clean Environment Income Fund), has a mediocre five-year track record (4.1% CAGR to August 31, 1999) and the new Acuity Bond fund is too new to assess.

Y2K Agnostic

Clean Environment Balanced Fund. Fund has come off a poor year in which it lost 49% for the year ended August 31, 1999 and has barely broken even over the two years ended the same period. But in a Y2K-uncertain climate, the fund's 26% exposure to bonds and cash and another 22% to income trusts should buffer much of the volatility. Note that the new Acuity Canadian Balanced Fund has a similar mix: 54% equity, 29% cash, 14% bonds, and 3% income trusts.

Availability

Selected full-service and discount brokers and dealers across Canada.

2. AGF FUNDS INC.

FRONT, REAR & LOW

Strengths	Canadian bonds
	Unique single country funds
Weaknesses	High MERs
	Confusing mix of bond and A.A. funds
Web Site	www.agf.com
RESPs?	Yes
Toll Free	1-800-268-8583

CANADIAN	Category	Rating	Fund Name	MER%	RRSP/Foreign
Money Market:		■	AGF Canadian Money Market Fund	1.42	RRSP
Fixed Income:	Long-term	▲ KO	AGF Canadian Bond Fund	1.93	RRSP
	Short-term	■	AGF Canadian High Income Fund	1.68	RRSP
Equity:	Mid-Large Cap	■	AGF Canada Class	2.63	RRSP
		■	AGF Canadian Stock Fund	2.46	RRSP
	Small Cap	■	AGF Canadian Growth Equity Fund Ltd.	2.8	RRSP
		■	20/20 RSP Aggressive Equity Fund	2.47	RRSP
		■	20/20 RSP Aggressive Smaller Companies	2.73	RRSP
	Resource	■	20/20 Canadian Resources Fund Ltd.	2.88	RRSP
	Other	■	20/20 Managed Futures Value Fund	3.69	RRSP
Tax Advantaged:	Dividend	★ OK	AGF Dividend Fund	1.87	RRSP
Multi-Asset:	Balanced	▲ AG	AGF Growth & Income Fund	2.5	RRSP
	Asset Allocation	■	AGF Canadian Tactical Asset Allocation Fund	2.42	RRSP
	AA Service	▲ KO	AGF Canadian Asset Allocation Service		RRSP

FOREIGN	Category	Rating	Fund Name	MER%	RRSP/Foreign
Money Market:		■	AGF U.S. Dollar Money Market Account	0.84	Foreign
Fixed Income:		■	AGF U.S. Income Fund	2.46	Foreign
		▲ KO	AGF Global Government Bond Fund	1.86	Foreign
		▲ KO	AGF RSP Global Bond Fund	1.97	RRSP
		■	AGF U.S. Short-term High Yield Fund	2.48	Foreign
		■	AGF International Short-Term Income Class	2.69	Foreign
Global Equity:	All-global	■	AGF World Equity Class	3.07	Foreign
		★ OK	AGF International Value Fund	2.77	Foreign
		▲ OK	AGF RSP International Equity Allocation Fund	2.45	RRSP
	EAFE	■	AGF International Stock Class	2.98	Foreign
		■	20/20 Aggressive Global Stock Fund	3.64	Foreign
	Specialty	■	AGF Global Real Estate Equity Class	New	Foreign
Regional Equity:	U.S. Large-cap	★ OK	AGF American Growth Class	2.78	Foreign
		▲ OK	20/20 Aggressive Growth Fund	2.55	Foreign
	U.S. Small-cap	■	AGF Special U.S. Class	2.86	Foreign
	Latin American	■	20/20 Latin America Fund	3.24	Foreign
	Emerging Market	■	20/20 Emerging Markets Value Fund	3.57	Foreign
	Far East	■	AGF Asian Growth Class	3.03	Foreign
	Japan	▲ OK	AGF Japan Class	3.07	Foreign
	Europe	■	AGF European Growth Class	3.03	Foreign
	Other	■	AGF China Focus Class	3.49	Foreign
		■	AGF Germany Class	2.99	Foreign
		■	20/20 India Fund	3.74	Foreign
Global Balanced:		■	AGF World Balanced Fund	2.46	Foreign
		★ OK	AGF American Tactical Asset Allocation Fund	2.56	Foreign
		■	AGF European Asset Allocation Fund	2.56	Foreign

AGF is one of the grand old Canadian fund companies. A glance at the fund matrix quickly reveals both its strengths and weaknesses. There is choice aplenty, perhaps too much, with some 40 distinct funds, including several unique regional funds—who else offers single-country funds covering Germany or India? There is a host of redundant domestic and foreign bond or asset allocation funds, making it quite a challenge to mix funds and still have a grip on your overall asset allocation.

Apart from that, you can see that AGF's Management Expense Ratios, or MERs, are decidedly at the high end of the range in Canada. Five of them top the already egregious 3.5% level. But despite this—or perhaps because of it—there are a number of money-losing nags in this stable.

Domestically, AGF leans to in-house investment management, with particular strength in its domestic bond funds. Here again, MERs are not cheap but they do at least get you the top-flight bond experience of both AGF chairman Warren Goldring and his able vice-president, Clive Coombs.

Globally, AGF goes the common route of contracting external advisors, which include top-notch value investors Brandes Investment Partners of San Diego; aggressive growth specialists Driehaus Capital Management Inc. of Chicago; San Francisco asset allocation experts Barclays Global Investors (formed from the 1996 merger of BZW and Wells Fargo Nikko), Deutsche Asset Management; Latin specialists Globalvest Management LP (still headed by Peter Gruber); Nomura Asset Management Co. of Japan; and New York-based PaineWebber and Salomon Smith Barney Inc. AGF is also developing its own international in-house investment teams: AGF Asset Management Asia Ltd. and Dublin-based AGF International Advisors Company Ltd. for its European investments.

AGF does possess some formidable strengths and, by sheer virtue of the quantity of its offerings, always manages to have several top-quartile performers.

AGF has never been a slouch in international equities. Goldring has always believed that fund products depend on strong markets. Thus, AGF was early in the American market (hence the original name, American Growth Fund) back when exciting high technology consisted of colour television, new wonder drugs, and jet airplanes. It has also been strong in Asia and single countries such as Japan and China.

For international equity investors with taxable (non-RRSP) portfolios, AGF, like C.I. and AIM Funds, is an especially attractive fund family. Investors can switch among the 11 funds in the AGF International Group without triggering a capital disposition. This also maximizes foreign-content capacity in an RRSP or RRIF, because the book value of the investments doesn't increase unless you leave the group.

Asset allocation has always been a strong suit of AGF, one strengthened by the addition of 20/20's regional tactical asset allocation funds; AGF pioneered strategic asset allocation with a service that juggles its domestic equity, bond, and money market funds.

Year 2000 Stance

AGF focused on the Year 2000 issue in 1996 when it converted its unitholder mainframe system to a new client/server platform. Like many financial services firms, it cannot vouch for the readiness of all vendors, suppliers, and customers. It says that "in part because of the uncertainty surrounding third-party Year 2000 readiness and notwithstanding the steps taken by AGF, there can be no assurance that AGF's business operations will not be materially and adversely impacted."

Y2K is also a factor taken into consideration by portfolio managers in evaluating firms whose stocks are held by the funds.

Smart Funds 2000

Y2K OK

AGF Dividend Fund. Back for its fourth consecutive year. This is a classic blue-chip equity fund that has been misnamed a dividend fund as it paid almost no distribution in 1998. Still a three-year compound return number of 15.8% as of August 31, 1999, demonstrates the merits of owning blue chips.

AGF American Growth Class. Steve Rogers continues to ride the wave of the hot large-cap growth stocks in the U.S. and has a five-year CAGR of 28.5% as of August 31, 1999.

AGF International Value Fund. A classic and one of a handful of five-time Smart Fund performers. This one has handily beaten the much larger Templeton Growth Fund with 16.6% five-year CAGR versus Templeton's 11.7%. Buy it and lock it in your RSP for the next 10 years.

AGF American Tactical Asset Allocation Fund. Has a stellar 17.3% five-year return. Asset calls have been great at lowering funds volatility. Fund has remarkable record for any 12-month period held.

Noteworthy Funds

Y2K OK

AGF RSP International Equity Allocation Fund. Managed by Barclay's Kathy Taylor. But this is not an asset allocation fund: it's an equity allocation fund that has been almost half in the U.S., 44% in Europe and the small balance in the Pacific Rim. 100% RRSP-eligible, fund has chalked up double-digit returns every year since 1995. Minimal exposure to the emerging markets that would be impacted by Y2K: fund underweight Japan and Hong Kong.

AGF 20/20 Aggressive Growth Fund. Richard Driehaus manages what is essentially a U.S. technology fund and has chalked up a 49.9% CAGR for the two years ended August 31, 1999. Lots of small- to mid-cap stocks, which may add to performance under a Y2K OK scenario but which could get hammered in a Y2K KO sell-off. Remember the warning label that is part of this fund's name: for "aggressive growth" investors only.

AGF Japan Class. Japan has been one of the few regions to show strong gains in 1999, suggesting that a bottom may have been reached after a decade in the doldrums. But we're not convinced that Japan has its Y2K act together. Monitor closely in December 1999.

Y2K KO

AGF Canadian Asset Allocation Service. This service—comprising three underlying Canadian funds—will take bigger asset allocation bets than AGF Growth & Income. Early in 1999 fund was very conservatively invested, with more than half in the AGF Canadian Money Market Fund, and the rest split between AGF Canadian Stock Fund and AGF Canadian Bond Fund. Fund has come off two mediocre years but is more likely to move to a defensive Y2K posture than are classic balanced funds.

AGF Canadian Bond. This consistent long-term performer's 1.93% MER is stiffer than we'd like for the long term but could be a relative safe haven for those who want to sit out the Y2K storm. Managed by AGF founder Warren Goldring and executive VP Clive Coombs. Annualized yield 5.5%. About two-thirds in Government of Canada bonds; the rest in provincials and some cash.

AGF Global Government Bond Fund. Managed by Clive Coombs and Scott Colbourne, global bond funds could fare better than Canadian bond funds if it's apparent that interest rates have further to fall in Europe and elsewhere.

AGF Global RSP Government Bond Fund. As above, but 100% RRSP-eligible at slightly higher MER. Allows investors to save their precious 20% foreign content for actively managed equity funds.

Y2K Agnostic

AGF Growth & Income. Classic balanced fund with Gerard Ferguson on stocks and Clive Coombs on bonds. Mix early in 1999 was 53% Canadian stocks, 10% foreign stocks, and 37% government bonds. Returns have been disappointing the last two years.

Availability

Through discount and full-service brokers, dealers, financial planners.

3. AIC LTD.

FRONT OR REAR

Strengths	Investing in the wealth industry Seg funds now available		
Weaknesses	Volatility in down markets		
Web Site	www.aicfunds.com		
RESPs?	Yes	**Toll Free**	1-800-263-2144

CANADIAN	Category	Rating	Fund Name	MER%	RRSP/Foreign
Money Market:		▲ KO	AIC Money Market Fund	1	RRSP
		■	AIC Money Market Segregated Fund	1.1	RRSP
Equity:	Mid-Large Cap	★ OK	AIC Advantage Fund	2.25	RRSP
		▲ OK	AIC Advantage Fund II	2.53	RRSP
		★ OK	AIC Diversified Canada Fund	2.35	RRSP
		▲ AG	AIC Diversified Canada Segregated Fund	2.8*	RRSP
Multi-Asset:		▲ AG	AIC Income Equity	2.49	RRSP
		■	AIC Income Equity Segregated Fund	2.94	RRSP

FOREIGN	Category	Rating	Fund Name	MER%	RRSP/Foreign
Global Equity:	All-global	▲ OK	AIC World Equity Fund	2.47	Foreign
		■	AIC World Equity Segregated Fund	3.07	Foreign
		■	AIC World Advantage	2.75	Foreign
		■	AIC World Advantage Segregated Fund	3.4	Foreign
Regional Equity:	U.S.	★ OK	AIC Value Fund	2.37	Foreign
		▲ AG	AIC Value Segregated Fund	2.97	Foreign
		■	AIC American Advantage	2.74	Foreign
		■	AIC American Advantage Segregated Fund	3.34	Foreign
Multi-Asset:	U.S.	■	AIC American Income Equity	2.49	Foreign
		■	AIC American Income Equity Segregated Fund	3.09	Foreign

AIC founder Michael Lee-Chin and sub-advisor Jonathan Wellum are true believers in the Warren Buffett school of buying excellent companies and holding them for the long run. This is reflected in AIC's well-considered slogan: Creating Portfolios of Excellent Businesses.

A related benefit is that, unlike many rival fund families, portfolio turnover in most AIC funds is low, which means triggering fewer taxable events for unitholders, a plus for non-registered portfolios in particular.

Throughout the 1990s bull market, the Advantage funds lived up to their names, making heroes of the financial advisors who recommended these funds early. Since the 1995 edition profiled ace manager Wellum, many *Smart Funds* readers should have received this advantage, which has been created by the shrewd decision to invest in the wealth management industry itself. The advantage then is to allow unitholders to profit from the generally high management expense ratios of other mutual funds, since AIC's Canadian funds tend to own as much as legally permitted of the stocks of rival Canadian fund companies.

The question for investors is whether a bear market would turn this advantage into a disadvantage, since fund company stocks tend to magnify market gains on the upside as well as declines on the downside.

Perhaps anticipating this, AIC management has introduced several segregated fund counterparts to its traditional equity funds. The higher MERs that make possible the money-back guarantee are shown in the matrix under the 100% minimum benefit guarantee option, which are generally 0.45% to 0.6% higher than the underlying funds. However, this extra insurance cost can be cut in half by choosing the 75% minimum benefit option.

In August 1998, AIC announced that it had decided to use permitted derivatives in some of its funds, of the kind mentioned in Canada's National Policy 39. The plan, which starts with AIC World Advantage and American Income Equity Fund and may eventually be applied to others, is to use derivatives in the form of debt-like securities or foreign currency forward contracts or options where it invests in non-Canadian securities.

AIC has come a long way with a brilliantly executed, simple original idea. With popularity and huge size, it remains to be seen how these complicated innovations will play out in the marketplace.

Year 2000 Stance

AIC says it considers the "possible implications of the Year 2000 issue on the Funds' investment portfolios to be very important." Inquiries about Y2K compliance are part of its normal due diligence. It observes that "earnings of individual companies in which the Funds invest may be affected by remediation costs, failures of critical internal systems or their customers' or suppliers' systems, and overall economic uncertainty about the Year 2000."

Smart Funds 2000

Y2K OK

AIC Advantage Fund I. Long-term track record is outstanding. Short-term, fund has lagged as financial stocks did poorly in 1999.

AIC Diversified. Solid buy and hold core holding with high tax efficiency. Fund will hold more than market weight in financial services stocks.

AIC Value. Neil Murdoch buys great American names and holds them for many years.

Noteworthy Funds

Y2K OK

AIC Advantage II. If you can, save 28 basis points on the MER with Advantage I version of this fund. If Advantage I is no longer available, then this is the closest thing to the top mutual fund in Canada the last 10 years.

AIC World Equity. This EAFE-mandated fund has had a rough year, but a stellar long-term track record of first quartiles over the two-, three-, four-, and five-year CAGR periods ending June 30, 1999 keeps it on the Smart Fund list.

Y2K Agnostic

AIC Diversified Canada Segregated Fund. As safe a harbour as you're likely to find in the AIC group, with good upside potential should the good times continue to roll.

Y2K KO

AIC Money Market Fund. Since most AIC funds are equity funds, there aren't many safe harbours in a full-scale market meltdown, apart from the new seg fund versions. A 1% MER is a bit stiff for a money market fund and there's little point in paying another 0.1% for a seg version.

Y2K Agnostic

AIC Income Equity. This is like the AIC Diversified Canada fund with a 37% cushion of cash and bonds. Greater portfolio turnover creates steady income stream but generates more taxable events outside registered plans.

AIC Value Segregated Fund. Stiff all-in MER of close to 3% but may be a reasonable price to pay for a downside hedge coupled with AIC's proven ability to generate upside from the overvalued American market.

Availability

Through full-service or discount brokerages across Canada, financial planners, and insurance companies.

4. AIM FAMILY OF FUNDS

FRONT OR REAR

Strengths "Some global funds, style switching"
Weaknesses "Temporarily, no free switches between fund groups"
High management expense ratios
RESPs? No
Web Site www.gtglobal.ca **Toll Free** 1-800-588-5684

CANADIAN	Category	Rating	Fund Name	MER%	RRSP/Foreign
Money Market:		■	AIM Canada Money Market Fund	0.76	RRSP
		■	AIM Cash Performance Fund	1.24	RRSP
Fixed Income:		■	AIM Canadian Bond Fund	2.55	RRSP
Equity:	Mid-Large Cap	★ OK	AIM Canada Growth Class	2.43	RRSP
	Mid-Large Cap	■	AIM Canadian Premier Fund	2.65	RRSP
	Mid-Large Cap	■	AIM Canada Value Class	2.9	RRSP
Tax Advantaged:	Dividend	★ KO	AIM Canada Income Class	2.11	RRSP
Multi-Asset:	Balanced	■	AIM Canadian Balanced Fund	2.55	RRSP

FOREIGN	Category	Rating	Fund Name	MER%	RRSP/Foreign
Money Market:		▲ KO	AIM Short-Term Income Class	1.82-2.31	Foreign
Fixed Income:		■	AIM Global Bond Fund	2.51	Foreign
Global Equity:	All-global	■	AIM International Value Fund	2.95	Foreign
	Specialty	▲ OK	AIM Global Theme Class	2.79	Foreign
		▲	AIM Global Infrastructure Class	2.81	Foreign
		■	AIM Global Natural Resources Class	2.96	Foreign
		★ OK	AIM Global Technology Fund	2.95	Foreign
		■	AIM Global Telecommunications Class	2.79	Foreign
		★ OK	AIM Global Health Sciences	2.64	Foreign
		▲ OK	AIM Global Health Care Class	2.75	Foreign
Regional Equity:	U.S.	■	AIM America Growth Class	2.81	Foreign
	U.S. Large Cap	■	AIM American Premier Fund	2.95	Foreign
	US Small Cap	■	AIM American Aggressive Growth Fund	2.95	Foreign
	Europe	▲ OK	AIM European Growth Fund	2.95	Foreign
	Latin American	■	AIM Latin America Growth Class	2.95	Foreign
	Far East	■	AIM Global Pacific Growth Class	2.99	Foreign
Global Balanced:		▲ AG	AIM Global Growth & Income Fund	2.85	Foreign

AIM is the Canadian unit that resulted from the April 1998 merger of what was formerly Lou Voticky's Admax Group of Funds, later AIM Funds Group Canada Inc., and Joe Canavan's GT Global Canada. Canavan went on to form Synergy, while GT Global Canada's parent company, LGT Asset Management, was acquired by UK-based Amvescap PLC. Therefore, AIM is part of a global equity powerhouse (managing C$360 billion worldwide) which employs 300 portfolio managers in 20 countries around the world.

The merger brought together firms that had several things in common: both were subsidiaries of global money management businesses, with most funds run by portfolio managers based outside Canada, and particularly in the United States. Both firms offered funds with a variety of styles, as well as more narrowly focused regional and sector funds. GT Global pioneered "theme investing" in Canada, a strategy since matched by C.I. Mutual Funds and Fidelity Investments Canada.

On the negative side, MERs both pre- and post-merger continue to be higher than we'd like. Nevertheless, the family offers a number of funds that so far have justified their fees. That should be the case for as long as a bull market endures.

Meanwhile, after standing pat on its fund line-up in the first year post-merger, the expected consolidation of redundant or underperforming funds began in earnest in a fund shake-up announced December 18, 1998.

Under Voticky, Admax had a strong focus on Asian funds, several of which were consolidated into the AIM International Fund. Therefore the old AIM Korea, AIM Nippon (Japan), and AIM Tiger funds are no longer separately available. The 100% RRSP-eligible AIM RSP Index Fund has been merged into AIM Canadian Premier Fund. The AIM Global RSP Income Fund has become the AIM Canadian Bond Fund. In a minor change, the name of AIM Europa Fund was changed to AIM European Growth Fund.

In February 1999, a management change on AIM Global Telecommunications Fund was announced. Former manager Michael Mahoney, who had managed the fund since inception in 1994, was replaced by Houston-based David Barnard. In April 1999, Paul Rogge, manager of AIM Canadian Premier Fund and AIM Canadian Balanced Fund, left the firm after eight years with AIM. The funds are now managed by existing managers Clas Olsson, with Bob Alley and Carolyn Gibbs on the fixed-income portion of the balanced fund.

AIM provides an interesting option for investors who like to switch among different regional or special equity funds, and particularly investors who are concerned about triggering capital gains in non-registered portfolios. AIM Global Fund Inc. consists of eight "classes"—in effect funds: the five theme classes, three regional classes, and the short-term income class. A similar structure is used for the domestic funds: AIM Canada Fund Inc. consists of AIM Canada Income Class, AIM Canada Value Class, and AIM Canada Growth Class.

For investors who are wary about sector funds, AIM Global Theme Class is like a "greatest hits" fund, taking the best ideas from the seven sector funds. Instead of dividing the world into geographical regions, it chooses stocks from health care, infrastructure, telecommunications, natural resources, financial services, consumer products, and technology.

Year 2000 Stance

AIM says the Y2K vulnerability of any given company and its degree of preparedness will determine in part whether it will continue to hold them in its portfolios. However, it adds that "AIM cannot guarantee that all the companies we own will be fully Y2K compliant by the end of 1999." Health sciences portfolio manager John Schroer notes that the issue for health care is provider and payor information systems. Operations for the industry should not be much of a problem as most are compliant and those that are not are prepared to go "paper." The pharmaceutical industry is kicking off an educational program to mute end-of-year drug stockpiling, but this could still be an issue, Schroer notes. From an investment psychology perspective, he believes that Y2K OK is the most likely outcome. "Y2K will not be a big issue. But that does not mean the bull market continues. There are more important things than whether the elevators and televisions operate—like interest rates, earnings, currencies, projected growth rates for GDP and valuations."

Smart Funds 2000

Y2K OK

AIM Canada Growth Class. This momentum style fund has been riding the Nortel Networks, BCE, JDS Uniphase, and Celestica train to great returns.

AIM Global Technology Fund. Spectacular triple-digit 12-month returns. This could spice up the growth portion of your portfolio.

AIM Global Health Sciences Fund. Be patient, short-term performance is off, but John Schroer's big weighting in pharmaceuticals will pay-off in the long run.

Y2K KO

AIM Canada Income Class. Buy this one for the income as it should generate a better return than GICs plus have capital appreciation. Cash yield is about 8% with its $0.038 monthly distribution.

Noteworthy Funds

Y2K OK

AIM Global Theme Class. This "seven theme funds in one" fund is less risky than any of the underlying funds and was first quartile in the global equity category in 1998, returning 33% for the year. Manager Dave Ellman departed for Merrill Lynch in July 1999.

AIM European Growth. Steven Chamberlain keeps hitting the ball out of the park. Fund is first quartile for 5 and 3 years end August 31.

AIM Global Health Care Class. Fund has been languishing in the third quartile after years of being in the second quartile. John Schroer took over the fund and we continue to view him as an asset.

Y2K KO

AIM Short-Term Income Class. Strictly a place to park cash short-term if the heat from various equity classes of AIM GT Global Fund Inc. gets too hot.

Y2K Agnostic

AIM Global Growth & Income. Global balanced fund was first quartile in 1997 and 1998. UK-based Michael Lindsell invests in blue-chip stocks and high quality bonds primarily from G7 countries. As of March it was 37% in bonds, 8% in cash, 5% in utilities, with the rest in stocks. Geographically about half in North America, 41% Europe, and only a nominal position in Asia.

Availability

Through full-service and discount brokers and dealers.

5. ALTAMIRA INVESTMENT SERVICES INC. NO LOAD

Strengths Some interesting funds: e-business and index
New low-MER index funds
Weaknesses High MERs on equity funds versus other no-loads
Web Site www.altamira.com
RESPs? Yes **Toll Free** 1-800-263-2824

CANADIAN	Category	Rating	Fund Name	MER%	RRSP/Foreign
Money Market:		■	Altamira T-Bill Fund	0.36	RRSP
Fixed Income:	Long-term	★ KO	Altamira Bond Fund	1.36	RRSP

	Medium-term	■	Altamira Income Fund	1	RRSP
	Short-term	■	Altamira Short Term Government Bond	1.36	RRSP
		■	Altamira Short Term Canadian Income Fund	0.54	RRSP
Equity:	Mid-Large Cap	■	Altamira Capital Growth Fund Limited	2	RRSP
		■	Altamira Equity Fund	2.33	RRSP
	Index	★ OK	Altamira Precision Canadian Index	0.5	RRSP
	Small Cap	■	Altamira Special Growth Fund	1.8	RRSP
	Gold/precious metal	■	Altamira Precious & Strategic Metal Fund	2.38	RRSP
	Resource	■	Altamira Resource Fund	2.34	RRSP
		■	AltaFund Investment Corp.	2.43	RRSP
Tax Advantaged:	Dividend	▲ AG	Altamira Dividend	1.62	RRSP
	Labour-sponsored	■	Triax Growth Fund	3.6	RRSP
Multi-Asset:					
	Tactical asset allocation	▲ AG	Altamira Balanced Fund	2	RRSP
		▲ AG	Altamira Growth & Income Fund	1.4	RRSP

FOREIGN	Category	Rating	Fund Name	MER%	RRSP/Foreign
Fixed Income:		■	Altamira Short Term Global Income Fund	1.3	RRSP
		■	Altamira Global Bond Fund	1.9	RRSP
		▲ AG	Altamira High Yield Bond Fund	1.94	Foreign
Global Equity:	Small-cap	■	Altamira Global Small Company	2.95	Foreign
	Index	■	Altamira Precision International RSP Index	0.5	RRSP
	Specialty	★ OK	Altamira Science & Technology Fund	2.31	Foreign
	Specialty	★ OK	Altamira e-business	2.79	Foreign
Regional Equity:	U.S. Large-cap	■	Altamira U.S. Larger Company Fund	2.3	Foreign
	U.S. Small-Med	■	Altamira Select American Fund	2.28	Foreign
	U.S. Index	■	Altamira Precision U.S. RSP Index	0.5	RRSP
	NAFTA/N.Am.	■	Altamira North American Recovery Fund	2.3	RRSP
	Emerging Market	■	Altamira Global Discovery Fund	2.95	Foreign
	Far East	■	Altamira Asia Pacific Fund	2.34	Foreign
	Japan	■	Altamira Japanese Opportunity Fund	2.37	Foreign
	Europe	■	Altamira European Equity Fund	2.32	Foreign
Global Balanced:		■	Altamira Global Diversified Fund	2	Foreign

To say 1998–99 was a period of big changes at one of Canada's best-known no-load fund companies doesn't quite cover it. After a troubled period in which many investors jumped ship, Altamira launched an offensive to try to win customers and recapture its past reputation as a fund industry innovator. New products were introduced, the company moved into new areas of business, and it even made an acquisition.

A bitter ownership battle and poor performance in some key funds had led many Altamira unitholders to pull their money out of the family. The company recognized that it had troubles: too much of its clients' money was concentrated in one fund, for example. So when the flagship Altamira Equity fund had poor performance under former manager Frank Mersch, Altamira clients lost confidence and redemptions spilled over into other funds.

No one said turning around a ship the size of Altamira would be easy, including president Gordon Cheesbrough, who was brought in to revive the firm in early 1998. But the company took steps to improve performance and introduced products that would attract investors' attention.

One of the most interesting moves for Altamira last year was the launch of a series of index funds that caused a stir when they were unveiled with the lowest annual management fees of any available in Canada. Almost immediately, Royal Bank Investment Management responded by lowering the fees on its index funds to match Altamira's. At 0.5% a year for either the Canadian, U.S., or global equity index fund, these are as cheap as you can get in Canada. Altamira's two foreign index funds have been structured to be fully RRSP-eligible, a definite advantage for investors who want more than the permitted 20% of their portfolio invested in foreign markets.

Also new is the Altamira e-business fund. The stars seemed to line up for Altamira on this one. It was launched in November 1998, just as the appetite for technology and e-business stocks really kicked in. The fund returned 56.9% for the six months, making it the top performer since its launch in this category. E-business refers to the use of electronic networks, such as the Internet, to purchase consumer goods and services and conduct business transactions. The fund is managed by Altamira's technology team, Ian Ainsworth, David Cooke, and Stephen Masson. And it is advised by Don Tapscott, who is considered an authority on the digital economy. As of the spring, it had attracted more than $145 million.

Gordon Cheesbrough, formerly chairman and CEO of ScotiaMcLeod and Scotia Capital Markets, has not stopped at new products. In December 1998, Altamira acquired Mutual Fund Direct, a no-load discount mutual fund seller based in London, Ontario, with a branch office in Calgary. Mutual Fund Direct sells load funds from 33 fund companies without charging the usual transaction fee to buy or sell. The company makes money by collecting the ongoing service fees paid to dealers by fund companies. For now it continues to operate separately from Altamira, but unitholders should benefit from the two companies' plans to coordinate accounts so Altamira clients have access to these other funds simply and cheaply.

As for some of Altamira's better-known funds, the performance of Altamira Equity has improved under the team management of Ian Ainsworth, Sue Coleman, and Shauna Sexsmith. The fund continued to underperform in 1998, but has recently shown signs of improvement. It was expected to take time before the group re-jigged the portfolio to reflect their theme style investing: buying stocks that they believe will benefit from fundamental changes in demographics, technology, and so on. The fund remains more expensive than the average with its 2.33% MER. When you consider that these funds are no-load, and don't have the cost of financing brokers' commissions that load funds do, they are expensive.

Altamira Bond, managed by Robert Marcus, returns as a Smart Fund this year. It was voted best bond fund of 1998 by the industry and has a lower-than-average 1.36% MER.

Altamira Science and Technology also benefited from the clamour for tech stocks. It was top quartile in 1998 and continues as a Smart Fund this year.

For those who don't want to put together their own portfolio, Altamira also launched the Managed RSP Portfolios. Seven combinations of Altamira funds give investors choices ranging between 100% income and 100% growth. The minimum investment is $2,500 and there is an annual fee of $50 for the service. The overall MER is a combination of what is charged by the underlying funds.

Year 2000 Stance

As part of its due diligence Altamira is looking at how companies are dealing with Y2K and says, "at a minimum, an audit of the current operating environment must have been undertaken, a plan to address any weaknesses delineated, and replacement or redesign of suspect systems and processes in progress."

Altamira has a Y2K Investment Compliance Team that is monitoring the readiness of all companies it is invested in, or is considering buying. The company is paying close attention to higher-risk regions but made no mention of plans to adjust asset allocation.

Smart Funds 2000

Y2K OK

Altamira Precision Canadian Index Fund. Finally low MER index funds are available to Canadians. Just in time to ride Nortel Networks and BCE and outperform almost all funds.

Altamira Science & Technology Fund. Ian Ainsworth and his team have rode the technology boom to a four-year CAGR of 44.4%, tops in the category.

Altamira e-business. Ainsworth uses this fund to play the Internet revolution. Currently risky, but may be a core holding by 2005.

Y2K KO

Altamira Bond. Continues to be a top bond fund over the long term, investing in long-term and stripped coupon bonds. Managed by Robert Marcus, it returns as a Smart Fund. An MER of 1.36% is below the 1.66% average for this type of fund. The one-year return to June 30 was 1.6%, but it remains first quartile over the long term.

Noteworthy Funds

Y2K Agnostic

Altamira Dividend. This high-quality dividend fund remains appropriate for non-registered accounts or for those seeking a conservative equity fund in their RRSPs. The MER of 1.62% is well below the category average of 2.11%. Returns over the long term have been well above average. Over one year to August 31, 1999, the fund gained 8.9%.

Altamira Balanced, Altamira Growth & Income. These funds go down the middle with roughly equal portions of stock and bond exposure.

Altamira High Yield Bond Fund. Global "junk bond" fund, returned 6.6% over one year to August 31. It has a solid long-term record, being top quartile on a three-year basis. It uses up the 20% foreign-content limit in RRSPs or RRIFs. Not recommended for a Y2K KO scenario, where a flight to quality bonds would hurt funds like these.

Availability

Directly from Altamira or some full-service and discount brokers and dealers on request. Minimum investment $1,000 or $50 through Automatic Investment Plan.

6. @RGENTUM MANAGEMENT & RESEARCH CORP.

LOAD

Strengths	Market neutral fund High net worth offerings		
Weaknesses	MERs mid-high "$5,000 minimum investments"		
RESPs?	No		
Web Site	www.argentum.com	**Toll Free**	1-877-274-3688

CANADIAN	Category	Rating	Fund Name	MER%	RRSP/Foreign
Money Market:		■	Short Term Asset Portfolio	0.79	RRSP
Equity:	Small Cap	▲ OK	Canadian Performance Portfolio	2.86	RRSP
		■	Discovery Portfolio	1.96	RRSP
	Mid-Large Cap	■	Canadian Equity Portfolio	2.76	RRSP
Multi-Asset:		▲ AG	Income Portfolio	2.25	RRSP
	Balanced	■	Quebec Balanced Portfolio	1.5	RRSP

FOREIGN	Category	Rating	Fund Name	MER%	RRSP/Foreign
Global Equity:	All-global	▲ OK	International Master Portfolio	2.95	Foreign
Regional Equity:	U.S.	■	U.S. Master Portfolio	2.86	Foreign
		★ KO	Market Neutral Portfolio	2.86	Foreign

New to Smart Funds with this edition is this Montreal-based start-up oriented to sophisticated high-net-worth investors. One reason for its selection was that it is one of the few fund families that has a market-neutral "hedge fund" that can profit from market downturns, whether triggered by Y2K or some other non-foreseeable event. See @rgentum's extensive analysis of Y2K investing issues under the entry Year 2000 Stance, below.

Founder, president, and CEO Frederick Pye is a former senior executive of Fidelity Investments Canada Ltd. Pye recognized a need for investment products that were both consistent as well as capable of generating superior, more predictable performance. The company attempts to achieve this through a blend of traditional fundamental-based money management and modern computer-based quantitative analysis.

The "@" in @rgentum is no typo but part of the name. The word itself is derived from the Latin word for money. @rgentum has alliances with Hillsdale Investment Management Inc. of Toronto and C.A.S.E. Management Inc. of Boca Raton, Florida, both experts in technology-based quantitative analysis.

@rgentum also caters to the high-net-worth market, offering segregated investment management to those with portfolios of more than $1 million. Asset classes include North American traded stock and Canadian income trusts and bonds.

Year 2000 Stance

@rgentum says it started studying the Year 2000 problem long before it was discussed in the mass media. In fact, "once it reached the front pages, we knew the problem would likely fizzle out." It considers North American corporations and world-class foreign ones as "essentially prepared" to deal with the issue, because of the time and capital most have already invested. “We have interviewed numerous corporations on this subject and have yet to find one whose answers would cause us serious concern.”

That said, it reports that “we do not take the issue lightly.” Its best-case scenario involves Y2K weighing heavily on the markets in the closing months of 1999, followed by the actual century change proving to be a “non-event.” This would result in the markets “taking off” in January 2000, with long-term interest rates falling and bond and stock prices rising. Such a scenario would imply holding no cash or short-term bonds and maximizing equities.

Under @rgentum’s worst-case scenario, Y2K would create major disruptions in many corporate and public processes and services, such as a breakdown of the North American power grid. It notes, “Outside North America, effects could be more catastrophic.” Under this scenario, which it views as “quite unlikely,” investors would hold only paper cash and gold bullion.

The Y2K KO Smart Fund is @rgentum Market Neutral Portfolio, which is designed to perform in down markets and marketed by advisors as a defensive strategy in the event of a Y2K market meltdown or a general market downturn triggered by some other event.

@rgentum expects Y2K to “cast a pall over the markets during the fall months of 1999” but believes the issue will not prove to be “seriously damaging.” Therefore it recommends gradually adopting a more aggressive stance as 1999 closes in order to benefit from an eventual relief rally early in 2000.

Smart Funds 2000

Y2K KO

Market Neutral Portfolio. Managed by Hillsdale, the fund combines both long and short positions in U.S. equities and tries to capitalize on opportunities found through variations in security valuations, regardless of the market’s general direction. In an up market, market neutral funds will sacrifice maximum performance but could rise even when the stock market is falling. Minimum investment of $150,000, available to sophisticated investors through an offering memorandum. Fund is up 5.7% for one year, but lost 11.3% for the six months ended August 31, 1999.

Noteworthy Funds

Y2K OK

Canadian Performance Portfolio. Active, style-neutral stance. Holds 40 quality growth companies from the TSE 200. All @rgentum funds have $5,000 minimum, except the Market Neutral Portfolio.

International Master Portfolio. Invests in companies in highly developed countries. Geographic weightings track a global index; with quantitative systems supplementing stock selection.

Y2K Agnostic

Income Portfolio. Invests in quality fixed-income and dividend-yielding investments.

Availability

Through investment advisors. Minimum investment is $5,000 with the exception of the Market Neutral Portfolio, which has a $150,000 minimum and is available to sophisticated investors through an offering memorandum.

7. ATLAS ASSET MANAGEMENT INC.

NO LOAD OR FRONT OR DEFERRED LOAD

Strengths	Style diversification (value and growth) Access to many external advisors
Weaknesses	Complexity of fund types High MERs
RESPs?	No
Web Site	www.atlasfunds.ca
Toll Free	1-800-463-2857

CANADIAN	Category	Rating	Fund Name	MER%	RRSP/Foreign
Money Market:		▲ KO	Atlas Canadian Money Market Fund	1.11	RRSP
		■	Atlas Canadian T-Bill Fund	1.31	RRSP
Fixed Income:	Long-term	■	Atlas Canadian Bond Fund	1.93	RRSP
	Short-med	■	Atlas Canadian High Yield Bond Fund	1.87	RRSP
Equity:	Mid-Large Cap	★ OK	Atlas Canadian Large Cap Growth Fund	2.43	RRSP
		■	Atlas Canadian Large Cap Value Fund	2.56	RRSP
	Small Cap	■	Atlas Canadian Emerging Growth Fund	2.61	RRSP
		■	Atlas Canadian Small Cap Value Fund	2.67	RRSP
		■	Atlas Canadian Small Cap Growth Fund	2.77	RRSP

Tax Advantaged:	Dividend	■	Atlas Canadian Income & Growth Fund	2.25	RRSP
	Income	■	Atlas Canadian Income Trust Fund	1.89	RRSP
Multi-Asset:	Balanced	▲ AG	Atlas Canadian Balanced Fund	2.19	RRSP

FOREIGN	Category	Rating	Fund Name	MER%	RRSP/Foreign
Money Market:		■	Atlas American Money Market Fund	1.13	Foreign
Fixed Income:		■	Atlas World Bond Fund Fund	2.12	RRSP
Global Equity:	All-global	■	Atlas Global Value Fund	2.73	Foreign
		■	Atlas International Large Cap Growth Fund	2.8	Foreign
	Index	■	Atlas International RSP Index Fund	2	RRSP
Regional Equity:	U.S.	■	Atlas American Large Cap Growth Fund	2.52	Foreign
		■	Atlas American Advantage Value Fund	2.55	Foreign
	U.S. index	★ OK	Atlas American RSP Index Fund	1.5	RRSP
	Latin American	■	Atlas Latin American Value Fund	2.95	Foreign
	Emerging Market	■	Atlas International Emerging Markets Growth	3.5	Foreign
	Far East	■	Atlas Pacific Basin Value Fund	2.9	Foreign
	Europe	■	Atlas European Value Fund	2.58	Foreign

The 24 Atlas Mutual Funds bring a style-based approach to a competitive market, with both value and growth versions in many fund categories and, in some cases, small- and large-cap versions too. Such a surfeit of choice normally creates the need for a financial planner, which makes sense since the group is Merrill Lynch Canada's in-house mutual fund family. As a result, assets have been rising at a healthy clip, with Atlas's market share tripling over the past three years.

Under four sales options, investors can choose no load with a one-year clawback, no load with no clawback, front load with a negotiable commission of 0 to 5%, or a redemption schedule that declines from 5.5% to 1.5% over six years.

As with most load groups engaging multiple external advisors, MERs tend to be on the high side. The 1.31% MER charged to the Treasury Bill Fund and 1.93% charged to the Atlas Canadian Bond Fund are excessive for those asset classes, as is the 3.5% for the Emerging Markets Growth Fund. On the other hand, it is one of the rare load groups to carry lower-cost index funds. These include three foreign funds that beat the 20% foreign-content rule for RRSPs and RRIFs. The Atlas American RSP Index Fund, with a 1.5% MER, constitutes the best of all worlds—unlimited exposure to the U.S. market and a reasonable MER. The Atlas International RSP Index Fund provides similar unlimited exposure to international markets at a reasonable 2% MER, and the Atlas World Bond Fund does the same for global bonds at 2.12%.

Atlas makes much of its role as a "manager of managers" and indeed chose to replace several managers in 1998. In October 1998, it replaced Salomon Brothers Asset Management Ltd. with Laketon Investment Management for the above-named Atlas World Bond Fund. It also appointed Merrill Lynch Asset Management LP, Atlas' corporate affiliate, on the money market funds.

Later that month, it replaced Vancouver-based Deans Knight Capital Management Ltd. with Calgary's Bissett & Associates on the Atlas Canadian Emerging Growth Fund. And in November 1998, Singapore-based Global Value Investment Portfolio Management Pte Ltd. replaced IAI International Ltd.

Internationally, Atlas provides access to some credible managers, albeit at fairly stiff MERs. Marvin & Palmer Associates Inc. manages the Asian and Emerging Markets funds; Bankers Trust, the Latin fund; and Pictet International Management Ltd., the European fund.

High-net-worth investors may want to investigate the Horizons program of individually managed accounts provided by Merrill Lynch Asset Management Group Canada, available for Merrill Lynch clients with at least $500,000 of investable assets. Managers include Bissett, Mulvihill Capital, BonaVista, Acuity, Jarislowsky Fraser, Goodreid Investment Counsel, Brandes Investment Partners L.P., and Morgan Stanley.

Year 2000 Stance

Atlas was unable to articulate its Y2K investment policies at the time of writing, which should sound alarm bells for some unitholders concerned about this possible problem.

Smart Funds 2000

Y2K OK

Atlas Canadian Large Cap Growth. Managed by Bissett & Associates, Fred Pynn, the two-time Smart Fund Manager of the Year, but at a higher MER than would be obtained directly from Bissett. Seeks companies with strong balance sheets and reasonable valuations. Fund returned 15.3% in year ended August 31, 1999, slightly worse than the 26.6% gain of the TSE 300 index.

Atlas American RSP Index Fund. Low-MER index funds are rare among Canadian broker-sold funds. Managed by Newcastle Capital Management Inc., this index fund has a reasonable MER of 1.5% and 100% RRSP eligibility to boot. Asset mix is 70% the S&P 500 index, 20% the mid-cap S&P 400 index, and 10% the Nasdaq 100 index. Consider also the Atlas International RSP Index Fund also managed by Newcastle.

Noteworthy Funds

Y2K KO

Atlas Canadian Money Market Fund. Under a Y2K KO scenario, most of Atlas's fixed income funds have onerous MERs. The 1.11% is also high for a money market fund but hopefully you plan to "park" your funds only for a short time. Invested 80% in commercial paper with balance in Canadian T-bills and term deposits. Consider also the 100% RRSP-eligible Atlas World Bond Fund.

Y2K Agnostic

Atlas Canadian Balanced Fund. First quartile over one-, two-, three-, and five-year periods to August 31, 1999. Classic balanced fund managed by Jarislowsky Fraser Ltd. At the time of writing it was roughly 50% invested in equities and 50% in bonds and cash.

Availability

Most full-service and discount brokerages and financial planners, and Laurentian Bank offices.

8. BANK OF MONTREAL FIRST CANADIAN FUNDS **NO LOAD**

Strengths	Declining fees for large volume of assets MatchMaker asset allocation service
Weaknesses	Index fund MERs too high
RESPs?	Yes
Web Site	www.bmo.com/fcfunds **Toll Free** 1-800-665-7700

CANADIAN	Category	Rating	Fund Name	MER%	RRSP/Foreign
Money Market:		■	First Canadian Money Market	1.12	RRSP
		■	First Canadian T-Bill	1.16	RRSP
		▲ KO	First Canadian Premium Money Market	0.4	RRSP
Fixed Income:	Long-term	■	First Canadian Bond	1.51	RRSP
	Income	■	First Canadian Monthly Income	New	RRSP
	Mortgage	▲ KO	First Canadian Mortgage	1.41	RRSP
Equity:	Large Cap	▲ OK	First Canadian Equity	2.21	RRSP
	Small-Mid Cap	■	First Canadian Special Equity	2.22	RRSP
	Index	■	First Canadian Equity Index	1.22	RRSP
	Gold/precious metal	▲ KO	First Canadian Precious Metals	2.07	RRSP
	Resource	■	First Canadian Resource	2.28	RRSP
Tax Advantaged:	Dividend	★ AG	First Canadian Dividend	1.66	RRSP
Multi-Asset:	Asset Allocation	▲ AG	First Canadian Asset Allocation	1.94	RRSP

FOREIGN	Category	Rating	Fund Name	MER%	RRSP/Foreign
Money Market:	U.S. Dollar	■	First Canadian U.S. Dollar Money Market	New	Foreign*
Fixed Income:	U.S. Dollar	■	First Canadian U.S. Dollar Bond	New	Foreign*
		■	First Canadian International Bond	2.01	Foreign
Global Equity:	EAFE	■	First Canadian International Equity	2.01	Foreign
	Specialty	▲ OK	First Canadian Global Science & Technology	1.96	Foreign
	Index	■	First Canadian International Index RSP	New	Foreign
Regional Equity:	U.S. Large cap	▲ OK	First Canadian U.S. Growth	2.18	Foreign
		■	First Canadian U.S. Value	2.01	Foreign
	U.S. Small cap	■	First Canadian US. Special Equity	1.96	Foreign
	U.S. index	▲ OK	First Canadian U.S. Equity Index RSP	1.22	RRSP
	U.S. Dollar	■	First Canadian U.S.Dollar Equity Index	New	Foreign*
	NAFTA/N.Am.	■	First Canadian NAFTA Advantage	2.06	Foreign
	Latin American	■	First Canadian Latin America	2.34	Foreign
	Emerging Market	■	First Canadian Emerging Markets	2.18	Foreign
	Far East	■	First Canadian Far East	2.2	Foreign
	Japan	▲ AG	First Canadian Japanese	2.23	Foreign
	Europe	■	First Canadian European	2.06	Foreign

* Not available for RRSP

The United States has been the market with the biggest payoff through most of the 1990s' bull run. Over the past year, Bank of Montreal's First Canadian Funds have been exploiting that fact. To its existing 25 no-load mutual funds, it has added three U.S.-dollar funds to accommodate investors wishing to hold assets denominated in U.S. dollars. In this it is aided by subadvisor Harris Investment Management Inc. of Chicago, which already directs investments in the older First Canadian U.S. equity funds. Harris is also advisor to the new First Canadian U.S. Dollar Money Market, U.S. Dollar Bond, and U.S. Dollar Equity Index Funds, all launched in October 1998.

Because they are new, the MERs are not shown in the matrix. But the management fee is 1% on the first $50,000 for the U.S. Dollar Money Market Fund and U.S. Dollar Equity Index, and 1.25% on U.S. Dollar Bond. Like other First Canadian funds, these fees ratchet down to as low as 0.5% and 0.7% at over $1 million.

First Canadian is also making it easier for RRSP and RRIF investors to maximize their foreign content with global securities. In March 1999, it launched the First Canadian International Index RRSP Fund, a 100% RRSP-eligible fund that uses derivatives, including futures, forwards, and options, to track the MSCI EAFE index (Morgan Stanley Capital International—Europe, Australia, and the Far East). The new fund is managed by State Street Global Advisors.

Also new is the First Canadian Monthly Income Fund, which invests in corporate and government debt instruments, preferred and common shares, real estate investment trusts, royalty trusts, and other high-yielding instruments. Jones Heward Investment Counsel, which advises other First Canadian domestic funds, is manager of the new income fund.

Some of the names on the matrix have been changed slightly: the word "growth" has been omitted on a number of fund names to better reflect a "value" orientation. Thus, for example, Japanese Growth Fund has been renamed the Japanese Fund.

On the personnel front, veteran Bill Belovay, who joined Jones Heward last year, is now manager of the First Canadian Resource and First Canadian Precious Metals Fund. In October 1998, Jones Heward also appointed Lesley Marks as advisor to the First Canadian Special Equity Fund.

Intuition, the Registered Education Savings Plan (RESP) launched in May 1998, has proven the attraction of government grants (a 20% grant for each $2,000 annual purchase of an RESP per child): more than 20,000 Intuition accounts have been opened.

Another popular service is the MatchMaker Strategic Investment Service, first announced early in 1996 and which has attracted more than $3 billion in net fund assets. MatchMaker is the centrepiece of BMO's "It doesn't have to be complicated" brand positioning. The capability of automatic rebalancing of portfolios to reflect a customer's original risk/return profile is attractive in the kind of volatile markets experienced in the fall of 1998 and which could recur under a Year 2000 downturn.

First Canadian continues to be almost alone among the big bank no-load groups to give a price break to large investors. In a feature that should be adopted by its competitors if they wish to retain the high-net-worth client, BMO's declining management fee schedule kicks in starting with a $50,000 investment in a fund. The 2% fee that small investors pay on First Canadian Growth would, for example, fall to 1.6%, then 1.4%, 1.2%, 1.1%, and finally 1% on amounts greater than $1 million. If performance in funds generally falls to single digits in the near future, this feature may strengthen returns for large portfolios.

Year 2000 Stance

First Canadian Funds reports that all investment advisors consider Y2K readiness when assessing a new or continued investment in a company. All interviews held with company management include the question of Y2K readiness. The fund family "considers Year 2000 issues as part of our due diligence in monitoring our managers. It is our intention to minimize the risk of investment in companies that are not taking adequate steps to mitigate their exposure to the Year 2000 issue."

Thus, fund managers continually assess the Y2K readiness of stocks held in the fund portfolios. Companies found not to be Y2K compliant may be sold, particularly those that operate in critical industries such as utilities.

However, First Canadian describes the situation in non-developed markets as "more complex." Many firms in Asia and Latin America have only recently computerized and so have Y2K-ready equipment. Non-Y2K-ready companies add to the risk factors assessed by fund managers as to whether to purchase a company.

Smart Funds 2000

Y2K Agnostic

First Canadian Dividend. Returning Smart Fund, managed by Jones Heward's Michael Stanley. First quartile over two and three years.

Noteworthy Funds

Y2K OK

First Canadian Equity. Formerly First Canadian Growth Fund, fund has been in first quartile over one-, two-, three-, and five-year periods ended August 31, 1999. MER of 2.21% is no screaming bargain.

First Canadian U.S. Growth. Second quartile over the last three years, this Harris-advised fund is now in its sixth year. So far the MER of 2.18% has been justified, relative to the index version, also managed by Harris.

First Canadian U.S. Equity Index RSP. MER of 1.22% is attractive for investors wanting U.S. market exposure without using up foreign-content room in registered plans.

First Canadian Global Science & Technology Fund. Global equity fund that intends to have at least 50% invested in each of science (health care) and technology sectors. Fund's two-year CAGR is 41.3%. Has preference for companies that have displayed repeatable, sustainable, and predictable earnings. Advised by Harris' Dan Sido.

Y2K KO

First Canadian Premium Money Market. Launched in late 1997, this fund offers safe parking at an MER of just 0.4% for investors who can ante up the minimum $150,000 investment. For those with smaller amounts, the two alternative money market funds charge more than 1%.

First Canadian Mortgage. Returns to first-quartile performance, this fund should generate higher yields than money market funds and expose unitholders to less risk than long-term bond funds. Long history: launched in 1974 with good long-term results: first quartile over 10 years and five years.

First Canadian Precious Metals. Manager Bill Belovay has plenty of experience as a mining analyst. Aggressive investors worried about Y2K may find a small position in this fund could offset losses in the general market, should they arise.

Y2K Agnostic

First Canadian Japanese. If you believe that Japan has undergone its worst period and want to reduce exposure to overvalued North American markets, this fund may be one contrarian play for aggressive investors. Advised by J.P. Morgan since January 1998, and first quartile since the change, this employs sector-neutral stock selection based on J.P. Morgan's proprietary dividend discount model.

First Canadian Asset Allocation. Another middle-of-the-road choice for Y2K agnostics

Availability

Bank of Montreal branches across Canada, Nesbitt Burns, InvestorLine, Investores, mbanx, and through the First Canadian Call Centre. $500 minimum initial investment for funds, $1,000 for MatchMaker or Intuition portfolios.

9. BISSETT & ASSOCIATES

NO LOAD

Strengths "Low MERs, No-Load"
Small-cap equities

Weaknesses Retirement of David Bissett
"Minimum $10,000 investments"

RESPs? No

Web Site www.bissett.com **Toll Free** (888)-247-7388

CANADIAN	Category	Rating	Fund Name	MER%	RRSP/Foreign
Money Market:			Bissett Money Market Fund	0.5	RRSP
Fixed Income:	Mixed-term	★ KO	Bissett Bond Fund	0.75	RRSP

	Category	Rating	Fund Name	MER%	RRSP/Foreign
Equity:	Large-cap	■	Bissett Large Cap Fund	New	RRSP
	Mid-Large Cap	★ OK	Bissett Canadian Equity Fund	1.19	RRSP
	Small Cap	▲ OK	Bissett Small Cap Fund	1.78	RRSP
	Micro Cap	■	Bissett Microcap Fund	2.5	RRSP
Tax Advantaged:	Dividend	★ AG	Bissett Dividend Income Fund	1.31	RRSP
	Income Trust	▲ AG	Bissett Income Trust Fund	1.25	RRSP
Multi-Asset:	Portfolio of Funds	★ AG	Bissett Retirement Fund	1.31	RRSP

FOREIGN	Category	Rating	Fund Name	MER%	RRSP/Foreign
Global Equity:	All-global	★ OK	Bissett Multinational Growth Fund	1.34	Foreign
	EAFE	■	Bissett International Equity Fund	2	Not RRSP eligible
Regional Equity:	U.S.	■	Bissett American Equity Fund	1.44	Foreign

When this fund family was perhaps at the pinnacle of its popularity, founder David Bissett announced his retirement in June 1999. His announcement comes as this popular Calgary-based money manager extended the availability of his funds nationwide, now including Quebec, and a year after going public. Top management holds 66% of the stock.

Bissett now manages more than $5 billion for various institutional pension plans and wealthy individuals. And its popular low-MER, no-load retail funds have been making more ordinary Canadians wealthy, provided they can ante up the minimum $10,000 investment per fund.

While the impact of David Bissett's departure is potentially a concern, the succession plan seems to have been implemented smoothly. Long-time Bissett senior executive Kevin Wolfe is now president and chief executive officer, Gene Vollendorf—who joined in 1996—is continuing as small-cap and micro-cap manager, and Leslie Lundquist—who joined in 1992—is continuing as income trust manager. Fred Pynn, profiled in last year's edition, and other popular fund managers remain in place.

Because the company spends little on marketing, MERs are below 1.5% for most of its equity funds, with the exception of 2% for its international equity fund, 2.5% for the microcap fund, 1.9% for the small-cap fund, 0.75% for the bond fund, and 0.5% for the money market fund. There are no switching fees.

Bissett's emphasis remains on North American equities. The fund line-up is unchanged from the previous year, but with one addition: the new Bissett Large Cap Fund, launched in June 1999, which will invest in the top 120 market capitalization stocks in Canada and will be benchmarked against the S&P/TSE 60 index.

Bissett is popping up as the advisor to other well-known money managers. Fidelity Pensions now offers Bissett Funds as part of its FundsNet program and continues to be advisor to external funds such as Atlas Canadian Growth. Canada Life and Industrial Alliance have put insurance seg wrappers on some Bissett funds.

Year 2000 Stance

In addition to the usual assurances as to its own internal readiness, Bissett's equity research teams are reviewing the funds' investments from a Year 2000 perspective. It states that its "conclusions could lead to buy/sell decisions of existing and potential securities that are deemed to be vulnerable to Year 2000 issues."

It has reviewed "the majority" of Canadian and U.S. securities held in its equity accounts and is comfortable there is a high level of awareness of the problem and "willingness to take actions to mitigate any risks involved."

Smart Funds 2000

Y2K OK

Bissett Canadian Equity Fund. Fund fared no better than most Canadian equity funds the past year but the MER of 1.19% is hard to match. Lead manager Fred Pynn includes some small- and mid-cap firms with the mostly large-cap stocks in this conservatively managed fund.

Bissett Multinational Growth. First quartile over three years and five years ended August 31, 1999.

Y2K KO

Bissett Bond Fund. Almost equal split of corporate and federal bonds, with slightly fewer provincial issues. Lead manager Michael Quinn uses a moderate term-to-maturity approach rather than trying to anticipate interest rates.

Y2K Agnostic

Bissett Dividend Income. Steady first- or second- quartile performance year in and year out, with MER of just 1.31%

Bissett Retirement Fund. This fund of other Bissett Funds was 40% weighted to the bond fund as of June 30, 1999. MER is 0.23% on top of the underlying funds MERs. A pretty good deal for this consistent first- and second-quartile performer.

Noteworthy Funds

Y2K OK

Bissett Small Cap Fund. This fund has been demoted from Smart Fund status, partly because of David Bissett's retirement, and also because it lost 13.3%, substantially more than the average small-cap fund, for the two years ended August 31, 1999.

Y2K Agnostic

Bissett Income Trust Fund. This is billed as providing tax-effective cash flow but it lost money, 6% for the two years ended August 31, 1999, and more than the average dividend fund.

Availability

Directly from the company on a no-load basis for investors in all provinces, now including Quebec. Also available through all full-service and discount brokerage firms and most planners. Brokers may charge a 2% front load. Minimum investment has been increased to $10,000 per fund.

10. BPI CAPITAL MANAGEMENT CORP. FRONT OR REAR

Strengths	Legacy seg funds New RSP-eligible foreign funds
Weaknesses	Load structure tends to be high Equity fund MERs still high
RESPs?	Yes
Web Site	bpifunds.com
Toll Free	1-800-937-5146

CANADIAN	Category	Rating	Fund Name	MER%	RRSP/Foreign
Money Market:		■	BPI T-Bill Fund	0.65	RRSP
		■	BPI Legacy T-Bill Segregated	0.7	RRSP
Fixed Income:	Long-term	■	BPI Canadian Bond Fund	1.5	RRSP
		■	BPI Legacy Canadian Bond Seg	1.65	RRSP
	Corporate Bond	■	BPI Corporate Bond Fund	1.5	RRSP
Equity:	Large-Cap	▲ OK	BPI Dividend Equity Fund	New	RRSP
	Mid-Large Cap	■	BPI Canadian Equity Value Fund	2.46	RRSP
		■	BPI Legacy Canadian Equity Value Seg	2.71	RRSP
	Mid-cap	■	BPI Canadian Mid-Cap Fund	2.76	RRSP
		■	BPI Legacy Canadian Mid Cap Seg	3.16	RRSP
	Small Cap	■	BPI Canadian Small Companies Fund	2.78	RRSP

	Resource	■	BPI Canadian Resource Fund Inc.	2.99	RRSP
	Other	■	BPI Canadian Opportunities RSP Fund	2.47	RRSP
		■	BPI Canadian Opportunities II Fund	1.94	RRSP
Tax Advantaged:	Dividend	★ OK	BPI Dividend Income Fund	1	RRSP
		▲ KO	BPI Legacy Dividend Income Seg	1.15	RRSP
	Div/High yield	★ AG	BPI High Income Fund	1.25	RRSP
		■	BPI Legacy High Income Seg	1.45	RRSP
	Labor-sponsored	■	VenGrowth	3.9	RRSP
	Labor/Manitoba	■	ENSIS Growth Fund	New	RRSP
Multi-Asset:	Balanced	■	BPI Canadian Balanced Fund	2.2	RRSP
	Div/Bal'd	▲ AG	BPI Income & Growth Fund	2.5	RRSP
		■	BPI Legacy Income & Growth Seg	2.65	RRSP

FOREIGN	Category	Rating	Fund Name	MER%	RRSP/Foreign
Money Market:		■	BPI U.S. Money Market Fund	0.65	Foreign
Fixed Income:		■	BPI Global RSP Bond Fund	1.5	RRSP
Global Equity:	All-global	★ OK	BPI Global Equity Value Fund	2.43	Foreign
		■	BPI Legacy Global Equity Value Seg	2.78	Foreign
	Small-cap	■	BPI Global Small Companies Fund	2.61	Foreign
	Specialty	■	BPI Global Opportunities Fund	2.56	Foreign
	EAFE	■	BPI International Equity Value Fund	2.47	Foreign
		■	BPI Legacy International Equity Value Seg	2.82	Foreign
Global Equity:	U.S. Mid-large	★ OK	BPI American Equity Value Fund	2.37	Foreign
		■	BPI Legacy Amer. Equity Value Seg	2.77	Foreign
	U.S. Small-cap	■	BPI American Small Companies Fund	2.63	Foreign
	Emerging Market	■	BPI Emerging Markets Fund	2.82	Foreign
	Far East	■	BPI Asia Pacific Fund	3.25	Foreign

After much speculation about a pending merger, on August 19, 1999, C.I. Fund Management Inc. purchased BPI Financial Corp., parent of BPI Mutual Funds. That deal created a combined company that is now the 10th-largest fund operation in Canada with assets of $17 billion. There is no doubt this is a significant event for BPI unitholders. Several fund mergers and management changes will likely result from the deal already underway as of fall 1999. BPI has been completely absorbed by C.I. and its Canadian funds will likely be renamed, possibly with the C.I. Signature brand. The international funds will retain the BPI name to reflect the management of BPI's U.S. operation in Orlando, Florida.

This deal is likely a blessing and a burden for BPI investors, although there should be more pluses than minuses over the long term. Through C.I. investors have access to an even greater selection of funds including some classic Smart Funds. And C.I. says the greater economies of scale will result in lower management expense ratios. On the downside, investors might feel overwhelmed by the more than 100 funds the combined family now offers.

What follows is the commentary on the BPI funds prepared prior to the merger. Because many changes will likely be implemented, be sure to understand how the funds have changed prior to purchasing them.

BPI's strength used to be small-cap equity funds, both domestically and globally. For a long time, these carried hefty MERs, but were worth it. But the Canadian Small Companies Fund run internally by Steven Misener has continued to struggle. It lost 18.6% in 1997 and another 35% in 1998. This fund has been hit with a double whammy: it has been a tough period for all small caps, as the market has favoured their larger brethren. And it has been at the bottom of the category. BPI has tried to address the problem by reassigning responsibilities among the Canadian team, thus giving Misener more time to focus on the fund. Andrew Waight now manages the BPI Canadian Mid-Cap Fund. And Robert Lyon is managing BPI Canadian Resources. The lighter load seems to be helping; as we update this book, the fund appears to be turning around, performing ahead of the rebound of the small-cap sector.

BPI's varied global equity and American equity funds are run in-house by its subsidiary, BPI Global Asset Management LLP of Orlando, Florida. Several of these funds have kept pace with or beat their benchmarks justifying their higher-than-average expense ratios.

BPI also made changes to its American Small Companies Fund this year. In March 1999, Paul Holland took over management of that fund, along with all of BPI's U.S. equity portfolios. Working with him are Jon Sorensen and John Bichelmeyer.

BPI has two high-net-worth hedge funds, known as the Opportunities Funds. Global Opportunities Fund continued on its positive run with a strong 67.7% return over one year to August 31. In November, BPI Canadian Opportunities RSP Fund, with its lacklustre performance, was merged into BPI Global Opportunities. And the other Canadian fund, Canadian Opportunities II, was changed to a global mandate and renamed BPI Global Opportunities II. This closed-end fund continues to trade on the Toronto and Montreal exchanges (as BOI.UN) and is managed by Dan Jaworski and Paul Holland from BPI's Orlando office.

Ironically, given BPI's aggressive tendencies, its strength has appeared increasingly in its more conservative domestic income and balanced funds. The BPI Income and Growth Fund absorbed the BPI Global Balanced Fund in December 1998. This fund continues to perform above average with a 14.7% gain over one year to August 31. Its MER remained at 2.48%.

BPI did a good job of offering a variety of product that could appeal to many investors and those continue to be available through C.I.

Mutual Funds. The addition of the RSP-eligible foreign funds will appeal to the many investors moving more money outside Canada.

Year 2000 Stance

Fred Dalley, BPI's executive vice president of portfolio management, acknowledges that there are limitless scenarios in which there could be Y2K problems with companies that money managers invest in. But good diversification of the funds should shield investors from being overexposed to any particular crisis, he argues. As well, BPI claims to stick to "the highest quality companies within each sector or asset class." These companies are the most likely to be prepared and their strong cash flow should allow them to deal quickly with any unexpected problems.

Smart Funds 2000

Y2K OK

BPI Dividend Income. One of the best in its class. Fund pays 4.5 cents per unit per month.

Y2K Agnostic

BPI High Income. A bit more yield than the Dividend Income with a payout of 6.5 cents per unit per month. Roughly 7.5% yield makes this one good for investors needing higher income from their fund.

BPI American Equity Value. Over one year to August 31, the 60.8% gain of this fund was well ahead of the U.S. benchmark S&P 500 index of 33.1%. It is managed by BPI's global asset office in Orlando.

BPI Global Equity Value. Continues its first-quartile performance over all long-term periods.

Noteworthy Funds

Y2K OK

BPI Dividend Equity. Eric Bushell, manager of the "Smart" High Income Fund, buys large-cap Canadian stocks that pay dividends and some foreign companies that do the same. It was a year old at May 31. As of the end of June 1999, it returned 29.5% over one year, well ahead of the TSE 100 index.

Y2K KO

BPI Legacy Dividend Income Seg. Low MER, conservatively invested in quality dividend-paying stocks and a seg guarantee of initial principal.

Would provide more upside than other Y2K KO havens in this family: the T-Bill Fund or Legacy Canadian Bond Seg Fund.

Y2K Agnostic

BPI Income & Growth. Managed by Wally Kusters and Chris Roy, this balanced fund had about 32% in bonds at August 31, 1999. With its sizeable weighting in equity markets, it managed to perform better than many of its competitors.

Availability

Only through full-service and discount brokers and dealers. Note that the three Opportunities Funds are subject to large minimum investment requirements under regulators' sophisticated investor guidelines, which vary by province.

11. CANADA LIFE ASSURANCE COMPANY **REAR**

Strengths	Guarantees of seg funds, but only 75% Multiple brand-name advisors
Weaknesses	Hard to mix with other funds unless advisor is dual licensed High MERs for brand-name seg funds
RESPs?	No
Web Site	www.canadalife.com **Toll Free** 1-888-252-1847

CANADIAN	Category	Rating	Fund Name	M.E.R.%	RRSP/Foreign
Money Market:		■	No-load Money Market Fund (Laketon)	0.85	RRSP
		■	Money Market Fund (Laketon)	1.30	RRSP
Fixed Income:		■	Canadian Bond Fund (AGF)	2.70	RRSP
		■	Fixed Income Fund (Bissett)	2.60	RRSP
		■	Fixed Income Fund (Laketon)	2.05	RRSP
Short-term:		■	Canadian Short-Term Bond Fund (Scudder)	2.15	RRSP
	Index	▲ KO	Indexed Canadian Bond Fund (TDQC)	2.00	RRSP
		■	International Bond Fund (Laketon)	2.05	RRSP
Tax Advantaged:		■	Dividend Fund (AGF)	3.05	RRSP
		■	Enhanced Dividend Fund (Laketon)	2.05	RRSP
Multi-Asset:		■	Balanced Fund (Bissett)	3.00	RRSP
		■	Harbour Growth & Income Fund (C.I.)	2.95	RRSP
		■	Canadian Asset Allocation Fund (Fidelity)	2.95	RRSP
		■	Managed Fund (Laketon)	2.30	RRSP
	Index	▲ AG	Indexed Balanced Fund (TDQC)	2.20	RRSP
		■	Balanced Fund (Trimark)	3.00	RRSP

Fund of Funds:					
	Asset Allocation Service	★ AG	Continuum Conservative Module	2.35	RRSP
	Asset Allocation Service	■	Continuum Moderate Module	2.52	RRSP
	Asset Allocation Service	■	Continuum Growth Module	2.77	RRSP
	Asset Allocation Service	■	Continuum Aggressive Growth Module	2.84	RRSP
	Asset Allocation Service	■	Continuum Maximum Growth Module	2.88	RRSP
Equity:	Small-mid cap	■	Canadian Equity Fund (AGF)	3.10	RRSP
		■	Canadian Equity Fund (AIC)	3.20	RRSP
		■	Canadian Equity Fund (Bissett)	2.80	RRSP
	Small cap	■	Small Cap Equity Fund (Bissett)	3.00	RRSP
		■	Harbour Canadian Fund (C.I.)	2.90	RRSP
		■	True North Fund (Fidelity)	2.85	RRSP
		■	Canadian Equity Fund (Laketon)	2.30	RRSP
		■	Canadian Equity Fund (Scudder)	3.10	RRSP
	Index	▲ OK	Indexed Canadian Equity (TDQC)	2.10	RRSP
		■	Canadian Equity Fund (Templeton)	3.15	RRSP
		■	Canadian Equity Fund (Trimark)	2.90	RRSP

FOREIGN	Category	Rating	Fund Name	M.E.R.%	RRSP/Foreign
Regional Equity:	U.S.	■	U.S. Value Fund (AIC)	3.50	Foreign
	U.S.	■	Growth America Fund (Fidelity)	3.10	Foreign
	U.S.	■	U.S. Equity Fund (Scudder)	3.25	Foreign
	Index	■	Indexed U.S. Equity Fund (TDQC)	2.30	Foreign
	European	■	European Equity Fund (Laketon)	2.45	Foreign
	European	■	Greater Europe Fund (Scudder)	3.90	Foreign
Global Equity:		▲ OK	World Equity Fund (AIC)	3.60	Foreign
	Specialty	▲ OK	Global Boomernomics Fund (C.I.)	3.50	Foreign
		■	International Portfolio Fund (Fidelity)	3.15	Foreign
		■	Global Equity Fund (Laketon)	2.45	Foreign
		■	Global Equity Fund (Scudder)	3.75	Foreign
	Index	■	Indexed Global Equity Fund (TDQC)	2.30	Foreign
		■	International Equity Fund (Templeton)	3.40	Foreign
		■	Global Equity Fund (Trimark)	3.15	Foreign
		■	Global Equity RSP Fund (C.I.)	3.30	RRSP

Fans of popular broker-sold firms such as AGF, AIC, C.I., Fidelity, Templeton, and Trimark, and no-load firms such as Bissett and Scudder, can gain access to "segregated" fund versions of some of their families through Canada Life, an insurance company with more than 150 years in Canada.

However, the accompanying MERs for such protection can come in higher than average, even for normally low-MER families such as Bissett and Scudder. Furthermore, the Canada Life versions offer only a 75% guarantee of principal over 10 years, unlike the 100% offered by many of the newer mutual fund/insurance company alliances unveiled in recent years. C.I., Templeton, and Trimark offer seg versions of their own funds; compare MERs and guarantees before deciding on the Canada Life or original version.

Since the last edition of *Smart Funds*, Canada Life has launched Generations, a new investment contract on the retail side of Canada Life's Investments and Pensions operations. It provides individual investors with access to more than 40 segregated funds managed by some of the above-named money managers.

Canada Life also launched the Continuum Fund, an asset-allocation service consisting of five modules, each tailored to investors with varying risk/reward tolerances. Most of the Generations funds invest in units of underlying mutual or pooled funds (except funds managed by Laketon that invest directly in individual securities).

Early in 1999, INDAGO Capital Management (formerly Canada Life Investment Management) merged with Laketon Investment Management. Some fund managers have changed as a result. Canada Life now names Laketon as the manager of its segregated funds. The management style for Laketon funds has not changed.

Canada Life funds are offered only on a DSC (deferred sales charge) basis, except Laketon's no-load money market fund. Two policies are available: the Flexible Investment Policy, available only for Laketon-managed funds (the Money Market Fund is excluded here); and the Generations Policy, which is available for purchasing any of the more than 40 segregated funds.

Year 2000 Stance

All of the funds offered under the Canada Life Flexible Investment Policy (Flex) are managed by Laketon Investment Management, which is 35% owned by Canada Life. According to Laketon, "The Y2K issue has been touted by some as a disaster waiting to happen, and by others as a non-event. What is certain is the high degree of uncertainty surrounding this issue and thus Laketon is proactively contacting all portfolio holdings, requesting reports on their Y2K readiness and how they are ensuring that their businesses will not be negatively impacted, insofar as it is within their control."

Laketon views the Y2K issue as an added element of risk that must be controlled to the extent possible. As of mid-1999, many companies still had to complete their Y2K readiness testing, Laketon reports, although most have plans in place. Laketon estimates that it will have a clearer assessment of the risks in the latter part of the third quarter.

Other considerations include portfolio trading activity at year end. Activity may be limited should the Y2K risks associated with custodians and the settlement process appear to be high. Laketon states that it does not believe that Y2K will be devastating to financial markets and is therefore not recommending any radical changes to clients' investment programs. It will, however, monitor the situation closely as events unfold. Laketon also manages some of the funds offered under Generations.

Smart Funds 2000

Y2K Agnostic

Generations Continuum Fund. Conservative Module. With a 2.35% MER, this most conservative of the Continuum Fund's asset allocation modules should weather a severe Y2K storm, especially when you consider that it also has the normal 75% seg fund principal guarantees. Fund consists 60% of three bond funds run by T.A.L., McLean Budden, and TD Quantitative Capital, with the balance Canadian, U.S., and global equity funds run by McLean Budden, Knight Bain Seath Holbrook, and INDAGO respectively.

Noteworthy Funds

Y2K OK

CL Generations Indexed Canadian Equity (TD Quantitative Capital). Index fund mirrors the TSE 300 total return index with a 2.1% MER that is no lower than the average for Canadian funds but is lower than alternatives in this family. When you add in the 75% capital guarantee, however, that makes this a reasonable bet for those who want market returns in Canada with some downside protection.

CL Generations Global Boomernomics Fund (C.I.). The 3.5% MER on this fund is too stiff for Smart Fund status. But C.I.'s Bill Sterling is on top of two important trends: the baby-boom demographic argument for rising stock prices, as well as the need to hold only Y2K-compliant stocks in a portfolio. With a seg fund guarantee as a hedge, there is at least a chance that this fund may justify its outrageously high MER.

CL Generations World Equity Fund (AIC). The 3.6% MER is 90 basis points higher than the underlying AIC World Equity Fund, but AIC has consistently shown that it is capable of justifying its MERs. Add Canada Life's 75% seg guarantee of initial principal and this fund may have some allure for "have your cake and eat it too" investors.

Y2K KO

CL Generations Indexed Canadian Bond Fund (TD Quantitative Capital). For investors oriented to preservation of capital, this fund mirrors the Scotia Capital Markets Universe bond index at an MER of 2%–pretty stiff for an indexed bond fund but lower than most of the other alternatives in this family. Mix is 60% Government of Canada bonds, 21% provincials, 16% corporate bonds, and 1% municipal bonds.

Y2K Agnostic

CL Generations Indexed Balanced Fund (TD Quantitative Capital). Indexed balanced funds are rare in Canada even though index-king John Bogle has declared that they are all an investor really needs. The 2.2% MER is nothing to write home about, considering the passive investment approach, but lower than most of the other funds in this family. Fund invests in the Emerald Balanced Fund, a pooled fund managed by TD Quantitative Capital and mirrors both major U.S. and Canadian stock indices as well as the Scotia Capital Markets Universe Bond Index and T-Bill Index. Asset mix was roughly 50% stocks to 50% bonds.

Availability

Across Canada through salespeople who hold an insurance licence. $1,000 minimum initial investment for Flex or Generations: $500 thereafter or $50 via PACs.

12. CANADA TRUST MUTUAL FUNDS

NO LOAD

Strengths 100% RRSP-eligible global funds
Index funds, Investment Planner Plus Asset Allocation tool
Weaknesses In-house equity management
RESPs? No
Web Site www.canadatrust.com **Toll Free** 1-800-386-3757

CANADIAN	Category	Rating	Fund Name	M.E.R.%	RRSP/Foreign
Money Market:		■	Canada Trust Money Market Fund	0.98	RRSP
		■	Canada Trust Premium Money Market Fund	0.57	RRSP

Fixed Income:	Long-term	■	Canada Trust Bond Fund	1.35	RRSP
		★ KO	Canada Trust Canadian Bond Index Fund	0.83	RRSP
	Short-term	■	Canada Trust Short Term Bond	1.38	RRSP
	Mortgage	▲ KO	Canada Trust Mortgage Fund	1.59	RRSP
Equity:	Mid-Large Cap	■	Canada Trust Stock Fund	1.87	RRSP
		■	Canada Trust Canadian Equity Index Fund	0.75	RRSP
	Small Cap	■	Canada Trust Special Equity Fund	2.15	RRSP
Tax Advantaged:	Dividend	▲ OK	Canada Trust Dividend Income Fund	1.90	RRSP
Multi-Asset:		■	Canada Trust Monthly Income Fund	new	RRSP
	Balanced	■	Canada Trust Balanced Fund	2.13	RRSP
		■	Canada Trust RIF Balanced Fund	1.69	RRIF

FOREIGN	Category	Rating	Fund Name	M.E.R.%	RRSP/Foreign
Fixed Income:		■	Canada Trust International Bond Fund	2.07	RRSP
	High-yield	■	Canada Trust High-Yield Income Fund	new	Foreign
Global Equity:	All-global	■	Canada Trust Global Growth Fund	2.05	RRSP
		■	Canada Trust International Equity Index Fund	0.53	Foreign
	EAFE	■	Canada Trust International Equity Fund	2.62	Foreign
Regional Equity:	U.S.	■	Canada Trust U.S. Equity Fund	2.34	Foreign
	U.S.	■	Canada Trust U.S. Equity Index Fund	0.85	Foreign
		▲ OK	Canada Trust AmeriGrowth Fund	1.39	RRSP
	NAFTA/N.Am.	■	Canada Trust North American Fund	1.85	Foreign
	Emerging Market	■	Canada Trust Emerging Markets Fund	3.22	Foreign
	Far East	■	Canada Trust AsiaGrowth Fund	2.48	RRSP
	Europe	■	Canada Trust EuroGrowth Fund	2.20	RRSP
Multi-Asset:	Global	▲ AG	Canada Trust Global Asset Allocation Fund	new	RRSP
	Global	★ AG	Canada Trust Balanced Index Fund	new	RRSP

The expanded fund matrix in this edition shows at a glance Canada Trust's new thrust into its so-called Investment Portfolios. This is a fund-of-funds concept that wraps together up to 10 mutual funds in various configurations, some of them 100% RRSP-eligible and others counting as foreign content.

The Canada Trust Fund Portfolio invests in underlying Canada Trust no-load mutual funds. The eight Canada Trust Alliance Fund Portfolios invest in funds from other major mutual fund firms. CT Investment Management Group (CTIMG) continuously monitors the portfolios and rebalances them to stay within predetermined asset allocation targets.

As is so often the case in such programs, fees are layered on top of fees and the net MERs of these portfolios come in at the high end of the MER range relative to the underlying funds, particularly in the Alliance series. This is a marked departure from Canada Trust's previous thrust into low-MER index products. Thus, both because of this and the fact that the portfolios are too new to have established track records, most of our Smart and Noteworthy designations are assigned to its lower-MER traditional line-up, known as the Investor Series.

CTIMG was formed four years ago as the investment manager for the Canada Trust Mutual Funds. In late 1998 and early 1999, it took over advisory services previously provided by Schroder Capital Management International Inc. on international bonds; State Street Global Advisors Ltd. in derivatives (including the 100% foreign derivatives funds such as AmeriGrowth and EuroGrowth); Bissett & Associates Investment Management Ltd. and Guardian Capital Inc. in Canadian small caps and mid caps; and Warburg Pincus Asset Management in U.S. small- and mid-cap equities.

Canada Trust has also selected Schroder as its sole external advisor and strategic partner for international and emerging markets equities.

Year 2000 Stance

CT IMG reports that it has reviewed the readiness of individual companies in which its funds invest and "identified key signposts that allow us to assess and monitor industry and market risk associated with the Year 2000." While it has developed various possible scenarios and corresponding strategies, its assessment is that "at least in the short term, this event will accentuate market volatility, due more to investor nervousness about Year 2000 than to any significant impact on the underlying fundamentals of businesses and economies." If the century change occurs without major disruption, which it believes will be "more likely than not," then the market recovery "could well be very early and rapid."

Its strategy continues to be diversifying by industry, geography, and currency.

Its advice to individual investors is "to let their investment plan be their guide." It cautions that "second-guessing the market's direction is difficult at the best of times." Y2K adds another level of complexity, so investors should ensure they have "a well-constructed plan that is diversified to meet their long-term goals and the level of risk they are comfortable accepting."

Smart Funds 2000

Y2K KO

Canada Trust Canadian Bond Index Fund. One of the few bond index funds in Canada. If anything, the argument for indexing is more powerful for bond funds than equity funds. Stingy 0.75% MER.

Y2K Agnostic

Canada Trust Balanced Index Fund. The first of its kind in Canada, this kind of low-cost passively managed fund is the kind of "one fund is all you need" specified by Vanguard Group indexing guru John Bogle. Low MER on the fund of the other CT Index funds. Seems to be working as fund is second quartile for the year ended August 31, 1999.

Noteworthy Funds

Y2K OK

Canada Trust Dividend Income Fund. Provides balance of consistent tax-advantaged dividend income and moderate growth opportunities through blue-chip Canadian common shares.

Canada Trust AmeriGrowth Fund. Reasonable MER and 100% RRSP-eligibility makes this fund attractive for investors who are convinced that Y2K won't stop the bull in its tracks. EuroGrowth and AsiaGrowth are higher-MER alternatives but only if those regions can prove they've licked the Y2K bug.

Y2K KO

Canada Trust Mortgage Fund. Low-volatility fund invests in residential first mortgages and spreads the risk by balancing maturities and geographical distribution.

Y2K Agnostic

Canada Trust Global Asset Allocation Fund. Reasonable MER and 100% RRSP-eligibility make this a reasonable choice for spreading risks globally and by asset class. A tactical asset allocation fund that can shift in a big way to any one asset class or currency if necessary, and has a multi-manager structure featuring Mellon Capital, J.P. Morgan, and CT Investment Management. Above average performer for the one year ended August 31, 1999.

Availability

Sold directly through Canada Trust branches, EasyLine, EasyWeb, and CT Securities' OneStop Fund Solutions. Not available in Northwest Territories. Some brokers may sell on request.

13. CIBC SECURITIES INC.

NO LOAD

Strengths	Nine low-fee Index fund; fees fall with assets Unique 5-year Protected funds Wealth management products
Weaknesses	Hard to choose from 44 funds
RESPs?	Yes
Web Site	www.cibc.com/MutualFunds **Toll Free** 1-800-465-3863

CANADIAN	Category	Rating	Fund Name	M.E.R.%	RRSP/Foreign
Money Market:		■ KO	CIBC Canadian T-Bill Fund	0.99	RRSP
		▲ KO	CIBC Premium Canadian T-Bill Fund	0.55	RRSP
		■	CIBC Money Market Fund	0.99	RRSP
Fixed Income:	Index Short-term	■	CIBC Canadian Short-Term Bond Index Fund	0.90	RRSP
	Mortgage	▲ AG	CIBC Mortgage Fund	1.69	RRSP
	Index (Long-term)	■	CIBC Canadian Bond Index Fund	0.90	RRSP
	Long-term	■	CIBC Canadian Bond Fund	1.59	RRSP
		■	CIBC Monthly Income Fund	1.10	RRSP
Equity:	Index (Large-Cap)	▲ OK	CIBC Canadian Index Fund	0.90	RRSP
	Mid-Large Cap	■	CIBC Core Canadian Equity Fund	2.25	RRSP
	Mid-Large Cap	■	Canadian Imperial Equity Fund	2.00	RRSP
	Small-Cap	■	CIBC Capital Appreciation Fund	2.40	RRSP
	Small-Cap	■	CIBC Canadian Small Companies Fund	2.00	RRSP
	Small-Cap	■	CIBC Canadian Emerging Companies Fund	2.00	RRSP
	Sector	▲ OK	CIBC Financial Companies Fund	2.45	RRSP
	Resource	■	CIBC Canadian Resources Fund	2.35	RRSP
	Energy	■	CIBC Energy Fund	2.35	RRSP
	Sector	■	CIBC Canadian Real Estate Fund	2.65	RRSP
	Gold/precious metal	▲ KO	CIBC Precious Metals Fund	2.25	RRSP
Tax Advantaged:	Dividend	■	CIBC Dividend Fund	1.89	RRSP
Multi-asset:	Balanced	■	CIBC Balanced Fund	2.27	RRSP

FOREIGN	Category	Rating	Fund Name	M.E.R.%	RRSP/Foreign
Money Market:		■	CIBC U.S. Dollar Money Market Fund	1.11	RRSP
Fixed Income:	Index/All-global	■	CIBC Global Bond Index Fund	0.90	RRSP
	All-global	■	CIBC Global Bond Fund	2.05	RRSP
Global Equity:	All-global	■	CIBC Global Equity Fund	2.51	Foreign
	Index/All-global	■	CIBC International Index Fund	0.90	Foreign
	Index/All-global	■	CIBC International Index RRSP Fund	0.90	RRSP
	Small-cap	■	CIBC International Small Companies Fund	2.50	Foreign
	Technology	▲ OK	CIBC Global Technology Fund	2.58	Foreign
Regional Equity:					
	Index/US large-cap	■	CIBC U.S. Index RRSP Fund	0.90	RRSP
	U.S. Mid-Large-cap	▲ OK	CIBC U.S. Equity Fund	0.90	Foreign
	Specialty	★ OK	CIBC North American Demographics Fund	2.49	Foreign
	Index/Europe	■	CIBC European Index Fund	.90	Foreign
	Europe	■	CIBC European Equity Fund	2.48	Foreign
	Japan	■	CIBC Japanese Equity Fund	2.40	Foreign
	U.S. Small-cap	■	CIBC U.S. Small Companies Fund	2.45	Foreign

	Emerging Market	■	CIBC Emerging Economies Fund	2.69	Foreign
	Far East	■	CIBC Far East Prosperity Fund	2.69	Foreign
	Latin America	■	CIBC Latin America Fund	2.5	Foreign

PROTECTED	Category	Rating	Fund Name	M.E.R.%	RRSP/Foreign
Fixed Income	Index/Long-term	■ KO	5-Year Protected Canadian Bond Index Fund	1.75	RRSP
Multi-asset	Index/Balanced	■ AG	5-Year Protected Balanced Index Fund	2.65	RRSP
Equity	Index/Large-cap	■	5-Year Protected Canadian Index Fund	2.84	RRSP
Regional Equity	U.S. Large-cap	▲ AG	5-Year Protected U.S. Index Fund	2.85	Foreign
Global Equity	Index/All-global	■	5-Year Protected International Index Fund	3.49	RRSP

Over the past two years, CIBC Securities Inc. has been innovating on several important fronts. It has responded to the growing demand for lower fees with nine passively managed index funds with just 0.9% MERs, and which fall dramatically as significant investor assets are accumulated. It has met consumer demand for downside protection with its new Protected Funds. And CIBC Trust has been innovating on the wealth management side, combining low-fee indexing with discretionary management, and bringing the minimum entry price for such products down to the $100,000 level.

In all, there are now 44 no-load funds from which to choose. Because the funds are no load, this permits a growth path from the regular mutual funds to the high-net-worth products, with no redemption charges to inhibit the transfer. The seven funds introduced since the last edition of this book include the CIBC Monthly Income Fund and CIBC European Index Fund, launched in August 1998, followed by the December 1998 unveiling of the only five-year Protected Mutual Funds in Canada.

Manager changes have been minimal the past year. Robert Tattersall of small-cap specialists Howson Tattersall has taken over management of CIBC Canadian Emerging Companies Fund. The indexing strategy recognizes two trends: a growing investor sensitivity to high management expense ratios (MERs) and the fact that most actively managed mutual funds fail to beat the index against which they are measured.

All nine CIBC index funds now have MERs of 0.9%—a far sight better than active funds' MERs and among the most aggressive of index funds in Canada. In addition, there is a unique Index Portfolio Rebalancing Service. New in the past year are management fee rebates on index funds for accounts with balances higher than $150,000. For balances between the minimum and $500,000, a 0.6% fee rebate on index funds provides investors with a net management fee of 0.3%. Above $500,000 the rebate is 0.65%, providing a net fee of just 0.25%. These low indexing fees are unprecedented in Canada and moving close to the standard set in the U.S. by index giant Vanguard Group, a non-profit company.

CIBC has been one of the leading banks to innovate, not only in indexing products, but also in mutual-fund-like products aimed at affluent baby boomers. Its index products bring down MERs but CIBC Trust's Professional Investment Management Services division has developed a suite of discretionary investment management services for investors with $100,000 to $1 million in combined household investable assets.

The discretionary investment management division provides a migration path from the retail no-load arm, as investors accumulate assets and look for more personalized service. In less than three years, under vice president discretionary investment management Louise Stonehouse, this division has gone from zero to $5 billion in assets.

The first service was unveiled in 1996—Personal Portfolio Services (PPS), which are actively managed private pooled funds advised by TAL. Investors choose from six investment profiles: income focused, very conservative, conservative, moderate, aggressive, and very aggressive. On the first $250,000, annual fees are 2% for the conservative portfolios, moving up to 2.25% for the most aggressive versions. After the first $250,000 and up to $1 million, the annual fee drops to 0.75%. The income-focused portfolio has a 1.5% fee for the first $250,000 and 0.75% for the next $750,000. Outside of registered plans, the fees are 100% tax-deductible.

In February 1998, CIBC Trust announced a new investment management service targeted to baby-boom investors that combines low-cost passive "indexing" style investing with the same discretionary approach to asset allocation. Called Index Portfolio Services (IPS), the CIBC claims to have brought together "two of the most popular trends in personal finance today—index investing and discretionary investment management."

CIBC Trust uses TAL as its investment advisor for the IPS. They actively monitor the investments and periodically adjust the asset mix on the investor's behalf, adjusting the proportions of cash, fixed income, and equities to reflect the economic environment. The result is an interesting product that at the entry level is competitive with mutual fund fees, and whose fees taper down to be competitive with more upscale pooled funds when assets reach significant levels.

Annual fees on the IPS have been reduced to 1.25% on the first $150,000, whether for the conservative or aggressive profile—about 0.75% cheaper than the actively managed pooled funds. The IPS fees drop to 0.75% for the next $850,000. It includes eight index funds, which track such indices as the TSE 300 and the Wilshire 5000. These fees are partially tax-deductible for non-registered plans.

CIBC also addresses the low end of the mass mutual fund market with its CIBC Choice, which chooses third-party mutual funds selected by author Gordon Pape, with performance monitored by TAL and pension consultants William M. Mercer Ltd. Choice requires only a $25,000 minimum investment and investors can choose from five different investment profiles. It is costlier than CIBC Trust services or CIBC's no-load index funds because an annual management fee is imposed above and beyond the management fees of the underlying funds. Like the higher-end products, Choice's fees taper down with higher asset levels.

Add it all up and CIBC provides an interesting low-cost entry level point for cost-conscious beginning investors, as well as a growth path for affluent investors who want to leave such high-level decisions as asset allocation and fund selection to professionals. As the section below shows, manager TAL is well aware of the Y2K wild card, and the five-year Protected Funds provide a nice capital-preservation floor for investors worried about Y2K. In addition, in August the discretionary investment management division announced a new protection feature for its PPS and IPS portfolios: which provides a 10-year market guarantee at a cost ranging from 75 to 125 basis points, depending on the risk profile. This can be turned on and off at any time.

Year 2000 Stance

CIBC Securities' lead manager, TAL Global Asset Management Inc., was one of the first high-profile Canadian money managers to recognize the potential problems of the Y2K issue. In May, in one of the first investment seminars sponsored by a Canadian fund manager, TAL announced that it was withdrawing from emerging markets because of the problem, and even went so far as to suggest that individuals who were concerned about the problem should overweight cash and bonds in their portfolios. In its official *Smart Funds* submission, TAL said: "While TAL acknowledges the gravity of the situation, TAL views Y2K as only one of many issues that will drive capital market returns over the course of the next 12 to 18 months." Other issues it sees are earnings deceleration, lower European interest rates, strengthening North American currencies, and volatile commodity prices.

TAL views Y2K as an increasing factor in the final months of 1999. It views Y2K as having two impacts on capital market returns: it could restrain economic growth by impacting spending patterns (if consumers stock up on household essentials), and it has also created considerable corporate spending to fix the problem. TAL views this as a positive point initially, with greater economic growth in the last two quarters of 1999 but a possible slowdown early in 2000. It also suggests that lack of preparedness could result in the failure of some firms or reduce earnings expectations.

TAL also recognizes that Y2K could negatively impact investor psychology, providing investors with an excuse to "lock in" the capital gains of the past five years.

In an asset-class impact statement, TAL sees minimal problem for money market funds or Canadian bonds. For Canadian equities, TAL sees Y2K impacting only smaller firms that have not spent enough to fix their computer systems. It sees minimal impact for U.S. equities, which it believes will be affected more by excessive valuations, decelerating earnings, and the growth trajectory of Internet stocks.

Outside North America, TAL sees some Y2K risk, particularly in Eastern Europe and other emerging markets.

Smart Funds 2000

Y2K OK

CIBC North American Demographics Fund. If you've read such bestselling books as *Boom, Bust and Echo* or *The Pig and the Python*, you'll understand where this fund is coming from. The fund uses demographic analysis to determine how the baby boomers, Generation X, and other generations will impact markets as they age. Initial focus is North America. Manager is TAL's Kenneth Woods, with input from demographers at The RAND Corp. of Santa Monica, California. A returning Smart Fund.

CIBC U.S. Equity Index Fund. This index fund replaces the former actively managed version, which had an MER of 2.3%, with a 0.9% MER passively managed fund that tracks the Wilshire 5000. CIBC is no longer an actively managed large-cap U.S. equity fund. If there is any caveat, it's that index funds do not protect investors from market downturns as much as actively managed or balanced funds. This fund uses up the 20% RRSP foreign-content room; there is a 100% RRSP-eligible U.S. equity fund. Second quartile for the one-, three-, and five-year periods ended August 31, 1999. Still Royal's and Altamira's are cheaper and are available at most discount brokers.

Noteworthy Funds

Y2K KO

Five-Year Protected Canadian Bond Index Fund. For those who believe Y2K could be deflationary with lower interest rates, bond funds make sense since they provide capital gains with every drop in rates. Because of the passive approach, the MER of 1.75%, while no steal, is better than many other Canadian fixed-income funds. The five-year Protection puts a floor on your initial capital, just in case interest rates surge and hurt bond prices. Unfortunately, these protected funds have been closed to new investors.

CIBC Premium Canadian T-Bill Fund. MER of 0.55% is one of lowest in category, making this a logical haven for those seeking shelter from the possible Y2K storm. First quartile in the two-year and three-year periods ended August 31, 1999.

Y2K OK

CIBC Canadian Index Fund. If you can't beat the TSE index with a manager, then why not match it through indexing and cut costs to a barebones 0.9%? There's something to be said for using an index fund for your core Canadian large-cap portfolio and then using managed funds for specialties such as resources or small caps.

CIBC Global Technology. CIBC saw a good thing when rival TD cleaned up with the GreenLine Science & Technology Fund and launched its own version in November 1995. Run by TAL's Stephen Kahn.

CIBC Financial Companies Fund. Uses the same idea as AIC's Advantage Fund, and the portfolio is similar, with holdings in other mutual fund companies and banks. Such funds are sector funds and normally shouldn't represent more than a 5% or 10% position in your total portfolio. The fund company stocks are relatively illiquid and in a major stock correction would fall back more than more diversified holdings.

Y2K KO

CIBC Precious Metals Fund. If Y2K takes down the general market, it's possible that precious metals and gold prices will soar. 100% RRSP-eligible Canadian funds like this one could do well. CIBC Global Bond Index Fund: Would provide global diversification for a bond portfolio, complementing CIBC Canadian Bond Index Fund, and with a reasonable 0.9% MER.

Y2K Agnostic

CIBC Mortgage Fund. A Smart Fund in the 1998 edition but noteworthy for 1999. If interest rates start rising, you don't want to be overcommitted to this asset class, but mortgage funds will have less exposure than long-term bond funds. MER is a reasonable 1.69%, but more than the index bond funds charge. Second quartile for the year ended August 31, 1999.

CIBC Five-Year Protected Balanced Index Fund. Balanced funds provide some upside if markets keep soaring despite Y2K, and some fixed income to buffer any downside. The five-year Protection guarantee provides further peace of mind, while the indexing aspect means the insurance does not cost you more than a normal managed fund.

Protected U.S. Index Fund. Fund will provide upside protection if the U.S. market shakes off Y2K; preserve initial capital if the market falls. Because of the lower cost of indexing, the insurance protection is available for roughly the same as actively managed funds. Unfortunately, these protected funds are now closed to new investors.

Availability

Through CIBC branches across Canada. Also available through full-service and discount brokers and dealers, including CIBC Investor's Edge Discount Brokerage and CIBC Wood Gundy. CIBC's "At Your Request Direct Trading" service allows investors to buy, sell, and exchange funds by calling a toll-free number: 1-800-465-3863.

14. C.I. MUTUAL FUNDS

FRONT OR REAR

Strengths	New segregated funds BEA & Associates
Weaknesses	Too many funds to choose from MERs on the high side
RESPs?	No
Web Site	www.cifunds.com
Toll Free	1-800-268-9374

CANADIAN	Category	Rating	Fund Name	M.E.R.%	RRSP/Foreign
Money Market:		■	C.I. Money Market Fund	0.75	RRSP
		■	C.I. Money Market Seg Fund	1.5	RRSP
		■	C.I. Sector Short Term	0.05	Foreign
Fixed Income:	Long-term	★ KO	C.I. Canadian Bond Fund	1.65	RRSP
Equity:	Small Cap	▲ OK	Harbour Explorer Fund	2.33	RRSP
		■	Harbour Sector Explorer	2.33	Foreign
	Mid-Large Cap	■	C.I. Canadian Growth Fund	2.35	RRSP
		■	C.I. Sector Canadian	2.4	Foreign
		★ OK	Harbour Fund	2.33	RRSP
		■	Harbour Sector	2.33	Foreign
		■	C.I. Harbour Seg Fund	3.05	RRSP
	Labor-sponsored	■	C.I. Covington Fund	4.4	RRSP
Multi-Asset:	Balanced	■	C.I. Canadian Balanced Fund	2.3	RRSP
		■	Harbour Growth & Income	2.33	RRSP
		■	C.I. Harbour Growth & Income Seg Fund	2.97	RRSP
	Dividend/Bonds	■	C.I. Canadian Income Fund	1.82	RRSP

FOREIGN	Category	Rating	Fund Name	M.E.R.%	RRSP/Foreign
Money Market:		■	C.I. U.S. Money Market Fund	0.85	Foreign
Fixed Income:		■	C.I. World Bond Fund	2.09	Foreign
		■	C.I. Global High Yield	2.19	Foreign
		▲ KO	C.I. Global Bond RSP	2.09	RRSP
Global Equity:	All-global	★ OK	C.I. Global Fund*	2.49	Foreign
		■	C.I. Sector Global	2.54	Foreign
		■	C.I. Global Equity RSP*	2.47	RRSP
		■	C.I. Global Seg Fund	3.44	Foreign
		▲ AG	Hansberger Value Fund*	2.49	Foreign
		■	C.I. Sector Hansberger Value	2.54	Foreign
		▲ AG	C.I. Hansberger Value Seg Fund	3.44	Foreign
Multi-Asset:		★ AG	C.I. International Balanced RSP*	2.43	RRSP
		■	C.I. International Balanced*	2.44	Foreign
		■	C.I. Global Boomeronics Sector*	2.45	Foreign
		▲ OK	C.I. Global Boomeronics RSP Fund*	2.45	RRSP
	EAFE	■	Hansberger International Fund	2.5	Foreign
		■	C.I. Hansberger International Sector	2.55	Foreign
	Small-cap	■	Hansberger Global Small Cap Fund	2.73	Foreign
		■	C.I. Hansberger Global Small Cap Sector	2.78	Foreign
	Specialty	▲ OK	C.I. Sector Health Sciences	2.46	Foreign
		▲ OK	C.I. Sector Financial Services	2.46	Foreign
		■	C.I. Sector Global Resource	2.45	Foreign
		■	C.I. Sector Technology	2.46	Foreign
		▲ OK	C.I. Sector Telecommunications	2.46	Foreign
		■	C.I. Sector Global Consumer Products	2.46	Foreign
		■	C.I. Global Energy Sector	2.45	Foreign
Regional Equity:	U.S.	■	C.I. American Fund*	2.41	Foreign
		■	C.I. Sector American	2.46	Foreign
		■	C.I. American Seg Fund	3.26	Foreign
		■	C.I. American RSP Fund*	2.38	RRSP
	Latin American	■	C.I. Latin American	2.79	Foreign
		■	C.I. Sector Latin American	2.84	Foreign
	Emerging Market	■	C.I. Emerging Markets	2.78	Foreign
		■	C.I. Sector Emerging Markets	2.83	Foreign
		■	Hansberger Developing Markets	2.84	Foreign
		■	C.I. Sector Hansberger Developing Markets	2.89	Foreign
	Far East	■	C.I. Pacific Fund	2.53	Foreign
		■	C.I. Sector Pacific	2.58	Foreign
		■	Hansberger Asian	2.79	Foreign
		■	C.I. Sector Hansberger Asian	2.84	Foreign
		■	C.I. Japanese Sector Shares	2.45	Foreign
	Europe	■	Hansberger European	2.48	Foreign
		■	C.I. Sector Hansberger European	2.53	Foreign

*These funds also available as GIF funds with higher MERs.

Just when you think C.I. Mutual Funds has every possible fund concept covered in its giant family, the innovative people at C.I. come up with some more. The family now has the outrageous total of 82 investment funds, including 17 new Guaranteed Investment Funds (GIFs), its second group of segregated funds. And the purchase of BPI Mutual Funds will bring that number over 100. (See section on BPI Mutual Funds.) At the same time, there's no denying that if you favour the one family approach, this one offers something for everyone.

C.I. introduced several new funds since the last edition. One of the most popular investment types in the 1999 RRSP season were RRSP-eligible foreign funds. C.I. was already well positioned for this trend with several funds that fit the bill. But just to be sure, an RSP-eligible version of its Global Boomernomics Fund was added, and debuts as Noteworthy. It invests in industries with growth potential based on demographic trends. As with the other RSP-eligible foreign funds, investors can ignore the usual 20% limit on foreign funds in their RRSP or RRIF.

Also new are the Signature Canadian Funds—an equity and a balanced fund. Both are managed by Wally Kusters, who jumped to C.I. from O'Donnell Investment Management, but earned his stripes at Trimark Investment Management Inc. Kusters invests with a value bias aiming for low volatility and a low turnover—good in a taxable portfolio. Also new is C.I. Global Energy Fund, another sector fund for the group. In the regional equity group, C.I. added a Japanese Equity fund at a time when the Japanese market was showing signs of a strong rebound.

C.I. Guaranteed Investment Funds, launched in February 1999, are C.I.'s second group of segregated funds offered in association with Transamerica Life. Seg funds have long been the life insurance industry's equivalents of mutual funds, but souped up with return-of-principal guarantees at maturity or death. Other benefits are potential creditor protection and no probate fees. Popular C.I. Funds such as C.I. Harbour and C.I. International Balanced RSP are available as GIF funds, along with 15 others. Investors in these will pay about 50 basis points (0.5%) more each year in the management fee.

In addition to the GIF funds, C.I. continues to offer its six C.I. Segregated Funds, launched with Toronto Mutual Life Insurance Company. These offer a tiered guarantee starting at 75%. These are more expensive, with the investor paying a hefty 80 or 90 basis point (0.8 to 0.9%) annual premium for the benefits—on top of significant management expense ratios (MERs) in the first place. The newer GIF funds are the way to go if you want a guarantee from C.I. funds: they're cheaper and offer more choice.

One of the drawbacks of the C.I. family is that its MERs are definitely on the higher-than-average side—and climbing. Although increases in the last year were very small in many cases, they were increases nonetheless. And that comes as this fund group's assets under management grew about 17% over one year to March 31, 1999. We thought bigger assets meant declining MERs because of greater economies of scale. Every year, however, C.I. manages to turn out several funds that justify those higher fees.

So how to assemble a coherent family of C.I. funds from this plethora of choices? The fund family approach used throughout this book should help you focus on these families within a family. A global value-oriented investor might gravitate to the Hansberger funds, managed by former Templeton boss Thomas Hansberger. The domestic Harbour Funds also use a value approach, spearheaded by Gerry Coleman.

If you're a top-down active investor with strong opinions about the markets, then C.I.'s global industry funds may appeal. Like Fidelity and AIM Funds, C.I. funds let you bet on technology, health sciences, telecommunications, natural resources, and even the financial services industry itself. The funds are managed by BEA Associates of New York, which manages several of the older C.I. Funds.

If you're a frequent switcher with a large taxable portfolio, the Sector Fund approach minimizes capital gains taxes incurred by switching. There are more than 20 funds within the C.I. Sector umbrella, as well as Hansberger regional funds, theme funds (Global Industry Shares), and some of the Harbour Funds.

Year 2000 Stance

To guard as much as possible against unpleasant Y2K surprises, C.I. money managers question corporate managements of their investments about their progress with Y2K compliance. C.I. identifies possible trouble spots as follows: industries that have not had enough lead time for complete compliance; embedded chips in relatively inaccessible locations; and uncertainty about compliance of customers and suppliers.

C.I. believes that the possibility of worst-case scenarios is small. There is a possibility of brief market volatility, the company says. But the managers have no plans to increase cash in anticipation of that. Instead they will watch for volatility and use it as a buying opportunity.

Smart Funds 2000

Y2K OK

Harbour Fund. Solid fund managed by Gerry Coleman and a long-time member of the exclusive Smart Fund list.

C.I. Global Growth. Managed by Bill Sterling, this stable performer returns again to the Smart Fund list.

Y2K KO

C.I. Canadian Bond. This fund, managed by Jeffrey Herold at J. Zechner Associates, has been either first or second quartile since its launch in 1993, returning 9.9% on average over five years and is first quartile over that period.

Y2K Agnostic

C.I. International Balanced RSP. Solid second-quartile performer in this fund that counts as Canadian content in your RSP. Very low volatility on this one.

Noteworthy Funds

Y2K OK

C.I. Global Telecommunications Sector. Another sector fund for investors wanting to invest to benefit from a rapidly changing world. This fund has been top quartile since its launch in July 1996. Over one year to August 31, it benefited tremendously from mergers and acquisitions in this sector and returned 92.7%.

C.I. Sector Global Health Sciences. This sector fund has also performed above average since its launch in July 1996. If you believe the changing demographics will drive the growth of the sector, this may be a specialty fund for a more aggressive portfolio. It is managed by William Priest of BEA Associates.

C.I. Sector Global Financial Services. Now three years old, this sector fund has benefited from a strong run among financial stocks. Over one year to August 31, 1999, it is up 5.4%, with a whopping 56.3% invested in Japan, and only 6.9% in the United States.

Harbour Explorer Fund. If you like the Harbour Fund philosophy of owning just 30 to 40 low-volatility stocks and low portfolio turnover, then this small-cap version of Harbour Fund could merit some of your growth dollars. Manager Stephen Jenkins maximizes the foreign content with U.S. small- to mid-caps. It's been a rough period for the volatile small caps but buying while they're still out of favour means the most upside potential when they inevitably rebound.

C.I. Global Boomernomics RSP Fund. This RRSP-eligible global fund revolves around three themes: demographics, the technology revolution, and the global trend toward market-based capitalism. It is managed by Bill Sterling and Stephen Waite of Trilogy Asset Management in New York.

Y2K KO

C.I. Global Bond RSP. Global bond funds could benefit more than Canadian bond funds if the expectation interest rates in Europe and other global spots have more to fall than in North America actually occurs. This version won't use up your precious foreign content in an RRSP or RRIF.

Y2K Agnostic

Hansberger Value, Hansberger Value Seg Fund. Value funds such of this have been out of favour since mid-1994 so the timing for this fund, launched in June 1996, has been unfortunate. But it's only a matter of time before value begins to matter to investors again and Thomas Hansberger has the experience to be among the top value funds when it does. Consider also the downside protection of the seg-fund version of this fund. In normal times you won't find funds with 3.44% MERs being recommended by us, but for the short period of the century change the extra cost of protection may be worth it.

Availability

Through full-service and discount brokers and other fund dealers.

15. CLARINGTON CAPITAL MANAGEMENT INC. FRONT OR REAR

Strengths	Broker loyalty to Terry Stone	
	Small-cap specialty funds	
Weaknesses	High expense ratios	
	No 100% RRSP-eligible global equity funds	
RESPs?	No	
Web Site	None	Toll Free 1-888-860-9888

CANADIAN	Category	Rating	Fund Name	M.E.R.%	RRSP/Foreign
Money Market:		▲ KO	Clarington Money Market Fund	0.62	RRSP
Fixed Income:		■	Clarington Canadian Income Fund	2.29	RRSP
Equity:	Mid-Large Cap	■	Clarington Canadian Equity Fund	2.76	RRSP
	Small Cap	■	Clarington Canadian Small Cap Fund	2.75	RRSP
	Micro Cap	■	Clarington Canadian Micro Cap	2.75*	RRSP
Multi-Asset:	Balanced	★ AG	Clarington Canadian Balanced Fund	2.76	RRSP

FOREIGN	Category	Rating	Fund Name	MER%	RRSP/Foreign
Global Equity:	All-global	■	Clarington Global Equity	2.96*	Foreign
	Non U.S.	■	Clarington International Equity	2.96*	Foreign
	Small Cap	■	Clarington Global Opportunities Fund	2.96	Foreign
	Technology	★ OK	Clarington Global Communications Fund	2.96	Foreign
Regional Equity:					
	U.S. Mixed cap	▲ OK	Clarington US Equity Fund	2.96	Foreign
	U.S. Small cap	■	Clarington US Smaller Company Growth Fund	2.96	Foreign
	Far East	■	Clarington Asia Pacific Fund	2.98	Foreign

* MERs estimated for new funds

Clarington Capital added two new international equity funds last year, bringing its fund count to 13. They are managed by six different external management firms located in different regions of North America.

Clarington is basically an all-equity shop that charges above-average MERs and attempts to deliver the performance to justify it. It has done this in returning Smart Fund Clarington Global Communications Fund, and even in the yet-to-be-Noteworthy Clarington Asia Pacific Fund (which had chalked up a sizzling 145.9% in the year ended August 31, 1999).

Even Clarington's domestic funds are managed externally—by Seamark Asset Management of Halifax, known for combining competitive performance with low volatility. On the fixed-income side, the Canadian Income Fund is designed for conservative investors who want to do slightly better than a GIC. The Canadian Small Cap fund is managed by QVGD Investors Inc. of Calgary, a start-up by Leigh Pullen, former manager of the acclaimed Mawer New Canada Fund. The focus is on companies with a market capitalization of less than $400 million. The newer Canadian Micro Cap Fund, managed by QVGD's Patrick Slater, is off to a slow start.

Globally, Clarington has assembled some interesting managers based on both coasts of the United States. Clarington sells two U.S. equity funds: a large cap managed by Fleming Capital Management of New York, and a small-cap U.S. equity fund managed by Boston's Evergreen Investment Management. Evergreen also manages the global small-cap fund Clarington Global Opportunities Fund.

The two new Oppenheimer global funds will have passed their first anniversary by the time this edition is out. So far, the more inclusive Global Equity Fund has outperformed the non-U.S. International Equity Fund.

In summary, Clarington offers conservative core Canadian funds, plus interesting special equity funds. Small-cap funds in Canada, the U.S., and the globe, and a telecom fund all carry the usual promise of higher performance at higher risk.

Year 2000 Stance

Clarington did not respond to our request for its Y2K views. However, its individual managers do refer to the issue and appear unconcerned. Oscar Castro, manager of the "Smart" Clarington Global Communications Fund, says simply, "The Y2K issue is not expected to adversely affect the Fund. ... We are relaxed about Y2K and we have asked the companies we are invested in of their plans and accomplishments in that area. We have only good feedback from that area. So, I don't think it's going to be much more than a hangover after a major party on December 31!" Let's hope so. Put Clarington in the Y2K OK camp.

Smart Funds 2000

Y2K OK

Clarington Global Communications Fund. Back again because of the renowned expertise of Oscar Castro.

Y2K Agnostic

Clarington Canadian Balanced Fund. A conservatively managed, low-volatility fund that can act as a core offering with exposure to both Canadian stocks and bonds. Annual portfolio turnover is 12% to 15%, for a long average hold of seven to eight years, making this a tax-efficient fund even outside the RRSP. Emphasis is on growth stocks, not necessarily dividend-paying stocks. First quartile for the two years ended August 31.

Noteworthy Funds

Y2K OK

Clarington US Equity Fund. Modelled after Fleming's American Fund, this value fund provides the combination of performance and low volatility that Clarington founder Terry Stone looks for. As of spring 1999, it was 54% in large caps, 29% medium caps, and 13% in small-cap stocks. Fleming is part of the huge $100 billion UK

Fleming organization. As of May 1999, manager Jonathan Simon felt that U.S. markets were still not overvalued, but was sticking to a strategy of owning unwanted names with price/earnings ratios below 12.

Y2K KO

Clarington Money Market Fund. Clarington is virtually an all-equity shop. While its value approach as seen in the U.S. Equity Fund bodes better than an aggressive growth style in any Y2K slow-down, it has few safe harbours of fixed-income products. Consider also the Canadian Income Fund—its MER of 2.29% is too high except for a temporary holding spot.

Availability

At most full-service and discount brokers and dealers.

16. DUNDEE MUTUAL FUNDS

NO LOAD

Strengths	Low MERs Conservative core fund approach
Weaknesses	Visibility Few aggressive foreign funds
RESPs?	No
Web Site	www.centrepost.com
Toll Free	1-800-268-9597

CANADIAN	Category	Rating	Fund Name	M.E.R.%	RRSP/Foreign
Money Market:		■	Dynamic Money Market Fund	0.72	RRSP
		■	Infinity T-Bill	1	RRSP
Fixed Income:	Long-term	■	Dynamic Income Fund	1.56	RRSP
		■	Power Bond Fund	1.5	RRSP
Equity:	Mid-Large Cap	■	Dynamic Fund of Canada	2.2	RRSP
	All-cap	■	Dynamic Canadian Growth Fund	2.34	RRSP
		▲ OK	Power Canadian Fund	2.25	RRSP
		■	Infinity Canadian	2.56	RRSP
	Small-Mid cap	■	Dynamic Small Cap Fund	2.56	RRSP
	Gold/precious metal	▲ KO	Dynamic Precious Metals Fund	2.55	RRSP
		■	Dynamic Canadian Resource Fund	2.25	RRSP
	Specialty	■	Infinity Wealth Management	2.67	RRSP
	Regional	▲ OK	Dynamic Quebec Fund	2.18	RRSP
Tax Advantaged:	Dividend	▲ OK	Dynamic Dividend Fund	1.49	RRSP
		■	Dynamic Dividend Growth Fund	1.56	RRSP
		★ KO	Dynamic Protected Dividend Growth	4.33	RRSP
		■	Infinity Income & Growth	2.67	RRSP
		■	Dynamic Canadian Real Estate Fund	2.31	RRSP

Multi-Asset:	Balanced	■	Power Balanced Fund	2.29	RRSP
	Asset Allocation	■	Dynamic Partners Fund	2.29	RRSP
		▲ KO	Dynamic Protected Partners Fund	2.99	RRSP
	Portfolio of Funds	■	Dundee Fund of Funds**	0.52	RRSP
		▲ AG	Dundee Dollar-Cost Averaging Fund	0.72	RRSP

FOREIGN	Category	Rating	Fund Name	MER%	RRSP/Foreign
Fixed Income:		▲ AG	Dynamic Global Bond Fund	1.73	RRSP
Global Equity:	All-global	■	Dynamic International Fund	2.5	Foreign
		■	Dynamic Protected International Fund	2.84	Foreign
		■	Infinity International	2.74	Foreign
	Specialty	■	Dynamic Global Resource Fund*	2.69	Foreign
		■	Dynamic Global Precious Metals Fund	2.88	Foreign
		▲ AG	Dynamic Real Estate Equity Fund	2.62	Foreign
Regional Equity:	NAFTA/N.Am.	■	Dynamic Americas Fund	2.35	Foreign
		■	Dynamic Protected Americas Fund	2.64	Foreign
		▲ OK	Power American Fund	3.13	Foreign
	Europe	▲ OK	Dynamic Europe Fund	2.46	Foreign
	Latin/Emerging	■	Dynamic Latin American Fund	2.87	Foreign
		■	Dynamic Far East Fund	3.37	Foreign
	Other	■	Dynamic Israel Growth Fund	3.18	Foreign
Global Balanced:					
	Asset Allocation	■	Dynamic Global Partners Fund	2.52	Foreign
		■	Dynamic Protected Global Partners Fund	2.7	Foreign
		■	Dynamic Global Income & Growth	2.02	Foreign

* MER higher after performance fees

** Plus MERs of underlying funds

Last year brought much change at Dundee Mutual Funds, starting with its name. Formerly Dynamic Mutual Funds, the name change came as part of the company's attempt to diversify its offerings with a multi-brand approach.

The Dynamic funds continue as they have been, managed with a bottom-up value investment style. In July 1999, the company launched the Power brand of four basic funds managed with a growth style with an emphasis on earnings momentum: Power Canadian, Power American, Power Bond, and Power Balanced. Preliminary results for the funds, led by Rohit Sehgal, look promising.

The company had already added the Dynamic Canadian Resource Fund in September 1998, in time for a resurgence in that sector.

Ned Goodman, chief executive of parent company Dundee Bancorp Inc., and the team have historically shown a knack for identifying interesting investment trends early and bringing to market funds that will appeal to investors' appetites. In December 1998, for example, it launched the Dynamic Protected Mutual Funds, a new twist on guaranteed funds that appeal to nervous investors. These five funds offer a 100% guarantee of capital if the investments are held for 10 years. But they aren't segregated funds—

these are mutual funds and can be sold by any fund-licensed salesperson. But like segregated funds, these charge higher annual management fees to pay for the risk taken on by the company. CIBC Securities launched a similar no-load fund product.

One of the more interesting moves for the Dundee/Goodman group in the past year was the acquisition of Infinity Mutual Funds and the business of its sister company, Fortune Financial Management Inc. The five Infinity funds are managed with a buy-and-hold style, using a growth-at-a-reasonable-price criterion. That gives Dundee a third brand.

The addition of the Fortune business, which has operations that sell funds, securities, and insurance, was a surprise to some in the industry, given that it has had some run-ins with regulators. But Ned Goodman is not one to be scared off by a challenge, and viewed Fortune as an opportunity to get into the sales side of the fund business.

Other changes to the funds include the name change of Dynamic Team Fund to Dundee Fund of Funds and Dynamic Dollar Cost Averaging to Dundee Dollar Cost Averaging. That move allows both funds to invest in both Dynamic and Power funds. The family, now with 40 funds in total up from 27 last year, is attempting to streamline its ballooning line-up. Dynamic Government Income Fund was merged into Dynamic Money Market and Dynamic International absorbed the Global Millennia. By the end of 1999, Dynamic Israel and Dynamic Latin American will also be merged into Dynamic International.

What do all these changes mean for investors? The addition of the new funds offers style diversification within one family, which is a positive move. Investing in funds managed with different styles is a growing trend that investors should consider as another way to smooth out market ups and downs.

The Infinity funds have much higher MERs than we'd like to see. Two of the five have performed well since their launch a few years ago: Infinity Canadian and Infinity Wealth Management, but they are still new and management has changed to the Dundee team. With their high MERs, we hold off recommending them for now.

Some past Dynamic strengths, such as precious metals, fixed-income and asset allocation, and even Canadian equities, continued to exhibit weakness in 1998 but were showing signs of improvement in 1999. These include Dynamic Canadian Growth and Dynamic Dividend Growth. The latter is available in the"protected" series.

After a poor year in 1997, precious metals performed above average versus other funds in 1998 but were back below average in the first few months of 1999.

Unfortunately, the two "Smart Funds" from the last edition also had a tough year in 1998. Long-time favourite Dynamic Europe, managed by Joe Evershed, was fourth quartile in 1998 and third quartile as of August 31, 1999. Looking at the last four calendar years, the fund performed above average only in 1996. That performance just can't justify its 2.56% MER, although it's just slightly higher than average, and the fund has been demoted to Noteworthy, pending improvement.

Dynamic Real Estate Equity also had a tough year in 1998, losing 18.0%. That put it near the bottom versus the comparable funds. But based on its outstanding 1997 performance, we were hopeful that it would turn around. It has not and has been demoted.

While some funds are still pricey, we are pleased to see that Dynamic continues to lower the MERs of some of its funds.

Note that a few Dynamic funds also pay the managers a performance bonus that can add to the stated MERs in the matrix. No performance fees were paid in 1998.

Year 2000 Stance

None given pertaining to investing approach.

Smart Funds 2000

Dynamic Protected Dividend Growth. Heavy MER of over 4% but you get equities with a guarantee.

Noteworthy Funds

Y2K OK

Dynamic Europe Fund. Demoted from Smart status based on its poor recent performance.

Dynamic Dividend Fund. Bit weighting in preferred and royalty trusts. It returned 9.1% over one year to August 31, better than the TSE 300, which fell 4.1% over the same period.

Dynamic Quebec Fund. Launched in February 1997, this unique regional Canadian equity fund is a contrarian fund targeting Quebec stocks that have become undervalued because of the constant separatist agitation in Quebec. It lags the TSE 300 over the year ended August 31.

Dynamic Power Canadian. This momentum style fund benefited from a market that was particularly kind to momentum- and growth-style managers. It achieved its first full year of performance in July 1999. As of August 31, 1999, it returned 44.5% over the past year. Manager Rohit Sehgal has a solid track record with London Life, where he managed money before joining Dundee.

Power American. Also managed with a growth/momentum style, this fund flew high above the benchmark S&P 500 index, and much of the competition gaining 55.7% for year ended August 31, 1999.

Y2K KO

Dynamic Protected Partners Fund. We don't normally mention funds with MERs of almost 3%. The underlying Partners Fund used to be a Smart Fund some editions back but has had mixed results lately. Still, in a Y2K KO scenario the triple combination of Dynamic's value approach, its singular asset allocation calls, and the principal guarantee feature should provide investors with some peace of mind over the century change. Once things settle down, the lower-MER Partners Fund would be alternative.

Dynamic Precious Metals. Dynamic used to be tops in this special equity class but has suffered with most managers over the depressed price of gold bullion. But if you believe that Y2K could survive gold's sagging fortunes, Dynamic's team is as good as any to find a way to profit from this sector.

Y2K Agnostic

Dynamic Real Estate Equity Fund. Anne McLean is trying to recapture the glory of 1996 and 1997.

Dundee Dollar Cost Averaging Fund. All funds can be dollar cost averaged through pre-authorized chequing plans. The twist here is that this fund is designed to appeal to squeamish investors by gradually transferring money over 52 weeks from short-term bonds to selected equity and asset allocation funds. Dynamic classifies this as a money market fund; we tend to view it as a multi-asset fund.

Dynamic Global Bond Fund. 100% RRSP-eligible, MER not too excessive. Global bond funds can provide some stability and currency hedging in a Y2K-turbulent environment.

Availability

Funds are sold by full-service and discount mutual fund dealers and financial planners across Canada. Minimum initial investment is $1,000. Pre-authorized purchase plans may begin with $100.

17. ELLIOTT & PAGE LTD.

FRONT, REAR & LOW

Strengths	Canadian equities
	Low MERs for a load family
Weaknesses	Low visibility
	No 100% RRSP-eligible global funds
RESPs?	No
Web Site	www.fundlib.com/ellpag.html **Toll Free** 1-800-363-6647

CANADIAN	Category	Rating	Fund Name	M.E.R.%	RRSP/Foreign
Money Market:		▲ KO	E&P Money Fund	0.24	RRSP
		■	E&P T-Bill Fund	1.72	RRSP
Fixed Income:	Long-term	■	E&P Bond Fund	1.92	RRSP
Equity:	Mid-Large Cap	▲	E&P Equity Fund	1.92	RRSP
		■	E&P Value Equity Fund	2.1	RRSP
Tax Advantaged:		▲ AG	E&P Monthly High Income Fund	2.11	RRSP
Multi-Asset:	Balanced	■	E&P Balanced Fund	1.78	RRSP

FOREIGN	Category	Rating	Fund Name	MER%	RRSP/Foreign
Fixed Income:		■	E&P Global Bond Fund	2.07	Foreign
Global Equity:	All-global	■	E&P Global Equity Fund	1.95	Foreign
Regional Equity:					
	U.S. Large-cap	★ OK	E&P American Growth Fund	1.39	Foreign
	U.S. Mid-Cap	■	E&P U.S. Mid Cap Fund	3.5	Foreign
	Emerging Market	■	E&P Emerging Markets Fund	3.49	Foreign
	Far East	■	E&P Asian Growth Fund	3.33	Foreign
Global Balanced:		■	E&P Global Balanced Fund	2.82	Foreign

Elliott & Page Ltd. may not be the household name that some of the larger fund families in this book are, but it has a long history as a pension manager and aims to spread the word about its low-profile fund group.

E&P turned 50 this year. It has roots going back to 1949, when it was the first investment counsellor registered in Ontario. Today it is a member of the Manulife Group of financial service companies, managing $16 billion for corporations, unions, pension funds, foundations, and individual investors.

The company made some significant changes to its line-up in the last year, launching five funds late in 1998 and closing three others in March 1999: Bond, Global Bond, and Balanced. Those changes result in an expanded line-up of 16 funds, including the highly advertised Generation Wave fund, a Canadian equity portfolio that invests in companies expected to benefit from demographic changes. Three of the other funds are Canadian: Growth Opportunities and Sector Rotation are equity funds and the new active bond fund on the fixed-income side. E&P also launched a European Equity fund managed by ABN AMRO Asset Management.

Although the line-up offers a good selection for investors, E&P has relinquished its former low-MER advantage. Fees on many existing funds and the new Canadian funds are now higher than the average. Emerging markets, for example, charged investors an eye-popping 4.84% a year as of December 1998, and Asian Growth was 3.81% for the same period. On the positive side, E&P American Growth rose only slightly to 1.44%, which is still a bargain for investors.

E&P uses both in-house managers and external advisors. While its domestic equity and balanced funds have been Smart Funds in the past, they have been flat performers of late, as the sector-rotation style was out of favour.

Some of the winners continue to be several of E&P's externally managed U.S. and global funds, notably E&P American Growth Fund (with a 30.4% return for the year ended August 31, 1999), which continues to perform among the top U.S. equity funds. It is managed by New York's Goldman Sachs Asset Management. The company also changed the manager on its U.S. Mid-Cap Fund bringing it in-house to be invested by Mark Schmeer and Rhonda Chang. Since taking over from Buffalo-based M&T Capital Advisors Group in December 1998, the fund's performance has improved, to above average. E&P continues to use other global sub-advisors including London-based Flemings and Hong Kong's Jardine Fleming.

Nereo Piticco of PCJ Investment Counsel in Toronto continues to manage the E&P Equity Fund, which uses the sector-rotation style. This approach, which tends to be more volatile than some, moves money in and out of different market sectors in an attempt to anticipate winners based on factors such as the economic cycle. The fund continued to struggle throughout 1998, landing in the bottom 25% versus the competition. It was closed to new investments at the end of 1998 after a tough year. Early in 1999, there are signs of improvement.

Investors should take care in choosing the load structure. In addition to the unusual low load option of 0% to 2% (typically with higher trailer fees), E&P's deferred load option features a novel declining redemption schedule that can be started anywhere from 2% to 6% redemption in year one, declining to nil after six years.

Year 2000 Stance

For domestic equity funds, portfolio managers are questioning company managements about Y2K readiness. The quality of company management is usually indicative of how adequately they have dealt with the issue. The focus of managers continues to be on fundamentals: strong balance sheets, industry position, and product differentiation.

On international investing, the question becomes more complex. Managers of global funds have shifted their focus to large-cap quality companies that have taken Y2K seriously. They are cautious on emerging markets. Generally they view the financial services sector to be low risk among the best-prepared countries. However, Japan, with its other problems, may not be treating Y2K as a top priority. They say that the same applies to Germany.

Smart Funds 2000

Y2K OK

Elliott & Page American Growth. Well managed by Goldman Sachs, holding great growth stock names and maintaining first-quartile performance.

Noteworthy Funds

Y2K KO

Elliott & Page Money. Consistent above-average money market fund most of the last 10 years. Manager has been Vice President Maralyn Kobayashi since inception in 1984. She uses an interest rate anticipation style. MER is a very low 0.24%.

Y2K Agnostic

Elliott & Page Monthly High Income Fund. This tax-advantaged dividend fund was second quartile versus like funds over one year to August 31, 1999. It was up 15.6%. Also consider the E&P Balanced Fund.

Availability

Full-service and discount brokers, dealers, and planners across Canada; $500 minimum purchase per fund.

18. ETHICAL FUNDS INC.

NO LOAD*, FRONT & REAR

Strengths	Funds for investors with a conscience
	North American equities managed by Alliance Capital
Weaknesses	MERs above averages
	Distribution
RESPs?	No
Web Site	www.ethicalfunds.com **Toll Free** 1-800-267-5019

CANADIAN	Category	Rating	Fund Name	M.E.R.%	RRSP/Foreign
Money Market:		■	Ethical Money Market Fund	1.33	RRSP
Fixed Income:	Medium-term	■	Ethical Income Fund	1.68	RRSP
Equity:	Mid-Large Cap	■	Ethical Growth Fund	2.24	RRSP
	Small Cap	▲ OK	Ethical Special Equity Fund	2.79	RRSP
Multi-Asset:	Balanced	▲ AG	Ethical Balanced Fund	2.11	RRSP

FOREIGN	Category	Rating	Fund Name	MER%	RRSP/Foreign
Fixed Income:	Global	▲ KO	Ethical Global Bond Fund	2.63	RRSP
Regional Equity:					
	N.A. Large-cap	★ OK	Ethical North American Equity Fund	2.39	Foreign
	Far East	■	Ethical Pacific Rim Fund	3.39	Foreign

* No load through credit unions; varies with funds

Ethical Funds continued to grow in the last year—a tough one for the mutual funds industry as a whole. The Vancouver-based company is attracting attention from investors who are interested in more than just investment returns; they are also asking "Where does my money go?" An aggressive ad campaign answers that question with vivid images of child labour and the illness smoking can cause. And the slogan—"Non pollution, non weapons, non nuclear and non tobacco"—brings the point home.

The no-load fund group now has about $2.3 billion in its eight funds. That maintains Ethical Funds as the largest group of "socially responsible" mutual funds in Canada.

The management at Ethical Funds say profits and principles can co-exist. In fact, it takes a fair share of the profits for themselves—management expense ratios are slightly above industry averages. Despite this, several of the funds have turned in impressive performances, most notably Ethical North American. It was one of the few funds that could keep pace with the S&P 500 index in 1998 and managed a stellar 62.6% in calendar 1998 versus 37.8% for the index. It is managed by Alliance Capital Management LP, and based on its above-average performance since 1995, it returns as a Smart Fund again this year.

All of the funds are managed externally. Connor, Clark & Lunn Investment Management Inc. of Vancouver, B.C., runs the flagship Ethical Growth Fund, while Co-operators Investment Counselling Ltd. runs the domestic fixed-income and balanced funds. The small-cap Ethical Special Equity Fund is managed by QVGD Investors Inc. of Calgary.

Last year, there were two manager changes on the foreign funds: Societe General Yamaichi is now managing Ethical Pacific Rim and Primus Capital Advisors advises Ethical Global Bond, with a slight change of mandate. It continues to be fully RRSP-eligible and tries to capture global bond returns by trading interest rate futures and currency forward contracts.

Year 2000 Stance

Portfolio managers are monitoring their investments and avoiding those they feel might be vulnerable. In the best-case scenario there will be minimal interruptions to business operations after the date change. In the worst-case scenario, Ethical Funds will take defensive positions where it identifies risks. It does not mention having done that so far. Overall, the company says it is positive about the new millennium being a catalyst for growth.

Smart Funds 2000

Y2K OK

Ethical North American Equity. First quartile for one, two, three, five and 10 years ended August 31, 1999 and number one in its category over five years! Repeats as a Smart Fund.

Noteworthy Funds

Y2K OK

Ethical Special Equity. Managed by QVGD Investors Inc., this fund has consistently performed above average versus the competition.

Y2K KO

Ethical Global Bond Fund. If interest rates fall around the world under a Y2K-induced recession, global bonds could fare well. This fund does not use up your 20% foreign content. MER is stiff for the asset class, so view this as a temporary holding pattern. Alternatively consider the income fund or money market fund.

Y2K Agnostic

Ethical Balanced Fund. Classic balanced fund with the stocks portion mirroring the all-equity Ethical Growth Fund.

Availability

Direct from the company, through credit unions, discount brokers, fund brokers, and dealers in every province except Quebec. It expects to expand to that province by early 2000.

19. FIDELITY INVESTMENTS CANADA LTD. FRONT, REAR OR LOW

Strengths	Clout of world's largest fund company
	Massive research capabilities
Weaknesses	Size of some funds
	MERs high on equity funds
RESPs?	Yes
Web Site	www.fidelity.ca **Toll Free** 1-800-387-0074

CANADIAN	Category	Rating	Fund Name	M.E.R.%	RRSP/Foreign
Money Market:		■	Fidelity Canadian Short Term Asset Fund	1.25%	RRSP
Fixed Income:	Long-term	▲ KO	Fidelity Canadian Bond Fund	1.34%	RRSP
	Short-term	■	Fidelity Canadian Income Fund	1.25%	RRSP
Equity:	Small-Mid Cap	★ OK	Fidelity Canadian Growth Company Fund	2.46%	RRSP
	Mid-Large Cap	■	Fidelity Capital Builder Fund	2.41%	RRSP
	All Cap	■	Fidelity Disciplined Equity Fund	2.40%	RRSP
	All Cap	▲ OK	Fidelity True North™ Fund	2.49%	RRSP
Asset Allocation:		★ AG	Fidelity Canadian Asset Allocation Fund	2.44%	RRSP
Balanced:	Balanced	▲ AG	Fidelity Canadian Balanced Fund	2.25%	RRSP

FOREIGN	Category	Rating	Fund Name	MER%	RRSP/Foreign
Money Market:		■	Fidelity U.S. Money Market Fund	1.25%	Foreign
Fixed-Income:		■	Fidelity North American Income Fund	1.75%	Foreign
		■	Fidelity Emerging Markets Bond Fund	2.31%	Foreign
Global Equity:	All-global	★ OK	Fidelity International Portfolio Fund	2.64%	Foreign
	EAFE	■	Fidelity Overseas Fund	New	Foreign
	Sector	■	Fidelity Focus Consumer Industries Fund	2.49%	Foreign
	Sector	■	Fidelity Focus Financial Services Fund	2.50%	Foreign
	Sector	■	Fidelity Focus Health Care Fund	2.50%	Foreign
	Sector	■	Fidelity Focus Natural Resources Fund	2.44%	Foreign
	Sector	■	Fidelity Focus Technology Fund	2.49%	Foreign

Regional Equity:	U.S.	★ OK	Fidelity Growth America Fund	2.31%	Foreign
	U.S. Small-cap	■	Fidelity Small Cap America Fund	2.54%	Foreign
	Latin American	■	Fidelity Latin American Growth Fund	3.09%	Foreign
	Emerging Market	■	Fidelity Emerging Markets Portfolio Fund	3.78%	Foreign
	Far East	■	Fidelity Far East Fund	2.88%	Foreign
	Japan	■	Fidelity Japanese Growth Fund	2.97%	Foreign
	Europe	★ OK	Fidelity European Growth Fund	2.64%	Foreign
Global Balanced:					
	Asset Allocation	★ AG	Fidelity Global Asset Allocation Fund	2.63%	Foreign

Fidelity's Boston-based parent company is the largest mutual fund company in the world and, after years of relatively low profile in the Canadian market, is now one of the most popular fund groups in Canada.

The 27 funds that Fidelity now sells in Canada, including nine Canadian ones, represents a fairly complete line-up. Since the last edition, three funds have been added and one, Fidelity RSP Global Bond Fund, has been merged into Fidelity Canadian Bond Fund.

Fidelity's in-house, global stock-picking research machine makes it a tempting choice for global equity funds for investors who prefer the broker channel and the slightly higher MERs that accompany it. But Fidelity seems oblivious to the growing preference of Canadian investors for lower MERs; in fact, several funds actually saw MERs rise in the past year (Far East rose from 2.79% to 2.86%; Emerging Markets Portfolio Fund from 3.53% to an exorbitant 3.78%).

Thus far, Fidelity has also failed to provide its own line of segregated funds or protected funds, which cautious Canadian investors seem increasingly inclined to embrace, despite their higher fees. Fidelity's main Canadian alternatives for strong global exposure—Templeton and Trimark—both offer seg funds. A handful of Fidelity funds are, however, available as Manulife Guaranteed Investment Funds.

Apart from its disinclination to lower fees, Fidelity does not yet offer high-net-worth investors a growth path to alternatives in managed money. Nor is there evidence that it plans to give investors with large amounts in their funds a fee break at certain thresholds, as is starting to occur with some of the no-load bank competitors.

On the new-fund front, Fidelity Canada added Fidelity Disciplined Equity Fund and Fidelity Canadian Balanced Fund to the line-up in September 1998. These are intended to be run within tight constraints as outlined in the prospectus and will look more like traditional pension funds with similar mandates. In May 1999, the Fidelity Overseas Fund was launched and it has an EAFE, or ex–North American, mandate.

In April 1999 there was a manager change on two of the group's strongest U.S. equity funds: Fidelity Growth America Fund and Fidelity Small Cap America Fund. Brad Lewis, manager on both of these funds since inception, has left day-to-day management of the funds to his protégés as he assumes the role of head of quantitative investing for Fidelity.

Fidelity Canada also announced a few administrative changes in the spring of 1999. As of April 2, 1999, it will base the deferred sales charge (DSC) calculations on the original cost of fund units, rather than on their current market value. As of the same date, the company also decided to base the 10% free annual redemption amounts for DSC funds on the original cost of units, rather than on their current market value. In ever-rising markets that would mean you would be able to free up relatively less from the DSC schedule than was previously the case.

Fidelity Canada also stated that fund distributions may be paid to investors in cash, rather than having them reinvested, under either the DSC or front-load sales charge options. Redemption fees will not be incurred for cash distributions. If the cash distributions exceed the allowable 10% free amount for redemptions, the 10% free amount will be reduced in the following calendar year.

The five Fidelity Focus funds unveiled in 1997 cover consumer industries, financial services, health care, natural resources, and high technology and are overseen by Bob Haber, a 14-year Fidelity veteran who is director of equity research. These all use up the 20% foreign-content limit in an RRSP or RRIF. While they can invest worldwide, they are heavily concentrated in the United States, which investors should keep in mind when making geographical and asset allocation decisions.

None of the Fidelity Focus funds are designated Smart Funds, since for anyone but highly experienced investors, sector funds are less diversified than we like funds to be. Fidelity dominates the U.S. sector fund market and a thriving industry has been built around market timers and frequent switchers between the different industries represented. That's not a strategy we encourage.

Fidelity Focus Technology Fund, which had a manager change in 1998 to Michael Tempero, concentrates on U.S. small- and mid-cap technology stocks. Given the volatility of the NASDAQ exchange and the healthy dose of technology already in Fidelity Small Cap America and Fidelity Growth America, we believe that these more diversified funds are the better bet for average investors.

The usual demographic arguments for aging baby boomers make Fidelity Focus Health Care Fund an intriguing fund.

Year 2000 Stance

As we noted in the Introduction, if Fidelity views the Y2K problem as serious for capital markets, it's keeping it close to its chest. Given its prominent position in the investment industry, it can scarcely do other than make only the barest of statements on the issue as required by regulators.

Fidelity's official line is that it "knows that the Year 2000 is an issue not only for financial services companies, but also for the portfolio companies in which mutual funds invest." It states that its portfolio managers have been briefed on Y2K and are "equipped with appropriate questions to ask senior management of these companies." It views Y2K information as "only one piece in the mosaic of information" it considers in making investment decisions.

What can we make of this? Because it is not a public company, this traditionally secretive fund company is evidently committed to a "Y2K OK stance" officially. To do otherwise would be harmful for capital markets around the world. Like Alan Greenspan and a handful of other key figures, a wrong statement by Fidelity on Y2K could hasten a negative self-fulfilling prophecy. How its managers behave in any fall correction will be critical, not only to its own unitholders, but also to mutual fund investors everywhere.

Smart Funds 2000

Y2K OK

These are all repeaters with multiple years on the Smart Fund list.

Fidelity Canadian Growth Company.

Fidelity Growth America. This one has always been a steady second-quartile performer.

Fidelity International Portfolio. Longtime first-quartile performer. Check out the new RSP clone, too!

Fidelity European Growth. We are watching the recent downturn in performance, but fund's long-term track record is too compelling to drop it just yet.

Y2K Agnostic

Fidelity Canadian Asset Allocation Fund. A great performer providing unitholders with equity-like returns, but with balanced fund-like volatility.

Fidelity Global Asset Allocation Fund. Like its Canadian sister, but this one ties up foreign content. There is now an RSP version on this one.

Noteworthy Funds

Y2K OK

Fidelity True North Fund. Popular Canadian equity fund managed by Alan Radlo. We still prefer his small-cap Canadian Growth Company Fund.

Y2K KO

Fidelity Canadian Bond Fund. Reasonable MER at 1.34% and consistent second-quartile performer.

Y2K Agnostic

Fidelity Canadian Balanced Fund. New domestic balanced fund has lower MER than the asset allocation version, though both are high given the fixed-income components. The asset allocation fund can make more radical asset class shifts.

Availability

Only through full-service and discount brokers and dealers.

20. GBC ASSET MANAGEMENT INC. **NO LOAD**

Strengths	Low fees; no load
	Small- and medium-cap growth
Weaknesses	$100,000 minimum
	Limited menu of funds
RESPs?	No
Web Site	www.gbc.ca

Toll Free 1-800-668-7383

CANADIAN	Category	Rating	Fund Name	M.E.R.%	RRSP/Foreign
Money Market:		■	GBC Money Market Fund	0.75	RRSP
Fixed Income:	Long-term	▲ KO	GBC Canadian Bond Fund	1.09	RRSP
	Small-Med Cap	★ OK	GBC Canadian Growth Fund	1.86	RRSP

FOREIGN	Category	Rating	Fund Name	MER%	RRSP/Foreign
Global Equity:	EAFE	■	GBC International Growth Fund	1.87	Foreign
Regional Equity:					
	NAFTA/N.Am.	■	GBC North American Growth Fund	1.9	Foreign

GBC is another high-performance no-load group, but something of an anomaly. GBC makes no attempt to cater to the average small investor; instead it targets a specific individual: someone with at least $100,000 to invest with the firm, and who is willing to take on the risk of small- and mid-cap North American stocks in return for the chance of extra returns.

GBC's small five-fund portfolio is the same as in previous editions of this book. Its funds, except for International Growth, have performed above average over the long term. Over one year to August 31, 1999, two performed in the top quartile. And the GBC Canadian Growth continues to perform very well, earning Smart Fund status again this year. Because it pays no trailer fees, these funds are more likely to be recommended by a fee-only planner than a commission-oriented one. One other fund, GBC Canadian Bond, is Noteworthy again this year.

GBC would be attractive to many investors who have begun to accumulate real wealth. Its unitholders enjoy access to portfolio managers through regular face-to-face meetings. However, while the MERs are slightly below those of the average broker-sold load fund, many investors who can afford the $100,000 entry ticket to the GBC funds could ultimately find cheaper alternatives in pooled funds and other high-net-worth vehicles offered by investment counselling firms. So, while elite as a mutual fund group, GBC occupies somewhat of a narrow niche between mass-market mutual funds and high-net-worth alternatives.

GBC has tried to address this issue with a rebate program. With the GBC Canadian Bond Fund, for example, investors earn a 0.25% (25 basis points) management fee rebate if they have at least $500,000 in the fund.

The GBC initials originally stood for Great Britain and Canada Corp., a closed-end fund established 71 years ago for British investors wishing to invest in North America. The key in-house investment management team, Pembroke Management of Montreal, was founded in 1968 by veterans Ian Soutar and Scott Taylor, who remain in place today. Their philosophy has remained consistent over those three decades: choosing growth stocks by seeking out and supporting at an early stage good companies run by good people Pembroke manages the North American stock picking, while the respected Greydanus, Boeckh & Associates Inc. run the bonds and money market fund.

Year 2000 Stance

GBC performs its own due diligence on every company in the stock portfolios to determine Y2K preparedness. Beyond this it specifies no strategy specific to the event, nor does it suggest worst-case scenarios or shifts in asset allocation.

Smart Funds 2000

Y2K OK

GBC Canadian Growth Fund. This one is first quartile over every CAGR period greater than one year! If you can afford the hefty entry amount and are looking for a solid small-cap fund, this might be the only one you need.

Noteworthy Funds

Y2K KO

GBC Canadian Bond. This fund has consistently performed above average versus similar funds and has a lower MER, as it should given the minimum required. It returned 3.8% over one year to August 31, 1999.

Availability

Directly from GBC on a no-load basis in Ontario and Quebec. Also available nationally through broker/dealers.

21. GLOBAL STRATEGY INVESTMENT FUNDS **FRONT OR REAR**

Strengths	Streamlined fund line-up Canadian equity managers
Weaknesses	Challenge of handling many external advisors High MERs, but coming down
RESPs?	No
Web Site	www.globalstrategyfunds.com **Toll Free** 1-800-387-1229

CANADIAN	Category	Rating	Fund Name	M.E.R.%	RRSP/Foreign
Money Market:		■	Money Market Fund	0.84	RRSP
Fixed Income:	Short-term	■	Bond Fund	1.5	RRSP
Equity:	Canadian Equity	■	Canada Growth Fund	2.57	RRSP
	Canadian Equity	▲ OK	Canadian Opportunities Fund	2.57	RRSP
	Small Cap	★ OK	Canadian Small Cap Fund	2.71	RRSP
	Gold/Precious Metals	▲ KO	Gold Plus Fund	2.75	RRSP
Multi-Asset:	Balanced	★ AG	Income Plus Fund	2.4	RRSP

FOREIGN	Category	Rating	Fund Name	MER%	RRSP/Foreign
Fixed Income:		■	World Bond Fund	2.1	Foreign
		▲ KO	Diversified World Bond Fund*	2.2	RRSP
Global Equity:	All-global	■	World Equity Fund	2.79	Foreign

		★ OK	World Companies Fund	2.79	Foreign
		▲ OK	Diversified World Equity Fund	2.37	RRSP
		■	World Opportunities Fund	n/a	Foreign
Regional Equity:	U.S.	■	U.S. Equity Fund	2.59	Foreign
	Japan	▲ OK	Diversified Japan Plus Fund	2.48	RRSP
	Europe	■	Europe Plus	2.79	Foreign
		■	Diversified Europe	2.51	RRSP
Global Balanced:		▲ AG	World Balanced Fund	2.32	Foreign

* Formerly Diversified Bond Fund

The family has lived up to its pioneering role in developing 100% RRSP-eligible foreign funds that undo the damage of the 20% foreign-content limit in RRSPs and RRIFs. Global Strategy was founded in 1983, chiefly for this purpose. Only recently have the many investors started to concede the value of maximum foreign content.

Ironically for Global Strategy, however, it is its Canadian funds that investors have embraced, led by Tony Massie in Vancouver and John Sartz in Toronto. The pair have each been in the investment industry for more than 25 years and therefore have a strong value orientation, regardless of market conditions.

Last year's edition noted that Global Strategy has also been efficient at cleaning up its fund family and simplifying the line-up of managers on its international funds—an effort that was completed in September 1998. Lately, the focus has been to return to its roots and build on the strengths of its global partner and partial owner, Rothschild Asset Management.

The four "Diversified" funds continue the 100% RRSP-eligible international tradition. Half of the 20% foreign-property basket in these funds can be invested in the corresponding multi-advisor fund. The latter, which are actively managed, 20% RRSP-eligible funds, draw upon several different global advisors.

This idea of using two or three different advisors on a single fund has been in place for five years at Global Strategy, and has only recently been adopted by other fund companies. The fruits have shown up in perennial Smart Funds such as the World Companies Fund, a Smart Fund for five years running, and which has a CAGR of 24.7% (to August 31, 1999) since its inception in January 1995.

Investor awareness of these strengths may be on the rise, now that Global Strategy has embarked on its first broadcast advertising, as of the 1999 RRSP season. Previously, the firm concentrated on raising awareness among brokers and dealers, which it achieved by using real journalists to deliver its bimonthly newsmagazine, *Global Stratagems*, the quarterly *Views* magazine, and daily e-mail and phone-delivered updates, formerly called Global Voice.

All of these services come at a price, in the form of management expense ratios. Global Strategy continues to inch down their MERs: most of the MERs shown in this edition's matrix are five or six basis points lower than in last year's edition.

While Global Strategy has focused on consolidating rather than expanding its fund line-up (its 18 funds are almost half the 30 it reached at one point), it did launch the 20% RRSP-eligible World Opportunities Fund in 1998, allowing domestic stock-picking ace John Sartz to take his value approach abroad. Unfortunately, Sartz did no better than other Canadian equity managers in a difficult year for the Canadian stock market, so his Canadian Opportunities Fund has been demoted.

Year 2000 Stance

Global Strategy recognized the importance of the Year 2000 "Y2K" problem in 1997 and began a project of identifying systems potentially affected by Y2K issues, and assessing associated risk factors. "Increasingly, regulators are becoming more concerned about the Y2K issue, and specifically with the securities and mutual fund industry's plans to address the problem." In December 1998 it implemented the Y2K-ready version of its mission-critical shareholder record-keeping system.

The firm did not comment on the implications for its equity fund holdings.

Smart Funds 2000

Y2K OK

Global Strategy World Companies. One of the top-performing global equity funds over the past four years.

Global Strategy Canadian Small Cap. The last time we doubted John Sartz he roared back to first quartile. We learned our lesson. If small caps are appropriate for your portfolio, then stick with the manager during the rocky periods.

Y2K Agnostic

Global Strategy Income Plus. A brief slump, but still a top long-term balanced fund with a little income for those needing the cash flow.

Noteworthy Funds

Y2K OK

Canadian Opportunities Fund. This has been demoted from Smart Funds status. The value orientation should be vindicated once the market's overvaluation corrects itself.

Diversified World Equity Fund. Second quartile, 100% RRSP-eligible global fund managed by Rothschilds, with the 20% foreign-content basket filled by World Companies and World Equity funds. Those with plenty of foreign content can consider the multi-advisor World Equity Fund, managed by Capital International, Schroder and Rothschild.

Diversified Japan Fund. Japan has been showing evidence of shaking off a 10-year depression. This is one of the few 100% RRSP-eligible Japan funds available in Canada.

Y2K KO

Diversified World Bond Fund. Modest return of 4.2% in year ended August 31, 1999 is above average, and this version does not use up your foreign content and could be a good alternative to global equity funds in a Y2K storm.

Gold Plus Fund. For more aggressive investors wanting to profit from a Y2K sell-off, Tony Massie could pull off some upside surprises here if the price of gold bullion ever rebounds.

Y2K Agnostic

World Balanced Fund. This fund isn't 100% RRSP-eligible, but will balance asset classes better than pure global equity funds.

Availability

Full-service and discount brokers and dealers across Canada. $500 minimum investments.

22. GREAT-WEST LIFE SEGREGATED FUNDS

NO LOAD OR REAR LOAD

Strengths	Traditional insurance guarantees Choice of five strong advisors
Weaknesses	MERs average to high Unspectacular performance
RESPs?	No
Web Site	www.gwl.ca

Telephone. 1-204-946-1190

CANADIAN	Category	Rating	Fund Name	M.E.R.*%	RRSP/Foreign
Money Market:		■	GWL Money Market Fund	1.24	RRSP
Fixed Income:		■	GWL Canadian Bond Fund	1.74	RRSP
		■	GWL Bond Fund (Beutel Goodman)	1.94	RRSP
		■	GWL Bond Fund (Sceptre)	1.93	RRSP
		■	GWL Government Bond Fund	1.76	RRSP
		■	GWL Income Fund	1.93	RRSP
	Mortgage	■	GWL Mortgage Fund	2.16	RRSP
Equity:	Large-Cap	■	GWL Canadian Equity Fund	2.37	RRSP
		■	GWL Larger Company Fund (Mackenzie)	2.65	RRSP
		■	GWL Equity Fund (Mackenzie)	2.58	RRSP
		■	GWL Equity Fund (Sceptre)	2.56	RRSP
	Index	▲ OK	GWL Equity Index Fund	2.23	RRSP
	Mid-Cap	■	GWL Mid Cap Canada Fund	2.49	RRSP
	Small-cap	■	GWL Smaller Company Fund (Mackenzie)	2.62	RRSP
		▲ OK	GWL Growth Equity Fund (AGF)	3	RRSP
	Specialty	■	GWL Canadian Opportunity Fund (Mackenzie)	2.76	RRSP
	Resource	■	GWL Canadian Resources Fund (AGF)	3.05	RRSP
	Real estate	■	GWL Real Estate Fund	2.7	RRSP
Tax Advantaged:	Dividend	■	GWL Dividend Fund	2.35	RRSP
		■	GWL Dividend/Growth Fund (Mackenzie)	2.66	RRSP
Multi-Asset:	Balanced	■	GWL Diversified RS Fund	2.37	RRSP
		■	GWL Balanced Fund (Mackenzie)	2.65	RRSP
		■	GWL Balanced Fund (Beutel Goodman)	2.51	RRSP
		▲ AG	GWL Balanced Fund (Sceptre)	2.56	RRSP
		■	GWL Growth & Income Fund (Mackenzie)	2.38	RRSP
		■	GWL Growth & Income Fund (AGF)	2.61	RRSP
		■	GWL Equity/Bond Fund	2.4	RRSP
		■	GWL Income Fund (Mackenize)	2.21	RRSP
	Fund of Funds	■	GWL Conservative Portfolio RS Fund	2.43	RRSP
		■	GWL Moderate Portfolio RS Fund	2.49	RRSP
		■	GWL Balanced Portfolio RS Fund	2.58	RRSP
		■	GWL Advanced Portfolio RS Fund	2.64	RRSP
		■	GWL Aggressive Portfolio RS Fund	2.7	RRSP

FOREIGN	Category	Rating	Fund Name	MER%	RRSP/Foreign
Fixed Income:		■	GWL International Bond Fund (Putnam)	2.46	Foreign
		▲ KO	GWL Global Income Fund (AGF)	2.38	RRSP
Global Equity:	EAFE	★ OK	GWL International Equity Fund (Putnam)	2.64	Foreign
		■	GWL International Opportunity (Putnam)	2.87	Foreign
Regional Equity:	U.S.	■	GWL U.S. Equity Fund	2.53	Foreign
		▲ OK	GWL American Growth (AGF)	2.92	Foreign
	NAFTA/N.A.	■	GWL North American Equity Fund (Beutel Goodman)	2.52	RRSP
	Europe	■	GWL European Equity Fund (Sceptre)	2.93	Foreign
	Asia	■	GWL Asian Growth (AGF)	3.03	Foreign

* MERs are for DSC versions: add 0.24% for no-loads

With mutual fund companies flooding the market with their own segregated funds, the quiet giant, Great-West Life Assurance Co. of Winnipeg, is faced with the challenge of keeping its own seg fund line-up competitive. That could be a challenge for the 108-year-old institution. But so far it has responded with innovative launches and continues to use several highly regarded managers as sub-advisors to its funds.

So-called "seg" funds are life insurance products governed by life insurance regulations, but are, for all intents and purposes, just like mutual funds from an investment perspective. For Y2K Agnostics, seg funds offer continued participation in equity markets plus some assurance of return of principal.

As stock markets climb, investors continue to rediscover the benefits of seg funds, the main one being that you can guarantee all or 75% of your initial capital if markets stay down 10 years, or in the event of death, your beneficiary would have that initial capital guaranteed. Seg funds also provide some potential creditor-proofing benefits and can allow assets to be transferred to a beneficiary without probate fees.

Several fund companies, such as Talvest, Templeton, and Trimark, are the latest to form alliances with insurance companies, which enables them to put an "insurance wrapper" around their own funds. Manulife Securities Inc. has taken a slightly different approach, putting a number of brand-name mutual funds under its Guaranteed Investment Fund (GIF encore) umbrella.

However, the ability to sleep at night carries with it a price; with most mutual fund/seg funds, the net MER is higher than the underlying funds.

This is why traditional insurance companies merit consideration for the seg-fund buyer. Great-West Life specifically merits special attention, for at least three reasons. First, GWL has one of the largest selections of seg funds among the traditional seg suppliers, with 42. Second, GWL's funds include several well-known mutual fund managers: AGF Management Ltd., Mackenzie Financial Corp., Beutel Goodman and Co. Ltd., Sceptre Investment Counsel Ltd., and Putnam Investments. And finally, GWL is planning to change its guarantee to give investors more choice. Subject to regulatory approval, by October 1999, it should have in place a new "rider" approach to guarantees. Clients will have the option of choosing the basic version which comes with a 75% guarantee or an enhanced guarantee that rises to 100% after the investment is held for five years. The higher guarantee will be more expensive, but investors at least have a choice.

As for managers of the seg funds, Beutel Goodman and Sceptre, both pension managers that have their own mutual funds, are also sub-advisors to Investors Group. On the international side, GWL opted for Putnam. Established in 1937, Putnam is one of the largest money management firms in the United States and runs almost $200 billion in assets worldwide. In 1994, GWL also created its own internal investment management subsidiary, known as GWL Investment Management Ltd., which it describes as a "top-down, growth-oriented manager." Perhaps so, but there are a lot of income and balanced funds in GWLIM's line-up, plus five Portfolio funds made up of other GWL funds.

A glance at the GWL fund matrix shows the all-in MERs are slightly higher than the average MERs of traditional load funds, but comparable to, or slightly below, the new fund company/life hybrid products. MERs on several funds have been lowered, albeit slightly in the last year. Unfortunately, those annual costs on several of the international funds jumped. GWL International Opportunity, for example, went from an MER of 2.52% to 2.87%.

Note too that the MERs in the matrix are for the DSC (rear-load funds). If you want the same funds no load, you will have to add 0.24% to the MERs shown in the matrix.

Generally, our Noteworthy designations derive from the corresponding funds in the other fund families, although in some cases the extra MER precluded the equivalent ranking.

As with other fund families with more than 40 funds, it's a bit of a challenge sorting out the line-up and a good advisor is really needed. GWL uses an asset allocation program called Discovery to help find the appropriate mix for investors. A questionnaire helps the agent decide on the right asset mix and funds. The matrix reveals plenty of duplication in Canadian equities, bonds, and balanced funds, while the global line-up tends to have only one entry in each category.

Year 2000 Stance

GWL has its own money managers but also uses the services of five outside managers, as mentioned above. GWL says each of those managers is taking Y2K scenarios under consideration; however, they aren't changing their styles to address them. (See sections on these firms in their respective fund family treatments elsewhere in this book for more on their strategies.)

GWL does not suggest any best- or worst-case scenario strategies for investors. Instead it recommends investors follow their long-term investment strategies and stick with those asset allocations. "Speculating about short- or near-term stock market prospects, whether related to Y2K scenarios or not, is not something we partake in," the company says.

Smart Funds 2000

Y2K OK

GWL International Equity Fund B. This one has the lower MER than its sister A fund. First-quartile performer for two, three, and four years ended August 31, 1999. This one is managed, with an EAFE mandate, by the outstanding Boston-based firm Putnam Investments and returns as a Smart Fund. Fund mandate excludes North America.

Noteworthy Funds

Y2K OK

GWL Equity Index Fund. For years, this was one of the few Canadian equity index funds available in the market. But the banks have entered this domain aggressively the past year and this fund's MER of 2.33% is much too high for an index fund.

GWL American Growth (AGF). This fund has been skilfully managed by Stephen Rogers at AGF. As we've said, guarantees are more worthwhile for riskier investment types, and the U.S. market, with its current valuations, could be considered one such investment type. And the guaranteed version is not much more expensive than the fund from AGF.

GWL Growth Equity (AGF). The corresponding AGF Canadian small-cap fund has almost the same MER. As with GWL American Growth, the small premium might be worth it to get some hedged exposure to an asset class—Canadian small caps—that can more than earn the fees.

Y2K KO

GWL Global Income Fund (AGF). 100% RRSP-eligible global bond fund managed by AGF, one of the better fixed-income managers. Alternatively, consider parking in any of the first seven funds shown in the top half of the fund matrix (one money market, six fixed income).

Y2K Agnostic

GWL Balanced (Sceptre). The underlying fund managed by Lyle Stein at Sceptre has been in a slump for almost two years now. This version with the guarantee is more expensive with an annual 2.56% MER.

23. GUARDIAN GROUP OF FUNDS

FRONT OR REAR

Strengths	Canadian funds 100% RRSP-eligible global funds
Weaknesses	Classic series lower MERs but high minimums
RESPs?	Yes
Web Site	www.guardianfunds.com **Toll Free** 1-800-668-7327

CANADIAN	Category	Rating	Fund Name	M.E.R.%	RRSP/Foreign
				Classic/Mutual Fund	
Money Market:		■	Guardian Canadian Money Market	0.81/1.48	RRSP
	Short-term bonds	■	Guardian Canadian Income	0.87/1.53	RRSP
Fixed Income:		▲ KO	Guardian Canadian Bond	1.10/1.70	RRSP
		■	Guardian High Yield	1.24/1.85	RRSP
Equity:	All Cap	▲ OK	Guardian Growth Equity	2.20/2.88	RRSP
	Small/Mid Cap	▲ OK	Guardian Enterprise	2.34/2.98	RRSP
	Large Cap	■	Guardian Large Cap	2.00/2.60	RRSP
Tax Advantaged:					
	Dividend Income	■	Guardian Monthly Dividend	1.31/1.93	RRSP
		■	Guardian Monthly High Income	1.54/2.16	RRSP
Multi-Asset:	Balanced	▲ AG	Guardian Canadian Balanced	1.71/2.78	RRSP
		▲ AG	Guardian Growth & Income	2.05/2.69	RRSP

FOREIGN	Category	Rating	Fund Name	MER%	RRSP/Foreign
Money Market:		■	Guardian US Money Market	0.87/1.53	RRSP
Fixed Income:					
	No hedging restrictions	▲ KO	Guardian International Income	2.12/2.72	RRSP
	Cannot hedge into C$	★ KO	Guardian Foreign Income	2.10/2.70	RRSP
Global Equity:	All-global	■	Guardian Global Equity	1.99/2.59	Foreign
	All global Small Caps	▲ OK	Guardian Global Small Cap	2.00/2.60	Foreign

Regional Equity:				
Emerging Markets	■	Guardian Emerging Markets	1.80/2.92	Foreign
US All Cap	★ OK	Guardian American Equity	2.05/2.63	Foreign
US Large Cap	■	Guardian American Large Cap	2.00/2.60	Foreign
Europe	■	Guardian European Equity	1.99/2.60	Foreign
Global Balanced:	▲ AG	Guardian International Balanced	2.00/2.88	Foreign

The Guardian Group has long positioned itself as the "risk management" specialist, a stance that should serve unitholders well in the volatile, overheated securities markets of 1999 leading up to the Y2K denouement. The emphasis on risk control, which is cleverly played up in its television commercials, in theory generates strong performance in good times and a defensive capital preservation approach in bear markets. The low volatility figures of its fixed-income funds and mixed-asset products such as the Canadian Balanced Fund demonstrate that there is a consistent investment management approach underlying the marketing campaigns.

Unlike some of the monster 50 fund families shown elsewhere in this book, Guardian's 21 funds cover the major bases, split evenly between 11 Canadian funds and 10 global funds. Three of its foreign funds are 100% RRSP-eligible, permitting investors to get around the usual 20% foreign-content restrictions of RRSPs and RRIFs.

Four new funds were launched on January 18, 1999:

1) Guardian Canadian Bond Fund aims to generate interest income from bonds and debentures issued by Canadian governments and corporations. It is managed by veteran Peter Hargrove, Guardian Capital's managing director of fixed-income investments.
2) Guardian Canadian High-Yield Fund seeks to generate a higher level of interest income by investing in high-yield bonds and debentures issued by Canadian governments and corporations. The Fund is managed by Stephen Kearns, a fixed-income investments portfolio manager with 10 years' investment experience.
3) Guardian Canadian Large Cap Fund is a new large-cap fund managed by James Lawson.
4) Guardian European Equity Fund complements Guardian's earlier entries in Asia and Emerging Markets with this all-Europe fund managed by Juliet Cohn of Dresdner RCM Global Investors. Cohn's 12-year track record was established

researching European companies for a major European investment firm.

The Guardian Asia Pacific Fund itself was recast in October 1, 1998, as the Guardian Global Small Cap Fund, with a mandate to invest in small- and mid-cap companies around the world. That coincided with the appointment of former BPI advisor Lazard Asset Management on the Guardian Emerging Markets Fund. Lazard Asset Management is a division of Lazard Freres and Co., established in 1848 and which is now manager of more than C$100 billion in assets. The manager is 14-year veteran James Donald.

Guardian's dividend income funds have also proved to be popular for income-oriented investors with large taxable portfolios. The conservative income stance does not generate the kind of performance as their pure growth equity counterparts but the Guardian Monthly Dividend Fund and Guardian Monthly Income Fund compare favourably with GICs and other guaranteed products on an after-tax basis.

As noted in last year's edition, the matrix shows two classes of Guardian fund, each with different MERs. Guardian Classic Funds are sold as front-load funds to investors with $50,000 or more. Guardian Mutual Funds without the Classic imprimatur are sold either on a DSC or front-load basis but carry higher MERs. Our Smart Fund selections are invariably the Classic version because of our preference for lower MERs where a choice exists.

Year 2000 Stance

Given its reputation for risk management, one would expect Guardian to carefully consider the possible investment implications of Y2K. Indeed, Guardian says it is taking the issue seriously. It cites the three-prong approach taken by the Ontario Securities Commission, which is raising awareness and educating the industry on the issue; monitoring Y2K activity and progress of testing programs; and encouraging firms to take the necessary corrective actions to remedy the situation. It notes too that the Toronto Stock Exchange has adopted a rule requiring listed companies to disclose material information regarding Y2K readiness and that the Canadian Institute of Chartered Accountants' Accounting Guideline on Y2K calls for factual and verifiable disclosure of Y2K issues in financial statements.

Guardian therefore views the public disclosure documents issued by public companies as the most appropriate source for Y2K compliance information. In addition, Guardian has instituted an internal program to review Y2K information for both the firms in which it invests as well as those it is considering investing in. It also makes a point of making verbal inquiries of company management's Y2K program and readiness when portfolio managers meet with them.

Like other fund companies, Guardian considers Y2K as one of many inputs in its bottom-up analysis, and does not intend to engage in market timing or sector rotation strictly because of Y2K. It concludes that it is "not currently able to target specific securities or sectors in Canada that seem to be at special risk. As we get closer to the year-end, we will likely get additional information regarding individual company's true state of readiness. At that time we may revise our estimate of the overall severity of the problem and take any investment action that we deem to be appropriate in the circumstances."

Smart Funds 2000

Y2K OK

Guardian American Equity. Managed by Michael Rome of Lazard, this value manager should hold up well in any correction.

Y2K KO

Guardian Foreign Income. First quartile over two, three, and five years; fund is back for its third appearance on the Smart Fund list.

Noteworthy Funds

Y2K OK

Guardian Enterprise Fund. Small caps have had a rough time lately and has been third quartile over the past 2.5 years. Fund gets demoted because of better funds from the competition.

Guardian Growth Equity Classic. Former Smart Fund (1998 edition) managed by John Priestman. Mid-large cap would be nice complement to Gary Chapman's small-cap Enterprise fund.

Guardian Global Small Cap. Formerly the Asia Pacific fund, this global small-cap fund now managed by Lazard Freres could do well long term if acquired in a Y2K down-dip.

Y2K KO

Guardian Canadian Bond Classic. New conservative bond fund managed by Peter Hargrove. MER of Classic version is far more reasonable than the non-Classic.

Guardian International Income. Slightly higher MER than Foreign Income. Both funds are 100% eligible, providing some currency diversification to Canadian fixed-income funds.

Y2K Agnostic

Guardian Canadian Balanced. This fund has been fourth quartile for each year 1995 through 1998, but rarely loses money.

Guardian Growth & Income. In a Y2K-uncertain environment, a multi-asset Guardian fund managed by John Priestman should provide a reasonable balance of safety, growth, and income.

Guardian International Balanced Fund. As above, with more global diversification.

Availability

Through full-service and discount brokers and dealers.

24. HSBC Asset Management (HONGKONG BANK MUTUAL FUNDS)

NO LOAD

Strengths	Far East equities HSBC on fixed income
Weaknesses	No 100% RRSP-eligible global funds
RESPs?	Under development
Web Site	www.hksi.com **Toll Free** 1-800-830-8888

CANADIAN	Category	Rating	Fund Name	M.E.R.%	RRSP/Foreign
Money Market:		■	HSBC Canadian Money Market Fund	0.91%	RRSP
	U.S. denominated	■	HSBC U.S. Dollar Money Market Fund	0.99%	RRSP
Fixed Income:	Mortgage	▲ KO	HSBC Mortgage Fund	1.42%	RRSP
	Mid to long-term	■	HSBC Canadian Bond Fund	1.12%	RRSP
Equity:	Mid to Large-Cap	■	HSBC Equity Fund	1.85%	RRSP
	Small-Cap	■	HSBC Small Cap Growth Fund	2.15%	RRSP
Tax Advantaged:	Dividend	▲ AG	HSBC Dividend Income Fund	1.85%	RRSP
Multi-Asset:	Balanced	▲ AG	HSBC Canadian Balanced Fund	1.79%	RRSP

FOREIGN	Category	Rating	Fund Name	MER%	RRSP/Foreign
Fixed Income:		■	HSBC World Bond Fund	2.00%	Foreign
Global Equity:	NAFTA/N.Am	★ OK	HSBC U.S. Equity Fund	2.09%	Foreign
	Europe	▲ OK	HSBC European Fund	2.12%	Foreign
	Far East	■	HSBC AsiaPacific Fund	2.22%	Foreign
	Emerging Market	■	HSBC Emerging Markets Fund	2.71%	Foreign
Multi-Asset:	Balanced	■	HSBC Global Equity Fund	0.45%	Foreign

Better known by the name Hongkong Bank Mutual Funds, this group and other global sister companies will be known henceforth by the moniker of the parent company, the HSBC Group, one of the world's largest banking and financial services organizations.

But except for the name change, it remains one of the lower-MER, low-volatility group of no-load funds in the Canadian universe.

The Vancouver-based investment team continues to manage the domestic funds, which include the HSBC Canadian Balanced and Equity Funds. The investment manager used to be known as M.K. Wong & Associates Ltd. and was renamed HSBC Asset Management (Canada) Ltd. after M.K. Wong was purchased by Hongkong Bank of Canada. The firm's presence in Canada began with the 1990 purchase of Lloyds Bank of Canada.

The foreign funds are managed by investment teams in other HSBCAM offices around the world—consistent with the group's investment philosophy that fund managers be located close to the markets in which they invest.

Since the last edition, Stephen Baker has been appointed Deputy Chief Executive Officer of HSBC Canada. He has added members to the domestic investment team: Duncan McCrindell, portfolio manager, Canadian equities, and Jamie McKeough, analyst, Canadian equities.

Apart from below-average MERs, many of the HSBC Canada funds are in the first and second quartile; that is, the top half of their respective fund groups in the performance rankings. While the line-up of funds is just 14, most of the bases are covered.

HSBCAM also offers discretionary money management for high-net-worth individuals, with both pooled funds and segregated accounts. The 11 pooled funds correspond to most of the no-load mutual funds but have a different fee schedule that falls with the amount of money invested.

Year 2000 Stance

HSBC Asset Management says its investment teams are monitoring and analyzing the potential effects of Y2K in light of "the impact it may have on economies and asset prices." It cautions that because of the uncertainties surrounding the issue, it is "extremely difficult to quantify the precise nature, location, and magnitude of this risk."

It is implementing a global policy that requires all investment teams to have sought and retained information from portfolio holdings concerning their internal Y2K risk, awareness of external supplier Y2K risk, and contingency planning.

Smart Funds 2000

HSBC U.S. Equity Fund. First-quartile U.S. fund in every period since inception in 1994, and with a reasonable 2.09% MER.

Noteworthy Funds

Y2K OK

HSBC European Fund. 23.9% CAGR for three years ended June 30, 1999, making this one of the better European funds in the Canadian marketplace. Reasonable 2.12% MER. Main caveat is to track Y2K progress in Europe, which cannot be assumed to be on par with North America.

Y2K KO

HSBC Mortgage Fund. Sixth best-performing mortgage fund in Canada over a five-year period. The 1.42% MER is lower than most comparable bond funds and the shorter-term underlying mortgage securities will have less interest rate risk than volatile long-term bond funds may experience during a period of Y2K financial uncertainty.

Y2K Agnostic

HSBC Canadian Balanced Fund. Ranked second quartile over two-, three-, five-, and ten-year periods ended August 31, 1999. MER of 1.79% is well below the average Canadian balanced fund. The fund was up 17.6% for the year ended August 31, 1999, for top quartile. It had a roughly classic balanced fund asset mix of 55% equities to 45% cash and bonds.

HSBC Dividend Income Fund. Launched in 1995, this fund has a three-year CAGR of 13.6% to August 31, 1999. Bias is toward defensive sectors such as utilities, pipelines, and financial services. Ranked in top quartile over two, and three years.

Availability

At HSBC branches in all provinces except PEI, and at select registered investment dealers and discount brokers. $500 minimum initial investment; less on PACs.

25. INVESTORS GROUP INC.

LOAD

Strengths	Conservative, long-term approach
	Now extensive choice globally
Weaknesses	Hard to mix with other fund families
	Complexity of 5 families & 50 funds
RESPs?	Yes
Web Site	www.investorsgroup.com **Toll Free** 1-888-746-6344

CANADIAN	Category	Rating	Fund Name	M.E.R.%	RRSP/Foreign
Money Market:		■	Investors Canadian Money Market Fund	1.07	RRSP
	Segregated	■	IG/GWL Money Market Segregated Fund	1.3	RRSP
Fixed Income:	Long-term	■	Investors Government Bond Fund	1.89	RRSP
		■	Investors Corporate Bond Fund	1.89	RRSP
		■	IG Sceptre Canadian Bond Fund	2.29	RRSP
	Segregated	▲ KO	IG/GWL Government Bond Segregated Fund	2.1	RRSP
	Mortgage	■	Investors Mortgage Fund	1.9	RRSP
Equity:	Mid-Large Cap	■	Investors Canadian Equity Fund	2.46	RRSP
		■	Investors Retirement Mutual	2.42	RRSP
		■	Merrill Lynch Canadian Equity	2.83	RRSP
		■	GS Canadian Equity Fund	2.79	RRSP
		■	IG Sceptre Canadian Equity Fund	2.84	RRSP
		■	IG Beutel Goodman Canadian Equity Fund	2.9	RRSP
	Segregated	■	IG/GWL Canadian Equity Segregated Fund	2.65	RRSP
	Small Cap	■	Investors Canadian Small Cap Fund	2.57	RRSP
		■	Investors Canadian Small Cap Fund II	2.55	RRSP
		■	IG Beutel Goodman Canadian Small Cap	2.88	RRSP
	Resource	■	Investors Canadian Natural Resource Fund	2.54	RRSP
	Ethical	■	Investors Summa Fund	2.47	RRSP
	Quebec	■	Investors Quebec Enterprise Fund	New	RRSP
Tax Advantaged:	Dividend	■	Investors Dividend Fund	2.36	RRSP
	Div-Seg	▲ AG	IG/GWL Dividend Segregated Fund	2.65	RRSP
	Real Estate	■	Investors Real Property Fund	2.37	RRSP
Multi-Asset:	Balanced	★ AG	Investors Mutual of Canada Fund	2.36	RRSP
		▲ AG	GS Canadian Balanced	2.78	RRSP
		▲ AG	IG Sceptre Canadian Balanced Fund	2.81	RRSP
		■	IG Beutel Goodman Canadian Balanced Fund	2.79	RRSP
	Asset Allocation	■	Investors Asset Allocation Fund	2.72	RRSP
	Portfolio of Funds	■	Investors Growth Portfolio	2.45	Foreign
		■	Investors Growth Plus Portfolio	2.45	Foreign
		■	Investors Income Portfolio	2.06	RRSP
		■	Investors Income Plus Portfolio	2.29	RRSP
		■	Investors World Growth Portfolio	2.62	Foreign
		■	Investors Retirement Plus Portfolio	2.41	RRSP
		■	Investors Retirement Growth Portfolio	2.45	RRSP
		■	Investors High Growth Portfolio	New	RRSP

FOREIGN	Category	Rating	Fund Name	MER%	RRSP/Foreign
Money Market:		■	Investors U.S. Money MarketFund	1.19	Foreign
Fixed Income:		■	Investors Global Bond Fund	2.19	Foreign
		■	Investors North American High Yield Bond Fund	2.23	Foreign
		■	Merrill Lynch World Bond Fund	2.26	RRSP
		■	GS International Bond	2.79	RRSP
Global Equity:	All-global	■	Investors Global Fund	2.19	Foreign
		■	GS International Equity	2.83	Foreign
	Sci-Tech	▲ OK	Investors Global Science & Technology Fund	New	Foreign
Regional Equity:	U.S.	■	Investors U.S. Growth Fund	2.4	Foreign
		■	GS American Equity	2.94	Foreign
	U.S. small cap	■	Investors U.S. Opportunities Fund	2.56	Foreign
	NAFTA/N.Am.	■	Investors North American Growth Fund	2.38	Foreign
	NAFTA small-cap	■	Investors Special Fund	2.39	Foreign
	Latin American	■	Investors Latin American Growth Fund	3.1	Foreign
	Emerging Market	■	Merrill Lynch Emerging Markets	3.28	Foreign
	Far East	■	Investors Pacific International Fund	2.55	Foreign
	Japan	■	Investors Japanese Growth Fund	2.46	Foreign
	Europe	■	Investors European Growth Fund	2.47	Foreign
Global Balanced:		■	Merrill Lynch World Allocation	2.91	Foreign
	U.S. Balanced	■	Merrill Lynch U.S. Allocation Fund	2.85	Foreign

* No-load on equity funds if more than $10,000 with Investors Group

Investors Group Inc. of Winnipeg is the largest, as well as one of the oldest, mutual fund firms in Canada. It has assets of more than $37 billion spread among more than five fund families and 57 funds. In total, 3,700 representatives serve one million customers from 100 financial planning centres across Canada.

But as earlier editions of *Smart Funds* have noted, because of Investors' "proprietary" approach to selling its in-house funds, it has been difficult to mix and match its funds with other rival families. Investors started to address this when it created new Investors' funds run by external advisors, such as Beutel Goodman, Sceptre, Rothschild, and Merrill Lynch. In 1999, it went a step further, with new alliances with Templeton, Scudder Maxxum, AGF, and even sister company Great-West Life Assurance.

In effect, then, Investors Group offers a completely separate distribution network than independent broker-dealers that offer traditional access to the big brand-name load firms such as Fidelity, Mackenzie, and Trimark. It offers a slightly different mix of some of the best-known fund families available in Canada.

Until recently, Investors Group did not sell segregated funds because these were the exclusive domain of GWL. This changed on January 12, 1999, however, when Investors Group decided to offer four seg funds in conjunction with GWL: the IG/GWL Canadian Equity Segregated Fund, and the similarly named dividend, government bond, and money market funds. Why one would pay an insurance premium for a seg version of a money market or bond fund is debatable but Investors plans to provide more seg funds later in 1999. While many rival firms have emphasized the guarantees on initial principal, Investors views the chief appeal as the death benefit or potential creditor protection. Like most old-time seg funds, the IG/GWL seg funds have only a 75% maturity benefit but 100% death benefit for beneficiaries.

Investors Group also beefed up its global funds, with Templeton Management Ltd. advising on a new series of Investors Group funds effective April 1999. That's in addition to its previous global two-punch of Rothschild and Merrill Lynch.

Domestically, the Scudder/Maxxum alliance that was also announced in April will result in new Scudder Maxxum Co. funds created for Investors Group's sales network. Whether the low-MER versions of the Scudder funds remain intact in their Investors Group incarnations remains to be seen. High-performing Janus Capital may not be available. If they become available, ask your Investors Group representative to include it in your portfolio.

Since the last edition, Investors also expanded its Portfolio Funds series, which use a "fund of funds" approach to asset allocation, providing various fund combinations that range from a capital preservation risk profile to aggressive growth. The latest and eighth addition to the series is in the latter category—the Investors Retirement High Growth Portfolio Fund, which became available in January 1999. It also reopened the Beutel Goodman Canadian Small Cap Fund, which had been closed to new investors in January 1998.

Investors Group also expanded its investment management into Montreal, Quebec, and appointed Christine Decarie as partner and portfolio manager. A new Quebec-focused fund was also planned for launch in mid-1999, pending regulatory approval.

As the matrix shows, there is considerable duplication in certain fund categories. Confusion can be minimized by working with an Investors representative, which comes with the package. As the new Scudder Maxxum funds come on board, this task will become even more difficult. Apart from the externally advised funds, there are still the many proprietary Investors Group in-house funds to consider. There is no fee to switch between the various fund families. The funds are no load if you have a minimum $10,000 in Investors' funds. Otherwise, there is a 2.5% front-end sales charge on equity funds.

Generally, Investors Group dodges the issue of high cost from its funds' medium-to-high MERs. As we note in the matrix, despite the ridiculous amount of redundant choices it offers, it does not provide investors with the choice of low-MER index funds. And to date there is not much evidence that Investors Group has delivered consistent performance to go along with its expensive actively managed funds.

Year 2000 Stance

Investors Group investment team is assessing the Year 2000 preparedness strategies of companies for the more than 600 companies whose shares are owned by its mutual funds. It has asked those organizations to report on the steps being taken to address Y2K compliance and the deadlines set for completion.

Investors notes that Y2K is "an issue that can affect a company's ability to operate, their subsequent performance and share value, which is why we need to pay close attention to the steps these companies are taking."

Investors Group has a Year 2000 section on its web site and questions can be e-mailed to yr2000@investorsgroup.com.

Smart Funds 2000

Y2K Agnostic

Investors Mutual of Canada. Hard picking in this family with such high MERs. This one is in the average expense range and is an above average performer.

Noteworthy Funds

Y2K OK

Investors Global Science & Technology Fund. Investors was long overdue to introduce a global technology fund, which have been available for several years in the independent broker-dealer channel. You can expect the MER to clock in well north of 2.5%. The fund will be geographically diversified and includes small caps but mainly medium- and large-cap sci-tech stocks. Targeted sectors include computer services, telecom, semiconductors, networking, biotech, pharmaceuticals, wireless, and e-commerce. Launched in October 1998, the fund was up 51.3% for the eight months ended August 31, 1999. As long as the U.S. bull market and the tech-heavy NASDAQ exchange stay aloft, this fund should participate in the festivities.

Y2K KO

IG/GWL Government Bond Segregated Fund. Double protection here for a Y2K meltdown. While it may not make a lot of sense to use seg-fund versions of bond funds in normal times—unless you were looking for the death or creditor features—the 75% market guarantee could conceivably be useful if interest rates went in the wrong direction for bond fund values. A 2.1% MER is a high price to pay for a Canadian bond fund so this should not be a long-term measure but rather a place to park until the Y2K storm clouds pass.

Y2K Agnostic

IG/GWL Dividend Segregated Fund. New Great-West Life managed seg fund offers a normally conservative dividend fund approach with an insurance guarantee of 75% of initial principal should markets seriously decline. The all-in MER of 2.65% is high for domestic dividend funds but typical of Canadian seg funds.

IG Sceptre Canadian Balanced Fund. Since this fund has dropped into the fourth quartile, we are dropping it to Noteworthy.

Rothschild Select. GS Canadian Balanced. Has the solid Smart Fund, Global Strategy Income Plus as its core underlying investment, but at an MER of almost 40 basis points higher. Manager Tony Massie's value approach, long experience, and knowledge of the gold market (he also runs Global Strategy's Gold Plus fund) should serve investors well in a Y2K Agnostic or Y2K KO scenario.

Availability

Exclusively from 3,700 Investors' reps.

26. JONES HEWARD GROUP OF FUNDS FRONT OR REAR

Strengths	Half a century of pension experience Low-MER money market fund
Weaknesses	No global funds (except U.S.) Relatively high MERs
RESPs?	No
Web Site	www.jonesheward.com **Toll Free** 1-800-361-1392

CANADIAN	Category	Rating	Fund Name	M.E.R.%	RRSP/Foreign
Money Market:		▲ KO	Jones Heward Money Market Fund	0.5	RRSP

Fixed Income:	Long-term	■	Jones Heward Bond Fund	1.75	RRSP
	Small-Large cap	■	Jones Heward Fund Ltd.	2.5	RRSP
Multi-Asset:	Balanced	■	Jones Heward Canadian Balanced Fund	2.4	RRSP

FOREIGN	Category	Rating	Fund Name	MER%	RRSP/Foreign
Regional Equity:	U.S.	▲ OK	Jones Heward American Fund	2.5	Foreign

Jones Heward is one of the few fund groups that has been content with its small line-up—a different approach from the many rival fund companies that scramble to launch every specialty fund concept that comes along. This family, part of the Bank of Montreal Group of Companies, remains tightly focused with five funds. The line-up includes the basic vanilla fund types, but has no global or international fund. The only foreign-content fund is a U.S. equity portfolio. Recent executive changes at the Bank of Montreal Group of Companies may bring more attention to this small fund family.

While its MERs are comparable to any of the big load groups, the money market fund designated Noteworthy carries a reasonable 0.5% MER, half the usual price for this fund type.

The five funds are regular load funds, with optional front-end commissions negotiable to 9% and rear loads of 5%, declining to nil after seven years. Its Canadian funds are average performers but, except for the money market fund, we see little evidence that their fairly high MERs have created extra value added. Perhaps recognizing this, in 1997 the firm shook up the venerable Jones Heward Fund, which is approaching its 60th birthday. The fund performed below average again in 1998, although more recent performance has shown signs of improvement.

The stand-out was Jones Heward American Fund, a top performer in 1997, 1998, and so far in 1999. Over one year to August 31, 1999, it returned 46.8%.

Year 2000 Stance

Each of the portfolio managers has their own strategy for assessing securities in their portfolios. Most are questioning management in interviews or questionnaires. If a company is behind in its Year 2000 preparations, a closer examination will be made to determine what position to take on the security.

Smart Funds 2000

None

Noteworthy Funds

Y2K OK

Jones Heward American. A top performer over the last few years, manager Graeme Bretall, of Harris, Bretall, Sullivan & Smith focuses on large, blue-chip stocks. Over three years to August 31, 1999, it returned 32.3% just behind the 32.4% gain of the S&P 500 index.

Y2K KO

Jones Heward Money Market Fund. The 0.5% MER makes this the most cost-effective buy in the group and the place to park if it seems as though the Y2K storms may rage. Y2K Agnostics would consider the Jones Heward Balanced Fund.

Availability

Through brokers and dealers, primarily Nesbitt Burns. $1,000 minimum initial purchase.

27. LEITH WHEELER INVESTMENT COUNSEL LTD.

NO LOAD

Strengths	Low MERs
	Route to high-net-worth products
Weaknesses	Limited number of funds
	Not available in all provinces
RESPs?	No
Web Site	none
Toll Free	1-888-292-1122

CANADIAN	Category	Rating	Fund Name	M.E.R.%	RRSP/Foreign
Money Market:		■	Money Market Fund	0.6	RRSP
Fixed Income:	Long-term	■	Fixed Income Fund	0.75	RRSP
Equity:	Large-cap	▲ OK	Canadian Equity fund	1.4	RRSP
Multi-Asset:	Balanced	★ AG	Balanced Fund	1.1	RRSP

FOREIGN	Category	Rating	Fund Name	MER%	RRSP/Foreign
Regional Equity:	U.S.	▲ OK	U.S. Equity Fund	1.25	Foreign

This is the second edition in *Smart Funds* for this 18-year-old Vancouver-based, employee-owned investment counselling firm. The strength of its low-MER, no-load funds makes it well worth including, despite the $50,000 minimum that can be invested in any combination of its five funds. While the firm's mutual funds operation is small relative to much of the competition, it manages another $2.5 billion for pension funds, wealthy individuals, charities, and foundations.

For those who can meet the minimum, the MERs are tough to beat: the Balanced Fund, with a 1.1% MER, is a Smart Fund again this year. It's also the oldest Leith Wheeler Fund, having been created in 1987: the other four were started up in 1994 and now have five-year track records. The Canadian Equity Fund, with a 1.4% MER, and U.S. Equity Fund, at 1.25%, are designated Noteworthy again although their relative performance slumped a bit in 1998 and into early 1999.

The Leith Wheeler funds also provide an entry level and growth path to the even lower-fee high-net-worth products normally offered by investment counselling firms. At Leith Wheeler, discretionary "segregated" portfolio management is available at a $1 million minimum, while a "portfolio of funds" service is available at a $500,000 threshold. For a full explanation of these terms, investors in this category can refer to the *National Post*'s *The Wealthy Boomer: Life After Mutual Funds.*

Leith Wheeler's approach is to eschew attempts to "time" the stock market. It looks for stocks it thinks are undervalued and will grow; the managers typically expect to hold a stock for two to four years.

Year 2000 Stance

Leith Wheeler believes that no investment manager is in a position to offer the assurance that every company they own will smoothly enter the year 2000. It relies on the fact that competent management have analyzed operations and are dealing with issues that arise. According to the company, it is the financial services area where the risks appear the highest. In Canada, the actions of the banks provides them with a reasonable level of comfort that they will be ready to deal with this. But nothing is certain.

As a value investor with a three-year time horizon, Leith Wheeler believes that Y2K may have a short-term impact on company earnings and stock prices and would view that as a buying opportunity.

Smart Funds 2000

Y2K Agnostic

Leith Wheeler Balanced Fund. 1.1% MER is well below the category average. Similarly, low-MER havens for Y2K KO believers will be the money market or fixed-income funds.

Noteworthy Funds

Y2K OK

Leith Wheeler Canadian Equity Fund. MER of 1.4% is well below the category average. Created in 1994, this mostly large-cap fund is broadly spread across the major economic sectors: 20% resources, 38% in financial services, 14% consumer products, and 9% in industrials. Stocks are purchased with the intention of holding them for two to four years.

Leith Wheeler U.S. Equity Fund. 1.25% MER is lower than most comparable retail-level funds. The managers are cautious about record valuations and seek companies in industries where sentiment has turned negative, or which have encountered a short-term difficulty that can be overcome, or stocks that managers believe other analysts have overlooked or misunderstand. That more prudent approach caused it to underperform much of the competition in 1998 and early 1999 as the S&P 500 index soared.

Availability

$50,000 minimum initial investment. Not available in Quebec or Atlantic Canada.

28. LONDON LIFE FREEDOM FUNDS

FRONT OR REAR

Strengths	Canadian equities
	Janus on global funds
Weaknesses	Volatile specialty funds
	MERs no longer below average
RESPs?	No
Web Site	www.maxxumfund.com **Toll Free** 1-888-462-9986

CANADIAN	Category	Rating	Fund Name	M.E.R.%	RRSP/Foreign
Money Market:		■	LL Money Market Fund (LLIM)	1.2	RRSP
Fixed Income:		■	LL Government Bond Fund (GWLIM)	1.75	RRSP
		★ KO	LL Mortgage Fund (LLIM)	2	RRSP
		■	LL Bond Fund (LLIM)	1.75	RRSP
Equity:	Mixed-cap	▲ OK	LL Canadian Equity (LLIM)	2.35	RRSP
		■	LL Canadian Equity (GWLIM)	2.35	RRSP
		■	LL Canadian Equity Growth (Maxxum)	2.4	RRSP
	Large-cap	■	LL Larger Company (Mackenzie)	2.5	RRSP

	Mid-cap	■	LL Mid Cap Canada (GWLIM)	2.35	RRSP
		■	LL Equity (Mackenzie)	2.5	RRSP
		■	LL Growth Equity Fund (LLIM)	2.35	RRSP
		■	LL North American Equity Fund (Beutel Goodman)	2.45	RRSP
		■	LL Equity Fund (Sceptre)	2.45	RRSP
	Specialty	■	LL Canadian Opportunity Fund (Mackenzie)	2.5	RRSP
		■	LL Growth Equity Fund (AGF)	2.9	RRSP
		■	LL Natural Resource Fund (Maxxum)	2.65	RRSP
		▲ KO	LL Precious Metals Fund (Maxxum)	2.65	RRSP
Tax Advantaged:	Dividend	■	LL Dividend Fund (LLIM)	2.25	RRSP
		■	LL Dividend Fund (Maxxum)	2.3	RRSP
	Real Estate	■	LL Real Estate Fund (GWLIM)	2.7	RRSP
Multi-Asset:	Balanced	■	LL Income Fund (LLIM)	1.9	RRSP
		■	LL Income Fund (Mackenzie)	2.05	RRSP
		■	LL Equity/Bond Fund (GWLIM)	2.35	RRSP
		■	LL Balanced Fund (Sceptre)	2.45	RRSP
		■	LL Balanced Fund (Beutel Goodman)	2.45	RRSP
		■	LL Growth and Income (Mackenzie)	2.3	RRSP
		■	LL Growth and Income (AGF)	2.5	RRSP
		■	LL Balanced Growth (LLIM)	2.35	RRSP
		■	LL North American Balanced (LLIM)	2.35	RRSP
		■	LL Canadian Balanced (Maxxum)	2.4	RRSP
		■	LL Income Fund (Maxxum)	1.8	RRSP
	Fund of Funds	▲ AG	LL Diversified Fund (LLIM)	2.35	RRSP

FOREIGN	Category	Rating	Fund Name	MER%	RRSP/Foreign
Global Equity:	All-global	★ OK	LL Global Equity Fund (Maxxum)	2.6	Foreign
		■	LL Global Equity Fund (LLIM)	2.5	Foreign
		■	LL International Equity Fund (Fleming)	2.5	Foreign
Regional Equity:	U.S. equity	★ OK	LL American Equity Fund (Maxxum	2.6	Foreign
		▲ OK	LL US Equity Fund (LLIM)	2.55	Foreign
		■	LL American Growth Fund (AGF)	2.7	Foreign
	Europe	■	LL European Equity (Sceptre)	2.65	Foreign
		▲ OK	LL Asian Growth Fund (AGF)	2.6	Foreign

New to *Smart Funds* with this edition, and reflecting our increased coverage of major segregated fund families, is London Life Freedom Funds, which were launched in July 1998. London Life was acquired in 1997 by Great-West Life, the seg fund sister company of Winnipeg-based Investors Group. The 33 Freedom Funds provide access to several top Canadian and foreign money managers, including AGF, Beutel Goodman, Mackenzie, Maxxum, and Sceptre.

The Freedom Funds are segregated funds but the all-in MERs, as shown in the matrix, are no more than many actively managed equity funds with no downside protection. Of course, like most traditional seg funds, the capital guarantee is only 75%, not the 100% that the newer mutual fund/insurance company alliances have developed. In addition to the maturity and death benefit capital guarantees (which are 100%) common to all seg funds, these type of funds provide creditor protection possibilities and the ability for the value of the assets to be transferred without probate fees to a named beneficiary. There are no trustee fees when setting up an RRSP and there are no transfer fees for switching between funds.

London Life views seg funds not merely as niche products but rather as "the investment and retirement solution" for all of its clients. As our initial selection of Smart and Noteworthy funds shows, we view several Freedom funds as worthy of consideration for anyone concerned that Y2K may be more than just a brief glitch in the financial markets.Younger, less conservative investors looking for maximum growth and who are convinced Y2K is a mirage can look for more aggressive fund families portrayed elsewhere in this guide.

Year 2000 Stance

Low-MER seg funds would be attractive in Y2K-turbulent financial markets. Should the century change pass without incident, segregated equity funds could soar in a Y2K relief rally. If, on the other hand, markets did swoon, the capital guarantee could help investors sleep; however, like all seg funds, you'd have to wait 10 years for the guarantee to kick in.

Because London Life offers six different investment management firms, each may respond differently to Y2K scenarios. Check the Y2K stance of each of the appropriate fund families if you are considering their versions of the London Life funds. London Life reports that "each of our managers is taking Y2K scenarios under consideration. However, they are not changing their styles in order to address them."

It suggests that investors should follow long-term strategic asset mixes, as determined by its Investment Voyager process, that match investment profile to investors' goals and risk tolerance. Therefore, London Life counsels, "Changing portfolios in order to meet scenarios that may or may not materialize is not a behaviour we endorse." It likens Y2K to the Quebec referendum.

Smart Funds 2000

Y2K OK

London Life American Equity Fund (Maxxum). A seg fund that owns units of the high-flying Smart Fund Maxxum American Equity fund managed by star manager Warren Lammert of Janus Capital.

London Life Global Equity (Maxxum). A seg fund that owns units of the Maxxum Global Equity fund run by superstar manager Helen Young Hayes of Janus Capital.

Y2K KO

London Life Mortgage Fund (LLIM). A seg mortgage fund that's never lost money over almost a quarter century and with a reasonable MER. And it will be less sensitive to violent swings in interest rates, which could cause longer-term bond funds to lose money. First quartile over the three years ended August 31, 1999. What more do you want under a Y2K KO scenario?

Noteworthy Funds

Y2K OK

London Life U.S. Equity (LLIM). This fund now has a 10-year track record and is second quartile for the three years ended August 31, 1999. It invests in mid-large cap U.S. stocks with a GARP (Growth at a Reasonable Price) style.

London Life Canadian Equity Fund (LLIM). This long-time warhorse has been around since 1961. GARP and generally has no foreign content. Also provides some dividend income. The top three holdings—BCE, CIBC, and Royal Bank—tell you where the fund managers are coming from. Shoot out the lights? No. Sleep at night and steady growth? Quite likely. Manager change in 1998 is the main caveat.

Y2K KO

London Life Precious Metals Fund (Maxxum). Maxxum has always been a strong precious metals/natural resources manager. Gold has been a volatile and losing investment in recent years but could benefit in a Y2K meltdown. If not, at least you have some capital preservation under the seg guarantee, which is something that is available in very few other precious metals funds.

Y2K Agnostic

London Life Diversified Fund (LLIM). This fund of funds is invested 20% to 45% in the LLIM-managed Canadian Equity Fund, 15% to 20% in the U.S. Equity Fund and Fleming-managed International Equity Fund, and 40% to 60% in the LLIM-managed bond, mortgage, and money market funds. With a reasonable though not bargain-priced MER of 2.35% and the usual 75% capital protection guarantees, this should allow investors to both eat well if markets shake off Y2K uncertainty, and to sleep well if they do not.

Availability

Only through London Life representatives. $300 minimum initial investment or $25 PAC.

29. MACKENZIE FINANCIAL CORP.

FRONT OR REAR

Strengths Ivy and Universal families
STAR asset-allocation service
Weaknesses Industrial family
MERs could be lower
RESPs? Yes
Web Site www.mackenziefinancial.com **Toll Free** 1-800-387-0614

CANADIAN	Category	Rating	Fund Name	M.E.R.%	RRSP/Foreign
Money Market:		▲ KO	Industrial Cash Management	0.5	RRSP
		■	Industrial Short Term	1.25	RRSP
Fixed Income:	Long-term	■	Industrial Bond	1.83	RRSP
	Mortgage	■	Industrial Mortgage Securities	1.81	RRSP
		■	Ivy Mortgage	1.84	RRSP
Equity:	Mid-Large Cap	■	Industrial Growth	2.35	RRSP
		■	Industrial Horizon	2.33	RRSP
		■	Ivy Canadian	2.32	RRSP
		■	Cundill Canadian Security	2.38	RRSP
		★ OK	Universal Canadian Growth	2.34	RRSP
	Small Cap	■	Industrial Equity	2.43	RRSP
		▲ OK	Ivy Enterprise	2.33	RRSP
	Gold/precious metal	▲ KO	Universal Precious Metals	2.4	RRSP
	Resource	▲ OK	Universal Canadian Resource	2.35	RRSP
	Technology & Resources	▲ OK	Universal Future	2.33	RRSP
Tax Advantaged:	Dividend	▲ OK	Industrial Dividend Growth	2.33	RRSP
Multi-Asset:	Balanced	■	Industrial Balanced	2.32	RRSP
		■	Industrial Income	1.82	RRSP
		★ AG	Industrial Pension	2.33	RRSP
		■	Ivy Growth & Income	2.07	RRSP
		▲ AG	Universal Canadian Balanced Fund	2.32	RRSP
		■	Cundill Canadian Balanced	New	RRSP
	Asset Allocation	■	STAR service		RRSP & Foreign
		■	Keystone service		RRSP & Foreign

FOREIGN	Category	Rating	Fund Name	MER%	RRSP/Foreign
Money Market:		■	Universal U.S. Money Market	1.25	Foreign
Fixed Income:		★ KO	Universal World Income RRSP	2.1	RRSP
		■	Universal World Tactical Bond Fund	2.19	Foreign
		■	Universal World High Yield Fund	2.2	Foreign
Global Equity:	All-global	▲ OK	Ivy Foreign Equity	2.33	Foreign
		■	Cundill Value Fund	2.37	Foreign
		▲ OK	Universal World Growth RRSP	2.38	RRSP
		■	Universal World Value Fund	2.55	Foreign
		■	Universal RSP Select Managers Fund	New	RRSP
		■	Ivy RSP Foreign Equity Fund	New	RRSP
		▲ OK	Universal Select Managers Fund	New	Foreign
		■	Cundill Recovery Fund	New	Foreign
	Specialty	▲ OK	Universal World Science & Technology Fund	2.39	Foreign
		■	Universal World Real Estate	2.5	Foreign
Regional Equity:					
	U.S. Large-cap	■	Industrial American	2.34	Foreign
	U.S. Small-cap	■	Universal U.S. Emerging Growth	2.35	Foreign
	NAFTA/N.Am.	■	Universal Americas	2.47	Foreign
	EAFE	■	Universal International Stock Fund	2.37	Foreign
	Emerging Market	■	Universal World Emerging Growth	2.5	Foreign
	Far East	■	Universal Far East	2.57	Foreign
	Japan	■	Universal Japan	2.5	Foreign
	Europe	★ OK	Universal European Opportunities	2.43	Foreign
Global Balanced:		■	Universal World Asset Allocation	2.41	Foreign
		★ AG	Universal World Balanced RRSP	2.36	RRSP

Nothing stays the same for long at giant Mackenzie Financial, one of the largest load fund groups in Canada. Not being ones to sit on the sidelines while competitors jump on the latest investing trend, Mackenzie launched several new funds in the past year. It has focused on straight 20% eligible international funds as well as the 100% RRSP-eligible variety to which many investors have turned their attentions after Canadian equity markets lagged other regions of the world in 1998.

Among the new offerings are Universal Select Managers Fund, invested by five managers from three firms: Brian Ashford-Russell and Stephen Peak of Henderson Investors in the U.K., Peter Cundill of Vancouver-based Cundill Investment Research, and Paul Baran and Jim Broadfoot at Mackenzie U.S. Each selected approximately 10 stocks for the fund, giving it a concentrated portfolio of 50 names.

For those who want more than 20% of the tax-sheltered investments in foreign stocks, Universal RSP Select Managers Fund is fully RRSP-eligible and mimics the returns of the regular version of this fund. It uses forward contracts to gain indirect exposure to the returns of the fund, yet qualifies as domestic content for tax-sheltered RRSPs or RRIFs.

Also new is Ivy RSP Foreign Equity, which uses the same technique. Unfortunately for Mackenzie, highly regarded Bill Kanko, manager of the underlying Ivy Foreign Equity, left the firm in April 1999, to join rival Trimark Financial Corp., his former employer. Good news for Trimark, bad news for Mackenzie.

In July 1998, Mackenzie announced that it was buying the Cundill Funds, thereby creating a fourth brand to its line-up. Since then it has launched Cundill Recovery Fund and Cundill Canadian Balanced and renamed Cundill Security Fund the Cundill Canadian Security Fund. It also launched a series "C" share for that fund, which allows investors to buy on a deferred-load basis.

Several changes occurred in the growth-oriented Universal family last year. Richard Gluck was hired as lead manager of Universal World Income RRSP. He moved to Mackenzie's Boca Raton office from his previous position with U.S. firm Oppenheimer. And Paul Baran joined Mackenzie to manage Universal Americas Fund and co-manage Universal World Value and Universal Select Managers.

In the Ivy brand, with the departure of Bill Kanko, Jerry Javasky took on the management of Ivy Foreign Equity, which he had managed from October 1992 to June 1997. There's no doubt that Javasky has proven himself a talented money manager. His Ivy Canadian Fund was a Smart Fund in 1997 and 1996 when Gerry Coleman managed it. But he now has a lot on his plate managing foreign equities while he continues to be the $5-billion man, managing that much money in Ivy Canadian. For that reason, we've demoted Ivy Foreign Equity from "Smart" status until it becomes clear who will manage it. The company has inferred that Javasky is managing it temporarily until they find a more permanent solution. For unitholders already invested in the fund, there's no reason to move. But new investors considering the fund may want to wait to see how the reassignments shake out.

In all, then, 46 funds are spread over Mackenzie's four families, all with distinct styles. Investors who find it difficult to choose a few entrees from this buffet can delegate the task to Gordon Garmaise's STAR fund portfolio optimization service, which now holds several billion dollars' worth of Mackenzie funds. The alternative Keystone portfolios offer similar asset allocation services, using the funds of several Mackenzie competitors.

Past *Smart Funds* readers will be aware that the Universal family has long had the lion's share of Smart Funds and the Industrial family almost none. That is the case again this year.

Year 2000 Stance

In Mackenzie's "Millennium-Bugged" information sheet, available to investors, it says the consensus is that large companies will be Y2K compliant by New Year's Eve. But uncertainty remains over the readiness of suppliers and customers and this is of significant concern. The problem is most critical in industries and economies that are highly automated, Mackenzie says. Industries where systems are "mission-critical" include banking, airlines, telecommunications, securities brokers, and retail. Within these industries, addressing the problem has been a top priority and Mackenzie expects most companies to be ready well ahead of the deadline. Still, Y2K and contingency planning will increase cost to these industries. Mackenzie notes, "There is little doubt the millennium bug will have some impact on the global economy in the form of production disruptions. And in many instances, corporate earnings will take a hit in the short term as a result of revenue shortfalls and compliance cost overruns." Mackenzie expects long-term implications to be minimal, but says the date change may increase volatility in markets.

Mackenzie money managers are evaluating existing and potential companies on a case-by-case basis, considering everything they usually evaluate, as well as Y2K compliance.

Smart Funds 2000

Y2K OK

Universal Canadian Growth. Recent slump shouldn't worry fans of Dina DeGeer and Dennis Starritt.

Universal European Opportunities. Back again, this fund is first quartile for one, two, three, and four years ended August 31, 1999.

Y2K KO

Universal World Income RRSP. Global bonds could be a harbour if the Y2K storm rages longer than expected and interest rates start falling. This version does not consume foreign-content room.

Y2K Agnostic

Industrial Pension Fund. Bill Procter has fallen behind the competition over the last 18 months, but fund has a great long-term track record so we are keeping it a Smart Fund for this edition. This one is heavier on equities, so more volatile.

Universal World Balanced RRSP Fund. Steady performing Smart Fund that counts as Canadian content. Fund has outperformed the average Canadian balanced fund over the past five years.

Noteworthy Funds

Y2K OK

Universal World Science & Technology. This is the only true global sci-tech fund and has lagged its U.S. competitors. The international exposure should provide increased diversification and therefore lower volatility. Look at RSP edition, too!

Ivy Foreign Equity. Demoted from Smart status following the departure of manager Bill Kanko to Trimark. For now the fund is managed by the very capable but busy Jerry Javasky, who is also manager of Ivy Canadian. We will wait to see who gets assigned to the fund on a permanent basis. Look at the RSP edition, too.

Universal World Growth RRSP Fund. Participate in world markets without tying up foreign content. May be better off buying the RSP version of Ivy Foreign Equity.

Universal Select Managers. About 50 stocks from the best managers Mackenzie can access. Fund was launched on September 17, 1998, and gathered $500 million by July 1999. The RSP version of this now has over $300 million.

Ivy Enterprise Fund. Fund has had mixed results since Chuck Roth took over in late 1997.

Universal Canadian Resource. 1998 was another tough year for resources but things are looking up for the sector, and this fund, in 1999. It performed above the average in 1997 and 1998.

Universal Future Fund. A 100% RRSP-eligible technology fund, with the added diversification of an equal weighting of natural resource stocks. It is managed by John Rohr and has had solid long-term performance.

Industrial Dividend Growth. This tax-friendly fund managed by Bill Procter was second quartile over the year ended August 31, 1999. Over three, and five years to August 31, it's still had above-average returns.

Y2K KO

Industrial Cash Management. One of the better money market funds, with a tolerable MER.

Universal Precious Metals. In the worst-case Y2K scenario of economic turbulence, the price of gold bullion could rise significantly from its 20-year lows, and with it funds like this. Even the recommended maximum 5% in this asset class could help buffer losses elsewhere, should Y2K prove more than the expected hiccup.

Y2K Agnostic

Universal Canadian Balanced. This fund, managed by the dynamic duo of Dina DeGeer and Dennis Starritt of Bluewater Investment, was top quartile in 1997 and 1998.

Availability

Available through full-service and discount brokers, dealers, and a growing list of life insurance agents. The funds can't be sold in the United States.

30. MANULIFE GUARANTEED INVESTMENT FUNDS

NO LOAD

Strengths	Hedge against market losses
	Choice of major families
Weaknesses	MERs stiff
	No need for GIFs on bond, balanced funds
RESPs?	No
Web Site	www.manulife.com **Toll Free** 1-888-626-8543

CANADIAN	Category	Rating	Fund Name	M.E.R.%	RRSP/Foreign
Money Market:		■	Manulife Elliott & Page Money Market GIF Encore	1.35	RRSP
		▲ KO	Manulife Elliott & Page Money Market GIF Encore	1.25	RRSP
Fixed-Income:	Long-term	■	Manulife AGF Canadian Bond GIF Encore	2.35	RRSP
		■	Manulife AGF High Income GIF Encore	2.35	RRSP
		■	Manulife Fidelity Canadian Bond GIF Encore	2.15	RRSP
	Short-term	■	Manulife Talvest Income GIF Encore	2.25	RRSP
Equity:	Mid-Large Cap	■	Manulife AGF Canadian Stock GIF Encore	3.20	RRSP
		■	Manulife AIM Canada Growth Class GIF Encore	3.00	RRSP
		■	Manulife C.I. Harbour GIF Encore	3.00	RRSP
		■	Manulife Elliott & Page Equity GIF Encore	2.75	RRSP
		■	Manulife Elliott & Page Value Equity GIF Encore	2.80	RRSP
		■	Manulife Fidelity Capital Builder GIF Encore	3.00	RRSP
		▲ AG	Manulife Fidelity True North GIF Encore	3.00	RRSP

		■	Manulife O'Donnell Canadian GIF Encore	3.00	RRSP
		■	Manulife O'Donnell Select GIF Encore	3.00	RRSP
		■	Manulife Sceptre Canadian Equity GIF Encore	2.80	RRSP
		■	Manulife Trimark Select Canadian Growth GIF Encore	2.98	RRSP
	Index	▲ AG	Manulife Canadian Equity Index GIF Encore	1.75	RRSP
Tax Advantaged:	Dividend	■	Manulife AGF Dividend GIF Encore	2.80	RRSP
		■	Manulife Dynamic Dividend Growth GIF Encore	2.94	RRSP
Multi-Asset:	Balanced	■	Manulife AGF Growth & Income GIF Encore	2.95	RRSP
		■	Manulife Atlas Canadian Balanced GIF Encore	3.05	RRSP
		■	Manulife C.I. Harbour Growth & Income GIF Encore	2.95	RRSP
		■	Manulife Dynamic Partners GIF Encore	3.37	RRSP
		■	Manulife Elliott & Page Balanced GIF Encore	2.75	RRSP
		■	Manulife Fidelity Canadian Asset Allocation GIF Encore	2.95	RRSP
		■	Manulife Sceptre Balanced Growth GIF Encore	3.05	RRSP
		■	Manulife Talvest Canadian Asset Allocation GIF Encore	2.95	RRSP
		■	Manulife Trimark Select Balanced GIF Encore	2.97	RRSP
		■	Manulife Conservative Asset Allocation GIF Encore	2.50	RRSP
		■	Manulife Moderate Asset Allocation GIF Encore	2.60	RRSP
		■	Manulife Balanced Asset Allocation GIF Encore	2.70	RRSP
		■	Manulife Growth Asset Allocation GIF Encore	2.85	RRSP
		■	Manulife Aggressive Asset Allocation GIF Encore	3.10	RRSP

FOREIGN	Category	Rating	Fund Name	MER%	RRSP/Foreign
Fixed-Income:		■	Manulife AGF Global Government Bond GIF Encore	2.35	Foreign
		■	Manulife Dynamic Global Bond GIF Encore	2.45	RRSP
Global Equity:	All-global	■	Manulife Fidelity International Portfolio GIF Encore	3.38	Foreign
		■	Manulife Merrill Lynch Global Growth GIF Encore	2.60	Foreign
		■	Manulife Trimark Select Growth GIF Encore	3.33	Foreign
Regional Equity:					
	U.S. Large-cap	▲ AG	Manulife AGF American Growth Class GIF Encore	3.25	Foreign
		■	Manulife AIM Global America Growth Class GIF Encore	3.15	Foreign
		▲ AG	Manulife Elliott & Page American Growth GIF Encore	3.05	Foreign
		▲ AG	Manulife Fidelity Growth America GIF Encore	3.15	Foreign
		■	Manulife Merrill Lynch U.S. Basic Value GIF Encore	2.90	Foreign
		■	Manulife Talvest Value Line U.S. Equity GIF*	3.15	Foreign
	Index - U.S.	■	Manulife U.S. Equity Index GIF Encore	1.80	Foreign

With more than $3.8 billion in the Guaranteed Investment Funds and another $285 million in the newly launched GIF Encore funds, there is little doubt that Canadians like the concept of guarantees against losing money. And they don't mind paying extra for it. That fact has not been lost on the fund industry, with most of the largest fund companies launching their own segregated or "seg" versions of their mutual funds, moving in on turf that was previously that of insurance companies only.

Manulife's GIF concept offers investors brand-name funds from companies such as AGF, Fidelity, and Trimark, but with an added insurance "guarantee" wrapped around them. Technically they are segregated funds, not mutual funds, but investors receive the return of the underlying funds, less fees.

With Manulife's launch of a new line of GIFs, GIF Encore early in 1999, the company closed to new investors the original GIF group of funds launched with much fanfare in January 1997. Existing unitholders in the original GIF funds can continue to invest in them.

The differences between the two are minor. The original GIFs guaranteed 100% of invested capital at death or maturity (after 10 years), plus any increase in value of the portfolio. GIF Encore goes a step further with its death benefit, which guarantees that the principal will earn a return of 4% a year. For example, if an investor dies after one year in a GIF Encore fund, the designated beneficiary would receive at least 104% of what was invested—more if the investment had appreciated beyond that. If they had been invested for 10 years, they would receive 140%. As with most segregated funds, when a beneficiary is named in the contract, the money passes to the client's heirs, thereby avoiding the normal estate and probate fees. Sounds good, but that guarantee is a death benefit only. The maturity benefit is a 100% return of capital, as with the original GIFs. The other difference between the two is that the GIF Encore does not have the reset feature where investors can lock in gains and the 10-year clock starts ticking all over again. The original GIF had that reset but the company said not many people used it.

For this year's overview of Manulife, we have updated the matrix to include just the GIF Encore funds, as they are the only ones available to new investors. If you take a look at the revised fund matrix, you'll notice two things. First, we've designated several Noteworthy funds but no Smart Funds; second, these funds charge high MERs.

What's going on here? The public is certainly voting with their feet, and telling the industry that they're willing to pay more to protect their initial capital against loss if markets fall.

We can understand the allure of these funds. And while at first glance the concept makes sense, we suggest that investors consider whether it's realistic that stock markets would go down and stay down for a decade, which is how long it would have to be for the GIF Encore fund guarantees to be worthwhile. History tells us that is unlikely, although certainly possible.

The bottom line is we don't think it makes sense to pay higher MERs for this so-called "protection" on money market funds, bond funds, or even balanced funds. However, the extra premium may be worth it in the case of U.S. stock or global stock funds or certain aggressive equity funds. That is why we have designated some of the

GIF Encore funds as Noteworthy. These correspond to the underlying fund that may be Smart or Noteworthy in their respective fund family, elsewhere in this book. And certainly if there was ever a time when the extra insurance cost of seg funds was justified, it would be in this unique period of the century change and the Y2K problem examined throughout this book.

For business owners, seg funds might also be appealing because it is a little easier to protect your assets from creditors (but not if you're already faced with financial problems).

With the introduction of Encore, Manulife expanded the line-up to include some funds that weren't available as GIFs: Sceptre Canadian Growth Equity, Sceptre Balanced Growth, and Merrill Lynch U.S. Basic Value.

Also new are five asset allocation GIF Encore portfolios, ranging from conservative to growth. Each is managed by a combination of several money managers that buy securities directly for the portfolios. These do not invest in units of existing funds. The managers are Elliott & Page, Sceptre Investment Counsel, AGF Management, Templeton Management Ltd., McLean Budden, and TAL Investment Counsel.

In addition, Manulife has its own in-house Cabot Funds, a group of seven no-load funds launched in February 1994. This family is predominantly Canadian equity, with one pure global fund, Global Equity.

Year 2000 Stance

None provided by Manulife, despite our request. Generally, as noted above, seg funds provide more protection to downside moves of pure equity funds than is available to regular mutual fund investors. Also check the section of the fund family treatments elsewhere in this book that correspond to the underlying managers.

Generally, if you're convinced that a Y2K OK scenario is most likely, you would seek the underlying funds, not the GIF Encore version with higher MERs. Most of our Noteworthy selections are oriented to Y2K Agnostics: pure equity funds with a seg guarantee of principal. As elsewhere in the book, Y2K KO believers would examine money market or bond funds.

Smart Funds 2000

None

Noteworthy Funds

Y2K KO

Manulife Elliott & Page Money Market GIF Encore. The underlying E&P money market funds is one of the country's better ones in this class. The GIF mark-up negates what is otherwise a low MER. However, for Y2K KO believers, this version is probably a more cost-effective place to park funds than other Y2K KO possibilities: the various fixed-income and balanced funds shown in the matrix.

Y2K Agnostic

Manulife Fidelity True North GIF. So far manager Alan Radlo continues to justify the 3% MER on this fund as a GIF. It returned 25.3% over one year ended August 31, 1999, versus 28.1% for its benchmark the TSE 300 index.

Manulife Canadian Index GIF. If managers can't beat the TSE 300 index, why pay for them? This should do as well as any actively managed large-cap Canadian equity fund, and while the MER of 1.75% looks expensive compared with the Royal and Altamira index funds, you get the peace of mind of downside protection. Managed by Elliott & Page.

Manulife AGF American Growth Class GIF. Underlying AGF fund is a Smart Fund again this year but at 3.25% this is a hefty annual fee. Consider the Manulife U.S. Equity Index GIF at 1.8%.

Manulife Elliott & Page American Growth GIF. This fund outperforms most of the competition. It returned 28.7% for the year ended August 31, 1999, which puts it below the S&P 500 index, as was the case with most actively managed funds recently. It is managed by Goldman Sachs Asset Management in New York City.

Manulife Fidelity Growth America GIF. The underlying fund run by Fidelity's Steve Snider continues as a Smart Fund despite the departure of manager Brad Lewis. Snider was co-manager with Lewis for one year before it changed hands.

Availability

Life insurance agents and "dual-licensed" brokers and dealers.

31. MAWER INVESTMENT MANAGEMENT **NO LOAD**

Strengths	Low MERs (but inching up) Mawer New Canada Fund
Weaknesses	Limited distribution Low profile
RESPs?	No
Web Site	www.mawer.com

Toll Free 1-800-889-6248

CANADIAN	Category	Rating	Fund Name	M.E.R.%	RRSP/Foreign
Money Market:		▲ KO	Mawer Canadian Money Market Fund	0.7	RRSP
Fixed Income:	Long-term	■	Mawer Canadian Bond Fund	1.03	RRSP
	Short-term	■	Mawer Canadian Income Fund	1.03	Not RRSP-eligible
	Corporate	■	Mawer High Yield Bond Fund	1.61	RRSP
Equity:	Mid-Large Cap	■	Mawer Canadian Equity Fund	1.35	RRSP
	Small Cap	▲ OK	Mawer New Canada Fund	1.48	RRSP
Multi-Asset:	Balanced	▲ AG	Mawer Canadian Balanced Retirement Savings Fund	1.02	RRSP

FOREIGN	Category	Rating	Fund Name	MER%	RRSP/Foreign
Global Equity:	EAFE	■	Mawer World Investment Fund	1.44	Foreign
Regional Equity:	U.S.	▲ OK	Mawer U.S. Equity Fund	1.3	Foreign
Multi-Asset:	Balanced	■	Mawer Canadian Diversified Investment Fund	1.12	Foreign

This Calgary-based, no-load firm, like its fellow Alberta-based competitor Bissett, does minimal marketing and passes along the savings with low management expense ratios. The MERs of both its Canadian and global equity funds are at the low end of their category averages, although several have edged slightly higher since the last edition of this book. There are no switching charges.

The firm's 10 mutual funds are registered in all provinces and territories. No new funds have been added since the last edition.

Mawer celebrates its 25-year anniversary this year. It was founded in 1974 as a high-net-worth investment counsellor, and in 1987 expanded into mutual funds. It does not subcontract sub-advisors, even in its international funds (which also helps keep fees down). All funds are managed by its in-house team.

There has been a change in the manager of the New Canada Fund, a Canadian small-cap equity fund. As of December 1998, it is managed by Martin Ferguson, a partner and portfolio manager of Canadian equities at Mawer. Also, the company's management team has expanded to include Michael Barkley. It now employs nine in-house investment managers, with an average 15 years each in the business.

Mawer describes itself as having a "value" approach to equity investing. The Canadian funds, also like Bissett, tend to have strong western Canada representation, particularly in oil and gas and other natural resources. That may make it attractive to investors concerned about possible Quebec separation. Several of the funds have reached their 10-year anniversaries, including the Canadian Balanced, Canadian Diversified Investment, and New Canada. Performance has been above average for those funds. Asset allocation for several funds is handled by partner Don Ferris, a 21-year veteran who manages the Canadian Balanced Retirement Savings Fund and Canadian Diversified Investment Fund.

Mawer Investment Management provides discretionary investment management for individuals with a minimum $500,000 to invest. Segregated portfolios are available for private clients with at least $2 million.

Year 2000 Stance

None provided: never a good sign.

Smart Funds 2000

None

Noteworthy Funds

Y2K OK

Mawer New Canada Fund. 1998 and early 1999 were a dismal time for Canadian small-caps. For the year ended August 31, the Nesbitt Burns Small-Cap index returned 27.8%. This small-cap portfolio did worse. It beat the index by a considerable margin in 1996 and 1997 out of the last five. The fund is now managed by Martin Ferguson, formerly a co-manager.

Mawer U.S. Equity Fund. Like many U.S. equity funds, this portfolio couldn't keep pace with the S&P 500 in 1998 and into 1999. The rise of the S&P was concentrated among a small number of large stocks. Because mutual funds must be more diversified, they couldn't keep up. But with a stingy 1.30% MER, and good performance over the longer term, this is worth consideration. Manager Darrell Anderson invests in 40 to 50 U.S. stocks of mixed market capitalization.

Y2K KO

Mawer Canadian Money Market Fund. Reasonable MER for parking funds during a Y2K storm.

Y2K Agnostic

Mawer Canadian Balanced Retirement Savings Fund. In early 1998, this balanced fund passes the 10-year mark and has proven in most years it can better a benchmark of the combined TSE 300 and ScotiaMcLeod Bond Universe Index. No doubt the low 1.02% MER helps.

Availability

Through selected discount brokers and investment dealers in all provinces and territories, with minimum $5,000 investment per fund. Residents of Alberta and Saskatchewan can purchase directly from Mawer, with minimum initial investment of $25,000.

32. MD MANAGEMENT LTD.

NO LOAD

Strengths Performance with low fees
Strong subadvisors
Weaknesses Not available to general public
RESPs? Soon
Web Site www.cma.ca **Toll Free** 1-800-267-2332

CANADIAN	Category	Rating	Fund Name	M.E.R.%	RRSP/Foreign
Money Market:		■	MD Money Fund	0.53	RRSP
Fixed Income:	Long-term	▲ AG	MD Bond Fund	1.03	RRSP
	Short-term	■	MD Income Fund*		RRSP
	Short-term	▲ KO	MD Bond and Mortgage Fund	1.1	RRSP
Equity:	Mid-Large Cap	▲	MD Equity Fund	1.27	RRSP
	Mid-Large Cap	▲	MD Select Fund	1.29	RRSP
Tax Advantaged:	Dividend	■	MD Dividend Fund	1.29	RRSP
Multi-Asset:	Balanced	▲ AG	MD Balanced Fund	1.28	RRSP

FOREIGN	Category	Rating	Fund Name	MER%	RRSP/Foreign
Fixed Income:		■	MD Global Bond Fund	1.19	Foreign
Global Equity:	All-global	★ OK	MD Growth Fund	1.28	Foreign
Regional Equity:	U.S.	★ OK	M.D. U.S. Equity	1.28	Foreign

* Not a fund but a deferred group annuity contract

If you've ever wondered where your family doctor invests, it may well be in this exclusive family of low-MER no-load funds. It features the best of both worlds: some of the industry's most respected money managers—including Templeton, TAL, and McLean Budden—at among the lowest MERs in the Canadian industry. The catch is that

MD Management Limited is a subsidiary of the Canadian Medical Association and the funds are sold only to CMA members and their families. Approximately 80,000 physicians and their families are customers and over $8 billion worth of their money is managed by it.

The fund family matrix is virtually unchanged since last year's edition, but MD Emerging Markets has been omitted: effective December 31, 1998, the fund was merged into Templeton Emerging Markets. One of the managers on MD Equity Fund, O'Donnell, has been replaced by Acuity as the mid-cap manager. That accounts for just 16% of the fund: the rest is managed by McLean Budden, J.R. Senecal & Associates, and Templeton Management Ltd.

MD Management's already low MERs continue to inch down a few basis points. Those investors in high-MER funds should take a look at MD Management's prospectus, entitled *Investment Guide for MD Management Mutual Funds.* It contains some eye-opening data on the true costs of mutual funds.

Since the last edition, it has introduced a Registered Education Savings Plan.

In July 1999 it also introduced on-line trading, building on the introduction in September 1998 of on-line account access. MD Management also sells a broader package of services, including GICs, financial planning, medical practice management services, and MF Family Trust, a tax-effective way to save for family members. And it has been doing so for more than a quarter century. In fact, in the early 1950s the CMA was an early advocate of government-endorsed retirement savings plans, which were introduced in 1957 as RRSPs.

In 1969, the CMA established Lancet Management Ltd., a wholly owned financial subsidiary offering three funds. Lancet was renamed MD Management Ltd. in 1971. Some funds were renamed and more added, with the count currently at 10, plus a pooled annuity contract. In 1998, MD was named as one of Canada's 50 Best Managed Private Companies for the fourth consecutive year.

Today, several of the funds are top performers. This should not be surprising since they are managed externally by some of the best load fund enterprises in the business, namely Guardian Capital, Mackenzie, TAL Investment Counsel, and Templeton. Even better, for those who qualify for this exclusive club, management fees are much lower than the equivalent load funds.

On the administration front, MD is making it easier for physicians to get access to their financial consultants. MD Classic Plus allows creation of a portfolio of MD funds and more than 200 non-MD mutual funds, as well as guaranteed term deposits. MD

Portfolio Access lets clients view their accounts over the Internet.

The MD Consolidated Portfolio is a self-directed investment service that lets investors consolidate their investments, including MD funds and 850 third-party mutual funds, stocks, and fixed-income products.

As the matrix shows, MD does not have everything. It lacks seg funds, 100% RRSP-eligible foreign funds, and index funds. On the other hand, the MERs on its actively managed funds are almost as low as most index funds.

Year 2000 Stance

MD Management says all its fund managers "have been directed to include potential Y2K impact as part of their stock selection process and to avoid stocks they believe could be significantly impacted by any Y2K events."

MD managers take a long-term view of investing and many of them believe "Y2K will be a blip in the investment life cycle of a long-term investor and that efforts to time the market usually tend to be less than successful."

Smart Funds 2000

Y2K OK

MD Growth Fund. First quartile over the three, five, and 10 years ended August 31, 1999. Five-time Smart Fund.

MD U.S. Equity. For those not in the medical profession who want the talents of Alliance Capital Management, buy the Ethical North American Fund. This one managed by Al Harrison is the number two fund in the category for the five years ended August 31, 1999.

Noteworthy Funds

Y2K KO

MD Bond & Mortgage. Multiple fixed-income managers on this fund, all at a 1.1% MER. Invests in domestic and international bonds, and residential first mortgages with terms of one to five years.

Y2K Agnostic

MD Balanced. Managed by Connor Clark & Lunn and WorldInvest, this balanced fund has a 1.28% MER and both Canadian and global stocks, as well as domestic bonds.

MD Bond. Managed by TAL Investment Counsel at a reasonable 1.03% MER, the fund invests in Canadian government bonds, corporate bonds, and some foreign bonds.

Availability

Available only to members of the Canadian Medical Association and their immediate families and sold through a network of more than 150 financial planners in 40 offices across Canada.

33. NAVIGATOR FUND COMPANY LTD. LOAD

Strengths	A capital-preserving Asian fund A Canadian technology fund
Weaknesses	No broad global funds High MERs
RESPs?	No
Web Site:	www.navigator.ca **Toll Free** 1-888-240-2220

CANADIAN	Category	Rating	Fund Name	M.E.R.%	RRSP/Foreign
Money Market:		▲ KO	Navigator Money Market	1.00	RRSP
Fixed income:	Corporate	▲ AG	Navigator Cdn. Income	2.45	RRSP
Equity:	Small Cap, value	■	Navigator Cdn. Focused Growth*	2.99	RRSP
	Mid/ large cap, growth	■	Navigator Cdn. Growth	2.75	RRSP
	Technology	▲ OK	Navigator Cdn. Technology	2.85	RRSP
Multi-Asset:	Balanced	■	Navigator Cdn. Growth & income	2.75	RRSP

FOREIGN	Category	Rating	Fund Name	MER%	RRSP/Foreign
Regional Equity:					
	Asia ex Japan, Australia	■	Navigator Asia-Pacific	3.01	Foreign
	U.S. large-cap value	▲ AG	Navigator American Value Investment	2.99	Foreign
	U.S. small/mid-cap growth	■	Navigator American Growth	2.99	Foreign

* Formerly Value Investment Retirement Fund

This small Vancouver-based fund family has a new majority owner in the privately held Nova Bancorp Group also the owner of the old Centre-Post funds. The only new addition to the stable of funds is a money market fund.

This family should be regarded as a specialty boutique, with all its money management farmed out to external subadvisors located in Canada, the United States, and Hong Kong. The main attractions are, in theory, Wayne Deans on Canadian equities, Doug Knight on Canadian fixed income, and American equities. Deans' fund has received a name change from Navigator Value Investment Retirement to Navigator Focused Canadian Growth. Performance continues to be disappointing for investors hoping for the returns that Deans used to generate for the Marathon Equity Fund.

What excitement there is revolves around the Navigator Canadian Technology Fund, one of the few such 100% RRSP-eligible funds available in the Canadian market. Manager Duncan Stewart is frequently quoted by Canadian technology writers.

The two American equity funds—both managed by Roxbury Capital Management of Santa Monica, California—now have three-year track records under their belt: Anthony Browne's American Value Investment Fund has so far outperformed Al Lockwood's American Growth Fund. The MERs of just under 3% are on the high side for the category.

Navigator Asia-Pacific, demoted last year from Smart Funds status in the 1998 edition of this book, continues to disappoint.

Year 2000 Stance

Like most fund companies, Navigator's focus on equity funds makes it more appropriate if the Y2K OK scenario comes to pass. The new money market fund could offer a safe harbour under a Y2K KO outcome, although a 1% MER for a money market fund is not cheap protection.

As for the equity funds, Navigator says it will not invest in questionable Y2K-compliant companies, particularly for its Asia-Pacific fund. It says that in a worst-case Y2K scenario, non-G7 investments would be primarily affected, which would have minimal impact on its mostly North American funds.

Its advice to investors on asset allocation is that "given the small proportion of investments likely to be questionable from a Y2K perspective, radical changes in asset allocation or fund holdings are not advisable" and could in fact detract value from portfolio.

Smart Funds 2000

None

Noteworthy Funds

Y2K OK

Navigator Canadian Technology. 100% RRSP-eligible technology fund. Tera Capital Corp of Toronto specializes in technology and biotechnology investing. Fund returned 98.6% for the year ended August 31, 1999, as JDS and Nortel rocketed the tiny fund.

Y2K KO

Navigator Money Market. New fund to placate market timers. 1% MER is no bargain.

Y2K Agnostic

Navigator Canadian Income. Doug Knight's high-yield bond fund that invests mostly in corporate bonds. 8.8% CAGR for five years to August 31, 1999, is reasonable, although the 2.45% MER is on the high side for the category.

Navigator American Value Investment. Blue-chip American equity fund managed by Anthony Browne returned 26.1% for year ended August 31, 1999, and has three-year CAGR of 22.8%. With top 10 names like Cisco, Microsoft, Oracle, MCI, Texas Instruments, Intel, Sun Microsystems, we're not sure how the fund was given the "value" moniker.

Availability

Through full-service and discount brokers and planners. Minimum $2,000 initial investment required.

34. NOVA MUTUAL FUNDS (FORMERLY CENTREPOST) NO LOAD

Strengths Low MERs
Conservative core fund approach
Weaknesses Visibility
Few aggressive foreign funds
RESPs? No
Web Site www.centrepost.com **Toll Free** 1-800-268-9597

CANADIAN	Category	Rating	Fund Name	M.E.R.%	RRSP/Foreign
Money Market:	Short Term	■	Nova Short Term	0.75	RRSP

Fixed Income:	Medium Term	■	Nova Bond	1.00	RRSP
Equity:	Mid to Large Cap	▲ OK	Nova Canadian	1.00	RRSP
Multi-Asset:	Balanced	▲ AG	Nova Balanced	1.00	RRSP

FOREIGN	Category	Rating	Fund Name	M.E.R.%	RRSP/Foreign
Global Equity:	Mid to Large Cap	■	Nova Foreign	1.75	Foreign

The firm behind Nova goes back to 1974. Formerly the OHA Group of Funds, it was a division of the Ontario Hospital Association. It managed the Hospitals of Ontario Pension Plan, and over the years, added more than 100 health care foundations and institutions as clients.

In early 1997, OHA Investment Management Ltd. became independent and soon changed its fund family name to CentrePost, which is intended to evoke the image of a solid, core, balanced approach to investments. And that's about what you'll get with this family, along with some aggressively low MERs. Like several other "Smart" no-load outfits in this book, you may not hear the Nova name advertised much, which allows it to keep its marketing costs down.

The MERs on its Canadian Equity Fund and Balanced Fund remain a stingy 1%, about 50% below the category averages.

Unlike MD Management Funds, however, Nova funds are not restricted to the health care community. Any Ontario investor can buy them directly, or if you live in any province except Quebec they can be purchased through brokers and dealers.

It's interesting that Nova management invokes the fund family approach to mutual funds in its own industry positioning statement. Naturally, it suggests that its own funds serve for the 50% of a portfolio that should be conservative, steady and secure—with low MERs. Then it suggests that investors can look outside the Nova family for specialty funds and higher-risk vehicles.

Since many large-cap equity funds perform like the indices, why pay 2% plus? These funds are priced like passively managed index funds and should do about the same in bull markets. In down markets, investors will take comfort that a human manager is around to make defensive adjustments.

Year 2000 Stance

The company says large North American corporations are best positioned to deal with potential Y2K problems. This is due both to the timely recognition of this problem and the available resources—both technical and financial. While there cannot be guaranteed certainty of a smooth year-end transition, from an investment perspective a well-diversified portfolio concentrating on blue-chip investments in North American markets is probably as well insulated from potential Y2K problems as can be expected.

Nova says its mutual funds have traditionally been invested conservatively, in large-cap, blue-chip equity investments. It does not believe in the overweighting in sectors or specific corporations from a Y2K perspective. A broadly diversified portfolio is likely better insulated from whatever disruptions may result from this event than is a specifically targeted portfolio. Corporations have gone to great lengths to deal with potential computer problems and can be expected to be prepared for the event. Consequently, computer related disruptions will therefore likely be random in nature and would, by definition, have been unforeseen.

It advises clients who are concerned with the impact of Y2K on their investments to consider fixed-income portfolios, such as the Nova Bond Fund (formerly CentrePost Bond Fund), which are highly concentrated in government securities. As it believes that emerging markets will be the hardest hit due to lower readiness levels when compared to North America, it advises caution with respect to foreign investment exposure. From an overall investment perspective, it believes that heading into year-end there may well be a slowdown in investment activity as uncertainty regarding the actual magnitude of the Y2K problem grows. Securities issuance and corporate spending will likely taper off in the fourth quarter and the risk premium on corporate investments will likely increase.

Smart Funds 2000

None

Noteworthy Funds

Y2K OK

Nova Canadian. If you want large-cap Canada with a low 1% MER, this fund is an alternative to the average 2.1% MER Canadian funds. The fund is a fourth-quartile performer for the three and five years ended August 31, 1999, although its longer-term results have been satisfactory.

Y2K Agnostic

Nova Balanced. Like the pure Canadian equity fund, this equity/bond fund is fourth quartile. Performance has improved in 1999 however and it also has a 1% MER.

Availability

Directly by Ontario residents on a no-load basis. Also available through brokers and dealers in all provinces but Quebec and the Territories, with sales charges negotiable. $1,000 minimum investment.

35. PHILLIPS, HAGER & NORTH LTD. **NO LOAD**

Strengths	Performance
	Low MERs
Weaknesses	Marketing
	$25,000 minimum
RESPs?	No
Web Site	www.phn.ca

Toll Free 1-800-661-6141

CANADIAN	Category	Rating	Fund Name	M.E.R.%	RRSP/Foreign
Money Market:		■	PH&N Canadian Money Market Fund	0.45	RRSP
Fixed Income:	Long-term	★ KO	PH&N Bond Fund	0.56	RRSP
	Short-term	■	PH&N Short Term Bond & Mortgage Fund	0.62	RRSP
Equity:	Mid-Large Cap	★ OK	PH&N Canadian Equity Fund	1.07	RRSP
		■	PH&N Canadian Equity Plus Fund	1.16	RRSP
	Small Cap	■	PH&N Vintage Fund*	1.73	RRSP
Tax Advantaged:	Dividend	★ OK	PH&N Dividend Income Fund	1.16	RRSP
Multi-Asset:	Balanced	★ AG	PH&N Balanced Fund	0.89	RRSP

FOREIGN	Category	Rating	Fund Name	MER%	RRSP/Foreign
Money Market:		■	PH&N $U.S. Money Market Fund	0.52	RRSP
Regional Equity:	U.S.	▲ OK	PH&N U.S. Equity Fund	1.11	Foreign
	NAFTA/N.Am.	■	PH&N North American Equity Fund	1.16	Foreign
	Europe	▲ OK	PH&N Euro-Pacific Equity Fund	1.39	Foreign

* Closed to new investors

Growing consumer awareness of the importance of low management expense ratios (MERs) has played into the hands of Vancouver-based Phillips, Hager & North Ltd. This employee-owned no-load outfit may not advertise, but after 30 years, it hardly constitutes a secret any more. Its good long-term performance and low MERs mean PH&N continues to garner more than its fair share of Smart Funds.

Whether the accompanying popularity forces its larger funds into a "regression to the mean" syndrome remains to be seen. PH&N continues to require high minimum initial investments as a way to keep its fees as low as possible. For RRSP accounts for clients dealing directly with the firm or through a broker or advisor, the minimum is $10,000. The minimum initial investment for RRIF accounts is $50,000.

No new funds were added in the past year, although the International Equity Fund had a name change. It is now called the Euro-Pacific Fund because the company felt that more clearly reflects the EAFE investment mandate of the fund.

PH&N also has an unusually low turnover of its money managers. Whether it is the Vancouver lifestyle or allure of a smaller privately owned firm, money managers that go there rarely seem to leave, except to retire, as is starting to occur. Co-founder Richard Bradshaw retired from the firm in March 1999 as part of a planned transition. And senior management at the firm seem to take turns in the president's seat. Tony Gage stepped down as president and will oversee a team of money managers. Meanwhile, Tom Bradley became president and chief executive in September 1999, giving up his former duties with the Canadian equity team.

PH&N's core business is pension investing and running segregated management and pooled funds for high-net-worth individuals. Due, in part, to the funds' low MERs, even its wealthy clients use the same family of no-load funds. That tells you one of the most respected independent investment counsellors in Canada thinks the diversification and other benefits of mutual funds is appropriate for almost anyone. But the company is dedicating more resources to its fast-growing mutual fund business. For instance, they are trying to get the word out to clients that they can offer advice, even though these are no-load funds.

PH&N's investment style is focused on finding good North American companies, based on specific criteria, such as a consistently above-average rate of return on shareholder equity, and companies that are industry leaders and in the growth phase of their life cycles.

Nevertheless, PH&N may not be for everyone. If you want to beat RRSP or RRIF foreign-content limitations or want regional equity funds concentrated in such exotic locales as Latin America or the riskier emerging markets, PH&N is not the place to be. The proven PH&N funds are ideal for building a low-cost, above-average core holding in North American stocks and bonds.

Year 2000 Stance

PH&N has what it calls its Stock Watch program to monitor Y2K compliance of stocks in its portfolios. Each organization is assigned a risk score based on available information and is then designated either off-track or on-track. So far PH&N has done Y2K assessments on more than 440 organizations.

The firm is not recommending asset allocation changes based solely on Y2K. They believe the outlook for the pre- and post-Year 2000 will be short term and not affect the underlying value of a company.

Smart Funds 2000

Y2K OK

PH&N Canadian Equity Fund. Performance has slipped in the last two years. But we expect this talented firm to get the fund back on its long-term, above-average performance. MER of 1.1% is tough to find anywhere in Canada.

PH&N Dividend Income Fund. A five-time Smart Fund that is first quartile over two, three, four, five, and 10 years ended August 31, 1999. Fund actually has a very low yield and acts more like a conservative Canadian equity fund. Its 21.7% three-year return handily beat the TSE.

Y2K KO

PH&N Bond Fund. Top-quartile fund with a 0.57% MER!

Y2K Agnostic

PH&N Balanced Fund. First quartile for one, two, three, and five years ended August 31, 1999, and another five-time Smart Fund.

Noteworthy Funds

Y2K OK

PH&N Euro-Pacific Equity. This EAFE (Europe, Australia, and Far East) index fund has a lower-than-normal expense ratio for its category because PH&N acts on the premise that most of the performance from global equity funds comes primarily from country selection, which can be achieved through local stock indices. It calls this approach "active country allocation/passive stock selection." The fund is exposed to about 20 industrial economies, with all industry groups in the chosen countries represented. Its total stock exposure is 300 to 700 companies, and the fund has full exposure to foreign currencies. It performed below average in 1997, 1998, and 1999, proving that stock-picking matters.

PH&N U.S. Equity Fund. This perennial Smart Fund has slipped a bit, falling to the third quartile in 1997, 1998, and the first part of 1999. But U.S. equities have proven to be the world's asset class of choice and this fund's MER of 1.11% is hard to beat. Still, the incredible competition of this category means this one gets demoted.

Availability

Directly from PH&N or through some brokers. Funds available across Canada: a prospectus had been filed in every province as of May 1998. $10,000 minimum initial investment, whether purchased directly or through third parties.

36. ROYAL MUTUAL FUNDS INC. **NO LOAD**

Strengths Low-MER strategic index funds
Style diversification
Weaknesses Billion-dollar funds,
RESPs? Yes
Web Site www.royalbank.com **Toll Free** 1-800-463-3863

CANADIAN	Category	Rating	Fund Name	M.E.R.%	RRSP/Foreign
Money Market:		■	Royal Canadian T-Bill Fund	0.92	RRSP
		■	Royal Canadian Money Market Fund	0.95	RRSP
		▲ KO	Royal Premium Money Market Fund*	0.3	RRSP
Fixed Income:	Long-term	■	Royal Bond Fund	1.39	RRSP
	Mortgage	■	Royal Mortgage Fund	1.54	RRSP
		▲ AG	Royal Monthly Income Fund	1.16	RRSP
Equity:	Mid-Large Cap	■	Royal Canadian Equity Fund	1.97	RRSP
		■	Royal Canadian Growth Fund	2.27	RRSP
		■	Royal Canadian Value Fund	2	RRSP
	Small Cap	■	Royal Canadian Small Cap Fund	2.27	RRSP
	Gold/precious metal	▲ KO	Royal Precious Metals Fund	2.53	RRSP
	Resource	■	Royal Energy Fund	2.34	RRSP
	Index	■	Royal Canadian Strategic Index Fund	1.5	RRSP
		▲ OK	Royal Canadian Index Fund	0.5	RRSP
		■	Royal Premium Canadian Index Fund*	0.3	RRSP
Tax Advantaged:	Dividend	★ OK	Royal Dividend Fund	1.75	RRSP
Multi-Asset:	Balanced	■	Royal Balanced Fund	2.2	RRSP
		■	Royal Balanced Growth Fund	2.25	RRSP
		■	Royal Trust Advantage Income Fund	1.58	RRSP
		■	Royal Trust Advantage Balanced Fund	1.72	RRSP
		■	Royal Trust Advantage Growth Fund	1.87	RRSP

FOREIGN	Category	Rating	Fund Name	MER%	RRSP/Foreign
Money Market:		■	Royal $U.S. Money Market Fund	1.1	Foreign
Fixed Income:		▲ KO	Royal Global Bond Fund	1.86	RRSP
Global Equity:	EAFE	■	Royal International Equity Fund	2.63	Foreign
	Large-Cap	■	Royal Global Education Fund	1.95	Foreign
	Technology	▲ OK	Royal Life Science and Technology Fund	2.74	Foreign
Regional Equity:					
	U.S. Large-cap	▲ OK	Royal U.S. Equity Fund	2.11	Foreign
	U.S. Small-cap	▲ AG	Zweig Strategic Growth Fund	2.49	Foreign
	Index	■	Royal U.S. Value Strategic Index Fund	1.5	Foreign
		■	Royal U.S. Growth Strategic Index Fund	1.5	Foreign
		▲ OK	Royal U.S. Index Fund	0.5	Foreign
		■	Royal Premium U.S. Index Fund*	0.3	Foreign
		★ OK	Royal U.S. RSP Index Fund	0.5	RRSP
	Latin American	■	Royal Latin American Fund	2.99	Foreign
	Far East	■	Royal Asian Growth Fund	2.97	Foreign
	Japan	■	Royal Japanese Stock Fund	2.63	Foreign
	Europe	▲ OK	Royal European Growth Fund	2.48	Foreign
	Index	▲ OK	Royal International RSP Index Fund	0.5	RRSP
Global Balanced:		▲ AG	Zweig Global Balanced Fund	2.75	Foreign

* $250,000 minimum

This continues to be Canada's largest no-load mutual fund family, although maybe not as large as it would like, given the merger between its parent the Royal Bank of Canada and the Bank of Montreal was not permitted by the federal government.

In theory, the size of this group and its many multi-billion-dollar funds should bring greater economies of scale and drive down management expense ratios (MERs). However, there's been little evidence so far of that at Royal Mutual Funds. The mammoth $7.4-billion Royal Balanced Fund has an MER of 2.2%, equal to the average for all balanced funds.

On the positive side, Royal has shown that it will be competitive where investors demand it. In August 1998 it launched five passively managed index funds: Royal Canadian Index, Royal Premium Canadian Index, Royal U.S. Index, Royal Premium U.S. Index, Royal U.S. RSP Index, and Royal International RSP Index. The fees at launch were the lowest available: 0.55% on the regular index funds and 0.3% on the two "Premium" index funds. The Premium versions have lower fees because they require a $250,000 minimum, as does the Premium Money Market fund.

These funds appealed to what many investors are looking for: low-cost access to the potential growth of stock markets, and fully RSP-eligible foreign investments.

Not long after the launch, Altamira Investment Services Inc. came out with its index funds, which were even cheaper with a 0.5% MER. Royal wasted no time in matching that lower fee and Canadian investors benefited from what was the first real competition on fee pricing for funds in Canada.

There is no doubt that index funds are appealing. With their low fees, and the fact that most active managers can't consistently achieve better returns than the index, they are a good option, at least for part of a portfolio. On the other hand, actively managed funds generally do a better job of protecting investors in "bear" markets. Royal's marketing materials concede that "in falling equity markets, index funds often lose relatively more value." It's also worth noting that outside registered plans, index funds generate fewer capital gains because they don't actively trade stocks. For investors who like the idea and understand the down-side, these funds may be a good alternative to regular actively managed equity funds. They require a $2,500 minimum investment.

The new index funds are not to be confused with Royal's "Strategic Index" funds, launched a year earlier with the promotional backing of David Chilton, speaker and author of *The Wealthy Barber*. The maximum MER of these funds has been set at 1.5%, which is no screaming bargain. But these passively managed funds do have a component of active management. Royal has trademarked the phrase "strategy indexing" to describe an investment approach developed by James P. O'Shaughnessy, who runs the Greenwich, Connecticut investment advisory firm bearing his name. A computer-based set of screens select promising stocks that are held for a year, after which the portfolio is rebalanced and stocks reselected.

Because these were not index funds, Royal scrapped the goofy name and now call them O'Shaughnessy Funds.

Also new since the last edition is the Global Education Fund, launched in October 1998. This global equity fund invests in shares of large, widely recognized companies throughout the world: American Express Company, Sony Corp., and DaimlerChrysler AG. The idea is that this fund is an ideal investment for a savings plan for a child's education. It is suitable for a long-term horizon because it is in equities, and has the growth potential of stocks, but the stability of the world's most well-established companies. The fund is being conservatively managed by Royal Bank's Christine Poole. It will have very large cash positions while waiting for the right investment at the right time, rather than rushing to get all the money invested. Still, it charges a 1.95% MER, so you wouldn't want to see too much of the money sitting in cash.

Most of Royal's Canadian and some of its U.S. funds are managed internally by Royal Bank Investment Management. RBIM also has a Global Investment Group, so the international funds are managed partly through its internal resources and partly through externally contracted subadvisors. However, some of the global funds have moved to in-house management.

Investors with more than $50,000 also have the option of a discretionary investment management service called Personal Asset Management Services, which is managed by Royal Trust Investment Counsel. The service holds $1 billion in Royal Mutual Funds. RTIC also provides other discretionary products for larger-sized portfolios.

Year 2000 Stance

The year 2000 poses investment risks in mutual funds, according to Royal Mutual Funds. Although money managers receive information relevant to Y2K from companies they invest in, "it is not possible to be certain that all the Year 2000 related risks and uncertainties affecting the funds will be fully resolved or mitigated." Royal Mutual Funds says it is taking steps designed to address Y2K, including "contingency planning" where appropriate. The bank did not elaborate on its plans beyond that.

Smart Funds 2000

Royal Dividend. Solid blue-chipper that was first-quartile performer in 1996, 1997, and 1998.

Royal U.S. RSP Index Fund. Low-MER index funds are arguably the best way to play the highly liquid U.S. large-cap market. This offering is doubly alluring because it doesn't use up the 20% foreign-content limit in RRSPs or RRIFs. However, beware going overboard with that possibility because the overvalued U.S. market has potentially farther to fall should Y2K prove not to be OK. Managed by State Street, the get-out-of-Canada mood has been demonstrated by the fund's growth to over $150 million since its launch in October 1998.

Noteworthy Funds

Y2K OK

Royal Canadian Index, Royal U.S. Index. These index funds are the cheapest available in Canada—along with Altamira's—and require a $2,500 minimum investment. For investors disillusioned with how tough it is for active managers to beat the market, these offer an alternative. On the flip side, beware that these offer no insulation against market drops, but you are fully invested when it bounces back.

Royal European Growth. This fund continued in the top quartile in 1998 and into 1999. As of August 31, it was up 9.7% over one year. Manager Ross Youngman of BT Fund Managers (International) Ltd. focuses on the developed European countries but also has the flexibility to invest in Eastern Europe. Note that if Y2K is serious, Europe's attempts to fix the Euro ahead of Y2K could impact all European equity funds.

Royal U.S. Equity. A solid if unspectacular performer. Has a 20% five-year CAGR to August 31, 1999. Trouble now is that Jim Young left for Trimark.

Royal Life Science & Technology. This health care and technology fund can invest around the world but was heavily weighted in U.S. stocks recently. It performed above average versus similar funds in 1997 and 1998. Relative performance was well behind its peers for the first six months of 1999. This fund is not cheap with its 2.74% annual MER. Manager Jim Young left for Trimark.

Y2K KO

Royal Premium Money Market Fund. Those with hefty portfolios can "park" a minimum $250,000 in this low-MER (0.3%) money market fund. Subsequent investments are a minimum $5,000.

Royal Global Bond Fund. In a Y2K meltdown scenario, governments may lower interest rates to reprime the economic pump. If that happens, bond funds would make capital gains. Global bonds may provide greater gains and also a measure of currency diversification. This one is 100% RRSP-eligible.

Royal Precious Metals. It was a tough go for gold and other precious metals in 1998. For investors who want to invest this sector as a hedge to other asset classes, manager John Embry is among the top managers in this category. Some Y2K bears expect gold to soar if Y2K has a worse impact on financial markets than has been anticipated.

Y2K Agnostic

Royal Monthly Income Fund. This fund pays monthly by investing in high-yielding debt and equities. It has a reasonable 1.16% MER. Based on interest rate declines in 1998, the fund reduced its monthly income stream from $0.045 per share each month to $0.0425 per month.

Zweig Strategic Growth Fund. The U.S. fund for cautious bulls, this market-timing strategy means manager David Katzen will move 100% to cash if deemed advisable. The Zweig model uses monetary measures, sentiment indicators, and market momentum to make its calls. Still waiting for this one. With consistent below-average performance, Royal may want to merge this one into the U.S. equity fund.

Zweig Global Balanced Fund. As above, with a greater assurance of exposure to the major asset classes. Seems the Zweig model works in the global arena with first-quartile performance over three and two years to August 31, 1999.

Availability

Royal Bank and Royal Trust branches; RBC Dominion Securities and many other discount brokers.

37. SAXON FUNDS

NO LOAD

Strengths	No frills, low fees, no-load
	Small-cap value niche
Weaknesses	Limited range of funds
	Profile and marketing
RESPs?	No
Web site:	www.saxonfunds.com/~saxon **Toll Free** 1-888-287-2966

CANADIAN	Category	Rating	Fund Name	M.E.R.%	RRSP/Foreign
Equity:	Mid-Large Cap	▲ OK	Saxon Stock Fund	1.75	RRSP
	Small Cap	★ OK	Saxon Small Cap	1.75	RRSP
Tax Advant:	Income Trust	▲ AG	Saxon High Income Fund	1.25	RRSP
Multi-Asset:	Balanced	■ AG	Saxon Balanced Fund	1.75	RRSP

FOREIGN	Category	Rating	Fund Name	MER%	RRSP/Foreign
Global Equity:	All-global	▲ OK	Saxon World Growth	1.75	Foreign

Saxon Funds has only five funds in its stable,. In past years a number of those were designated Smart Funds. Once available in a limited number of provinces, they can now be purchased across the country, either directly from the company or through brokers and dealers.

The essence of this family continues to be investment management by the in-house manager Howson Tattersall Investment Counsel Ltd., which also does pension and private client investment management, with pooled accounts for investors with $250,000 or more. The company's two principals remain in place. Bob Tattersall has been a Saxon principal since the firm's founding 13 years ago. Rick Howson has been on board for 10 years and also handles segregated portfolio management for private clients with accounts of more than $1 million. As sole owners, both managers can be expected to be with the firm for the long term. The funds are managed with a value approach that insists that stocks be cheaper than what the manager believes is their true value. The companies they like usually have minimal debt, low market-to-book ratio, low price-to-cash-flow ratio, and low price to sales. Saxon views themselves as investors in companies, not traders in shares. That results in low portfolio turnover, which is especially attractive for taxable portfolios.

The management fees for this no-load fund group remain lower than much of the competition. The annual management fee for four of the funds is 1.75%, which is also the MER, since the managers absorb all other expenses. Saxon High Income has a 1.25% MER.

Saxon Small Cap continues to stand out as the gem of this fund group and receives a Smart Fund designation again this year. It was also recognized by an industry award as the best in its category.

The newest addition, Saxon High Income, was launched in November 1997 and had a good first year in that it performed above average in 1998. Its return was still only 0.9% in the year, but that was in addition to meeting its objective to provide a consistent cash flow along with the tax advantages of return of capital.

Year 2000 Stance

The company feels that with Y2K being a well-publicized event, the stock market has already discounted possible problems and will continue to do so as the time draws closer. Saxon managers have no plans to "market time" in anticipation of the event. The managers continue to buy stocks that are, on average, well below the fundamental valuations of the market.

Smart Funds 2000

Saxon Small Cap. The award-winner at the Annual Mutual Fund Awards. It somehow side-stepped the small-cap massacre and is the number one fund in its category for the three years ended August 31, 1999.

Noteworthy Funds

Y2K OK

Saxon Stock. Managed by Richard Howson, this Canadian equity fund mixes some small caps with large caps. Over the long term this fund has showcased Howson's stock-picking ability. Its performance was below average in 1998 but was moving into above-average returns in 1999.

Saxon World Growth. This former Smart Fund remains Noteworthy as intense competition pushed it into the fourth quartile in 1998. That followed below-average performance in 1997. It was back to first quartile for the eight months ended August 31, 1999.

Y2K Agnostic

Saxon High Income Fund. This tax-advantaged income trust fund pays out distribution income every quarter, including some return of capital. Saxon projects that the fund will generate a pre-tax return of more than 7%, or about 5.5% after taxes. The fund had a difficult first year in 1998, with weak commodity prices, such as oil. The fund is managed by Richard Howson.

Availability

Directly from Saxon or discount brokers at no-load, or through dealers and financial planners at a 2% front load. The funds are now available across the country. There is a $5,000 minimum initial purchase.

38. SCEPTRE MUTUAL FUNDS

NO LOAD

Strengths	High performance with low MERs
	No-frills marketing
Weaknesses	No specialty funds
	Low profile
RESPs?	No
Web Site	www.sceptre.ca
Toll Free	1-800-265-1888

CANADIAN	Category	Rating	Fund Name	M.E.R.%	RRSP/Foreign
Money Market:		■	Sceptre Money Market Fund	0.75	RRSP
Fixed Income:	Short-term	★ KO	Sceptre Bond Fund	0.94	RRSP
Equity:	Mid-Large Cap	■	Sceptre Canadian Equity Fund	1.65	RRSP
	Small-med Cap	▲ OK	Sceptre Equity Growth Fund	1.44	RRSP
Multi-Asset:	Balanced	★ AG	Sceptre Balanced Growth Fund	1.43	RRSP

FOREIGN	Category	Rating	Fund Name	MER%	RRSP/Foreign
Global Equity:	All-global	■	Sceptre International Fund	2.09	Foreign
Regional Equity:	U.S.	▲ OK	Sceptre U.S. Equity Fund	1.72	Foreign

The combination of strong performance and reasonable MERs propelled Sceptre past $1 billion in assets last year. The MERs are even inching down on some of the funds, as should be the case with greater economies of scale. However, performance has surprisingly turned south.

The simple seven-fund matrix is only slightly changed from last year: it reflects the closure of Sceptre Asian Growth Fund in January 1999. It also shows the two July 1998 additions, Sceptre Canadian Equity and Sceptre U.S. Equity, which have now been around long enough to list their MERs: 1.65% and 1.72% respectively.

Sceptre Investment Counsel has been well known in the pension fund world since 1955, with almost $20 billion now under management. Its Canadian funds were its strength but it also does a credible job of managing international investments from its base in Toronto. While the fund is off from its top-quartile performance earlier in the decade, Sceptre International manager Lennox McNeely still believes in over-weighting areas, with promising long-term economic growth. That area used to be Asia but is now evidently the more obvious choice of the United States. The proportions of the international fund reflect the closure of the Asia fund and launch of a U.S. fund: the international fund is 45% in the United States, with most of the rest in Europe, Japan, and Australia. This may also reflect Sceptre's view of the Y2K problem (see below) and its growing aversion to emerging markets.

Sceptre is committed to keeping its MERs among the 25% least expensive. Although it now pays a small service fee to brokers and discount brokers, it has not raised MERs to subsidize that cost.

Although Sceptre is no longer a well-kept secret, the company has not changed its winning formula. It still shies away from big-budget advertising campaigns and road shows aimed at wooing brokers and planners. It remains focused on what it does: money management.

Year 2000 Stance

Sceptre says it has attended various presentations from Y2K consultants over the past 18 months and is therefore "keenly aware" of the issue. It acknowledges that obtaining pertinent information on the status of particular companies "has been a concern" and that it must rely on the disclosures mandated by securities commissions and stock exchanges. It also discusses the issue with its normal interviews with management of investee companies. It views North America as leading the pack in dealing with the problem, and Europe as six to 12 months behind. Other countries may be further behind but have newer systems that could be more likely compliant. Nevertheless, while Sceptre views Y2K as just one factor among many in making investment decisions, it has "significantly reduced" its exposure to emerging markets and Southeast Asia: "Y2K was one factor in this decision, as we felt those markets were least prepared."

Sceptre expects "some hitches" and perhaps "a slowdown in corporate earnings levels." It recognizes that opinions vary as to the possibility of a general recession "or worse if a combination of investor panic and system failures force markets into an aberrant pattern." But it has no plans to halt trading or change its asset mix. Even without Y2K, Sceptre would have had a "slightly conservative" posture at this point in the economic cycle.

Smart Funds 2000

Y2K KO

Sceptre Bond. First quartile as you'd expect a low-MER bond fund to be. Manager Ian Lee joined Sceptre in 1996 and has 24 years' experience in investing. Two-thirds of portfolio is government bonds.

Y2K Agnostic

Sceptre Balanced Growth. Fund has slipped to fourth quartile but Lyle Stein (see profile in *Smart Funds 1999*) should be as adept at anyone at rejigging asset classes if Y2K becomes a storm. Stocks allocation was just 48% at the end of August 1999. The 6.0% weighting in the fourth-quartile performing Sceptre International fund has killed this fund. We hope that Lyle returns to the first-quartile performance of 1995, 1996, and 1997 or it will be demoted after four straight years as a Smart Fund.

Noteworthy Funds

Y2K OK

Sceptre Equity Growth Fund. Performance of this Allan Jacobs fund has slipped over the past 2.5 years. It seems many have voted with their feet as the fund is down to $250 million from $460 million at December 1997.

Sceptre U.S. Equity Fund. Small new fund managed by Stephen Douglas still must prove itself. Fund limits itself to 20 to 40 blue chips such as IBM, Xerox, and Bristol Myers Squibb. Blend of value and growth styles. Fund holds 10% in S&P Index. Not much effort there!

Availability

Directly on no-load basis in Ontario, British Columbia, and now Manitoba, or through discount brokers across Canada. Funds also available through full-service brokers, dealers, and financial planners, who may levy an acquisition charge of up to 2%. Minimum $5,000 investment required for new accounts, $1,000 thereafter.

39. SCOTIA MUTUAL FUNDS

NO LOAD

Strengths	Balanced funds 100% RRSP-eligible global funds
Weaknesses	Some global funds still finding their way Few small-cap offerings
RESPs?	No
Web Site	www.Scotiabank.ca
Toll Free	1-800-268-9269

CANADIAN	Category	Rating	Fund Name	M.E.R.%	RRSP/Foreign
Money Market:		■	Scotia T-Bill Fund	1.00%	RRSP
		▲ KO	Scotia Premium T-Bill Fund	0.52%	RRSP
		■	Scotia Money Market Fund	1.00%	RRSP
Fixed Income:	Mortgage	■	Scotia Mortgage Income Fund	1.56%	RRSP
	Short-term	■	Scotia Canadian Short-Term Income Fund	1.32%	RRSP
	Long-term	■	Scotia Canadian Income Fund	1.14%	RRSP
Equity:	Index	▲ OK	Scotia Canadian Stock Index Fund	0.87%	RRSP
	Large-cap	■	Scotia Canadian Blue Chip Fund	1.91%	RRSP
	Mixed-cap	■	Scotia Canadian Growth Fund	2.09%	RRSP
	Mid-cap	■	Scotia Canadian Mid-Large Cap Fund	1.48%	RRSP
	Small-cap	■	Scotia Canadian Small Cap Fund	2.37%	RRSP
	Gold/precious metal	▲ KO	Scotia Precious Metals Fund	2.19%	RRSP
Tax Advantaged:	Dividend	■	Scotia Canadian Dividend Fund	1.11%	RRSP
Multi-Asset:	Balanced	★ AG	Scotia Canadian Balanced Fund	1.65%	RRSP
	Asset Allocation	■	Scotia Total Return Fund	2.27%	RRSP
	Asset Allocation Service	■	"Solo, Copilot and Destination Accounts"		

FOREIGN	Category	Rating	Fund Name	MER%	RRSP/Foreign
Money Market:		■	Scotia CanAm U.S.$ Money Market Fund	1.00%	RRSP
Fixed Income:		■	Scotia CanAm U.S. $ Income Fund	1.60%	RRSP
		■	Scotia CanGlobal Income Fund	1.80%	RRSP
		■	Scotia Global Income Fund	1.99%	Foreign
Global Equity:	All-global	■	Scotia International Growth Fund	2.23%	Foreign
Regional Equity:	U.S. Index	▲ OK	Scotia American Stock Index Fund	0.89%	Foreign
	U.S. Index	▲ OK	Scotia CanAm Stock Index Fund	1.34%	RRSP
	U.S. Large-cap	■	Scotia American Growth Fund	2.06%	Foreign

Europe	■	Scotia European Growth Fund	2.26%	Foreign
Far East	■	Scotia Pacific Rim Growth Fund	2.43%	Foreign
Latin American	■	Scotia Latin American Growth Fund	2.39%	Foreign
Emerging Markets	■	Scotia Emerging Markets Fund	2.76%	Foreign

The 27 Scotia Mutual Funds are the newly integrated and consolidated family of the 21 Scotia Excelsior Funds and 13 National Trust funds. Several pairs of similar funds were combined and renamed, with a nod to the fund with the better long-term performance and lower MERs. The name Scotia Mutual Funds is a return to the bank group's original no-load funds, which had a name change four years ago to accommodate a similar merger of the Montreal Trust Excelsior Funds.

During this activity, we have been reluctant to make too many of the funds Smart Funds, since it typically takes time for funds to settle down after such activity. Star manager Denis Quellet departed for TAL, adding to its uncertainty. The merger activity occurred not only at the administrative level but also at the investment management level: in August 1998, Scotia Investment Management Ltd. (SIML) merged with Cassels Blaikie Investment Management, forming the new firm Scotia Cassels Investment Counsel, based in Toronto. It manages all the funds except three: Montrusco Bolton Inc. of Montreal manages Scotia Total Return Fund, Scotia Canadian Growth Fund, and Scotia International Growth Fund.

Among the bright spots that came with the National Trust funds are a growing line-up of lower-MER index funds. The Canadian Stock Index, from the N.T. stable, boasts a competitive 0.87% MER, while investors now have a choice between a 100% RRSP-eligible U.S. index fund and a lower-MER U.S. index fund that counts as 20% foreign content.

It's increasingly apparent that two of the biggest components of strong investment performance are low costs and asset allocation. In addition to beefing up its index offerings, as have most of its bank competitors, Scotiabank is also placing renewed emphasis on asset allocation services. In fact, investors with at least $5,000 can choose from three Scotia Asset Allocation Services: Solo, Copilot, or Destination. As the name suggests, Solo leaves much of the choosing to individual investors, who select the percentage of the portfolio to be invested in any particular fund. The fund mix is then rebalanced quarterly by Scotiabank to maintain the investor's original allocation of asset classes.

Copilot accounts grant more discretion to portfolio managers at Scotia Cassels Investment Counsel Ltd., who monitor assets and funds and adjust proportions to market and economic changes.

Destination accounts are for registered accounts only and are designed to "mature" after a certain number of years. Portfolio managers monitor the fund and asset mix, and the risk profile of the overall portfolio is gradually reduced until the maturity date is reached. Both Copilot and Destination are managed by Scotia Cassels.

Year 2000 Stance

From Scotia's web site:

> The Bank has prepared contingency plans to cover situations where, for whatever reason, a key component is not operational in the Year 2000.
>
> How will Y2K affect your investments?
> *"Scotia McLeod's efforts have been focused on ensuring that our clients' assets are safe and that there is no impact to the way our Investment Executives can provide service."*
> James Werry, Managing Director
> Head of Private Client Financial Services
> Scotia McLeod Inc
>
> Scotia Mutual Fund portfolio managers and ScotiaMcLeod's research team consider the issue of Y2K readiness when evaluating a company for investment. In some cases, analysts speak directly to the senior management of a company about their plans to ensure that they are ready for the Year 2000.

Smart Funds 2000

Y2K Agnostic

Scotia Canadian Balanced Fund. Reasonable 1.65% MER is below average for a domestic balanced fund that should weather Y2K storms better than a pure equity or index equity fund. First-quartile performer over the two, three, four, and five years ended August 31, 1999.

Noteworthy Funds

Y2K OK

Scotia Canadian Stock Index Fund. MER of 0.87% isn't the lowest for bank index funds but is a far sight better than MERs of actively managed funds. Second and third quartile in recent years.

Scotia CanAm Stock Index Fund. 100% RRSP-eligible U.S. index fund, with decent 1.34% MER. Second quartile over the last three years. Still Altamira, Royal, and CIBC offer a better product.

Scotia American Stock Index Fund. Counts as 20% foreign content. MER of 0.89% is lower than the 1.34% sported by the 100% RRSP-eligible Scotia CanAm Stock Index Fund. First or second quartile in recent years.

Y2K KO

Scotia Precious Metals Fund. Gold has been a terrible investment in recent years and this fund has languished against many of its peers. But if you believe that a Y2K economic downturn is good for gold bullion prices, this fund should share in the spoils.

Scotia Premium T-Bill Fund. If you must park in cash, best to do it with a 0.52% MER, but that's available only to investors with at least $100,000.

Availability

Across Canada, through branches of Scotiabank, Scotiabank & Trust, Montreal Trust, National Trust, Scotia Discount Brokerage Inc., and ScotiaMcLeod Inc. Premium T-bill fund has minimum $100,000 investment requirement; the other money market funds have a $2,500 minimum each. Most other funds are $500 minimum.

40–41. SCUDDER MAXXUM CO. — NO LOAD

Strengths Global equities
Low MERs, though rising
Weaknesses Brokers not motivated to sell family
RESPs? Yes*
Web Site www.scudder.ca **Toll Free** 1-800-850-3863

CANADIAN	Category	Rating	Fund Name	M.E.R.%	RRSP/Foreign
Money Market:		■	Scudder Canadian Money Market	0.5	RRSP
		■	Maxxum Money Market	0.85	RRSP
Fixed Income:	Short-term	★ KO	Scudder Canadian Short Term Bond Fund	1	RRSP
	Long-term	■	Scudder Canadian Bond Fund	0.85	RRSP
	Long-term	■	Maxxum Income Fund	1.75	RRSP
Equity:	Mid-Large Cap	★ OK	Scudder Canadian Equity Fund	1.5	RRSP
	Mid-Large Cap	▲ OK	Maxxum Canadian Equity Growth	2.15	RRSP
	Small-cap	■	Scudder Canadian Small Company	2	RRSP

	Gold/precious metal	▲ KO	Maxxum Precious Metals Fund	2.25	RRSP
	Resource	▲ OK	Maxxum Natural Resource Fund	2.25	RRSP
Tax Advantaged:	Dividend	★ OK	Maxxum Dividend Fund	1.75	RRSP
Multi-Asset:	Balanced	▲ AG	Maxxum Canadian Balanced Fund	2.15	RRSP

FOREIGN	Category	Rating	Fund Name	MER%	RRSP/Foreign
Global Equity:	All-global	★ OK	Scudder Global Fund	1.75	Foreign
	All-global	★ OK	Maxxum Global Equity Fund	2.5	Foreign
Regional Equity:	U.S. Large cap	▲ AG	Scudder U.S. Growth & Income Fund	1.5	Foreign
	U.S.	★ OK	Maxxum American Equity Fund	2.5	Foreign
	Emerging Market	▲ OK	Scudder Emerging Markets Fund	2.5	Foreign
	Far East	■	Scudder Pacific Fund	2	Foreign
	Europe	▲ OK	Scudder Greater Europe Fund	2	Foreign

* Currently only available with Scudder funds.

It was with mixed feelings that we heard the news of the merger between no-load company Scudder Funds of Canada and load group Maxxum Group of Funds in April 1999. Although we acknowledge this is probably a good move for Scudder as a company, given the realities of the market, we can't help but wonder whether investors may lose out as Scudder merges with the "load" side of the business. Then again, maybe we'll be pleasantly surprised.

When Scudder came to Canada four years ago, its low annual management fees coupled with a depth of management experience in the U.S. caused a stir. Could this be the company that forced the no-load giants to become more competitive and lower their prices? At first, business was tough for the established U.S. company that was virtually unknown in Canada. With solid performance numbers and a big advertising campaign, this small company struggled to attract clients for three years and apparently it could not continue as a stand-alone direct seller.

The merger was scheduled to close in the summer of 1999, subject to regulatory approval, and essentially sees the operations of the two companies merged into one: Scudder Maxxum Co. This union will likely mean more change for the Scudder funds than the Maxxum funds; exactly how much change remains to be seen. The new company is jointly owned by Winnipeg-based fund giant Investors Group Inc. (which already owned Maxxum) and Scudder's U.S. parent, Scudder Kemper Investments, Inc. The company will be run by John Wood, chief executive of Maxxum (and former president and CEO of 20/20 Funds) with Scudder's president, Gale Caruso, out of the picture. She has moved up in the Scudder Kemper hierarchy. Look for Mr. Wood to expand the line-up and perhaps add more funds managed by the spectacular Janus Capital!

For now, existing Scudder funds will continue to be sold exactly as they are: as no-load funds. Caruso is adamant that existing Scudder investors will be unaffected by the merger except that the statements they receive will now say Scudder Maxxum.

Likewise, the Maxxum funds will continue to be sold primarily through full-service brokers and dealers.

There are no plans to merge any of Scudder's 10 funds and Maxxum's nine funds. Therefore this will become a multi-brand fund group just as Mackenzie is. The key difference will be Scudder Maxxum's "multi-distribution approach." Existing funds will continue to be sold as they have been. To buy a Maxxum fund, you pay a commission, either at the time of purchase or through a deferred sales commission unless you use a discount broker like CT Securities that will offer it at zero commission. And existing Scudder funds continue to be sold as no-load funds—without commission. But to expand its distribution to the full-service brokerage network, a new version of the Scudder funds will be launched to be sold through brokers. These will carry higher annual management expense fees as most load funds do, to cover the cost of the brokers' commission fees and ongoing service fees. These may be branded as the "Kemper" Funds.

For investors who already own Scudder Funds, we don't see any reason to switch as long as the company says there will be no changes to those funds. In calendar 1998, performance of all funds was above average, with the exception of Scudder U.S. Growth and Income. Unfortunately, the once-refreshingly frugal MERs of the Scudder funds have been inching their way upward in the last two years, although they're still cheaper than most load funds—as they should be. The MERs on the Canadian and fixed-income funds are still a good deal.

Management of the Scudder funds continues by Scudder Kemper. The Canadian Equity Fund continues to do well, managed with a quantitative approach. A complex computer program chooses stocks based on historical stock market and economic data. This fund has clearly outperformed when the market has gone down.

The global research team has extensive research resources and delivers some original thinking on macro global equity trends. If global equity markets slow to single-digit growth rates, Scudder's reasonable MERs should give its funds some performance edge. And in the event of major stock market corrections, Scudder's value focus and evident caution could prove to be even more valuable to investors.

Originally known as Prudential Fund Management, Maxxum was purchased by London Life Insurance Co. three years ago and renamed. Then, in August 1997, Great-West Life, a sister company to Investors Group, purchased the London Insurance Group.

No new Maxxum funds have been added in the last year. But 1998 turned out to be a terrific year for the fund group. Every one of its funds performed in the first or second quartile, meaning they were all above-average performers. That was a big turnaround from 1997 when several were at the bottom of the barrel. Performance is more varied so far this year.

The special equity funds, with a high exposure to gold and resource stocks, were always high on the risk/reward spectrum. The portfolio managers running them have provided consistency throughout the changes in ownership: head of the investing department, Martin Anstee, has been in place for 29 years, bond manager Gerry Boychuk for 12 years. and Canadian equities manager Jackee Pratt for almost four years.

While most of Maxxum's investment management is performed in-house—that is, in its domestic equity and fixed-income funds—a definite strength are its two foreign equity funds: Global Equity and American Equity, managed since 1995 by Janus Capital Corp. of Denver. Janus is a bottom-up, growth-oriented investment firm and is currently one of the top fund companies in the United States. Both are Smart Funds this year.

Managed by Warren Lammert of Janus, Maxxum American Equity Fund continues as a Smart Fund this year. The fund gained an astounding 73% over one year to August 31, largely on the backs of the ever-rising technology/Internet stocks. The fund had over 35% in that sector and one of its biggest single positions was 6.1% in Internet bookseller Amazon.com Inc.

Year 2000 Stance

Neither the Scudder nor Maxxum management groups offered any information on how they are addressing concerns over Y2K. However, high-profile economic strategist Robert Frodich has commented in public appearances that the issue is over-hyped and the major markets and firms are prepared.

Smart Funds 2000

Y2K OK

Maxxum Global Equity Fund. The other strong Maxxum fund managed by Denver's Janus Capital. Morningstar named manager Helen Young Hayes the 1997 international fund manager. Fund returned 23% for year ended August 31, 1999. The fund has continued to add to its U.S. weighting over the last year and had more than 35% there at the end of August. It has also moved into Japan, which is now the third-largest country allocation at 9.4%.

Maxxum American Equity Fund. Simply one of the hottest funds around. Clones the top-performing Janus Mercury Fund. Look for 100% eligible version.

Maxxum Dividend Fund. Another of the blue-chip stock funds, with a fairly low yield that gets categorized as a dividend fund. Solid above-average performer.

Scudder Canadian Equity Fund. Top quartile over the two- and three-year periods. This fund does a remarkable job of outperforming the market when the market goes down.

Scudder Global Fund. Top-performing fund over two and three years. Has a 40% weighting in the U.S., all with a 1.75% MER.

Y2K KO

Scudder Canadian Short Term Bond. Consistent first-quartile performance that pays five cents per unit per month.

Noteworthy Funds

Y2K OK

Maxxum Natural Resource Fund. Finally a turnaround for Canadian resource funds; this one was up 45.4% for the year ended August 31, 1999, which was still better than average. It has about 10% in gold and precious metals.

Maxxum Canadian Equity Growth Fund. Managed by Jackee Pratt, this is usually more volatile than others in the large-cap category. It returned 31.7% over one year to August 31, well ahead of the TSE 300 index over the same period. And the fund was fully invested with only 2.6% in cash.

Scudder Greater Europe. An above-average performer since its launch, the fund is managed by Carol Franklin and Joan Gregory. They invest in both western and eastern Europe. The fund's 2.0% MER is lower than the 2.49% average MER. Because Europe put Euro conversion ahead of Y2K, do not assume that its compliance is the same as North America's.

Scudder Emerging Markets. In normal years, a Smart Fund. This year, we suggest Scudder Global, given the abysmal level of Y2K compliance in many emerging markets. (See entries for Talvest and

CIBC.) If in the new year, emerging markets are still intact and at lower value, this would be one of the first emerging markets funds we'd consider for re-entry.

Y2K KO

Maxxum Precious Metals Fund. As with other gold funds in this guide, Y2K bears tend to be gold bugs and believe the price of bullion could soar if Y2K puts a spanner in the works of the economic system. Risky, so don't go overboard or put more than 5% or 10% of a total portfolio in such funds.

Y2K Agnostic

Maxxum Canadian Balanced Fund. The performance of this portfolio improved in the last year after a disappointing 1997. It was above average in 1998 versus other balanced funds and continues to be so this year; however, the 2.13% MER makes it expensive if performance should fall.

Scudder U.S. Growth & Income Fund. The MER has been hiked 25 basis points since last edition but this fund, based on five-star Morningstar-rated U.S. version, could hold its own in Y2K-uncertain times. It buys stocks with dividend yields 20% higher than the yield on the unmanaged S&P 500. In an era where growth slows, such attention to yield could be a plus for unitholders.

Availability

Scudder Funds. The existing no-load funds can be purchased directly from Scudder Canada in Alberta, British Columbia, Saskatchewan, Ontario, and Manitoba. $1,000 minimum investment; $500 for registered accounts. There are no account set-up fees. As of the summer 1999, a line-up of Scudder "load" funds will also be available through full-service and discount brokers and fund dealers. Investors Group also plans to sell its own line of Scudder funds through its sales people.

Maxxum Funds. Through some full-service and discount brokers and financial planners, registered London Life agents, and other insurance agents with a mutual fund licence.

42. SPECTRUM UNITED MUTUAL FUNDS FRONT OR REAR

Strengths	Small-cap funds in U.S., Canada and Europe Relationship with McLean Budden
Weaknesses	Some funds sub-par
RESPs?	Yes
Web Site	www.spectrumunited.ca **Toll Free** 1-800-263-1851

CANADIAN	Category	Rating	Fund Name	M.E.R.%	RRSP/Foreign
Money Market:		■	Spectrum United Canadian Money Market Fund	0.98	RRSP
Fixed Income:	Long-term	■	Spectrum United Long-Term Bond Fund	1.66	RRSP
	Medium-term	■	Spectrum United Mid-Term Bond Fund	1.6	RRSP
	Short-term	▲ KO	Spectrum United Short-Term Bond Fund	1.5	RRSP
Equity:	Large-cap	▲ OK	Spectrum United Canadian Equity Fund	2.38	RRSP
		■	Spectrum United Canadian Stock Fund	2.38	RRSP
		▲ OK	Spectrum United Canadian Investment Fund	2.38	RRSP
	Small-mid Cap	▲ OK	Spectrum United Canadian Growth Fund	2.39	RRSP
		■	Spectrum United Canadian Small-Mid Cap	2.45	RRSP
	Resource	■	Spectrum United Canadian Resource Fund	2.45	RRSP
Tax Advantaged:	Dividend	■	Spectrum United Dividend Fund	1.65	RRSP
Multi-Asset:	Balanced	■	Spectrum United Diversified Fund	2.18	RRSP
	Asset Allocation	■	Spectrum United Asset Allocation Fund	2.25	RRSP
	Portfolio of Funds	▲ AG	Canadian Income Portfolio	1.93	RRSP
		■	Canadian Conservative Portfolio of Funds	2.06	RRSP
		■	Canadian Balanced Portfolio	2.2	RRSP
		■	Canadian Growth Portfolio	2.36	RRSP
		■	Canadian Maximum Growth Portfolio	2.51	RRSP

FOREIGN	Category	Rating	Fund Name	MER%	RRSP/Foreign
Money Market:	U.S.	■	Spectrum United U.S. Dollar Money Market	1.2	Foreign
Fixed Income:		■	Spectrum United Global Bond Fund	2.08	Foreign
		■	Spectrum United RRSP International Bond Fund	2.03	RRSP
Global Equity:	Large-cap	■	Spectrum United Global Equity Fund	2.41	Foreign
	Small-cap	■	Spectrum United Global Growth Fund	2.41	Foreign
	Telecom	▲ OK	Spectrum United Global Telecommunications Fund	2.6	Foreign
Regional Equity:					
	U.S. Large-cap	■	Spectrum United Optimax USA Fund	2.41	Foreign
	U.S Mixed cap	▲ OK	Spectrum United American Equity Fund	2.38	Foreign
	U.S. Small-mid cap	★ OK	Spectrum United American Growth Fund	2.39	Foreign
		■	Spectrum United American Growth-US$	2.39	Foreign
	Emerging Market	■	Spectrum United Emerging Markets Fund	2.75	Foreign
	Far East	■	Spectrum United Asian Dynasty Fund	2.65	Foreign
	Europe Small-cap	■	Spectrum United European Growth Fund	2.6	Foreign
Global Balanced:		■	Spectrum United Global Diversified Fund	2.41	Foreign
	Portfolio of Funds	■	Global Growth Portfolio	2.5	Foreign

A year after the departure of president Allen Marple, Spectrum United has had to endure considerable flux among its fund managers. But that's to be expected when you have so many overlapping funds as Spectrum United—33, if you count the six Portfolios of Funds.

The basic line-up of funds is more or less intact despite the news April 1999, that top manager Catherine (Kiki) Delaney left to become advisor for Trimark, and with her, small-cap ace Lynn Miller. The funds they advised, the automatically demoted Smart Fund Spectrum United Canadian Equity Fund and Miller's Spectrum United Canadian Growth Fund, will be managed by McLean Budden Ltd., effective May 25, 1999. A year earlier, Spectrum's parent company, Sun Life, purchased a 60% interest in McLean Budden, which has been in business since 1947.

The decision to reposition Canadian Growth Fund (which Miller managed) as a multi-manager, small-mid cap fund could be a positive one for unitholders. The fund has been third and fourth quartile over the past three years and now features small-cap value managers Howson Tattersall Investment Counsel (see Saxon Funds entry) and growth managers Mulvihill Capital Management Inc., with the foreign component managed by Mercury Asset Management.

In January 1999, Kim Shannon left AMI Partners for ML Asset Management (Canada). However, due to a strange turn in events, Spectrum United unitholders will not be deprived of her management. She had been lead manager of Spectrum United Canadian Investment Fund. Management of that fund has moved to Mercury Asset Management, which is owned by Merrill Lynch. Thus, effective June 14, 1999, Kim Shannon returns as manager of the fund, along with Gaelen Morphet.

Effective September 1, 1998, MFS Institutional Advisors became portfolio advisor to Spectrum United Global Equity Fund and Asian Dynasty Fund. Modelled after the Morningstar four-star-rated MFS Global Equity Fund, lead manager David Mannheim picks a "best ideas" portfolio of large-cap companies in local contexts.

Early in 1999, the lead manager for the American Equity Fund, Kevin Parke, was promoted to Chief Equity Officer of MFS Institutional Advisors. John Laupheimer, a 17-year veteran of MFS, replaces Parke on day-to-day management of the fund.

Finally, the Canadian Stock Fund is now managed by Massachusetts Financial Services (MFS). *Mutual Funds* magazine has called MFS, with more than $150 billion of assets under management, "the hottest fund family in the universe." Clearly their own hyperbole, as Janus would beg to differ!

Generally, Spectrum United's strength is the diversity of its domestic and global equity managers. Investors have the choice of multiple managers offering multiple styles. External management in the broker-sold "load" channel normally is expensive, and Spectrum United's MERs are typical of this class. Nor has the firm responded to consumer desire for lower MERs by doing what the bank no-load groups now do in abundance—provide low-cost index funds.

Year 2000 Stance

Spectrum United says that its managers "have discussed possible scenarios" involving the Year 2000 computer problem. In the best case, "Y2K would be a non-event and investors are well advised to stick with an appropriate long-term asset mix."

In the worst case, to which it assigns a low probability, "investor hysteria caused mostly by the media could trigger panic in equity markets, resulting in a sell-off." In this case, Spectrum United managers would see this as the proverbial "buying opportunity."

Most Spectrum United fund managers expect Y2K to be a non-event but in equities there may be a preference to large-cap stocks for perceived security.

Smart Funds 2000

Y2K OK

Spectrum United American Growth. Either first or second quartile every year since 1994 makes you first quartile over all the periods out to 10 years ended August 31, 1999. Five-year CAGR of 25.8%. Fund is no longer a small-cap fund.

Noteworthy Funds

Y2K OK

Spectrum United Canadian Investment Fund. Kim Shannon guides this to top quartile over the past 3 years.

Spectrum United American Equity. Conservative U.S. fund with 21% five-year compound return.

Spectrum United Canadian Equity. Former Smart Fund demoted because of departure of manager Catherine (Kiki) Delaney to Trimark. The new manager, McLean Budden Ltd., is a proven growth manager with a track record of more than half a century. Both growth and value styles are incorporated in the investment approach.

Spectrum United Canadian Growth Fund. As noted above, fund has lost Lynn Miller, but appointment of Howson Tattersall as small-cap manager and Mulvihill Capital as growth managers could turn out well for unitholders.

Spectrum United Global Telecommunications. Fund returned 73.1% over the year ended August 31.

Y2K KO

Spectrum United Short-Term Bond Fund. The MERs of all Spectrum United income are high, based on John Bogle's rule of thumb that 1.5% should be the highest MER for bond funds. If you want to park until the Y2K storm passes, this fund has the lowest MER of the bond funds and the least interest rate risk. The alternative is Canadian Money Market fund, whose 0.98% MER is excessive.

Y2K Agnostic

Spectrum United Canadian Income Portfolio. The 1.93% MER is high for income funds but this portfolio of funds has some equity exposure: 15% to 25% Canadian and global equities plus another 20% to 25% in units of the Dividend Fund. The rest is a mix of short- and mid-term bond funds and global bonds.

Availability

Full-service and discount brokers, financial planners, and representatives of Sunetco Investment Services Inc.

43. STANDARD LIFE SEGREGATED FUNDS

NO LOAD & REAR

Strengths Seg fund guarantees
Weaknesses Limited product line
RESPs? No
Web Site None **Toll Free** N/A

CANADIAN	Category	Rating	Fund Name	M.E.R.%	RRSP/Foreign
Money Market:		■	Standard Life Money Market Mutual Fund	0.9	RRSP
		■	Ideal Money Market Fund	1	RRSP
Fixed Income:		■	Standard Life Bond Mutual Fund	1.5	RRSP
		■	Ideal Bond Fund	1.7	RRSP
Equity:		■	Standard Life Equity Mutual Fund	2	RRSP
		■	Ideal Equity Fund	2.2	RRSP
		■	Standard Life Growth Equity Mutual Fun	2	RRSP

	Specialty	■	Standard Life Natural Resource Mutual Fund	2	RRSP
Multi-Asset:	Balanced	■	Standard Life Balanced Mutual Fund	2	RRSP
	Balanced	■	Ideal Payout Balanced Fund	2.25	RRSP
	Balanced	▲ AG	Ideal Balanced Fund	2.25	RRSP
Tax Advantaged:	Dividend	■	Standard Life Canadian Dividend Mutual Fund	1.5	RRSP
	Dividend	■	Ideal Canadian Dividend Fund	2.25	RRSP

FOREIGN	Category	Rating	Fund Name	MER%	RRSP/Foreign
Fixed Income:		▲ KO	Standard Life International Bond Fund	2	Foreign
Global Equity:		■	Standard Life International Equity Mutual Fund	2	Foreign
		■	Ideal International Equity Fund	2.5	Foreign
Regional Equity:	U.S.	■	Standard Life U.S. Equity Mutual Fund	2	Foreign
	U.S. Large Cap	■	Ideal U.S. Equity Fund	2.35	Foreign

When they were introduced in 1992, the Standard Life Mutual Funds were at first available only through a subsidiary of the Standard Life Assurance Co. As of 1999, however, availability was widened to include fund dealers, brokers, and trust companies. In addition to selling mutual funds, the Canadian division of this global insurance company also sells the "Ideal" line of segregated funds, an additional four of which were introduced in January 1999. The new seg funds include a new U.S. equity and international equity fund, as well as new domestic dividend and balanced funds. The Ideal Canadian Dividend Fund, Ideal U.S. Equity Fund, and Ideal International Equity Fund are wrap funds that invest in underlying Standard Life Mutual Funds.

While the seg funds are of the old-time, 75% guarantee-of-principal variety, the additional insurance coverage generally clocks in at only 20 basis points higher than the regular unguaranteed mutual funds. In both cases, MERs are slightly below average for their respective categories.

The in-house investment team, Standard Life Portfolio Management, is part of Standard Life Investment Management, the Edinburgh-based investment manager for the worldwide Standard Life Group. SLPM takes a team approach to security selection, with 75% of the research conducted in-house. There have been no major manager changes since the last edition.

Generally, performance of the funds compares favourably with other seg funds in the industry. For younger, aggressive investors who believe that Y2K is no problem, the regular mutual funds of other fund families shown in this book may be more suitable. But conservative investors who are concerned about fees and wishing seg fund or other guarantees in a Y2K-uncertain climate may find a few safe harbours in Standard Life's offerings, as noted in the Noteworthy funds flagged below.

High-net-worth investors should note that Standard Life may reduce fees for institutional, group, or individual investors with substantial holdings.

Year 2000 Stance

Standard Life believes that "we should not encounter major problems with year 2000." It is nevertheless considering Y2K issues as part of its investment management process so as to "reduce the risk of investment in companies that are not taking adequate steps to mitigate their risk of the Year 2000 issue."

Smart Funds 2000

None

Noteworthy Funds

Y2K KO

Standard Life International Bond. Not available in a seg version, this global bond fund lost 8.6% for the year ended August 31, 1999, and has a reasonable MER of 2%. Also consider the domestic seg fund, Ideal Bond fund, which has a 1.7% MER and a 75% return-of-principal guarantee should interest rates move in the wrong direction under a Y2K KO scenario.

Y2K Agnostic

Ideal Balanced Fund. Performance has more or less tracked the TSE 300 the last five years and compares favourably to other seg balanced funds. The 2.25% MER is reasonable for a seg balanced fund. The conservative classic balanced asset mix and the 75% guarantee of initial principal after 10 years should allow any investor to sleep well during any Y2K-induced economic uncertainties.

Availability

Through life agents and investment advisors with insurance licences. Their mutual funds are becoming available at many discount brokers.

44. STONE & CO. LTD.

FRONT OR REAR

Strengths McLean Budden as advisor
Weaknesses Limited line-up.
RESPs? No
Web Site www.stoneco.com **Toll Free** 1-800-336-9528

CANADIAN	Category	Rating	Fund Name	M.E.R.%	RRSP/Foreign
Money Market:		■	Flagship Money Market Fund Canada	1	RRSP
Equity:		■	Flagship Stock Fund Canada	2.88	RRSP
Multi-Asset:	Balanced	▲ AG	Flagship Growth & Income	2.85	RRSP

FOREIGN	Category	Rating	Fund Name	MER%	RRSP/Foreign
Global Equity:	All-global	■	Flagship Global Growth Fund	New	Foreign

Stone & Co. is a small player in a crowded field. Founded in 1994 by Richard Stone, formerly of the Guardian Group of Funds, until this year it had only three domestic funds, with MERs above average. On January 1, 1999, however, it rounded out its family with a new global equity fund, Flagship Global Growth Fund. It's too early to speculate how that fund may fare: its initial holdings are chiefly blue-chip stocks in Japan and Europe.

Stone's trademarked slogan, Pure Growth, pretty much sums up the family's approach to investing. That means a focus on Canada's global growth businesses rather than the traditional Canadian resource sector. Thus, expect to find "no rocks, no trees, and no golds" in these portfolios.

Its domestic funds contract investment management to 51-year-old pension/high-net-worth manager McLean Budden Ltd., which is now majority owned by Sun Life. In effect, four of the five no-load funds McLean Budden offers direct to investors can now be purchased through the advice channel of independent brokers and dealers. Investors who don't have enough assets to engage McLean Budden's private client service can do so through this fund family.

Year 2000 Stance

In a brief statement, company officials said that its investment strategy "will remain the same. We will not have radical shifts in stock-picking, asset allocation, and we predict little impact of the Y2K issue on our overall investment strategy."

Smart Funds 2000

None

Noteworthy Funds

Y2K Agnostic

Flagship Growth & Income Fund Canada. You could describe this fund as delivering "balanced growth" rather than pure growth. Classic balanced split of 60% equity to 40% bonds is maintained, with the growth component managed like Flagship Stock Fund Canada. Stone & Co. is paid a performance fee of 10% of the amount by which the fund beats a benchmark that is 45% the TSE 300, 15% MSCI world index, and 40% Scotia Capital Markets Universe bond index. The maximum performance fee is 0.3% of the fund's net asset value. MER of 2.85% is a bit stiff for a balanced fund.

Availability

Full-service and discount brokers, financial planners across Canada. $500 minimum investment.

45. SVC O'DONNELL CORP. FRONT OR REAR

Strengths	Choice of value & growth styles Aggressive small-mid cap growth funds
Weaknesses	MERs a tad high Spotty debuts for U.S. funds
RESPs?	No
Web Site	None
Toll Free	1-800-292-5658

CANADIAN	Category	Rating	Fund Name	M.E.R.%	RRSP/Foreign
Money Market:		■	Strategic Value Money Market	0.78	RRSP
		■	O'Donnell Money Market Fund	1.1	RRSP
Fixed Income:	Long-term	■	Strategic Value Income Fund	2.15	RRSP
		■	O'Donnell Short Term Fund	1.35	RRSP
	All-term	■	O'Donnell Canadian Bond Fund	New	RRSP
	Short-term	■	Strategic Value Government Bond Fund	2.18	RRSP
	Short-term	■ AG	O'Donnell High Income Fund	2	RRSP
		■	O'Donnell High Income Fund (US$)	1.98	RRSP
Equity:	All-cap	■	Strategic Value Canadian Equity Fund Ltd.	2.68	RRSP
	Large Cap	■	Strategic Value Canadian Equity Value Fund	2.72	RRSP

	Large-cap/Growth	■	O'Donnell Canadian Fund	2.75	RRSP
	Large-cap/Value	■	O'Donnell Select Fund	2.75	RRSP
	Medium Cap	▲OK	O'Donnell Growth Fund	2.75	RRSP
	Small-mid Cap	■	O'Donnell Canadian Emerging Growth Fund	2.75	RRSP
	Small Cap	■	Strategic Value Canadian Small Companies Fund	2.69	RRSP
Tax Advantaged:	Dividend	■	Strategic Value Dividend Fund Ltd.	2.68	RRSP
Multi-Asset:	Balanced	■	Strategic Value Canadian Balanced Fund	2.69	RRSP
	Balanced	▲AG	O'Donnell Balanced Fund	2.4	RRSP
		■	Strategic Value Global Balanced RSP Fund	3.02	RRSP

FOREIGN	Category	Rating	Fund Name	MER%	RRSP/Foreign
Global Equity:	All-global	■	Strategic Value International Fund Ltd.	2.69	Foreign
	All-global	■	O'Donnell World Equity Fund	2.9	Foreign
	Specialty	▲OK	Strategic Value Fund	3.5	Foreign
	Specialty	▲KO	O'Donnell World Precious Metals Fund	2.9	RRSP
Regional Equity:					
	U.S. Large-cap	■	Strategic Value American Equity Fund Ltd.	2.68	Foreign
	U.S. Mid-cap	▲OK	O'Donnell U.S. Mid Cap Fund	2.9	Foreign
	U.S. Small-cap	■	O'Donnell American Sector Growth Fund	2.9	Foreign
	Europe	■	Strategic Value Europe Fund	2.68	Foreign
	Asia Pacific	■	Strategic Value Asia Pacific Fund	2.57	Foreign
	Emerging Market	■	Strategic Value Emerging Markets Fund	2.94	Foreign
Global Balanced:		■	Strategic Value Commonwealth Fund Ltd.	2.69	Foreign
		■	Strategic Value Global Balanced RSP	2.65	Foreign

There are two ways to grow in the mutual fund business: by attracting more money to your funds through new sales or by acquiring your competitors. Mark Bonham has chosen the latter strategy and most recently surprised the industry and no doubt investors, by teaming up with high-profile fund industry executive Jim O'Donnell. The merger between Bonham's Strategic Value Corp. and O'Donnell Investment Management Corp. was announced in April 1999 and has since been finalized.

The result is a mid-size fund group with $3.3 billion in its total 31 funds. As of the early summer 1999, the company's plan was to continue to offer two distinct fund brands: the value-style Strategic value funds and the growth-style O'Donnell funds. With the merger complete, investors should soon be able to switch back and forth between the two brands. So on the plus side, the merger gives investors more choice and style diversification within the combined family.

What remains to be seen is the impact this will have on the funds themselves and investors. The merger combines two of the highest-MER fund families in the Canadian marketplace.

The newly combined firm did not wait long before firing O'Donnell's former star managers, Wayne Deans and Doug Knight of

Deans Knight Capital Management in Vancouver. Deans' Canadian Emerging Growth continued to suffer in 1998, losing 33.8%. It was also a poor performer in 1997. All the funds, previously managed by Deans Knight, have been taken over, for now, by the management team at Bonham & Co., sister company to SVC. The company declined to name specific managers so they may be looking for a more permanent solution to management of the funds.

As of mid-June, no other changes had been announced, but several duplications exist between the fund families and we expect some mergers of funds will follow.

The two founders intended to run the company together, with Bonham overseeing the money management and overall operations and O'Donnell running the sales and marketing. Certainly these are their respective strengths and if these two very different people could work together, they would make a strong team. In the summer of 1999, however, O'Donnell resigned from the firm.

Jim O'Donnell, whose contacts go back a quarter century to the marketing heyday of Mackenzie Financial Corp., founded his firm in December 1995, just as mutual funds were really exploding in Canada. The Toronto-based firm exploded out of the gates, growing to $1 billion in assets faster than any Canadian fund company ever had. But as the industry has become more competitive and performance of some of O'Donnell's key funds fell behind, Jim began shopping for a partner. In walked Bonham to make a deal.

Before founding SVC in 1997, Bonham already had built one fund company. As one of the founders of BPI Mutual Funds, he engineered the company's famous "minnow that swallowed the whale" acquisition of Bolton Tremblay Funds Inc. in 1994. Bonham was ousted from BPI in 1996, and started all over again with the single high-net-worth Strategic Value Fund. He has grown Strategic in large part by acquisition, buying Laurentian Fund Management from Imperial Life Financial in May 1997.

The O'Donnell funds continue to be managed by both outside and in-house managers with some big names such as Marc Gabelli (Mario's son), who manages U.S. Mid-Cap and co-manages World Equity, and Elaine Garzarelli on American Sector Growth. Unfortunately these funds have disappointed of late, with below-average performance in 1998.

A blow to the O'Donnell funds since the last edition was the departure of Wally Kusters, who left to join C.I. Mutual Funds. He managed the O'Donnell Select Fund, which has been taken over by Glenn Inamoto. O'Donnell Canadian, also managed by Inamoto, was one of only two funds with above-average performance in 1998 and it continues to do so this year. This is worthy of note but its 2.75% MER kept it from official Noteworthy status in this guide.

While Mark Bonham has proven his management expertise and employs a consistent value approach, the funds are saddled with very expensive management fees. That is the main reason we can't give any of the funds "Smart" status this year.

Prospective investors should negotiate hard with their broker or financial planner on commissions on the Strategic Value funds (a broker can charge 0% to 9% on a front-load commission or 1% to 9% on a deferred-load sale. There is also a fixed deferred option that pays the broker a fixed 5.5%. And be wary of early redemptions, which can be as high as a 10% charge in the first year.

Year 2000 Stance

SVC says small-cap companies seem to be lagging the mid-sized and large companies in terms of being adequately prepared for Y2K. It also perceives some risk to investor sentiment during the second half of 1999. This will be unpredictable as to its effect on stock markets.

SVC had contacted all the companies invested in through its funds and expects to continue doing so on an ongoing basis until the end of the year.

Smart Funds 2000

None

Noteworthy Funds

Y2K OK

O'Donnell Growth Fund. Mid-cap mandate for Canadian stocks is more likely to justify a hefty MER than the new large-cap versions. Investors who waited for Wayne Dean's old fund to regain his magic touch on emerging-growth stocks may want to try this fund instead.

O'Donnell U.S. Mid-Cap Fund. Mario Gabelli is an oft-quoted guru on communications and media stocks and this fund rode that wave to a 43.1% return for 1997. Fund gained 33% over one year to August 31, 1999. Mid-caps are companies between US$2 billion and US$5 billion.

Strategic Value Fund. Fund is up 71.8% for the year ended August 31, 1999. But this highly volatile fund lost 34.4% in 1997. The 3.5% MER is awfully high. Owns 22% of Bank One Corporation.

Y2K KO

O'Donnell World Precious Metals Fund. Gold fund launched in late 1996 has languished with most similar funds and the price of gold bullion, which had sunk to 20-year lows in mid-1999. Manager Kjeld Thygesen is a U.K.-based mining analyst with a 30-year track record. As we note in similar entries throughout this guide, many Y2K bears are also gold bugs. But limit exposure to no more than 5% or 10% of total portfolio, and only if you are convinced that bullion has bottomed.

Y2K Agnostic

O'Donnell Balanced Fund. Not a lot of Y2K Agnostic harbours in this combined fund family so this basic balanced fund will have to do, though it lacks its former one-two punch of Wayne Deans and Doug Knight on stocks and bonds respectively. Y2K KO believers can look to the usual money market or fixed-income funds that abound in this family's line-up but the MERs are too high to justify anything but short-term parking of funds.

Availability

Through full-service and discount brokers and fund dealers and Imperial Life Financial networks. Minimum lump-sum investments of $500 for all except the high-net-worth Strategic Value Fund.

46. SYNERGY ASSET MANAGEMENT INC. FRONT OR REAR

Strengths Unique style approach
Weaknesses Above average MERs.
RESPs? No
Web Site www.info@synergyasset.com **Toll Free** 1-888-664-4784

CANADIAN	Category	Rating	Fund Name	M.E.R.%	RRSP/Foreign
			Synergy Canadian Fund Inc.		
Equity:		★ OK	Synergy Canadian Style Management Class	2.95%	RRSP
		■	Synergy Canadian Value Class	2.95%	RRSP
		■	Synergy Canadian Growth Class	2.95%	RRSP
		▲ OK	Synergy Canadian Momentum Class	2.95%	RRSP
	Small Cap	■	Synergy Canadian Small Cap Class	2.95%	RRSP
Fixed Income:	Short-term	▲ KO	Synergy Canadian Short-Term Income Class	1.95%	RRSP

FOREIGN	Category	Rating	Fund Name	MER%	RRSP/Foreign
			Synergy Global Fund Inc.		
Global Equity:	Global	▲ OK	Synergy Global Style Management Class	2.95%	Foreign
		■	Synergy Global Momentum Class	2.95%	Foreign
Multi-Asset:	Asset Allocation	▲ AG	Synergy Tactical Asset Allocation	2.95%	RRSP

Synergy Asset Management Inc. was new to *Smart Funds* in last year's edition and has been growing at a rapid clip ever since. Founder Joe Canavan brings a wealth of experience from stints at Fidelity Canada and GT Global Canada. Unlike the global equity emphasis at those firms, Synergy is focused on the Canadian market, but with a twist. The funds' unique strategy is an investment approach called Style Management: a departure from the usual strategies of diversifying by asset class or geographical region.

Two new funds have been launched since the last edition. Synergy says their introduction was accelerated to take advantage of the cheap valuations that occurred in the market downdraft of autumn 1998: Synergy Tactical Asset Allocation Fund and the Synergy Global Style Management Class.

Meanwhile, Synergy's original funds have been making an impact. It ended 1998 with two funds in the top 10: Synergy Canadian Growth Class ranked number 4 and Synergy Canadian Momentum Class ranked number 1 for the year ending December 31, 1998.

In April 1999 it launched the Synergy Global Momentum Class, extending the idea of the earlier Canadian version of the fund.

Synergy was planning to change the name of Synergy Tactical Asset Allocation Fund, to Synergy Canadian Asset Allocation Fund late in the summer of 1999.

On the administrative front, Synergy has introduced Formula One pricing, a response to the growing environment of discounting and fee rebating. A client is not charged an up-front sales commission, while the advisor receives a 1% up-front commission plus a 1% annual trailer commission, which is twice as high as the trailer payable under the DSC option. Clients using this option can shorten their redemption schedule from six to two years. Still, you can buy the funds at a zero commission discounter and avoid all the sales charges.

Year 2000 Stance

Synergy says it is systematically assessing each of its investment positions. It has sent out individual requests for confirmation of Y2K readiness and is assembling publicly available data on its positions.

It has also prepared a considerations document and checklist to be used by each of the portfolio managers in assessing their investments through meetings with management. These tools focus on common risk areas (underestimating costs and manpower requirements, inadequate testing, program reliance on third party supply chain, etc.), trending analysis (trend lines in responses to completion status, resources required, percentage of effort devoted to testing) and broad industry exposures (high-risk areas include date-intensive service industries [operational exposure], just-in-time companies [supply chain exposure], and IT hardware/software/service companies [litigation exposure]).

In the best case, Synergy suggests investors who feel unconcerned about Y2K and who are confident in their equity positions may want to consider reducing their portfolio exposure to companies whose revenues are driven by the sales of client server-based software and desktop and PC sales. In the worst case, "investors who are worried about their portfolios could consider moving equity positions into cash until enough confidence is generated to suggest recommitment to the equity market."

Generally, Synergy says speculation of Y2K-related market activity "provides no solid foundation on which to base any concrete investment decisions at this time." It says companies whose growth is directly attributable to sales of software and computer-related technology may suffer in the period leading up to Y2K.

Smart Funds 2000

Y2K OK

Synergy Canadian Style Management Class. It is still new, but the fund has been an above-average performer.

Noteworthy Funds

Y2K OK

Synergy Canadian Momentum Class. The momentum style is rare in Canada but offers an alternative to growth and value, at least in a strong bull market. Managed by Dave Picton.

Synergy Global Style Management Class. New fund applies globally the style management of Smart Fund Synergy Canadian Style Management.

Y2K KO

Synergy Canadian Short-Term Income Class. This short-term fixed income fund is an alternative to Synergy's family of mostly equity mutual funds. A 1.95% MER is pretty stiff for a fixed-income fund.

Y2K Agnostic

Synergy Tactical Asset Allocation Fund. TAA funds have more scope to shift 100% to cash or bonds if a protracted bear market seems imminent or likely to linger.

Availability

Through brokers, discount brokers, and dealers. Minimum investment is $500.

47. TALVEST FUND MANAGEMENT INC.

FRONT OR REAR

Strengths	Fixed income and asset allocation Technology & health funds
Weaknesses	High MERs
RESPs?	No
Web Site	www.talvest.com
Toll Free	1-800-268-8258

CANADIAN	Category	Rating	Fund Name	M.E.R.%	RRSP/Foreign
Money Market:		■	Talvest Money Fund	0.77	RRSP
		■	Talvest Cash Management Fund	1	RRSP
Fixed Income:	Long-term	▲ KO	Talvest Bond Fund	1.98	RRSP
		★ AG	Talvest High Yield Bond Fund	2.12	RRSP
	Short-term	▲ KO	Talvest Income Fund	1.69	RRSP
		■	Talvest Millenium High Income Fund	2.5	
Equity:	Mid-Large Cap	■	Talvest Canadian Equity Value Fund	2.58	RRSP
		★ OK	Talvest Canadian Equity Growth Fund	2.58	RRSP
	Small Cap	★ OK	Talvest Small Cap Canadian Equity Fund	2.7	RRSP
	Other	■	Talvest New Economy	2.5	RRSP
		■	Talvest Canadian Resource Fund	2.75	RRSP
Tax Advantaged:	Dividend	■	Talvest Dividend Fund	2.38	RRSP
	Labor-sponsored	■	Canadian Medical Discoveries Fund	4.7	RRSP
		■	Canadian Science & Technology Growth Fund Inc.	4.7	RRSP
Multi-Asset:	Asset Allocation	▲ AG	Talvest Canadian Asset Allocation Fund	2.44	RRSP
		■	Synchrony Performance RRSP Portfolio	3.15	RRSP
		★ KO	Synchrony Conservative RRSP Portfolio	3.01	RRSP

FOREIGN	Category	Rating	Fund Name	MER%	RRSP/Foreign
Fixed Income:		■	Talvest Foreign Pay Cdn. Bond Fund	2.17	RRSP
Global Equity:	All-global	■	Talvest Global Equity Fund	2.9	Foreign

		■	Talvest Global RRSP Fund	2.52	RRSP
	Specialty	▲ OK	Talvest Global Science & Technology Fund	2.53	Foreign
		▲ OK	Talvest Global Health Care Fund	2.9	Foreign
	Small-cap	■	Talvest Global Small Cap Fund	2.9	Foreign
Regional Equity:	U.S.	▲ OK	Talvest Value Line U.S. Equity Fund	3	Foreign
	Europe	■	Talvest European Fund	3	Foreign
	Far East	■	Talvest Asian Fund	3	Foreign
	China	■	Talvest China Plus Fund	3	Foreign
Global Balanced:		■	Talvest Global Asset Allocation Fund	2.9	Foreign
		■	Synchrony Performance Portfolio	3.2	Foreign
		■	Synchrony Conservative Portfolio	3.02	Foreign
		▲ AG	Synchrony Income & Growth Portfolio	2.84	Foreign

Talvest is the broker-sold sister company of the Canadian Imperial Bank of Commerce, which acquired Talvest's parent company, TAL Global Asset Management, in 1994. However, the operating shareholders retain management control. For now, the intention to take the company public, announced in 1998, is on hold.

TAL itself is gigantic, managing $48 billion for pensions and other clients and acts as subadvisor to some of the no-load funds at CIBC Securities Inc. The company decided to leverage its pension expertise into mutual funds and launched Talvest in 1985 as a broker-sold load fund company. Many of the TAL portfolio managers also manage similar funds for CIBC's no-load line-up.

With competition in the fund industry heating up and new sales becoming more scarce, Talvest has become busy trying to position itself to compete and it has made its presence known in the last year.

Shortly after *Smart Funds 1999* went to print, Talvest joined the fray of fund companies to launch segregated funds. Talvest's Synchrony Funds were launched in September 1998 with Maritime Life Assurance Company and they have tried to distinguish them by adding special bells and whistles such as a daily reset feature that automatically locks in gains in the funds. They are structured as fund-of-fund portfolios, holding a mix of Talvest funds combined to get different asset allocations, from conservative to growth oriented.

Talvest has also simplified its funds by dropping the "Hyperion" label, which was maintained after some Talvest and Hyperion funds were merged.

Talvest also recognizes that in the fund industry where costs are competitive, size matters. In October 1998, it announced that it was buying three mutual funds from Canadian investment counsellor Morrison Williams Investment Management Inc. Of those three small "Millennium" funds, two were merged into existing Talvest funds and one continues as a standalone fund. The Millennium Next Generation Fund was merged with Talvest Canadian Leading Industries Fund and is now managed by Les Williams of Morrison Williams. Millennium Diversified was merged into Talvest Canadian Asset Allocation, which continues to be managed by Jean-Guy Desjardins. Millennium Income Fund continues as is. It invests in royalty trusts, REITs, and other securities that provide investors with a steady income stream.

Talvest also continues to offer some very specialized funds. Both in Canada and globally, it has developed or hired expertise in the fast-growing science and technology and health sciences industries. This also extends to the venture-capital level, through the Canadian Medical Discoveries Fund and the Canadian Science & Technology Growth Fund Inc.

The company's specialty mutual funds have performed well. Talvest Global Science and Technology made strong gains in 1998 and into 1999 and returned 139.5% over one year to August 31, 1999. Talvest Global Health Care has also performed above average since its launch in November 1996.

Talvest has had a strong reputation in fixed-income funds. Of last year's Smart Funds, however, the Talvest High Yield Bond had a disappointing year. But it seems to be coming back nicely.

On the equity side, Talvest Canadian Equity Growth, launched in December 1996, has performed above average since inception. Managed by Denis Ouellet, the fund has been fully invested in Canada, although it can have as much as 20% in the U.S. or elsewhere and it returns as a Smart Fund.

Several funds also return as Noteworthy. One Noteworthy from last year, Talvest U.S. Index Small Cap Fund, was never launched.

Year 2000 Stance

We have been impressed by Talvest, which has been probably the most vocal fund company on how it is approaching investing with Y2K around the corner. As with most fund groups, it is questioning investments to determine which ones are as ready as possible. And they are taking some definite steps in their funds. The managers intend to sell emerging-markets positions as the time draws closer, not because they expect serious problems in those countries, but because they can't get the information they need to assure them that companies have properly dealt with the issue.

Talvest also offers some thoughts for investors, given best- and worst-case scenarios. If you believe in the best-case scenario, make no changes assuming that you are satisfied with your investments. If you want to prepare for the worst case, cashing out and moving back in could be a difficult timing exercise to get right. Instead, it suggests, focus on diversifying among many asset types and re-evaluate your tolerance for short-term market ups and downs. If you are very uncomfortable with the Y2K issue, you should be transferring only a portion of your portfolio into cash and/or a well-diversified balanced mutual fund. Finally, stay away from drastic market timing moves: the cost and opportunity lost are too great.

Smart Funds 2000

Y2K OK

Talvest Canadian Equity Growth. Denis Ouellet continues his top-quartile performance that we originally recognized when he was managing Scotia's Excelsior Growth. The two-year CAGR of 7.1% to August 31 is well ahead of the TSE.

Talvest Small Cap Canadian Equity. Managed by Sebastian von Berkum and fund is first quartile for three and five years ended August 31, 1999. A solid bottom-up stock picker for more than 20 years, we missed this one because Talvest told us last year that the fund would be closed to new investors. This closure was unnecessary when small caps got pummelled in 1998.

Y2K KO

Synchrony Conservative RRSP. See also Y2K Agnostic "Noteworthy" comments under Talvest Canadian Asset Allocation. Same thing applies here with the additional consideration of a seg fund guarantee of initial principal. Whether the 60 basis points premium for the insurance is worth it will depend on whether the unitholder really believes that Y2K could keep markets down for 10 long years. That has happened only in Japan in recent history. Also consider the Synchrony foreign portfolios for foreign-content or non-registered plans.

Y2K Agnostic

Talvest High Yield Bond. After a top performance in 1997, this fund disappointed in 1998, falling into the fourth quartile. We gave it Smart status again because the manager, Chris Currie, has a solid reputation, and focuses on mitigating risk as much as possible. He has returned the fund to first quartile in the first half of 1999. Unfortunately the MER, at 2.12%, is higher than we'd like to see—a definite handicap for it.

Noteworthy Funds

Y2K OK

Talvest Value Line U.S. Equity Fund. This is managed by Alan Hoffman of Value Line Inc., a well-respected U.S. research firm that ranks more than 1,700 U.S. growth funds. The heaviest weightings are expected to remain in technology, financial services, health care, and retail.

Talvest Global Science & Technology Fund. Another strong year for this global sector fund. It gained 139.5% over one year ended August 31, 1999. Managed in-house by TAL's Stephen Kahn, the fund's top 10 holdings include Dell Computer Corp., Sun Microsystems Inc., and Microsoft Corp. at the end of the first quarter 1999. The portfolio is concentrated, holding 30 to 40 stocks.

Talvest Global Health Care Fund. Managed by Edward Owens of Wellington Management Co. U.S. stocks continue to dominate this fund at about 78%, followed by Japan with about 14%. It performed better than average again in 1999, gaining 30.7%. The original of this fund offered by Vanguard has been closed to new investors.

Y2K KO

Talvest Bond. John Braive is considered one of the country's most astute fixed-income managers. His style of spread trading is less aggressive than that of those who try to anticipate interest rate moves. Unfortunately, the fund performed below average versus like funds again in 1998. It was also third quartile in 1996 and 1997.

Y2K Agnostic

Talvest Canadian Asset Allocation Fund. Of all fund families, Talvest is known for its strong emphasis on asset allocation. It has also proved to be one of the most realistic in assessing the risks of Y2K. It was early in calling the U.S. market overvalued and in eschewing emerging markets because of Y2K risk. Unlike a traditional balanced fund, asset allocation funds like this one can move 100% to any given asset class if the managers deem it advisable. That makes this fund the Y2K agnostic fund of choice for Talvest investors. Also consider global version for foreign-content or non-registered portfolios.

Synchrony Income & Growth Portfolio. Refer also to comments under Smart Fund Synchrony Conservative RRSP and to the above comment on Talvest Canadian Asset Allocation Fund. Those with foreign content available who want to stay partially invested in the equity markets but hedge their bets on Y2K may find this a reasonable compromise.

Availability

Full-service and discount brokers and dealers across Canada.

48. TD GREEN LINE FUNDS

NO LOAD

Strengths	Low-MER index funds T. Rowe Price foreign funds Education & support
Weaknesses	Choosing from 43+ funds
RESPs?	Yes
Web Site	www.greenlinefunds.com
Toll Free	1-800-268-8166

CANADIAN	Category	Rating	Fund Name	M.E.R.%	RRSP/Foreign
Money Market:		■	Green Line Canadian Money Market Fund	0.85	RRSP
		■	Green Line Canadian T-Bill Fund	0.85	RRSP
		■	Green Line Premium Money Market Fund	0.3	RRSP
Fixed Income:	Long-term	★ KO	Green Line Canadian Bond Fund	0.94	RRSP
		■	Green Line Real Return Bond Fund	1.53	RRSP
	Short-term	■	Green Line Short Term Income Fund	1.08	RRSP
	Index	▲ KO	Green Line Canadian Government Bond Index	0.8	RRSP
	Mortgage	■	Green Line Mortgage Fund	1.59	RRSP
		■	Green Line Mortgage Backed Fund	1.55	RRSP
Equity:	Mid-Large Cap	■	Green Line Blue Chip Equity Fund	2.25	RRSP
	Mixed cap	■	Green Line Canadian Equity Fund	2.1	RRSP
		■	Green Line Canadian Small-Cap Equity	2.35	RRSP
		■	Green Line Value Fund	2.1	RRSP
	Index	▲ OK	Green Line Canadian Index Fund	0.8	RRSP
Sector:	Gold/precious metal	▲ KO	Green Line Precious Metals Fund	2.12	RRSP
	Resource	■	Green Line Resource Fund	2.12	RRSP
	Other	■	Green Line Energy Fund	2.11	RRSP
Tax Advantaged:	Dividend	■	Green Line Dividend Fund	2	RRSP
		■	Green Line Monthly Income Fund	1.22	RRSP
Multi-Asset:	Balanced	■	Green Line Balanced Growth Fund	1.95	RRSP
		▲ AG	Green Line Balanced Income Fund	1.95	RRSP

FOREIGN	Category	Rating	Fund Name	MER%	RRSP/Foreign
Money Market:		■	Green Line U.S. Money Market Fund	1	RRSP
Fixed Income:		▲ KO	Green Line Global Government Bond Fund	2.08	Foreign
		▲ KO	Green Line Global RSP Bond	2	RRSP

Global Equity:	All-global	▲ OK	Green Line Global Select Fund	2.33	Foreign
	EAFE	■	Green Line International Equity Fund	2.33	Foreign
	EAFE Index	■	Green Line International RSP Index	0.9	RRSP
	Specialty	★ OK	Green Line Science & Technology Fund	2.58	Foreign
		■	GL Entertainment & Communications Fund	2.59	Foreign
		▲ OK	Green Line Health Sciences Fund	2.58	Foreign
Regional Equity:					
	U.S. Large-cap	▲ OK	Green Line U.S. Blue Chip Equity	2.33	Foreign
	U.S. Mid-cap	★ OK	Green Line Mid-Cap Growth Fund	2.33	Foreign
	U.S. Small-cap	■	Green Line U.S. Small-Cap Equity Fund	2.37	Foreign
	U.S. Index	■	Green Line Dow Jones Industrial Average Index	0.8	Foreign
		★ OK	Green Line U.S. Index Fund	0.63	Foreign
		■	Green Line U.S. RSP Index Fund	0.8	RRSP
	Latin American	■	Green Line Latin American Growth Fund	2.6	Foreign
	Emerging Market	■	Green Line Emerging Markets Fund	2.63	Foreign
	Far East	■	Green Line Asian Growth Fund	2.59	Foreign
	Japan	■	Green Line Japanese Growth Fund	2.6	Foreign
	Japan Index	■	Green Line Japanese Index Fund	0.9	Foreign
	Europe	■	Green Line European Growth Fund	2.58	Foreign
		■	GL European Index Fund	0.9	Foreign

After a busy year in 1997 and early 1998, TD was at it again in 1999. The bank announced the addition of four AGF and four Fidelity funds, through all 900 TD bank branches. A few other brand names were expected to be added by year end.

TD clients will open a special TD Asset Accumulator Account, which is administered by TD Waterhouse, TD's discount brokerage arm. The bank branch and all staff licensed to sell TD funds will also sell and advise on these outside funds. The bank will charge usual loads, either back-end or 2.5% upfront.

Since our last edition, TD launched a group of segregated funds, the TD Guaranteed Investment Fund (GIF) which can be purchased only at TD Waterhouse or TD Evergreen and are not available in the bank. When purchased as a portfolio of Green Line funds, the portfolios are automatically rebalanced so investors know they're getting a specific asset allocation.

(TD does boast one of the industry's more sophisticated staff-education programs, which includes an annual exam that all TD representatives must pass. For the fourth year, an independent survey found TD gave the best service of the financial institutions.) It's a good thing they place an emphasis on training, because investors need help choosing with this many funds.

In conjunction with its mutual funds, TD launched the Green Line Managed Assets Program (MAP) in December 1998. The MAP fund of fund portfolios combine a number of TD and third-party funds, the exact combination depends on the goals of the investor. The portfolios are rebalanced automatically and provide investors with semi-annual performance reports that include personal rates of return. This kind of low-maintenance investment plan seems to appeal to TD clients. Within months of the launch, 50,000 MAP accounts were opened with assets over $700 million. (A minimum $2,000 is required for a registered MAP and $5,000 for a non-registered account. The minimum is $25,000 for the fund portfolios that include third-party choices.) MAP portfolios charge a higher annual fee than do the underlying funds if purchased directly. It ranges from 0.60% to 1.05%. Research shows the right asset allocation is very important in getting the best return for the least amount of risk, but investors should consider whether this significant extra fee is worthwhile.

TD has stood firm on the MERs on its index funds. Both Royal Bank and Altamira came out with lower fee index funds last year, a move that some expected would spark a price war on index funds. Instead, TD has maintained its fees and continues to make its funds accessible to more investors by requiring a lower minimum of $100 in its index funds (for RRSP accounts) and $2,000 for non-RRSP accounts.

There were also a few portfolio manager changes since the last edition. Margot Naudie is now managing the resource and energy funds, along with the precious metals fund. She took over from Rob Cassels, who left TD. And Montgomery Asset Management of San Francisco is managing the International Equity Fund, replacing Schroder Capital Management. Scott McGlashan of Perpetual Portfolio Management also replaces Schroder on the Japanese Growth Fund.

TD's actively managed domestic funds are managed either internally by TD Asset Management Inc. or externally by Sceptre Investment Counsel Ltd. and McLean, Budden Ltd.

Generally, our Smart Fund and Noteworthy picks are funds with outside managers, particularly in its global funds. TD was the first bank to recognize that the quickest way to build competent foreign funds is to set up a number of outside subadvisors. It has 10 external advisors around the world, including such respected firms as Morgan Stanley Asset Management Inc. of New York (a pioneer in emerging markets) and T. Rowe Price Associates Inc. of Baltimore, manager of the Green Line Science & Technology. On the downside, external advisors tend to be more pricey—and some of TD's funds are.

Several Green Line funds return as Smart Funds this year, including the above-mentioned Science & Technology, which returned to the top quartile in 1998 and the beginning of 1999, rewarding those who hung in after a tough year in 1997.

Year 2000 Stance

Managers assess Y2K readiness and ask companies to fill out questionnaires. Some companies that were determined to be unprepared or at risk have been removed from portfolios. Alternatively, fund managers have decreased their investments in those questionable companies.

TD believes that the best strategy for individual investors is to have a diversified portfolio. However, it offers some thoughts on the areas of greatest and least risk. By region, and like Talvest, TD considers emerging markets and Asian companies to be higher risk due to a lack of contingency planning; continental Europe to be medium risk; and U.S. and Canadian companies to be lower risk. Fund suggestions to prepare for worst-case scenarios are Canadian and U.S. large-cap growth funds. Process-intensive industries such as banking, telecoms, and utilities are most vulnerable, they believe.

Smart Funds 2000

Y2K OK

Green Line Canadian Index Fund. MER has come down a bit to 0.80%, not quite to Royal's level. But this one has a long-term track record.

Green Line Science & Technology. This one has a five-year CAGR of 33.1% to August 31, 1999, the number one fund in Canada for that period. This is a five-time Smart Fund.

Green Line U.S. Index Fund. This one is priced in U.S. dollars, which makes it unique in Canada. The 0.63% MER is competitive for this fund with a 10-year track record.

Green Line U.S. Mid-Cap Growth Fund. T. Rowe Price manager Brian Berghuis buys rapidly growing, U.S. mid-cap companies. The version of this fund available to U.S. investors has the top five-star rating by the U.S.'s Morningstar rating service. Returns to Smart Fund list after missing in 1999. Fund has a great long-term track record while investing in small- and mid-cap names while the S&P large caps roared ahead.

Y2K KO

Green Line Canadian Bond Fund. Just keeps going as a first-quartile performer with a 0.94% MER.

Noteworthy Funds

Y2K OK

Green Line U.S. Blue Chip Equity. Also managed by T. Rowe Price, this invests in 100 of the biggest, best-known U.S. companies.

Green Line Health Sciences Fund. Managed by T. Rowe Price Associates, Inc., it has had a good run since its launch in October 1996. Most recently it returned 28.4% over one year to August 31.

Green Line Global Select Fund. This global equity fund is managed by Perpetual Portfolio Management Ltd. Investments are mostly large companies and geographic boundaries include Canada. It has performed above average over five years, with an average 13.7% gain at August 31, 1999.

Y2K KO

Green Line Canadian Government Bond Index. This fund tracks the performance of the Scotia Capital Markets Government Bond Index. It invests only in Canadian government bonds and provides income but takes some risk to try and grow the capital as well. It charges a 0.8% MER.

Green Line Global Government Bond Fund. First quartile over two years to August 31, 1999. It is managed by J.P. Morgan Investment Management Inc. in London.

Green Line Global RSP Bond Fund. This one is managed in-house by TD and is fully RRSP-eligible. It invests in Canadian government bonds primarily, but they're denominated in foreign currencies, hence the global exposure. Performance has been consistently above average.

Green Line Precious Metals Fund. For those who believe a Y2K economic crisis will see a recovery in the price of gold bullion.

Y2K Agnostic

Green Line Balanced Income Fund. For investors who want to own one fund with several asset classes, this one combines bonds, Canadian, and global equities. MER is 1.95% and the fund was above average again in 1998 with a 4.1% return. Over one year to June 30, 1999, it had dropped below average with a –1.3% return.

Availability

TD Bank branches and many dealers and full-service and discount brokers.

49. TEMPLETON MANAGEMENT LTD.

FRONT OR REAR

Strengths	All-global equities
	New 100% RRSP eligible global funds
Weaknesses	Canadian funds
	Loss of Michael Price
RESPs?	Yes
Web Site	www.templeton.ca
Toll Free	1-800-387-0830

CANADIAN	Category	Rating	Fund Name	M.E.R.%	RRSP/Foreign
Money Market:		▲ KO	Templeton Treasury Bill Fund	0.75	RRSP
		■	Templeton Treasury Bill GIF	0.8	
Fixed Income:	Long-term	■	Templeton Canadian Bond Fund	1.65	RRSP
Equity:	Mid-Large Cap	■	Templeton Canadian Stock Fund	2.44	RRSP
		■	Templeton Canadian Stock GIF	2.74	
Multi-Asset:	Balanced	■	Templeton Balanced Fund	2.06	RRSP
		★ KO	Templeton Canadian Balanced GIF	2.31	RRSP
	Asset Allocation	■	Templeton Canadian Asset Allocation Fund	2.15	RRSP

FOREIGN	Category	Rating	Fund Name	MER%	RRSP/Foreign
Fixed Income:		■	Templeton Global Bond Fund	2.18	Foreign
Global Equity:	All-global	★ OK	Templeton Growth Fund Ltd.	2.04	Foreign
		▲ AG	Templeton Growth GIF	2.44	
	EAFE	★ OK	Templeton International Stock Fund	2.51	Foreign
		■	Templeton International Stock GIF	2.91	
	Small-cap	■	Templeton Global Smaller Companies Fund	2.71	Foreign
Regional Equity:	U.S.	■	Mutual Beacon Fund	2.5	Foreign
		■	Mutual Beacon GIF	2.9	
	U.S. Small-cap	▲ OK	Franklin U.S. Small Cap Growth Fund	2.5	Foreign
	Emerging Market	▲ OK	Templeton Emerging Markets Fund	3.77	Foreign
Global Balanced:		■	Templeton International Balanced Fund	2.55	Foreign
		▲ AG	Templeton Global Balanced Fund	2.46	Foreign

If you need proof that growth stocks have left value stocks in the dust over the last few years, you need look no further than the global funds of Templeton Management Ltd. These funds, managed with a strict value style, all found themselves at the bottom of the performance scale in 1998, with only one exception, Templeton Emerging Markets. But as of the spring of 1999, the funds have returned to above-average performance as value stocks struggle to make a comeback. And with Y2K upping the chances of market volatility, value funds may not have as far to fall as growth funds in a correction.

The value lag may be hard to stomach in the short term; on the other hand, it proves that Templeton sticks to its philosophy. We think that diligence should win out in the long term. The Smart

Funds philosophy is to find stable, consistent, long-term performing funds that can be held over decades. In this respect, we believe Templeton fits the bill, particularly for global investing. For most investors, that means the 20% foreign-content portion of an RRSP or RRIF, or the unconstrained taxable portfolios.

One of the reasons for Templeton's lag has been its underexposure to the U.S. market. Templeton viewed the U.S. as highly overvalued and moved money out. As the market has continued to climb, it looked like a bad call. The same thing happened 10 years earlier when Japan was so highly valued. Templeton pulled out of the region and for a time appeared foolish—until the bubble burst.

Templeton's value approach to stock picking means it doesn't make "top-down" country-specific decisions at all. It just seeks bargain-priced stocks wherever in the world they might be. Investors get the benefit of a giant research team located in dozens of countries.

New to Templeton this year are a line-up of segregated funds offered with Allianz Insurance Company of North America. These six funds, launched in September 1998, guarantee 100% of the principal invested after 10 years or upon death. As with most segregated funds, investors pay a premium for that guarantee: 48 basis points, for example, in the case of Templeton Growth.

Management of the Templeton funds continues unchanged from a year ago, with one exception. New to Templeton's Toronto office is Jeffrey Sutcliffe, portfolio manager for Templeton Canadian Bond as well as the fixed-income portion of Templeton Canadian Asset Allocation Fund and Templeton Balanced.

In past editions, we have noted the absence of Templeton global funds designed to beat the 20% foreign-content limit in Canadian RRSP and RRIFs. Templeton is catching up to its competitors now and offering the Growth fund and International Stock fund RSP clones. These fund types are very popular as the Canadian market performs poorly relative to the world.

The Templeton Growth Fund Ltd. Linked Notes were issued by TD Bank in time for RRSP season. These notes are structured to provide holders with rates of return comparable to TGF, but are not considered to be foreign property under the Income Tax Act. On the downside, investors pay a sizeable premium over the usual 2.04% MER of the fund. The notes sold very well, so the companies may issue them again in 2000. Investors willing to pay a lofty price for foreign exposure can watch for those.

Despite a tough period, Templeton's core global equity funds are Smart Funds again this year. Templeton Growth, the largest fund sold in Canada with about $10 billion has a reasonable 2.04% MER, making it a prudent way to access 97% of the world's stock markets. Manager Mark Holowesko has a solid track record and has stuck to his style: he's said repeatedly that he would prefer to leave some gains behind than take on too much risk in highly valued markets.

Templeton International Stock has a more expensive 2.51% MER, but a sparkling track record up until 1998. In 1999, its year-to-date performance was back above average as of the end of June.

Templeton Emerging Markets has been demoted because of the Y2K risk to emerging markets and its costly 3.77% MER.

And Templeton's Canadian offerings? We're less enthusiastic about these with their average performance and above-average MERs. Nevertheless, we have designated the seemingly Y2K-bulletproof Templeton Canadian Balanced GIF as a new Y2K KO Smart Fund.

Year 2000 Stance

In developed countries such as the United States, managers are relying in part on documents filed with regulators but attempting to independently confirm how ready companies are by talking to the company's themselves, related companies such as suppliers, and securities analysts.

In emerging market countries, managers are relying on publicly available information as well as their own assessments. Those are made by asking companies critical questions about how ready they are. But these precautions are not guarantees, Templeton says: "As with much in emerging markets, information about an issuer's or an industry's Year 2000 readiness may be very spotty. Financial reporting and auditing standards are far less developed and formal than in the U.S. and developed markets." They add, "Even where personal relationships are good, the ability to independently verify information will be limited." But they expect the problems to be mitigated to some extent, by the lower level of computerization on the one hand and the newness of computer systems on the other. That's not to say the broader issue of infrastructure readiness should be minimized.

As long-term investors, Templeton believes that well-managed companies are more likely to have appropriate plans in place. But no company can assure readiness of all its suppliers, public utilities, and communication and transportation systems, Templeton points out.

Smart Funds 2000

Y2K OK

Templeton Growth. (If concerned about Y2K, buy the GIF version.)

Clearly this fund has struggled of late. See its competitor AGF International Value for how much it was behind. Still it is hard to bet against a 45-year track record of double-digit returns. MER just doesn't come down even though fund is now $10.9 billion. Which means the gross revenue to Templeton on this fund is over $20 million. Fund is a five-time Smart Fund. Look for RSP version.

Templeton International. We prefer Templeton Growth because it has more North American content and is therefore less exposed to Y2K downside risk in less developed and less prepared markets. This one is a four-time Smart Fund and is first quartile over the three, five, and 10 years ended August 31, 1999. Look for RSP version.

Y2K KO

Templeton Canadian Balanced GIF. Templeton's value approach, the traditional balanced fund asset mix and a downside insurance protection to boot, all at a tolerable 2.31% MER, provides a Y2K harbour to those who still want some upside from equity markets. For those who don't, retreat to the T-Bill fund or its seg equivalent.

Noteworthy Funds

Y2K OK

Franklin U.S. Small Cap Growth Fund. Managed by Edward Jamieson at Franklin Advisors Inc., this fund performed above the average U.S. small-cap portfolio over one and two years to August 31.

Templeton Emerging Markets. Demoted because of Y2K risk in emerging markets and a high MER. As TAL has demonstrated, most emerging markets countries are not Y2K ready and the risks of emerging markets funds without segregated protection are too great under any but a Y2K OK scenario.

Y2K KO

Templeton Treasury Bill Fund. Cash is king if you're an unvarnished Y2K pessimist.

Y2K Agnostic

Templeton Growth GIF. Templeton's global research team, value approach to investing and a seg fund guarantee, all at an MER comparable to rival global equity funds with no downside protection.

Templeton Global Balanced Fund. Better alternative than the EAFE version, because this has more North American content, and North

America is better prepared for Y2K. This consumes foreign content; for domestic content, consider Templeton's Canadian balanced funds, either in GIF or non-GIF format.

Availability

Full-service and discount brokers and planners across Canada. London Life distributes Templeton International, Emerging Markets and the Treasury Bill funds. $500 minimum initial purchase per fund; $2,500 for the Treasury Bill fund.

50. TRIMARK INVESTMENT MANAGEMENT INC. FRONT OR REAR LOAD

Strengths Reasonable MERs
New 100% RRSP eligible foreign funds.
New seg funds

Weaknesses Size of Canadian equity funds

RESPs? Yes

Web Site www.trimark.com **Toll Free** 1-800-387-9845

CANADIAN	Category	Rating	Fund Name	M.E.R.%	RRSP/Foreign
Money Market:		■	Trimark Interest Fund	0.75	RRSP
		■	Trimark Interest Segregated	0.75	RRSP
Fixed Income:	Long-term	▲ KO	Trimark Canadian Bond Fund	1.24	RRSP
		■	Trimark Canadian Bond Segregated	1.44	RRSP
		★ KO	Trimark Advantage Bond Fund	1.24	RRSP
		■	Trimark Advantage Bond Segregated	1.44	RRSP
	Short-term	■	Trimark Government Income Fund	1.24	RRSP
		■	Trimark Government Income Segregated	1.44	RRSP
Equity:	Mid-Large cap	▲ OK	Trimark Canadian Fund	1.52	RRSP
		■	Trimark RSP Equity Fund	2	RRSP
		■	Trimark Select Canadian Growth Fund	2.35	RRSP
		■	Trimark Select Canadian Growth Segregated	2.8	RRSP
		▲ OK	Trimark Enterprise Fund	New	RRSP
	Small-cap	■	Trimark Canadian Small Companies Fund	2.4	RRSP
		■	Trimark Canadian Small Companies Segregated	3.2	RRSP
		▲ OK	Trimark Enterprise Small Cap Fund	New	RRSP
	Resources	■	Trimark Canadian Resources Fund	2.4	RRSP
		■	Trimark Canadian Resources Segregated	3.2	RRSP
Multi-Asset:	Balanced	★ AG	Trimark Income Growth Fund	1.56	RRSP
		■	Trimark Select Balanced Fund	2.25	RRSP
		▲ KO	Trimark Select Balanced Segregated	2.7	RRSP

FOREIGN	Category	Rating	Fund Name	MER%	RRSP/Foreign
Global Equity:	All-global	★ OK	Trimark Fund	1.52	Foreign
		▲ OK	Trimark Select Growth Fund	2.35	Foreign
		■	Trimark Select Growth Segregated	2.81	Foreign
	Specialty	▲ OK	Trimark Discovery Fund	2.65	Foreign
		■	Trimark Discovery Fund Segregated	3.5	Foreign
Regional Equity:					
	NAFTA/N.Am.	■	The Americas Fund	2.7	Foreign
		■	The Americas Segregated	3.5	Foreign
	Far East	▲ OK	Trimark Indo-Pacific Fund	2.95	Foreign
		■	Trimark Indo-Pacific Segregated	3.75	Foreign
	Europe	■	Trimark Europlus Fund	2.5	Foreign
		■	Trimark Europlus Segregated	3.4	Foreign

What a year for Trimark! Facing redemptions out of its funds amounting to hundreds of millions of dollars each month, Canada's once-favourite fund company undertook an overhaul of its money management team in an attempt to win back investors.

As recently as 1997, Trimark ruled as the brokers' and investors' favourite and was considered to have a bulletproof brand. But in 1998 the consensus changed and the strong net sales turned into net redemptions for the first time since 1991. Many investors have already left Trimark but more investors have held on and they are already seeing some of the benefits of changes at Trimark, as well as a changing stock market that is starting to recognize some of the value stocks that Trimark buys.

After months of insisting there was no problem at the firm, Trimark executives finally took action in January 1999. In the midst of RRSP season, it replaced Vito Maida, VP of Canadian equities, who had spent several years managing Trimark's multi-billion-dollar Canadian equity funds. With Maida's departure, Trimark's Ian Hardacre and Carmen Veloso took over the Trimark Canadian Fund. As of October 1998, Trimark managers Keith Graham and Geoff MacDonald had taken over the Trimark RSP Equity Fund.

Trimark also added some new recruits to the team. In April 1999, Heather Hunter, wife of Mackenzie Financial's CEO Jim Hunter, joined Trimark from the Ontario Teachers' Pension Plan Board to manage the third fund, Trimark Select Canadian Growth.

But it didn't stop there. Trimark raided two of its competitors and managed to woo away several seasoned managers. To broaden its Canadian equity line-up, Catherine (Kiki) Delaney and her partner, Lynn Miller, were hired as advisors to two new funds: Trimark Enterprise and Trimark Enterprise Small Cap. Delaney Capital had to end its agreement with Spectrum United Mutual Funds to manage for Trimark. Working with Trimark was an offer too good to pass up, Delaney told the press. She uses an approach similar to Trimark's: investing in stocks that offer growth potential, but only at a reasonable price. Analysts say her style differs slightly because she gives more emphasis to growth potential and uses themes she sees in the market to guide her investments.

On the international side, the rehiring of Bill Kanko, also in April 1999, was a coup for Trimark. He had been lured away from Mackenzie Financial Corp., one of Trimark's biggest rivals. Kanko is well acquainted with Trimark. Between 1985 and 1994 he was lead manager on the Trimark Fund and Trimark Select Growth Fund. He will help to manage and oversee the international side, freeing up Trimark chairman Bob Krembil to oversee the entire investment team.

Also new to the international side, Trimark hired Judith Adams in March 1999 to help manage the Trimark Fund and Trimark Select Growth. She comes from Sceptre Investment Counsel Ltd., where she was responsible for European equity research and investing. The firm also lured Jim Young away from Royal Bank to launch a new U.S. equity fund.

With all this change, the question is, how soon will Trimark and investors see the results? As of late June 1999, some already have. With the beginning of a recovery of resource stocks, the three Trimark Canadian funds have performed very well so far in 1999. So well, in fact, that Trimark Canadian and Trimark Select Canadian Growth were once again top-quartile funds over one year to August 31.

One of Trimark's strengths continues to be the low MERs on many of its funds and many of those stayed put in the last year. Trimark Canadian, for example, is a relative bargain at 1.52%. It has been cheap because it is sold with a front load: investors pay the commission at the time of sale. But Trimark intends to make it available with a deferred load and that version will come with a higher MER, the company says. Existing investors will continue to pay the lower MER. For new investors buying this fund, we suggest the front-load version, with as low a transaction fee as you can negotiate with your broker (it is negotiable between 0% to 5%). If you buy the deferred version, you'll be paying the higher MER for as long as you own the fund, even after the sliding redemption scale expires down to 0%.

By contrast, some of the specialty international funds are more expensive, ranging from 2.5% for Europlus to 2.95% for Trimark Indo-Pacific. The Trimark Fund is still a bargain at 1.52%.

Trimark's 13 segregated funds had just been launched when last year's edition came out. The extra cost of the guarantee on the underlying Trimark funds varies depending on the fund. The cost is 20 basis points (0.20 of a percentage point) on the Advantage Bond fund, for example: 1.24% on the mutual fund and 1.44% on the segregated fund, up to an additional 80 basis points on specialty funds such as Trimark Indo-Pacific.

We know many investors have already left Trimark. For those that haven't, we believe they will benefit from a variety of managers. Trimark still does not offer the style diversification that other large families do, such as Mackenzie and C.I., and they have no plans to do so. Krembil says the company's problems led them to extensively review Trimark's value investing style and they remain dedicated to it. He says the company does not want to become the "Heinz 57 of mutual funds." Because value and growth styles come in and out of favour, we would suggest that Trimark investors, who own these funds alone, consider diversifying by style and include some growth-oriented equity funds from another family. For conservative investors, the value style may suit just fine because they tend to not fall as hard in market corrections. In October, Trimark announced 100% RRSP eligible versions of its Select Growth, Discovery, Americas, Indo-Pacific and Europlus Funds.

Year 2000 Stance

As part of the investment process, managers evaluate management. They have integrated Y2K concerns into the due-diligence process by asking management about Y2K readiness. Companies have also been asked to fill out surveys. As of May, Trimark had not seen fit to sell any of its investments due to concerns about Y2K. But the company will continue to monitor readiness by the companies it holds in the funds.

Smart Funds 2000

Y2K OK

Trimark Fund. The Trimark Fund maintains its Smart status. It had fourth-quartile performance in 1998, but is performing above average so far in 1999. The authors believe that even the best money managers have bad years, usually because the equity or bond market movements were opposite of their particular strategy. Also, the addition of Bill Kanko bodes well for all of Trimark's international funds. Five-time Smart Fund.

Y2K Agnostic

Trimark Income Growth Fund. Returns as a Smart Fund for its fifth appearance, based on it having one of the lowest MERs in the

Canadian balanced fund universe at 1.56%, and its long-term track record. Some recent investors in the fund may not agree, given that it performed well below average in 1997 and 1998. But performance is improving in 1999 as it has returned to first quartile for the year ended August 31, 1999.

Y2K KO

Trimark Advantage Bond Fund. Back for its third consecutive year on the Smart Funds list. Patrick Farmer has directed it to first-quartile performance over the three years ended August 31, 1999.

Noteworthy Funds

Y2K OK

Trimark Canadian Fund. A low MER, and a consistent value approach, the fund has been a top performer thus far in 1999 and is now managed by Ian Hardacre and Carmen Velosa.

Trimark Enterprise and Enterprise Small-Cap. These funds have just been launched, but they are Noteworthy based on the experience and track record of newly hired Catherine "Kiki" Delaney and her team. Unfortunately, their MERs are expected to be higher than some of the other Trimark favourites.

Trimark Discovery Fund. Rick Serafini's focus on U.S. technology firms has put this fund ahead of the U.S.-based Russell index. As of August 31, 1999, it had returned 84.8% over one year and 23% on average over three years.

Trimark Indo-Pacific Fund. A Smart Fund in previous years, we question why pay high MERs to make regional bets when the low-MER Trimark Fund has a great long-term track record. Note that emerging markets and Asian funds are vulnerable under any but a Y2K OK scenario.

Y2K KO

Trimark Canadian Bond Fund. Consistently an above-average performer and it is a bargain with a 1.24% MER.

Trimark Select Balanced Segregated. Short of retreating entirely to the Interest Fund, this one provides some growth possibilities through equities, plus a healthy mix of cash and fixed income, all underpinned by a seg fund guarantee. Total MER of 2.7% cannot be justified in any but a Y2K century-change transition. Once the dust settles, make new purchases in Y2K Agnostic Smart Fund Trimark Income Growth, which has a far more reasonable MER.

Availability

Full-service and discount brokers, financial planners across Canada, and through some insurance sales agents.

The 100 Smart Funds

Once an investment strategy is in place, the investor is faced with the difficult task of selecting the individual funds that will make up his or her portfolio. This section contains details of the 100 funds that we feel comfortable recommending to family and friends. We call these Smart Funds.

There are six criteria for selecting a Smart Fund. Although performance is a key criterion, it is not the only one. Furthermore, absolute performance is not that important. It is relative performance that is critical. We have represented this by ranking the Smart Funds against other funds in that asset category. This apples-to-apples comparison allows us to assemble the more than 2,000 funds sold in Canada into manageable groups. We can then maintain a watch over money managers with similar styles and mandates to determine who emerges as the best of the bunch.

We are renowned for our inclusion of funds with less than three years' performance history. In certain instances, this has forced a compromise of the criteria used on the more mature funds. However, we would be remiss if we did not identify some of the extraordinary money management talent that Canadian fund companies have developed or hired in recent years. Securities regulations make it difficult for fund companies to advertise the past track records of managers without including reams of disclaimers. This is appropriate, because past performance is not a guarantee of future performance, and the investing circumstances surrounding the new fund may be different from the old fund's. Still, we cannot ignore a manager's successful past, and we do have a bias towards managers who have proven track records.

SELECTION CRITERIA

Quartile ranking is the prime performance measure. Examining performance relative to a fund's category peers, both in compound and in annual returns, allows for a more broad-based evaluation than the use of raw return numbers. Consistent, top-quartile performance over several periods is sought. Quartile rankings are determined by ranking the funds by their return numbers and then grouping the top 25 per cent into the first tranche, or quartile, the next 25 per cent into the second quartile, and so on. A mutual fund that can consistently achieve first- or second-quartile rankings will generate superior long-term returns for its owners.

Management expense ratio (MER) is calculated by dividing the total annual expenses of the fund by the fund's assets. Currently, there is a wide range of MERs, even within the same asset classes. Good-quality management must come at a reasonable price. These expenses are always deducted from the fund before the returns are calculated. Recognizing that higher fees erode your returns, we will tilt to lower fees and have included good index fund choices for cost conscious investors.

Asset size is considered relative to the fund's asset type and its mandate. For example, small bond funds face a price disadvantage against larger bond funds, which, because of their size, can negotiate lower commissions. Likewise, small-cap funds with a large asset pool may find it difficult to move in and out of the stocks they want.

When funds are being selected for income-oriented portfolios, the distribution of income and capital gains is a key criterion. Monthly distributions are preferred.

The authors conduct interviews with hundreds of money managers a year. These meetings are designed to confirm stated positions on style, explore the reasons behind past success (or lack of it) and ensure adherence to a stated methodology. This qualitative process balances the other quantitative aspects of fund selection.

SMART FUND LEGEND

There are many different pieces of information that are important to an investor when he or she is selecting a fund. We have included only the most important in each Smart Fund overview. Most do not need an explanation, but we'd like to touch on a few.

Fund manager: The person or team listed is the principal decision maker on the fund–the individual responsible for achieving the fund's performance. You could call these the Smart Managers. These managers are the best in Canada and should be on anyone's all-star team. The individual named is in-house, unless a subadviser is noted.

RRSP eligibility: 100 per cent indicates that the fund is fully eligible; 20 per cent means it can be in an RRSP or RRIF as part of your foreign content. It is paramount that Canadian investors increase their international exposure to enhance their returns and lower their portfolio risk. Where applicable, we indicate if the fund has a 100% RSP-eligible clone with "RSP Version Available" in parentheses next to the fund's name.

Management style: *Equity style can be one of the following:*

- Bottom-up, growth. The manager selects stocks based on their growth potential.
- Bottom-up, value. The manager selects stocks based on price.
- Top-down, growth. The manager selects for the growth potential of an industry, sector or geographic region.
- Sector rotator. The manager moves between industry sectors to capture growth.
- Growth at a reasonable price, or GARP. This is a blend of growth and value.

Fixed-income managers can adopt one of two styles, or a blend of the two:

- Interest rate anticipation. Managers endeavour to predict the direction of interest rates, and structure the fund to take advantage of this movement.
- Spread trading. Managers trade bonds to capture the differences between the interest rates of bonds of different credit qualities.

We fear many Canadians do not consider style diversification when selecting funds. Often they own funds that are very similar in performance and volatility.

Risk: Most investors are uncomfortable with a fund that is volatile, one that changes in value frequently and dramatically, with loss of money being especially disturbing. Therefore, we look at the maximum loss that has been experienced by a fund over a three-month period of time. These quarters are not calendar quarters; they are rolling three-month periods: January, February, March would be the first quarter of the year; February, March, April would be the second rolling quarter; March, April, May the third rolling quarter. There are ten of these rolling quarters in a year.

REMEMBER: these only show paper losses. Actual losses for an individual only occur when a sale is realized and could also be affected by taxes and commissions. We have also indicated how the fund has done over any 12-month holding period. Keep in mind that these are short periods for holding equity funds, but still useful for demonstrating volatility. Investing in equity funds means accepting these short-term rocky rides in order to gain the long-term benefits.

We've also used the three-month time period to look at a fund's worst and best performances. The worst three-month performance for an older fund is often the three months ended September 1990. This risk indicator lets you see the fund at its worst and at its best.

Performance: The graph compares the growth of a $1,000 investment in the fund, an appropriate benchmark and Canada Savings Bonds. The dots on the graph represent the fund's quartile performance in each calendar year. Beneath the graph are the fund's annual returns for each of the past nine calendar years and for the eight months ending August 31, 1999. We have also calculated the compound returns for the period ending August 31, 1999.

Notice on the graphs where sometimes the index outperforms the fund. This usually means that the fund has recovered or made a manager change. When we talk long term it can be enlightening to see performance over long-term time periods.

Smart Fund History: Our goal is to provide our readers with a list of Smart Funds that investors are confident will be long-term consistent winners. Thus, we have included the fund's Smart Fund "track record" indicating in which years the Fund had been previously awarded the prestigious Smart Fund moniker.

CANADIAN EQUITY FUNDS

For most Canadians, a significant portion of their core portfolio should be in mid- to large-cap Canadian equity funds. This is not because the Canadian market has outperformed other markets (it has not), but because:

- most Canadian investors are investing ultimately to spend in Canadian dollars;
- there is a familiarity with the companies that are chosen for investment; and

- most investors are saving in their RRSPs, which are governed by foreign-content rules.

Over the longer term, Canadian equities have outperformed Canadian bonds, so a core equity base is essential for long-term wealth accumulation.

Small-cap stocks are not for the conservative investor, or at least not as a significant portion of a portfolio. Although they have a history of outperforming large-cap stocks over the long term, when they move down, they can go down a lot. However, Canada is becoming internationally recognized for its small-cap opportunities. Once dominated by junior oils, the sector is diversifying as our expertise in computer systems and software grows. But small-cap investing is a skill. The managers often rely on their own research, culled from a wide variety of services that help them find that company or niche which is still largely undiscovered. The attraction is the huge potential for growth when the manager is right. Mutual funds are a natural vehicle for most investors who want to participate in this area of the market. The stocks are volatile, and owning a diversified portfolio will lessen the impact.

CANADIAN DIVIDEND FUNDS

Generally, dividend funds should be considered only by those investors who need to generate income from their non-RRSP portfolios. This is because dividends are taxed at 75 per cent of the rate that applies to interest income from bonds and GICs. The major difference between dividend funds is the percentage of dividends coming from preferred stock. Preferred stock is issued with a fixed dividend rate, making it possible for an investor to determine what the return will be. And there is greater security in preferred stock. A company must first pay its debt (bond) holders, and next in line are the preferred shareholders. Common equity holders are last in this hierarchy. In slower economic times, companies can suspend common equity payments without any obligation to make these payments in the future. Rarely do they suspend preferred equity payments. If they do, they must pay the preferred dividends in arrears before any payments can be made to common shareholders. The trade-off is that, in good times, you could enjoy capital gains from common equity. The funds with a higher percentage of dividends from preferred stock will underperform in rising markets, but they are the choice for those who want a higher degree of income certainty and less price volatility.

SPECIALTY FUNDS

These funds must be considered only in the context of a diversified portfolio. They are volatile, but investing in these funds wisely can enhance performance and reduce risk, since many behave differently from broader market funds.

We have moved all regional and sector funds into one category. We are benchmarking these for a Canadian investor to the TSE300. These are personal risky asset allocations made by the investor, who could have just as easily bought a low-cost index fund.

BALANCED FUNDS

Holding balanced funds is convenient. Ideally, investors should make their own decisions about asset mix, and then invest with managers who specialize in equity or fixed income. If you do not have the time to do this, put the decision in the hands of those who do it for a living.

There are essentially two types of balanced funds. Most are strategic asset-allocation funds. These funds have fixed minimum and maximum percentages of stock and bond holdings. This type of fund is best suited to the more conservative investor. The tactical asset-allocation funds can make more extreme bets. Their managers can be 100 per cent in an asset class if they believe in it strongly enough to make such a decision. This type of balanced fund is clearly for the more risk-tolerant investor. International balanced funds have the same benefits as their domestic counterparts but include the benefit of geographic and currency diversification.

U.S. EQUITY FUNDS

Too often Canadians feel they have to look across an ocean to get international investing exposure. The truth is that just south of the border, Canada has the largest capital market in the world. For many, this market should represent a first step in global investing and serve as a significant portion of their international allocation over time.

The U.S. economy, in global terms, is not as big as it once was. However, it still represents approximately 40 per cent of the global economy. Many of the world's largest and most successful companies are headquartered in the U.S. Many are multinational and derive much of their revenue from international activity. By investing in them, managers get international exposure without having to invest in less-regulated markets.

In addition, the U.S. has a fertile small-cap market. The

entrepreneurial spirit in the U.S. is such that good ideas and talented people find the money to develop business propositions.

INTERNATIONAL EQUITY FUNDS

Global equity funds should be in almost everyone's portfolio. The Canadian equity market represents only 3 to 4 per cent of world capital markets, and it is prudent to look outside Canada when building a properly diversified portfolio. Yet with the potential for increased return comes the potential for increased risk. Therefore, we favour globally diversified funds rather than regionally specific funds. Investors can enhance their portfolio returns while minimizing their reliance on any one region. Another reason to invest internationally is to diversify away from the Canadian dollar. Many people are concerned about the loonie losing its competitiveness; international investing is one way of protecting against that loss.

Ideally, every growth-oriented portfolio should include some emerging market exposure. However, the volatility that will be experienced by these funds means that anyone who finds such movement unsettling should steer clear. Broad-based emerging market funds, rather than their region-specific cousins, are the best way to take advantage of the areas around the world that will experience greater economic growth than more mature economies. The political instability and economic crises that exist in these regions will continue to cause short- to mid-term performance to remain uncertain.

EUROPEAN EQUITY FUNDS

Europe is a region familiar to most investors; there is a sense of comfort with business practices and cultures there. We believe, however, that Europe represents the most conservative international step outside of North America. These countries are not in the same economic cycle at the same time. There is an opportunity to invest during times when the other mature markets are out of cycle, and thereby enhance a portfolio's return and lower its risk. Most of the funds in this section have looked at the eastern European markets and are at various stages of investing in them. However, these countries are considered emerging markets, and the area is still seen as risky. Europe itself is undergoing tremendous changes that bode well for investors. We don't know what the impacts of the European Monetary Union and a recent movement toward running companies in the interest of shareholders will mean, but it should be positive.

CANADIAN BOND FUNDS

Most of the excitement and glamour in mutual funds surrounds equity funds. But investing in bonds, mortgages and other fixed-income products can also be lucrative. This was certainly the case as rates came down in the early 1990s. The reverse is also true, as too many found out the hard way in 1994.

Just as there are many different types of equity funds, there are also differences among bond funds. The three key considerations are term to maturity, credit quality and style.

Average term to maturity measures a bond portfolio's sensitivity to interest rate fluctuations. The longer the bond fund's term to maturity, the more sensitive the fund is to these moves. Most bond fund managers have the flexibility to shorten or lengthen their term. There are a growing number that simply focus on short-term (five years and under), and a few that have remained committed to longer-term (eight years and more).

The second consideration is credit quality. Credit quality is expressed in terms of As and Bs. The highest quality is AAA. National governments often get this top rating. Most Canadian mutual funds invest across the range of A- to AAA-rated bonds.

Finally, there is style. There are two main styles in bond management: interest rate anticipation and spread trading. An interest rate anticipator has an opinion on where interest rates are headed. If the manager believes that rates are going up, he or she will shorten the average term to maturity. A spread trader focuses on credit quality and the prices of the bonds. The lower the credit rating, the higher the interest rate the issuer pays to compensate the investor for the increased risk.

In looking for a Smart Bond Fund, there are two more considerations: size and price. In fact, price (MER) usually goes down as the size goes up. The debt market is huge. Those who trade bonds make a little on each transaction. Those with bigger amounts to buy and sell can demand better prices. As a rule of thumb, a bond fund under $100 million is going to find it hard to compete. Ideally, a bond fund should have $500 million or more under management. Bond funds charging more than 2 per cent are not competitive; 1 per cent is ideal.

Tip: For those seeking higher yield, consider allocating a portion of your assets to bond funds that invest in corporates. Trimark Advantage and Talvest High Yield are both Smart Funds again this year.

INTERNATIONAL BOND FUNDS

The criteria reviewed in the Canadian bond funds section are also applicable to international bond funds. Currency is an important fourth variable. Today's securities markets make it possible to buy bonds issued in German marks or British pounds, without exposure to either of these currencies, through hedging. If, in the opinion of the manager, the currency of the bond is likely to be weak against the unit holder's currency, the international bond fund manager will try to manage the currencies defensively. The benefits of international bond investing are similar to those of international equity investing. Economic markets around the world are at different stages and hence will have interest rates that differ from Canada's. Global bond managers can take advantage of many more investment opportunities to hedge the return, or reduce the risk, in their portfolios.

Tip: Global bonds do offer diversification from our own market. Be careful using up valuable foreign content space in your RSP with foreign bonds. You want to use that slot for international equities. Our Smart Fund, Guardian Foreign Income is considered Canadian content.

MONEY MARKET FUNDS

For most investors, in most time periods, these funds should be used as a temporary parking place for money to be spent or invested in the near term. If cash is to be spent within two years, a money market fund is a low-risk investment vehicle until the purchase date arrives.

Often investors will sit on the sidelines, waiting for the right time to invest. We believe, and a number of studies in the U.S. confirm this view, that rather than trying to assess the right time, it is best just to make a move and get into the market. Market timing is a mug's game. Alternatively, for the cautious, a dollar-cost-averaging, automatic investment program could be used to gradually invest cash. Academic studies show that this type of dollar cost averaging under performs lump sum investing.

Our unique Year 2000 consideration has increased the interest in money market funds. We believe that those with an asset allocation in place for their long-term investment goals should stay the course. For the more wary, moving a large part of your portfolio to money market for the next several months may feel more comfortable. We don't advise this, but human nature being what it is, we accept some will choose this strategy. Our tip for those nervous investors, is be cautious of your potential tax liability before selling and pick a date now when you will reinvest the funds. Don't seduce yourself into thinking you can perfectly time when to get back into the market. No on can do that!

Money market funds generally invest in the highest quality, Government of Canada treasury bills. The net asset value per share (NAVPS) is fixed at $10, and the total return is from interest earned. Barring a sudden and severe shift in interest rates, the NAVPS should not fluctuate.

There are two things to keep in mind when shopping for a money market fund. If investing on a deferred sales charge (DSC) basis, use that fund family's money market fund to avoid redemption charges.

On the other hand, if you are looking only for a money market fund to hold some money prior to purchase, shop for the one that has the lowest fee, but that is still convenient to purchase. If this is the only investment you are making, you should not pay more than 0.75 per cent in annual fees.

Money market funds can also represent the cash component of a portfolio. Cash plays two important roles in building an investment portfolio. First, cash, or money market, is the safest mutual fund investment, and its low volatility will add stability to a portfolio that includes riskier funds. Second, money market funds provide liquidity. Investors can be left unprepared when a personal event occurs that requires a part of their portfolio to be sold. Money market funds can be sold quickly with no loss of principal, and when other investments may be temporarily down in price. Additionally, they will not generate a taxable capital gain. Without a money market fund, the alternative may be selling a fund with a good unrealized gain, only because of the emergency, leaving the investor exposed to a potential tax bill.

Tip: For most investors, the money market fund they use will be determined by the other mutual fund investments they make and by the major fund families they have selected. Therefore, we do not recommend any specific money market funds as Smart Funds. However, if you are shopping only for a money market fund, consider it a form of bond fund and pay attention to the size and MER of the fund.

THE TOP SIX FUND FAMILIES—OUR SELECT CIRCLE

There are a few fund families that stand out from the competition. We are less focused on the loads now because most discount brokerages have eliminated front-end commissions. However, the distinction is still important for the channel from which you buy.

Of the fund companies that sell through brokers and dealers, the companies we feel deserve special recognition are: **AIM Funds of Canada, Fidelity Investments, and CI.**

Of the no-load fund families, **Bissett** and **PH&N** are back again demonstrating consistent and often superior performance, low MERs and solid long-term management teams. **Scudder**, too is back again this year, but even stronger with the addition of its newly purchased sister company, Maxxum.

Our choices were based not only on the number of Smart or Noteworthy Funds each company held, although this was a significant factor, but also on the scope of funds in all asset classes, the range of management styles, the level of support to clients as determined by outside consultants, the depth of management talent and experience, and the extent of communications with clients and advisers.

Fidelity has the most momentum of any fund family. They have effectively leveraged off their strength as the world's largest mutual fund company and are now the dealers' choice. Fidelity has demonstrated strong performance across core asset classes like Canadian equities, Canadian balanced, International equities, U.S. equities and European equities with more Smart Funds, six than any other firm. It has started to bring down many of the MERs to be comparable to, if not slightly ahead, of its load competitors. Fidelity has a passion and commitment for equity performance and will not scrimp on expenses in its quest for excellence.

In previous years, both C.I. Funds and BPI had several Smart Funds. Independently, they were competitive, but never quite made it to our Select Circle. With the acquisition of BPI this past summer, CI has vaulted to the upper echelon of the fund industry. The combined force now has eight Smart Funds (although full transferability is not yet available), a plethora of seg funds, multiple manager styles and a solid group of noteworthy sector funds.

AIM has been quietly coming on in the Canadian scene. Month after month the firm has added assets in a tough mutual fund market. It has several high performing Smart Funds and has several noteworthy and up and coming funds. The Company's parent company AMVESCAP, plc. is committed to growing brand, presence and assets in Canada. Watch for more great things from this fund family over the next couple of years.

Bissett returns with its group of strong Smart Funds and has made a smooth transition with the retirement of founder David Bissett and evolving to becoming a publicly-listed company.

We have been big supporters of PH&N's quiet investment success from our first edition. The Company has the most 5-time Smart Funds and in the core Canadian categories they are hard to deny. The steep entry minimum, low availability through brokers and dealers combined with only average foreign content funds reinforces our fund family approach–you need more than one fund company to build a portfolio.

Scudder's low MERs made it attractive even if they couldn't gather assets. This could now be considered a hybrid as its funds will be offered through all channels with dealers being compensated. Future.MERs may be higher. The addition of Maxxum with Janus Capital as subadvisor, makes this one of the most compelling fund offerings in Canada.

Our hats off to Janus Capital as our fund subadvisor firm of the year with Smart Funds Maxxum Global Equity, Maxxum American Equity, London Life American Equity, London Life Global Equity. Warren Lammert phenomenal performance on the two American equity products makes him the 2000 Smart Fund Manager of the Year.

ABC FUNDAMENTAL VALUE

NO LOAD

Primary Objective: Growth
Sponsor: I.A. Michael Investment Counsel
Fund Manager: Irwin A. Michael
Style: Bottom-up
Size (MMs): $266.375
RRSP: 100%
Expense Ratio: 2.00%

COMMENTS

The ABC funds require an investment of $150,000 and are generally unavailable from dealers and discount brokerages. Irwin Michael has not disappointed his unitholders and has survived some rough short-term volatility in his sector, returning the fund to top performance. Mr. Michael's eclectic style finds him investing all over. Be clear, this is not a staid blue-chip fund with Bell Canada and the banks. With no money spent on marketing, the low number of unitholders, and no trailers paid to brokers, the MER seems a bit high at 2%. A top-quartile performer in almost every calendar year since 1990, this is a solid holding for the affluent. The fund's 10-year return number of 14% makes it the number two Canadian equity fund in the country. **Smart Fund History: 1999, 1998, 1997, 1996.**

RISK

How Often Money was Lost:.....41 of 116 Months
.....34 of 114 Quarters
.....19 of 105 Years
Worst 3 Months: .....-26.87% (1998)
Best 3 Months: 40.09% (1993)

ASSET ALLOCATION

Paper & Forest products 21.5
Financial services 13.1
Industrial products 12
Merchandising 11
Oil & Gas 10.1
Other 32.3

COMPARISON OF FUND TO INDEXES

$1,000 invested in the fund
$1,000 invested in the TSE 300
$1,000 invested in Canada Savings Bonds
Annual ranking against other funds in the same categoryx

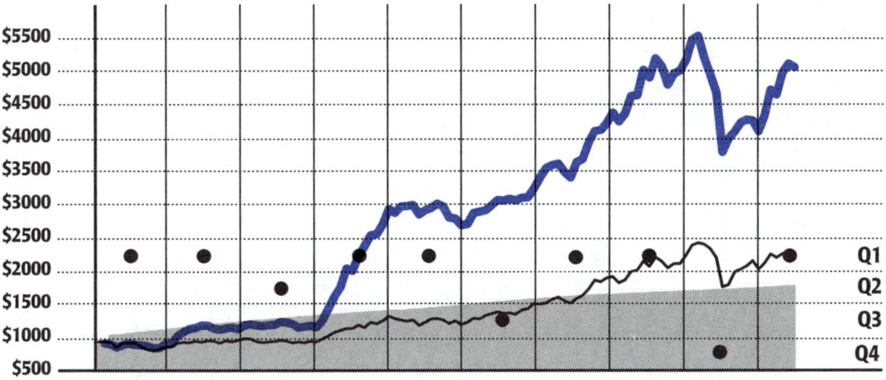

Annual Return (%)	1990		1992		1994		1996		1998	8/31/99
	-2.0	22.9	4.3	121.7	3.0	11.1	31.7	20.3	-13.8	18.1

Compound Return (%)	10 yr	9 yr	8 yr	7 yr	6 yr	5 yr	4 yr	3 yr	2 yr	1 yr
	17.9	20.4	19.8	21.6	14.3	11.2	13.1	11.4	1.5	33.0

AIC DIVERSIFIED CANADA

NO LOAD

Primary Objective: Growth
Sponsor: AIC Group of Funds
Fund Manager: Jonathan Wellum, Georgian Capital Partners
Style: Bottom-up, Growth
Size (MMs): $2,936.277
RRSP: 100%
Expense Ratio: 2.26%

COMMENTS

This fund still holds a bias to financial stocks, which is the prime reason for its dramatic underperformance in the category. Over the past year, major holdings such as Berkshire Hathaway, TD Bank, Newcourt Credit, and Fairfax Financial have disappointed. We like the tax-efficient, buy-and-hold philosophy in a concentrated portfolio that Wellum applies and have confidence that this fund will return to the upper echelon. Investors over the past two years have been largely disappointed, although the fund's four-year return of 25.1% is near the top of its class. We feel that crystallizing those losses now would be unwise. This demonstrates the importance of diversifying among different management styles. We warned last year that it could not sustain 25%+ returns year in and year out. **Smart Fund History: 1999, 1998, 1997.**

RISK

How Often Money was Lost:.......16 of 56 Months
....12 of 54 Quarters
....6 of 45 Years
Worst 3 Months:..............................-18.85% (1998)
Best 3 Months:..................................24.77% (1996)

ASSET ALLOCATION

Industrial products 21.8
Insurance 13.0
Cash & equivalent.......................12.6
Communications..........................11.7
Banks & trusts..............................11.7
Other 29.2

COMPARISON OF FUND TO INDEXES

$1,000 invested in the fund
$1,000 invested in the TSE 300
$1,000 invested in Canada Savings Bonds
● Annual ranking against other funds in the same category

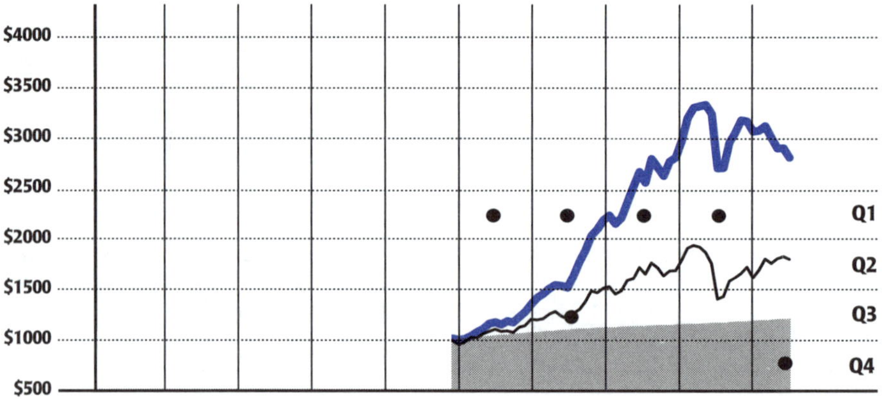

Annual Return (%)	**1990**		**1992**		**1994**		**1996**		**1998**	**8/31/99**
						26.2	65.1	32.1	14.9	-11.7
Compound Return (%)	**10 yr**	**9 yr**	**8 yr**	**7 yr**	**6 yr**	**5 yr**	**4 yr**	**3 yr**	**2 yr**	**1 yr**
							25.1	19.9	4.8	3.9

AIM CANADA GROWTH CLASS

LOAD

Primary Objective: Growth
Sponsor: AIM Funds Management Inc.
Fund Manager: Derek Webb
Style: Momentum
Size (MMs): $871.213
RRSP: 100%
Expense Ratio: 2.41%

COMMENTS

This fund uses a disciplined security selection process that focuses on corporate earnings growth. Webb analyzes earnings growth projections, analyst expectations, and price momentum. Negative moves in any of these areas often leads to a holding being sold. The model was back-tested with favourable results and now has a four-year track record of 16.5%. The fund will always have a good portion of foreign content. The fund has bopped around a bit and was dropped from Smart Fund status in 1998. It is our choice for momentum-style investing, which can be volatile and will necessarily have greater taxable distributions because of its high turnover. The fund acts as a good complement to other Canadian funds. **Smart Fund History: 1999, 1997.**

RISK

How Often Money was Lost:.......20 of 55 Months
....15 of 53 Quarters
....8 of 44 Years
Worst 3 Months:..............................-23.54% (1998)
Best 3 Months: 22.38% (1993)

ASSET ALLOCATION

Technology......................................21
Cash & equivalent........................11.5
Oil & Gas.......................................10.8
Communications 8.5
Other 48.2

COMPARISON OF FUND TO INDEXES

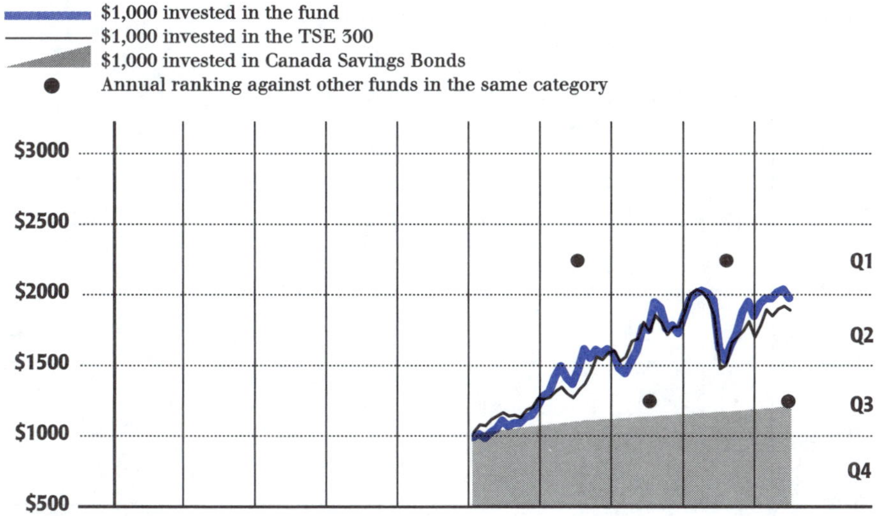

Annual Return (%)	1990		1992		1994		1996		1998	8/31/99
							38.1	12.4	5.2	5.2

Compound Return (%)	10 yr	9 yr	8 yr	7 yr	6 yr	5 yr	4 yr	3 yr	2 yr	1 yr
							16.5	10.3	6.3	21.8

ALTAMIRA PRECISION CANADIAN **NO LOAD**

Primary Objective:	Index
Sponsor:	Altamira Investment Service
Fund Manager:	State Street Global Advisors
Style:	Passive
Size (MMs):	$13.477
RRSP:	100%
Expense Ratio:	0.50%

COMMENTS

Index funds are gradually becoming popular as investors are frustrated with high fees and the mediocre performance of active managers. As BCE and Nortel Networks outperformed this past year and their weighting in the index grew to being more than 15% combined, many managers could not keep up with their more broadly diversified funds. We like Altamira's fund because of its low MER of 0.50%. Only two things matter in index investing: fees and tracking. We also like Royal Bank's fund, but you may find Altamira's more widely available through dealers and discount brokers. So far, this one is tracking very close to the TSE 100 index. **New Smart Fund.**

RISK

How Often Money was Lost: ....3 of 9 Months
..........1 of 7 Quarters
..........0 of 0 Years
Worst 3 Months: ....-1.02% (1999)
Best 3 Months: 8.69% (1999)

ASSET ALLOCATION

Financial services 19.8
Technology 13.5
Basic material 12.6
Communications 11.2
Energy 9.9
Other 33.0

COMPARISON OF FUND TO INDEXES

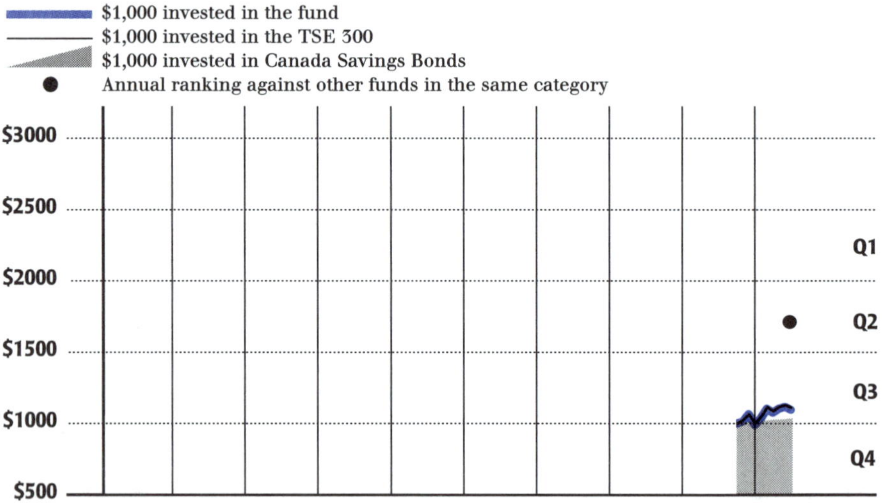

Annual Return (%)	1990		1992		1994		1996		1998	8/31/99
										8.1

Compound Return (%)	10 yr	9 yr	8 yr	7 yr	6 yr	5 yr	4 yr	3 yr	2 yr	1 yr

ATLAS CANADIAN LARGE-CAP GROWTH

LOAD

Primary Objective:	Growth
Sponsor:	Atlas Asset Management
Fund Manager:	Fred Pynn, Bissett & Associates
Style:	Bottom-up, Growth
Size (MMs):	$574.046
RRSP:	100%
Expense Ratio:	2.42%

COMMENTS

This is how to acquire the investment management team of Bissett & Associates from your advisor. Fred Pynn, Smart Fund Manager of the Year in 1998 and 1999, manages this fund and also co-manages the lower-MER Bissett Canadian Equity Fund (also a Smart Fund). Until this year, it had been a top-quartile performer since Pynn took over in July 1994. Using a growth-style of investing, Pynn selects solid companies on a bottom-up basis. Like many funds, it has experienced a rough 1999, but this is a long-term keeper. **Smart Fund History: 1999, 1998.**

RISK

How Often Money was Lost:.....48 of 116 Months
.....39 of 114 Quarters
.....28 of 105 Years
Worst 3 Months:.....-23.65% (1998)
Best 3 Months:.....17.95% (1997)

ASSET ALLOCATION

Industrial products	31.6
Financial services	16.4
Consumer products	13.6
Oil & Gas	12.4
Communications	7.1
Other	18.9

COMPARISON OF FUND TO INDEXES

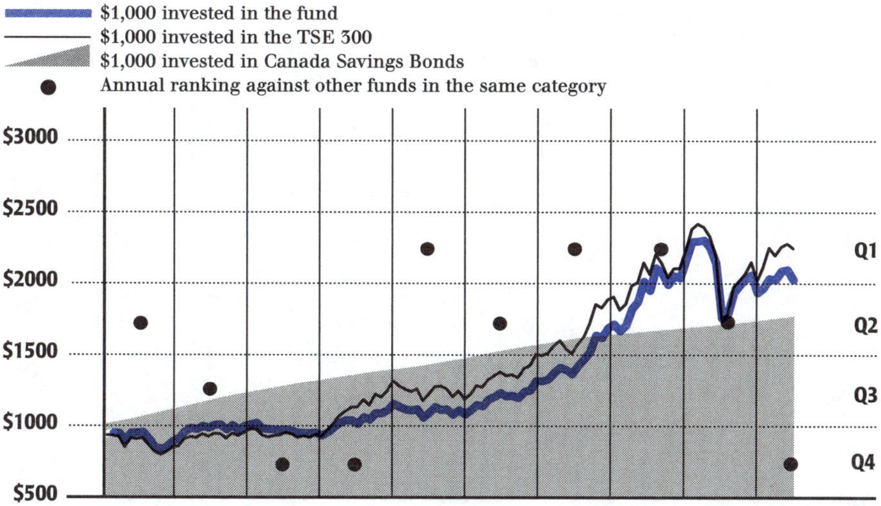

Annual Return (%)	1990		1992		1994		1996		1998	8/31/99
	-10.7	11.9	-4.7	16.6	0.0	12.5	29.7	26.7	-1.0	-0.1

Compound Return (%)	10 yr	9 yr	8 yr	7 yr	6 yr	5 yr	4 yr	3 yr	2 yr	1 yr
	7.1	9.4	9.1	11.2	11.4	12.4	13.8	12.5	2.0	15.3

BISSETT CANADIAN EQUITY

NO LOAD

Primary Objective:	Growth
Sponsor:	Bissett & Associates
Fund Manager:	Michael Quinn and Fred Pynn
Style:	Bottom-up, Growth
Size (MMs):	$572.604
RRSP:	100%
Expense Ratio:	1.18%

COMMENTS

Now available in most provinces, we again include this fund as a Smart Fund. A low MER combined with top-quartile performance over several periods make this a solid choice. This no-load fund is available from many dealers, who are entitled to charge an up-front commission. That's money well spent if your self-directed RRSP is with an advisor or discounter. Despite a minimum $10,000 investment and no trailers to brokers (enabling Bissett to keep the MER low), the fund has caught on, with assets almost tripling since 1997. Fund's five-year CAGR of 15.7% puts it near the top of the class. **Smart Fund History: 1999, 1998, 1997.**

RISK

How Often Money was Lost:.....42 of 116 Months
....33 of 114 Quarters
....15 of 105 Years
Worst 3 Months:........................-23.38% (1998)
Best 3 Months:..........................20.80% (1997)

ASSET ALLOCATION

Industrial products 26.4
Forest products 16.6
Consumer products 15.1
Oil & Gas 13.0
Communications 6.6
Other 23.3

COMPARISON OF FUND TO INDEXES

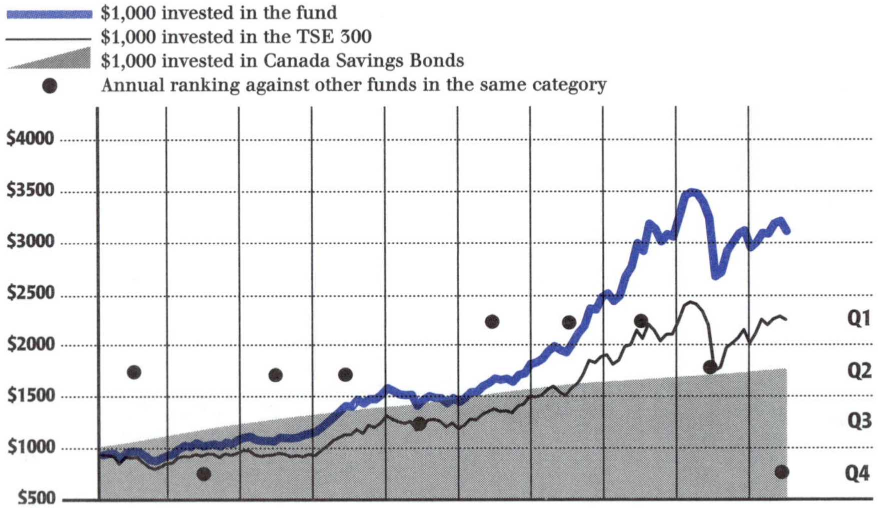

Annual	**1990**		**1992**		**1994**		**1996**		**1998**	**8/31/99**
Return (%)	-8.5	17.4	5.3	33.4	-2.3	16.4	36.0	31.5	0.1	0.8

Compound	**10 yr**	**9 yr**	**8 yr**	**7 yr**	**6 yr**	**5 yr**	**4 yr**	**3 yr**	**2 yr**	**1 yr**
Return (%)	12.0	14.4	14.8	16.1	13.3	15.7	17.0	15.5	3.3	16.6

C.I. HARBOUR

NO LOAD

Primary Objective: Growth
Sponsor: C.I. Mutual Funds
Fund Manager: Gerald Coleman
Style: Bottom-up, Value
Size (MMs): $869.448
RRSP: 100%
Expense Ratio: 2.36%

COMMENTS

Smart Funds has always been a leader in identifying strong new funds for investors. We bet on manager Gerry Coleman's outstanding track record—first at United, then at Mackenzie, when we made this a Smart Fund in 1998. Ivy Canadian was a Smart Fund in 1996 and 1997 when he managed it. The classic low-volatility, buy-and-hold style has generated solid if unspectacular returns year in and year out. With his judicious use of cash holdings it is rare for Coleman to lose any money for unitholders. This is our top pick for low-risk investors seeking a quality equity fund. Fund will not have a three-year number until the summer of 2000 yet it now has almost $900 million. Harbour and Ivy Canadian are neck and neck on their two-year CAGR, 5.3% vs. 5.5%. **Smart Fund History: 1999, 1998.**

RISK

How Often Money was Lost:.......10 of 26 Months
..........10 of 24 Quarters
..........9 of 15 Years
Worst 3 Months:..........-18.86% (1998)
Best 3 Months:..........11.85% (1998)

ASSET ALLOCATION

Canadian equities 67.7
Cash & equivalent..........23.5
U.S. equities 5.0
Foreign equities 3.8

COMPARISON OF FUND TO INDEXES

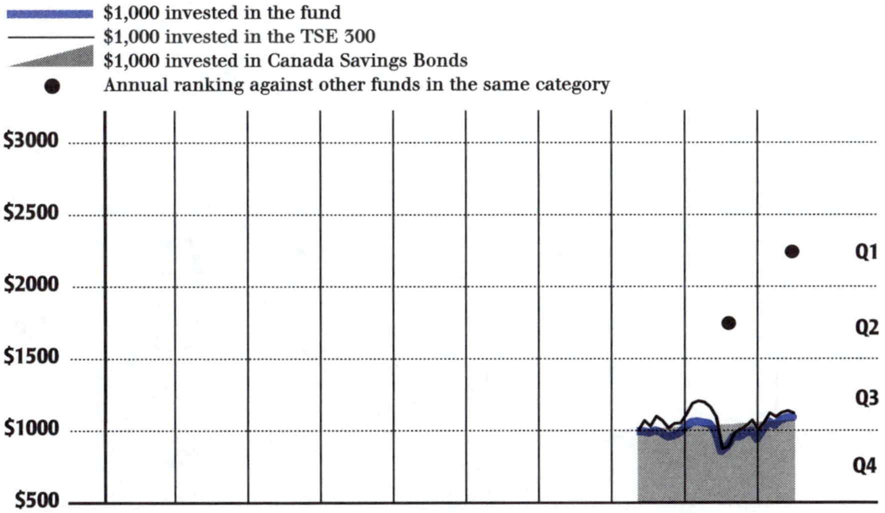

Annual Return (%)	1990	1992	1994	1996	1998	8/31/99
					1.7	11.2

Compound Return (%)	10 yr	9 yr	8 yr	7 yr	6 yr	5 yr	4 yr	3 yr	2 yr	1 yr
									5.3	27.5

PH&N CANADIAN EQUITY

NO LOAD

Primary Objective:	Growth
Sponsor:	Phillips, Hager & North Investment Management
Fund Manager:	Team
Style:	Bottom-up, Growth
Size (MMs):	$296.850
RRSP:	100%
Expense Ratio:	1.09%

COMMENTS

Fund has slipped a bit, dropping to second quartile over five- and ten-year periods ending August 31, 1999, making planners and brokers smile since they usually don't offer this one to their clients. We still believe in the team of managers with their minuscule 1.07% MER. You must invest a healthy minimum and, unless dealing directly with PH&N, you will be charged by brokers. Consistent style of picking growth stocks from the mid- and large-cap universe. The low-profile managers keep volatility low while generating solid above-average returns. Put this one in your RRSP, if you can. **Smart Fund History: 1999, 1998, 1997, 1996.**

RISK

How Often Money was Lost: .....47 of 116 Months
.....43 of 114 Quarters
.....25 of 105 Years
Worst 3 Months: .....-25.27% (1998)
Best 3 Months: 18.18% (1996)

ASSET ALLOCATION

Financial services 21.7
Industrial products 21.5
Oil & Gas 14.1
Communications 8.3
Utilities 6.4
Other 28.0

COMPARISON OF FUND TO INDEXES

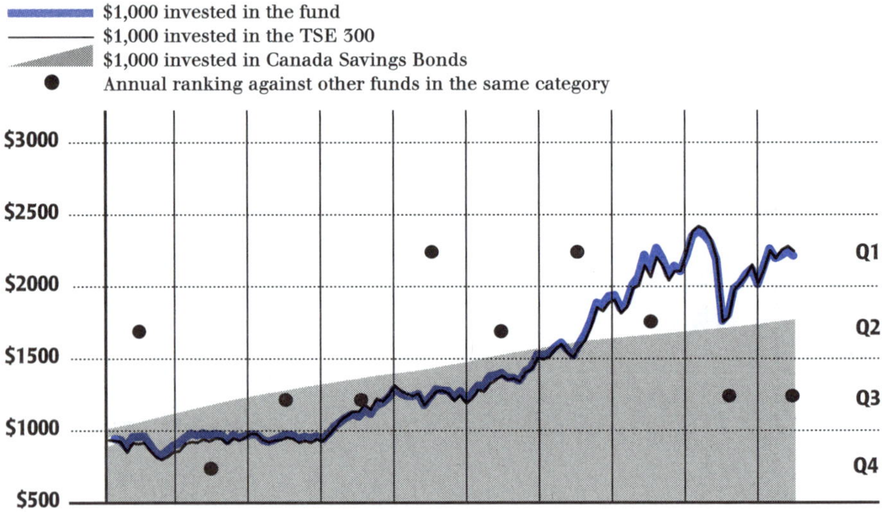

Annual Return (%)	1990		1992		1994		1996		1998	8/31/99
	-10.4	7.5	-0.2	27.6	3.9	13.1	30.0	14.2	-2.7	6.3

Compound Return (%)	10 yr	9 yr	8 yr	7 yr	6 yr	5 yr	4 yr	3 yr	2 yr	1 yr
	8.4	10.5	10.8	12.5	11.7	11.5	12.8	11.5	1.9	25.7

SCUDDER CANADIAN EQUITY **NO LOAD**

Primary Objective:	Growth
Sponsor:	Scudder Maxxum Co.
Fund Manager:	Phil Fortuna, Jennifer Carter & Josephine Chu
Style:	Bottom-up, Value
Size (MMs):	$282.079
RRSP:	100%
Expense Ratio:	1.50%

COMMENTS

Back-to-back first-quartile returns for 1996 and 1997 and a stellar three-year CAGR of almost 20% couldn't gather enough assets to keep the firm from being sold. Lead manager Fortuna and his team of Jennifer Carter and Josephine Chu use rigorous quantitative screens to generate a short-list of Canadian names. The fund's low MER of 1.50% gives it almost a 1% per year competitive advantage in the performance game. **Smart Fund History: 1999, 1998.**

RISK

How Often Money was Lost:	16 of 46 Months
	8 of 44 Quarters
	12 of 35 Years
Worst 3 Months:	-20.82% (1998)
Best 3 Months:	20.86% (1996)

ASSET ALLOCATION

Industrial products	18.7
Oil & Gas	18.0
Financial services	11.7
Communications	11.6
Merchandising	11.4
Other	28.6

COMPARISON OF FUND TO INDEXES

$1,000 invested in the fund
$1,000 invested in the TSE 300
$1,000 invested in Canada Savings Bonds
Annual ranking against other funds in the same category

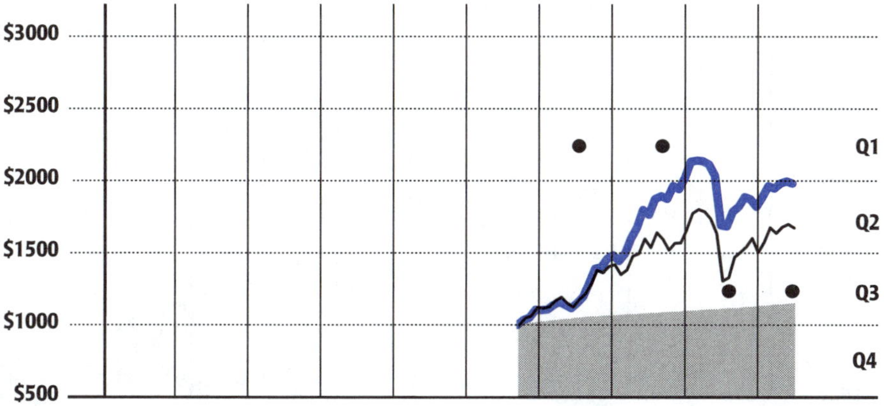

Annual Return (%)	1990		1992		1994		1996		1998	8/31/99
							33.4	40.2	-3.9	5.0

Compound Return (%)	10 yr	9 yr	8 yr	7 yr	6 yr	5 yr	4 yr	3 yr	2 yr	1 yr
								19.8	5.9	7.1

SYNERGY CANADIAN STYLE MANAGEMENT CLASS LOAD

Primary Objective: Growth
Sponsor: Synergy Asset Management
Fund Manager: Dave Picton
Style: Bottom-up, Blend
Size (MMs): $64.076
RRSP: 100%
Expense Ratio: 2.50% estimated

COMMENTS

A unique fund, since style diversification can reduce volatility over the long term. President Joe Canavan claims that many managers are guilty of style drift; strict adherence makes this fund different. Manager David Picton is responsible for ensuring that the underlying managers stick to their individual mandates of value, growth, momentum, and small-cap. The unique blending of different styles makes this theoretically less volatile. This one should act as a one-stop fund for people. Performance since inception puts it near the top of the class as its one-year to August 31 return is a first-quartile 28.8%. **Smart Fund History: 1999.**

RISK

How Often Money was Lost:.........7 of 20 Months
....5 of 18 Quarters
....4 of 9 Years
Worst 3 Months: ....-22.75% (1998)
Best 3 Months:..................................16.93% (1998)

ASSET ALLOCATION

Industrial products 20.7
Oil & Gas 9.4
Financial services 9.0
Consumer products 5.2
Communications 5.1
Other 50.6

COMPARISON OF FUND TO INDEXES

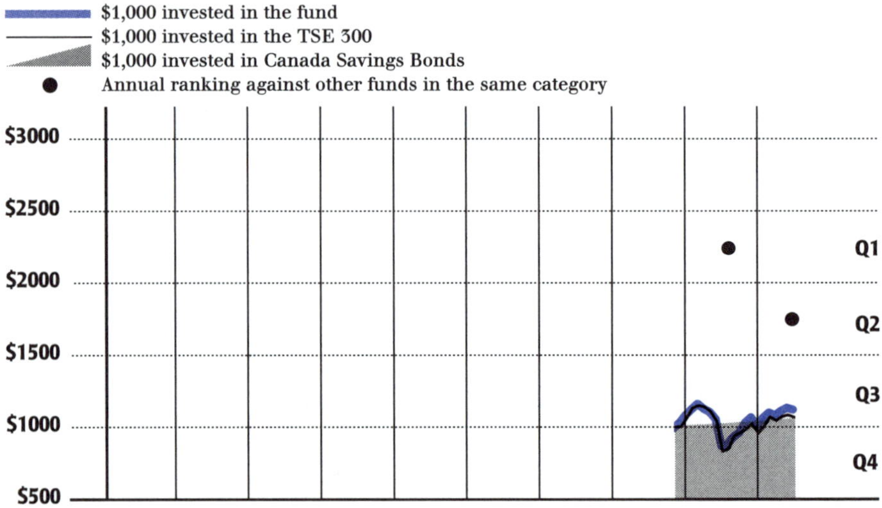

Annual Return (%)	1990		1992		1994		1996		1998	8/31/99
									3.6	8.9

Compound Return (%)	10 yr	9 yr	8 yr	7 yr	6 yr	5 yr	4 yr	3 yr	2 yr	1 yr
										28.8

TALVEST CANADIAN EQUITY GROWTH **LOAD**

Primary Objective:	Growth
Sponsor:	Talvest Fund Management
Fund Manager:	Denis Ouellet, TAL Investment Counsel
Style:	Bottom-up, Growth
Size (MMs):	$513.038
RRSP:	100%
Expense Ratio:	2.58%

COMMENTS

We had previously recognized manager Denis Ouellet in Smart Funds 1997 for his performance on Scotia Canadian Growth. Monsieur Ouellet is a bottom-up growth-stock investor and he continues to gather notice and accolades on this young fund. This fund was created for him when he joined Talvest in January 1997 and it has been first quartile ever since. This is just another example of keeping up with manager changes like Coleman, Kanko, and Michael Rome; you need to know if your Smart Manager is still running your fund. **Smart Fund History: 1999.**

RISK

How Often Money was Lost:.......10 of 32 Months
....9 of 30 Quarters
....9 of 21 Years
Worst 3 Months:..............................-27.09% (1998)
Best 3 Months:.................................19.88% (1997)

ASSET ALLOCATION

Industrial products 15.6
Oil & Gas.......................................13.8
Financial services 13.5
Merchandising.............................11.3
Communications 9.9
Other 35.9

COMPARISON OF FUND TO INDEXES

$1,000 invested in the fund
$1,000 invested in the TSE 300
$1,000 invested in Canada Savings Bonds
● Annual ranking against other funds in the same category

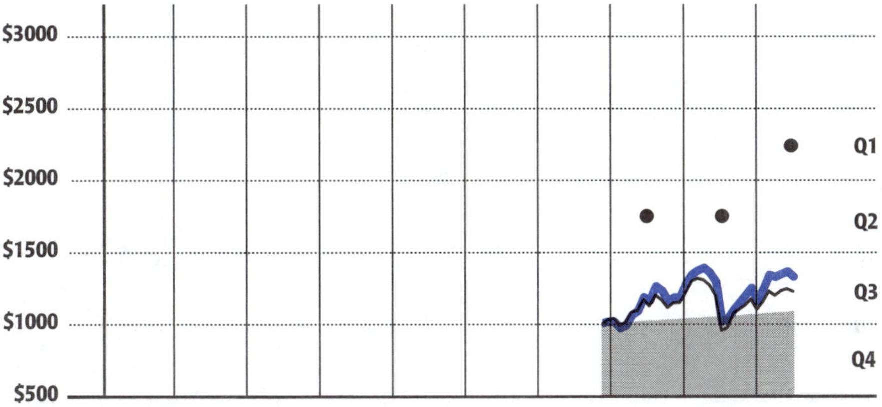

Annual Return (%)	**1990**		**1992**		**1994**		**1996**		**1998**	**8/31/99**
								18.0	1.2	11.1

Compound Return (%)	**10 yr**	**9 yr**	**8 yr**	**7 yr**	**6 yr**	**5 yr**	**4 yr**	**3 yr**	**2 yr**	**1 yr**
									7.1	31.0

UNIVERSAL CANADIAN GROWTH **LOAD**

Primary Objective: Growth
Sponsor: Mackenzie Financial
Fund Manager: Dina DeGeer & Dennis Starritt, Bluewater
Style: Bottom-up, Growth
Size (MMs): $1,815.895
RRSP: 100%
Expense Ratio: 2.30%

COMMENTS

The former Trimark team of Dina DeGeer and Dennis Starritt had outperformed their old company's Trimark Canadian significantly. Now the pendulum has swung back and the funds are about even over the past three years. This fund can be considered a core RRSP holding. Dennis and Dina buy good growth companies at attractive prices and hold them for several years. Their favourite stocks, such as TD Bank and Methanex, suffered in 1999, bringing down performance. Don't give up—they hold over 30% in cash and will redeploy that in the volatile times ahead to capture some bargains. **Smart Fund History: 1999, 1998.**

RISK

How Often Money was Lost:.......18 of 48 Months
....10 of 46 Quarters
....9 of 37 Years
Worst 3 Months:...............................-18.24% (1998)
Best 3 Months:....................................16.73% (1993)

ASSET ALLOCATION

Cash & equivalent........................31.0
Corporate..1.0
Canadian equities 50.0
U.S. equities....................................18.0

COMPARISON OF FUND TO INDEXES

$1,000 invested in the fund
$1,000 invested in the TSE 300
$1,000 invested in Canada Savings Bonds
● Annual ranking against other funds in the same category

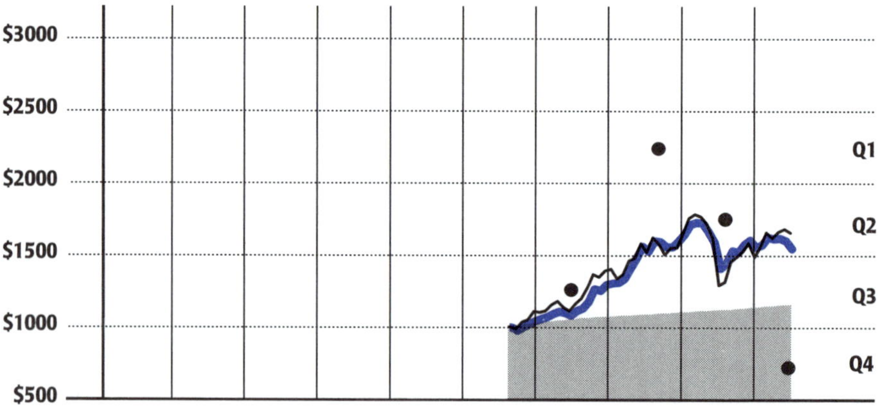

Annual Return (%)	1990		1992		1994		1996		1998	8/31/99
							22.8	24.3	1.1	-1.8

Compound Return (%)	10 yr	9 yr	8 yr	7 yr	6 yr	5 yr	4 yr	3 yr	2 yr	1 yr
							11.5	11.6	0.6	9.8

FIDELITY CANADIAN GROWTH COMPANY LOAD

Primary Objective:	High Growth
Sponsor:	Fidelity Investments Canada
Fund Manager:	Alan Radlo, Fidelity Management & Research
Style:	Bottom-up, Growth
Size (MMs):	$1,805.302
RRSP:	100%
Expense Ratio:	2.45%

COMMENTS

Manager Alan Radlo continues to do what he does best—picking solid growth companies and holding them. He and his analysts do their homework, visiting and interviewing company management teams to ensure that stated profits and cash flows are real. This fund has one of the best risk-adjusted returns in the category and its size forces it into larger stocks that will lower both the returns and the volatility. There is no evidence yet that he can't outperform many large-cap funds with reasonable risk, making this one a better deal than True North. Five-year CAGR of over 18.4% is near the top of its class. Fund is first quartile for five-, three-, and two-year returns ending August 31, 1999. **Smart Fund History: 1999, 1998, 1997, 1996.**

RISK

How Often Money was Lost:.......15 of 61 Months
.......11 of 59 Quarters
.......7 of 50 Years
Worst 3 Months: ....-20.87% (1998)
Best 3 Months:.......18.05% (1997)

ASSET ALLOCATION

Consumer products.......7.0
Industrial products 20.4
Communications.......16.2
Oil & Gas 8.5
Merchandising.......7.6
Other 40.3

COMPARISON OF FUND TO INDEXES

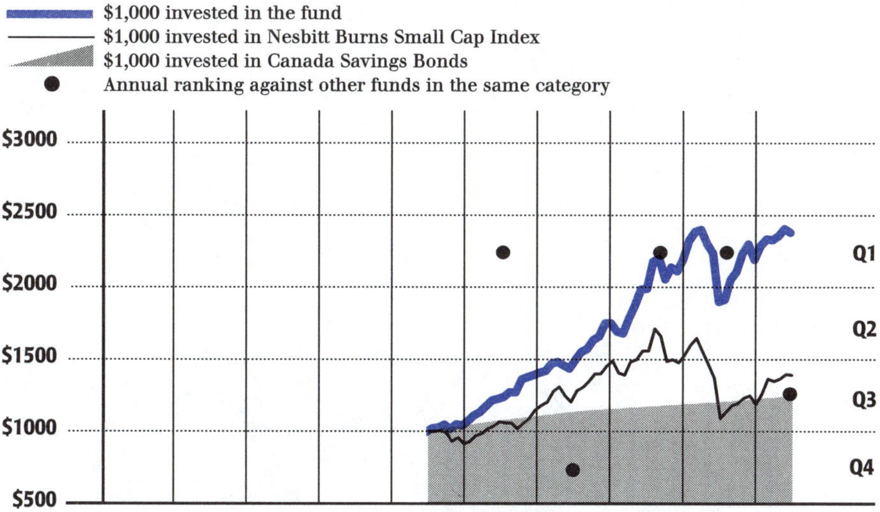

Annual	**1990**		**1992**		**1994**		**1996**		**1998**	**8/31/99**
Return (%)						31.1%	20.5%	28.8%	4.5%	6.6%
Compound	**10 yr**	**9 yr**	**8 yr**	**7 yr**	**6 yr**	**5 yr**	**4 yr**	**3 yr**	**2 yr**	**1 yr**
Return (%)							18.4%	16.7%	9.4%	25.3%

GBC CANADIAN GROWTH

NO LOAD

Primary Objective:	High Growth
Sponsor:	GBC Asset Management Inc
Fund Manager:	Ian Soutar, & Nicolas Chevalier
Style:	Bottom-up, Growth
Size (MMs):	$242.470
RRSP:	100%
Expense Ratio:	1.89%

CANADIAN SMALL-CAP EQUITY

COMMENTS

Sometimes performance makes a fund undeniable. Since 1993, this fund has been first or second quartile in every calendar year. That string equates to first-quartile performance for the ten-, five-, three-, two- and one-year periods ending August 31, 1999. This solid fund comes at a price and we don't just mean the 1.89% MER. GBC requires a $100,000 minimum investment. This very low-key fund company does not get much attention and is generally ignored by most dealers. Clearly, with this track record, Ian Soutar and his team deserve its Smart Fund recognition. **Smart Fund History: 1999.**

RISK

How Often Money was Lost:.....36 of 116 Months
.....32 of 114 Quarters
.....22 of 105 Years
Worst 3 Months: .....-3.92% (1998)
Best 3 Months:.....18.05% (1997)

ASSET ALLOCATION

Technology.....26.0%
Industrial products.....15.0%
Communications.....12.0%
Drugs & Medical.....12.0%
Oil & Gas.....10.0%
Other.....25.0%

COMPARISON OF FUND TO INDEXES

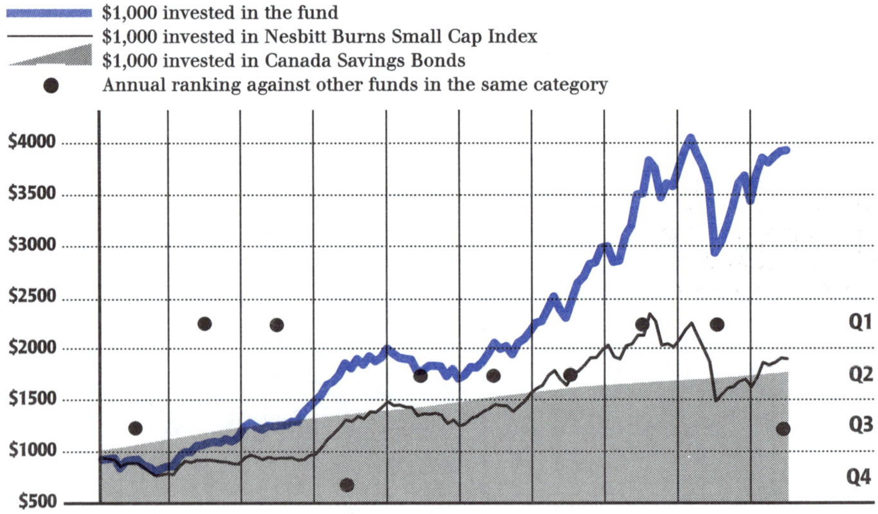

Annual Return (%)	1990		1992		1994		1996		1998	8/31/99
	-13.6	32.6	26.3	33.0	-5.8	16.1	35.3	27.0	0.2	8.7

Compound Return (%)	10 yr	9 yr	8 yr	7 yr	6 yr	5 yr	4 yr	3 yr	2 yr	1 yr
	15.7	18.1	17.2	17.6	12.8	16.4	18.3	16.6	5.8	33.9

GLOBAL STRATEGY SMALL CAP **LOAD**

Primary Objective: Growth
Sponsor: Global Strategy Financial Inc.
Fund Manager: John Sartz
Style: Bottom-up, Growth
Size (MMs): $267.312
RRSP: 100%
Expense Ratio: 2.64%

COMMENTS

After we prematurely removed this from the Smart Fund list in 1997, it blew the doors off in performance. Reinstated, it has dropped to fourth quartile since. During that period it has been closed and then reopened. After wringing our hands again, we decided to leave it as a Smart Fund and to watch it over longer periods. The fund's performance came despite being handcuffed with a punitive 2.64% MER, one of the highest in the class. Sartz has a track record in Canadian small caps that exceeds 20 years. He buys solid companies with consistent earnings and cash-flow streams, often in simple businesses, then holds them for what seems like forever. Those that own it should hold it and we will watch to see if Sartz comes back. **Smart Fund History: 1999, 1998, 1996.**

RISK

How Often Money was Lost:	22 of 56 Months
	17 of 54 Quarters
	14 of 45 Years
Worst 3 Months:	-22.44% (1998)
Best 3 Months:	21.15% (1997)

ASSET ALLOCATION

Industrial products	36.9
Oil & Gas	19.5
Merchandising	14.2
Consumer products	12.4
Communications	5.8
Other	11.2

COMPARISON OF FUND TO INDEXES

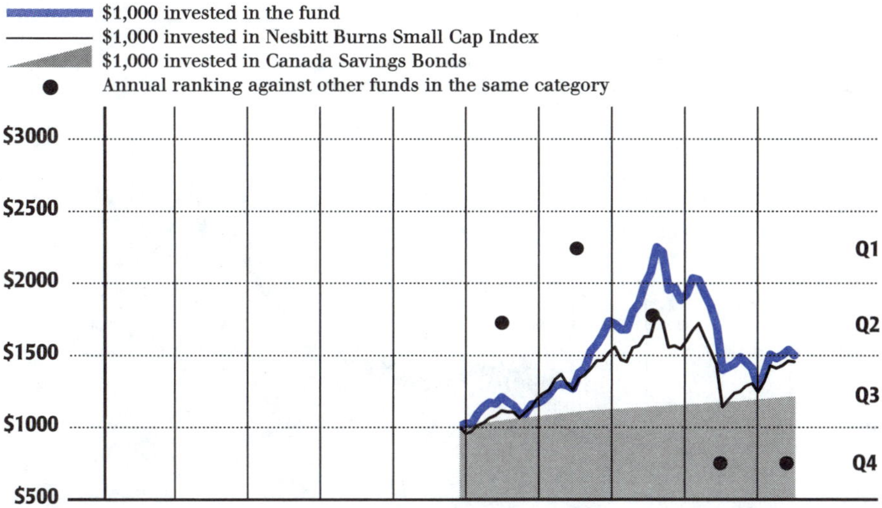

Annual Return (%)	1990		1992		1994		1996		1998	8/31/99
						14.2	42.7	19.8	-26.4	3.3

Compound Return (%)	10 yr	9 yr	8 yr	7 yr	6 yr	5 yr	4 yr	3 yr	2 yr	1 yr
								2.8	-15.0	7.2

SAXON SMALL CAP

NO LOAD

Primary Objective: High Growth
Sponsor: Saxon Funds
Fund Manager: Robert Tattersall, Howson Tattersall Investment Counsel
Style: Bottom-up, Growth
Size (MMs): $31.082
RRSP: 100%
Expense Ratio: 1.75%

CANADIAN SMALL-CAP EQUITY

COMMENTS

Saxon quietly gets recognition, even if it doesn't get assets. The fund won the Canadian Small Cap Fund of the Year at the 1998 Mutual Funds Awards. Manager Bob Tattersall is a bottom-up stock picker who has a portfolio of industrial products firms. Fund has an outstanding risk/return profile and sports one of the lower MERs in the small-cap class. No high-flying Internet stocks or junior resources here. This one is the number one small-cap fund on a three-year basis in what has been a tough small-cap period. Tattersall has generated a 19.3% three-year CAGR. **Smart Fund History: 1999.**

RISK

How Often Money was Lost:.....49 of 116 Months
.....41 of 114 Quarters
.....23 of 105 Years
Worst 3 Months:.....-20.08% (1998)
Best 3 Months:.....16.48% (1997)

ASSET ALLOCATION

Industrial products.....34.0
Consumer products.....13.0
Oil & Gas.....12.2
Paper & Forest Products.....11.3
Merchandising.....5.5
Other.....24.0

COMPARISON OF FUND TO INDEXES

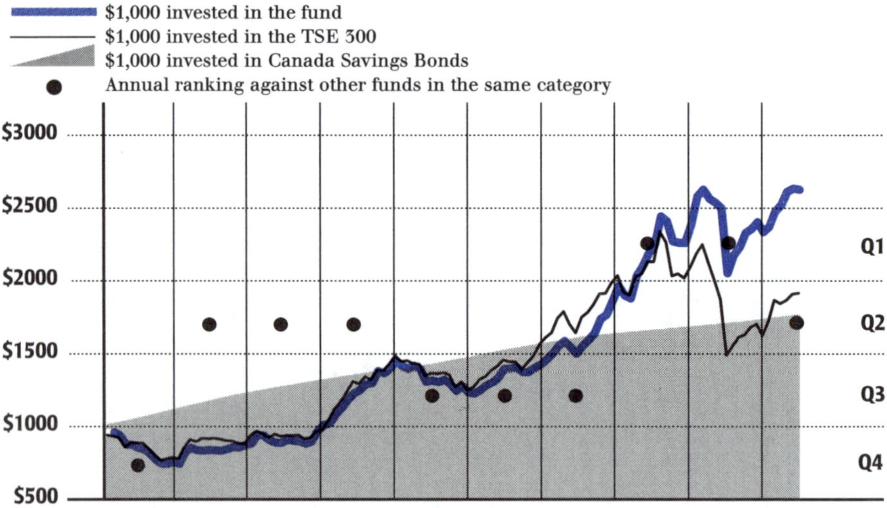

Annual Return (%)	1990		1992		1994		1996		1998	8/31/99
	-25.3	15.8	11.2	44.5	-8.7	9.9	26.2	28.1	4.2	11.5

Compound Return (%)	10 yr	9 yr	8 yr	7 yr	6 yr	5 yr	4 yr	3 yr	2 yr	1 yr
	9.9	14.0	15.5	16.6	12.6	15.1	17.2	19.3	8.1	28.1

TALVEST SMALL CAP CANADIAN EQUITY **LOAD**

Primary Objective: High Growth
Sponsor: Talvest Fund Management Inc.
Fund Manager: J. Sebastian van Berkom, Van Berkom & Assoc.
Style: Bottom-up, Growth
Size (MMs): $247.342
RRSP: 100%
Expense Ratio: 2.70%

COMMENTS

This fund makes its debut in this edition. We liked the fund last year, but Talvest was concerned about the rapid growth of the fund and indicated closure of the fund was highly probable. The small-cap correction last year eliminated that need and it should be open for some time now. Van Berkom is one of the top small-cap money managers in Canada whose disciplined style has produced top-quartile performance for three-year and five-year periods. When he gets a company he likes he will hold it for as long as he can. JDS Uniphase was one of his top picks and he also likes money management stocks. High MER of 2.70% is really rich for this $250 million fund. **New Smart Fund.**

RISK

How Often Money was Lost:.......26 of 67 Months
....26 of 65 Quarters
....16 of 56 Years
Worst 3 Months:................................-27.72% (1998)
Best 3 Months:...................................24.60% (1997)

ASSET ALLOCATION

Industrial products 30.4
Consumer products 22.7
Oil & Gas 12.4
Financial Services 11.8
Merchandising 10.0
Other 12.7

COMPARISON OF FUND TO INDEXES

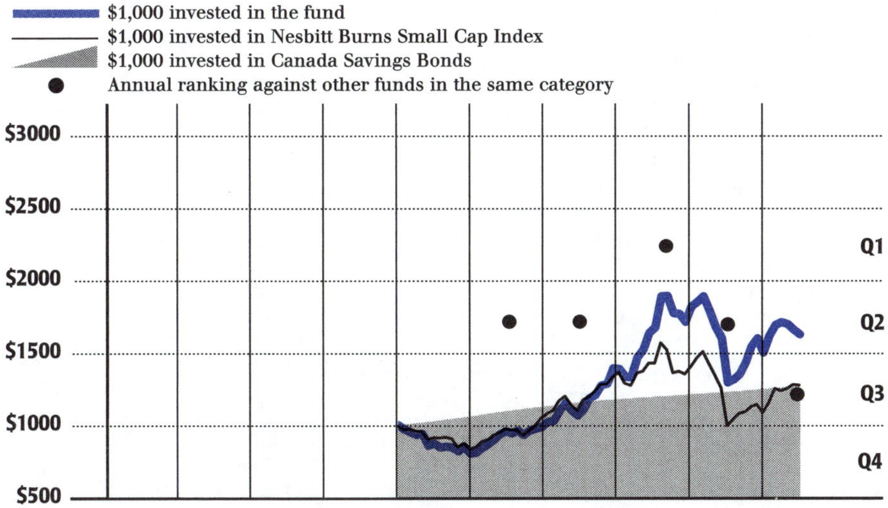

Annual Return (%)	1990		1992		1994		1996		1998	8/31/99
						14.6	13.1	37.6	-12.6	5.3

Compound Return (%)	10 yr	9 yr	8 yr	7 yr	6 yr	5 yr	4 yr	3 yr	2 yr	1 yr
						14.0	14.6	13.7	-1.5	25.8

AGF AMERICAN GROWTH CLASS LOAD

Primary Objective: Growth
Sponsor: AGF Funds Inc.
Fund Manager: Stephen Rogers, since 3/93
Style: Bottom-up, Growth
Size (MMs): $1,573.992
RRSP: 20%
Expense Ratio: 2.78%

COMMENTS

Available in RSP version

The American Growth Fund is where AGF got its name. Steve Rogers (see profile on page 20) keeps riding those dominant market-leading companies to top-quartile performance. This fund was recognized as U.S. equity fund of the year at the 1998 Mutual Funds Awards. AGF continues to charge its stiff 2.78% MER for a fund that uses in-house money management and has more than $1.5 billion in assets. Fund has been first or second quartile every calendar year since 1990, except 1997 when it returned only 29.7%! It is first quartile for every compound period out to 10 years ended August 31, 1999, with a blistering 18.2% 10-year CAGR. Top holdings like Dell Computer, Microsoft, Cisco, GE, and IBM. **Smart Fund History: 1999, 1998.**

RISK

How Often Money was Lost:.....43 of 116 Months
..........30 of 114 Quarters
..........2 of 105 Years
Worst 3 Months:..........-15.55% (1990)
Best 3 Months:..........27.65% (1998)

ASSET ALLOCATION

Technology	32.9
Financial services	14.5
Consumer products—growth	13.9
Health care	12.7
Capital goods	7.3
Other	18.7

COMPARISON OF FUND TO INDEXES

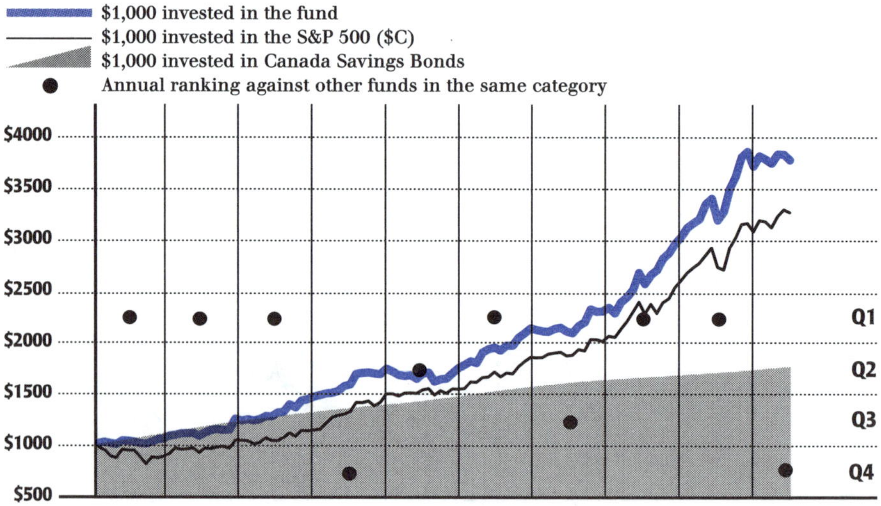

Annual Return (%)	1990		1992		1994		1996		1998	8/31/99
	-9.2	24.0	14.4	16.6	3.5	28.8	22.2	29.7	59.8	8.8

Compound Return (%)	10 yr	9 yr	8 yr	7 yr	6 yr	5 yr	4 yr	3 yr	2 yr	1 yr
	18.2	22.0	22.5	25.5	25.0	28.5	30.8	37.3	32.7	44.1

U.S. EQUITY

AIC VALUE

LOAD

Primary Objective:	Growth
Sponsor:	AIC Limited
Fund Manager:	Neil Murdoch
Style:	Bottom-up, Growth
Size (MMs):	$1,501.779
RRSP:	20%
Expense Ratio:	2.28%

COMMENTS

Available in RSP version

How the mighty can fall. This fund was the top U.S. equity fund at the Annual Mutual Funds Awards dinner in 1996 and 1997 by owning classics like Gillette, Johnson & Johnson, Coca-Cola, and Warren Buffett's Berkshire Hathaway. U.S. financial services stocks, such as Franklin Resources, Merrill Lynch, American Express, and T. Rowe Price, have helped fuel this fund to a strong 21.2% five-year return. Suddenly, all of these appear out of favour. Neil Murdoch continues to own great companies for the long run. Hang in, this one will come back. Fund has very low turnover, making it a good one to hold in taxable accounts. **Smart Fund History: 1999, 1998.**

RISK

How Often Money was Lost:.....38 of 114 Months
.....30 of 112 Quarters
.....10 of 103 Years
Worst 3 Months:.....-21.44% (1990)
Best 3 Months:.....30.41% (1991)

ASSET ALLOCATION

Consumer products	21.6
Financial services non bank	19.7
Health care	14.6
Financial services	14.2
Communications	9.9
Other	20.0

COMPARISON OF FUND TO INDEXES

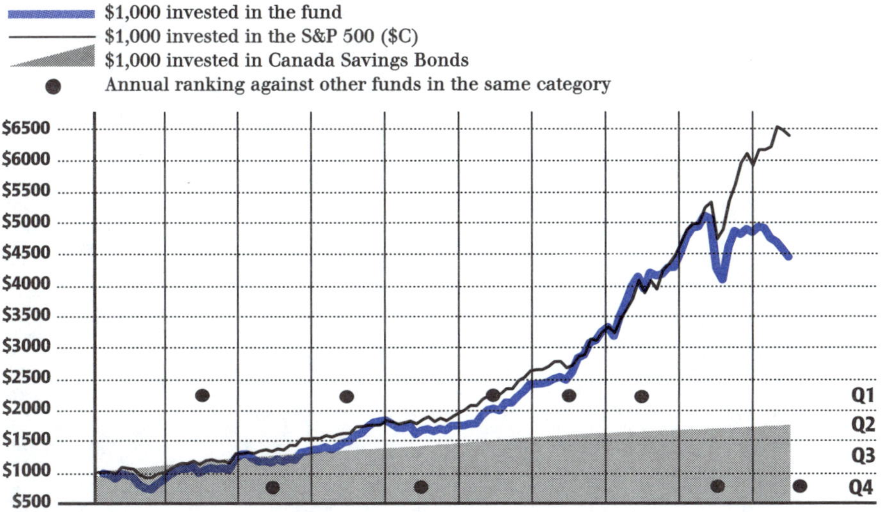

Annual Return (%)	**1990**		**1992**		**1994**		**1996**		**1998**	**8/31/99**
		37.5	10.0	35.9	-4.2	31.6	35.4	37.3	12.5	-7.6

Compound Return (%)	**10 yr**	**9 yr**	**8 yr**	**7 yr**	**6 yr**	**5 yr**	**4 yr**	**3 yr**	**2 yr**	**1 yr**
		20.7	19.3	20.8	17.3	21.2	22.2	19.5	6.3	4.3

U.S. EQUITY

ATLAS AMERICAN RSP INDEX

LOAD

Primary Objective:	Index
Sponsor:	Atlas Asset Management Inc.
Fund Manager:	David Patterson, Newcastle Capital Management
Style:	Passive
Size (MMs):	$213.091
RRSP:	100%
Expense Ratio:	1.53%

COMMENTS

The only RSP index fund offered by the load channel. Most planners and brokers are hesitant to sell index funds without some commission compensation. Given your advisor needs to be paid, the 1.52% MER is not bad considering it counts as Canadian content and returned 43% over the past year. **New Smart Fund.**

RISK

How Often Money was Lost:.......12 of 34 Months
....8 of 32 Quarters
....1 of 23 Years
Worst 3 Months: ....-13.45% (1998)
Best 3 Months: 23.55% (1998)

ASSET ALLOCATION

Foreign equities 79.4
Cash & equivalents 15.5
Index futures 2.1
Canadian equities...........................1.6
Other..1.4

COMPARISON OF FUND TO INDEXES

$1,000 invested in the fund
$1,000 invested in the S&P 500 ($C)
$1,000 invested in Canada Savings Bonds
Annual ranking against other funds in the same category

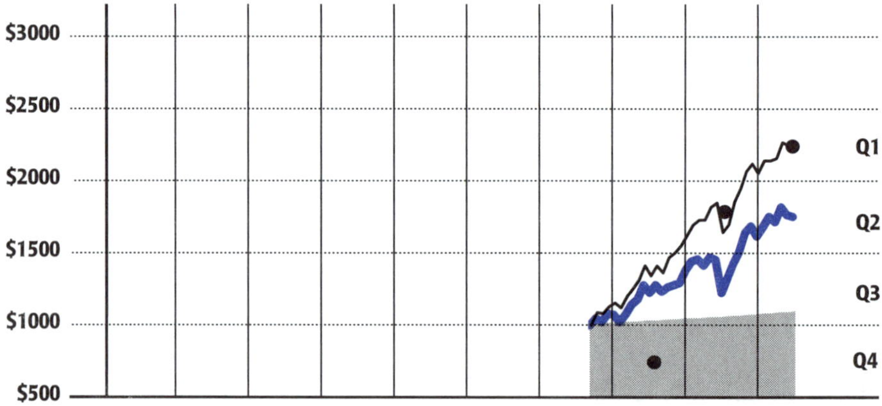

Annual	**1990**		**1992**		**1994**		**1996**		**1998**	**8/31/99**
Return (%)								25.3	28.3	6.8
Compound	**10 yr**	**9 yr**	**8 yr**	**7 yr**	**6 yr**	**5 yr**	**4 yr**	**3 yr**	**2 yr**	**1 yr**
Return (%)									19.6	43.1

BISSETT MULTINATIONAL GROWTH **NO LOAD**

Primary Objective: Growth
Sponsor: Bissett & Associates Investments
Fund Manager: Jeffrey Morrison with Fred Pynn
Style: Bottom-up, Growth
Size (MMs): $97.225
RRSP: 20%
Expense Ratio: 1.34%

COMMENTS

Bissett's version of a global equity fund features investments in mature multinational companies in the U.S., and Canada. Jeff Morrison has taken over lead on this fund and works with Fred Pynn seeking companies whose dividend growth rate is significantly above inflation. Many are household names like IBM, Johnson & Johnson, Nortel Networks, and Hewlett Packard. All companies in the portfolio are listed on North American stock exchanges. Fund is first quartile every year in the newly formed North American equity category. It's also no-load and has an MER of just 1.34%, and it could stay on the Smart Fund list for many years. **Smart Fund History: 1999, 1998.**

RISK

How Often Money was Lost:.......20 of 61 Months
.........9 of 59 Quarters
.........0 of 50 Years
Worst 3 Months: ....-12.27% (1998)
Best 3 Months:.........19.04% (1998)

ASSET ALLOCATION

USA	62.1
Canada	20.3
UK	10.0
Netherlands	4.9
Italy	2.7

COMPARISON OF FUND TO INDEXES

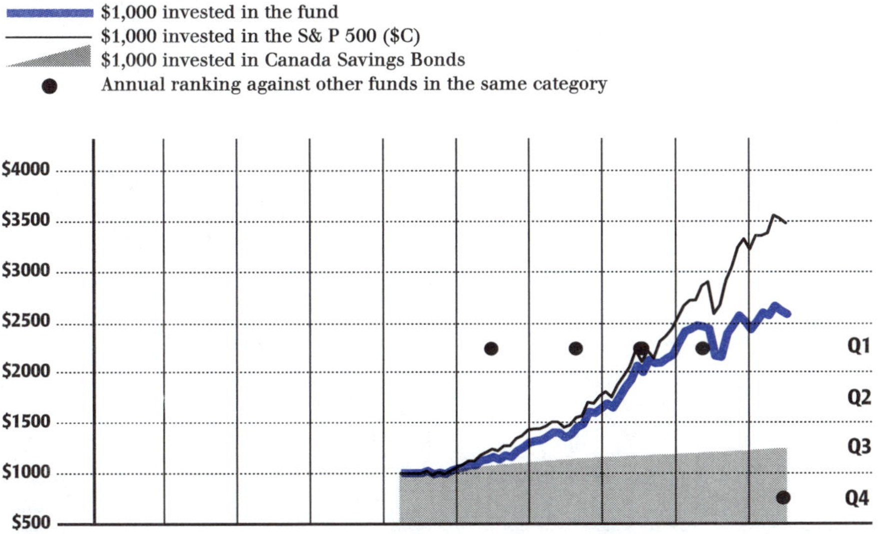

Annual Return (%)	1990		1992		1994		1996		1998	8/31/99
						22.0	27.5	33.9	19.7	0.5

Compound Return (%)	10 yr	9 yr	8 yr	7 yr	6 yr	5 yr	4 yr	3 yr	2 yr	1 yr
						20.2	22.7	23.0	13.4	19.1

U.S. EQUITY

BPI AMERICAN EQUITY VALUE

LOAD

Primary Objective:	Growth
Sponsor:	BPI Mutual Funds
Fund Manager:	Paul Holland & Jon Sorenson, BGAM
Style:	Bottom-up, Value
Size (MMs):	$293.100
RRSP:	20%
Expense Ratio:	2.51%

COMMENTS

Available in RSP version

Chief Investment Officer Dan Jaworski has built an energetic young team that keeps racking up great returns in both the U.S. and the global markets. The fund is now top quartile across all compound periods out to 10 years ended August 31, 1999, where it has achieved an 18.9% CAGR to rank as the number one fund in the category. GE, Microsoft, and Intel holdings indicate that this fund should be named a growth fund. MER is competitive for category, but not compelling. CI Funds is committed to retaining the relationship with BPI Global Asset Management. **Smart Fund History: 1999.**

RISK

How Often Money was Lost:.....42 of 116 Months
.....22 of 114 Quarters
.....1 of 105 Years
Worst 3 Months: .....-9.56% (1990)
Best 3 Months: 31.81% (1999)

ASSET ALLOCATION

Technology 20.6
Consumer products 18.2
Industrial products 16.7
Oil & Gas 8.6
Communications 8.1
Other 27.8

U.S. EQUITY

COMPARISON OF FUND TO INDEXES

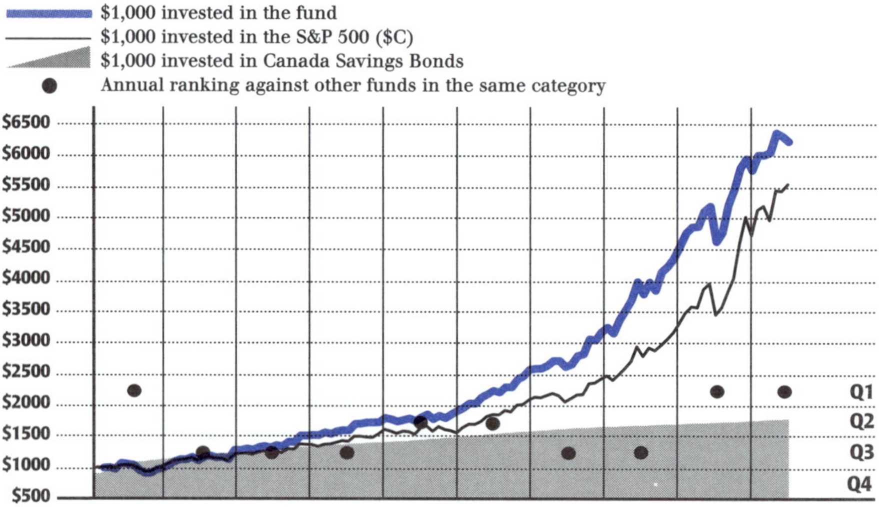

Annual	**1990**		**1992**		**1994**		**1996**		**1998**	**8/31/99**
Return (%)	0.3	19.7	13.8	12.5	3.5	26.4	17.4	29.7	50.5	20.5

Compound	**10 yr**	**9 yr**	**8 yr**	**7 yr**	**6 yr**	**5 yr**	**4 yr**	**3 yr**	**2 yr**	**1 yr**
Return (%)	18.9	21.1	21.5	24.0	24.4	27.3	31.8	38.1	41.2	60.8

CIBC NORTH AMERICAN DEMOGRAPHICS **NO LOAD**

Primary Objective: Growth
Sponsor: CIBC Securities Inc.
Fund Manager: Nancy Self, TAL Global Asset Mgmt.
Style: Top-down, Sector
Size (MMs): $92.039
RRSP: 20%
Expense Ratio: 2.45%

COMMENTS

After reading David Foot's bestselling *Boom, Bust & Echo*, many seek to invest in the demographic theme. We made this a Smart Fund in its debut year. It remains one of the best offerings from CIBC. The fund uses demographic analysis to determine how the baby boomers, Generation X, and other generations will impact markets as they age. Initial focus is North America. Managed by TAL, with input from demographers at the RAND Corporation. At August 31, the fund invested in Microsoft, Pfizer, Time Warner, and Cisco, to name a few. The fund was up 43% in 1997 and is up 20.7% since inception. **Smart Fund History: 1999, 1998.**

RISK

How Often Money was Lost:.......12 of 35 Months
.......5 of 33 Quarters
.......0 of 24 Years
Worst 3 Months:.......-15.81% (1998)
Best 3 Months:.......26.45% (1998)

ASSET ALLOCATION

Consumer services.......38.1
Health care.......15.1
Financial services.......12.4
Technology.......9.6
Consumer products—non durable....7.5
Other.......17.3

COMPARISON OF FUND TO INDEXES

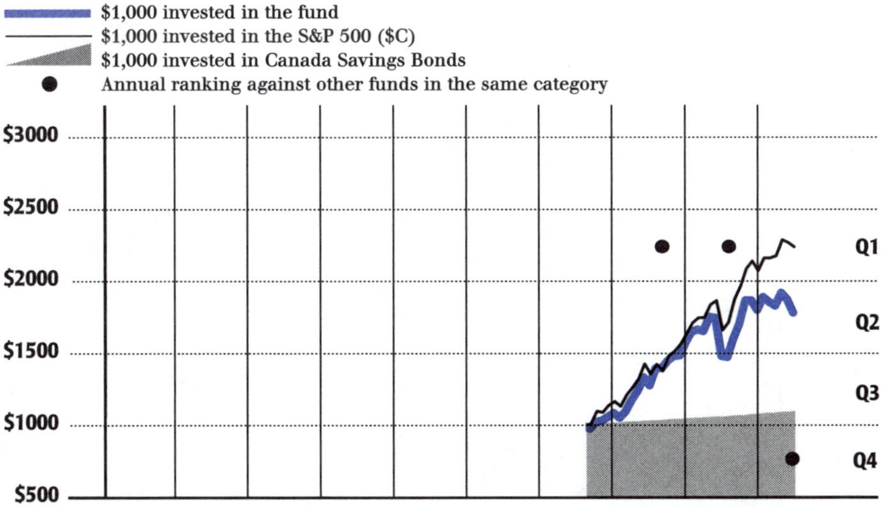

	1990		1992		1994		1996		1998	8/31/99
Annual Return (%)								43.2	26.0	-4.6

	10 yr	9 yr	8 yr	7 yr	6 yr	5 yr	4 yr	3 yr	2 yr	1 yr
Compound Return (%)									18.0	20.2

U.S. EQUITY

ELLIOTT & PAGE AMERICAN GROWTH LOAD

Primary Objective:	Growth
Sponsor:	Elliott & Page Ltd.
Fund Manager:	Robert Jones, Goldman Sachs
Style:	Bottom-up, Growth
Size (MMs):	$235.917
RRSP:	20%
Expense Ratio:	1.44%

COMMENTS

Still one of the lowest MERs in the load fund world at 1.44%. Robert Jones at Goldman Sachs continues to hold the large-cap growth stocks such as GE, Microsoft, AIG, and Citigroup. Fund's steady first- and second-quartile performance since 1995 has pulled the overall compound returns up to a first quartile 28.3% for the three years ended August 31, 1999. **Smart Fund History: 1999.**

RISK

How Often Money was Lost:.....41 of 116 Months
.....30 of 114 Quarters
.....2 of 105 Years
Worst 3 Months: .....-12.57% (1998)
Best 3 Months:.....22.70% (1998)

ASSET ALLOCATION

Technology 19.2
Financial services 16.2
Communications 11.4
Health care 10.2
Consumer products—non-durable 7.4
Other 35.6

U.S. EQUITY

COMPARISON OF FUND TO INDEXES

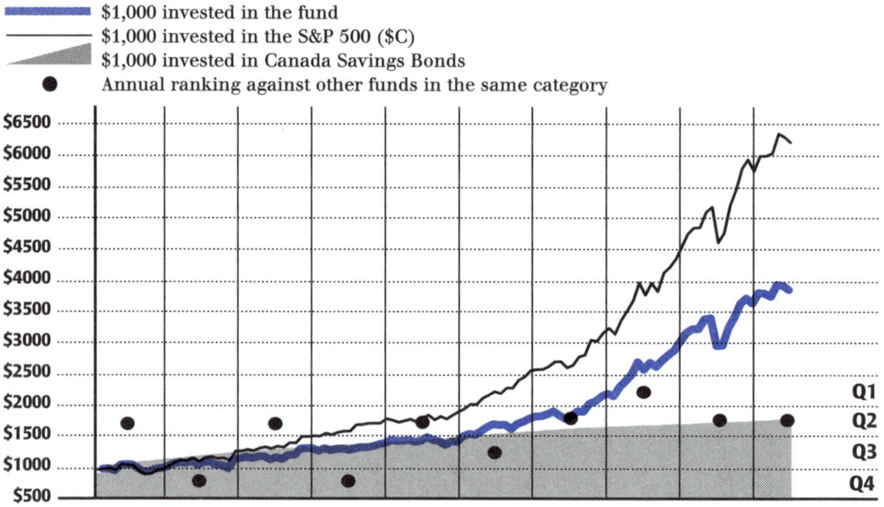

Annual Return (%)	1990		1992		1994		1996		1998	8/31/99
	-1.9	14.9	15.1	5.3	3.5	22.1	19.3	36.1	29.4	6.1

Compound Return (%)	10 yr	9 yr	8 yr	7 yr	6 yr	5 yr	4 yr	3 yr	2 yr	1 yr
	14.8	16.5	17.2	19.2	19.9	21.1	23.1	28.3	22.4	30.4

ETHICAL NORTH AMERICAN EQUITY **NO LOAD**

Primary Objective:	Growth with Ethical Screens
Sponsor:	Ethical Funds Inc.
Fund Manager:	Cynthia Frick, Alliance Capital since 5/93
Style:	Bottom-up, Growth
Size (MMs):	$324.584
RRSP:	20%
Expense Ratio:	2.39%

COMMENTS

Alliance Capital's Cindy Frick has steered this to a 28.9% CAGR for the five years ended August 31, 1999. Good enough for first overall in the category over that period. Ms. Frick manages this slightly differently than star manager Al Harrison on the MD U.S. Equity (also a Smart Fund). This one has ethical screens that the fund sponsor imposes, such as no tobacco or alcohol stocks. Frick holds "mostly companies which are highly liquid blue-chips, with a strong cost structure, strong leadership, high legal and accounting standards, and which are industry leaders." It's the execution that distinguishes this fund from the rest of the pack. **Smart Fund History: 1999.**

RISK

How Often Money was Lost:.....39 of 114 Months
.....27 of 112 Quarters
.....7 of 103 Years
Worst 3 Months:.....-10.55% (1990)
Best 3 Months:.....33.72% (1998)

ASSET ALLOCATION

Consumer products.....25.6
Financial services.....20.7
Communications.....8.3
Transportation.....0.6
Industrial products.....0.3
Other.....44.5

COMPARISON OF FUND TO INDEXES

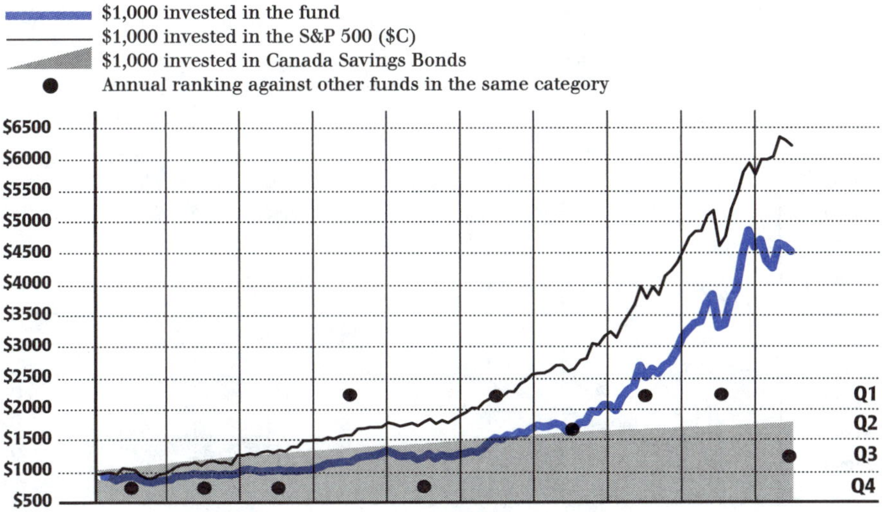

	1990		1992		1994		1996		1998	8/31/99
Annual Return (%)	-14.0	11.9	5.8	26.5	-4.2	29.8	21.2	41.8	62.6	1.1

Compound Return (%)	**10 yr**	**9 yr**	**8 yr**	**7 yr**	**6 yr**	**5 yr**	**4 yr**	**3 yr**	**2 yr**	**1 yr**
	16.3	20.2	21.4	24.1	24.6	28.9	31.7	39.7	34.4	37.2

U.S. EQUITY

FIDELITY GROWTH AMERICA

LOAD

Primary Objective:	Growth
Sponsor:	Fidelity Investments Canada
Fund Manager:	Steve Snider
Style:	Bottom-up, Growth
Size (MMs):	$2,064.030
RRSP:	20%
Expense Ratio:	2.30%

COMMENTS

Former lead manager Brad Lewis designed the sophisticated computer models that drive the stock selection on this fund. Mr. Lewis was promoted, leaving the day-to-day management of the fund to his protégé Steve Snyder. As always, a key part of their work is focused on avoiding stocks that will underperform. Fund's goal is to always be second quartile or better each calendar year. The fund invested in some value stocks and small caps, feeling their time had come. After performance was dragged into the third quartile, Mr. Snyder brought the fund back to the big growth names, GE, Microsoft, Hewlett Packard, and Wal-Mart. This fund is first quartile with its eight-year CAGR of 20.6%. **Smart Fund History: 1999, 1997, 1996.**

RISK

How Often Money was Lost:	34 of 107 Months
	22 of 105 Quarters
	2 of 96 Years
Worst 3 Months:	-11.89% (1998)
Best 3 Months:	24.18% (1992)

ASSET ALLOCATION

Financial services	16.1
Utilities	8.7
Technology	21.3
Health care	8.7
Retail & Wholesale	10.3
Other	34.9

COMPARISON OF FUND TO INDEXES

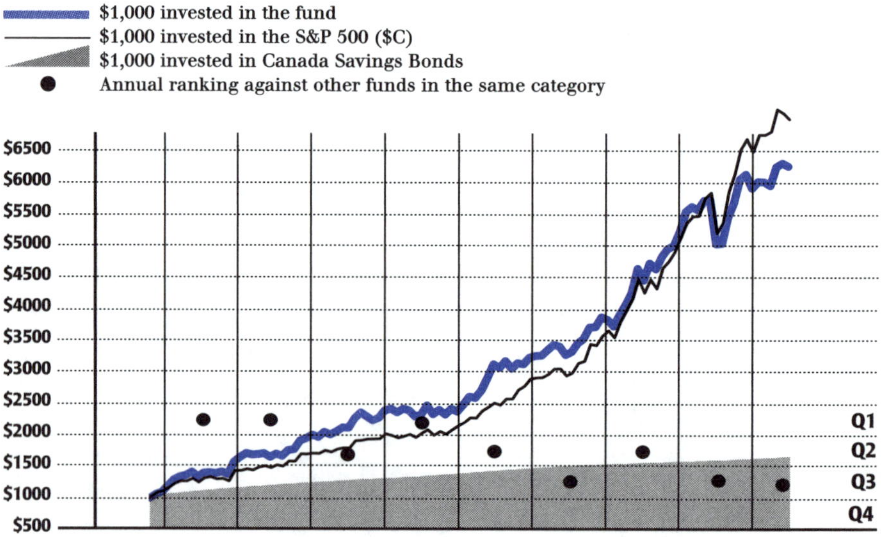

Annual Return (%)	1990		1992		1994		1996		1998	8/31/99
		44.3	27.3	17.2	6.2	29.3	18.9	33.6	22.2	3.4

Compound Return (%)	10 yr	9 yr	8 yr	7 yr	6 yr	5 yr	4 yr	3 yr	2 yr	1 yr
			20.6	20.9	18.5	20.5	19.6	23.6	18.6	24.4

U.S. EQUITY

GREEN LINE U.S. INDEX

NO LOAD

Primary Objective:	Index
Sponsor:	TD Asset Management
Fund Manager:	Team
Style:	Passive
Size (MMs):	$190.205
RRSP:	20%
Expense Ratio:	0.63%

COMMENTS

We formally recognized index funds last year. MERs are significantly less, they outperform most money managers, and they are tax-efficient. This one has been around a while and has a reasonable MER compared with some other Canadian pretenders. Remember, this one has its NAV quoted in U.S. dollars. No problem for Canadians: they have picked up the currency gain in addition to the soaring U.S. stock market. However, other Canadian dollar-quoted U.S. equity funds or the S&P 500 index reflected in Canadian-dollar terms appear to be outperforming the fund. Because it is bought in U.S. dollars, this is a good one for snowbirds. **Smart Fund History: 1999.**

RISK

How Often Money was Lost:.....36 of 116 Months
.....20 of 114 Quarters
.....2 of 105 Years
Worst 3 Months: .....-14.07% (1990)
Best 3 Months:.....21.77% (1998)

ASSET ALLOCATION

Technology 23.6
Financial services 14.5
Consumer products—staples 12.0
Health care 10.8
Consumer products—cyclical 8.4
Other 30.7

COMPARISON OF FUND TO INDEXES

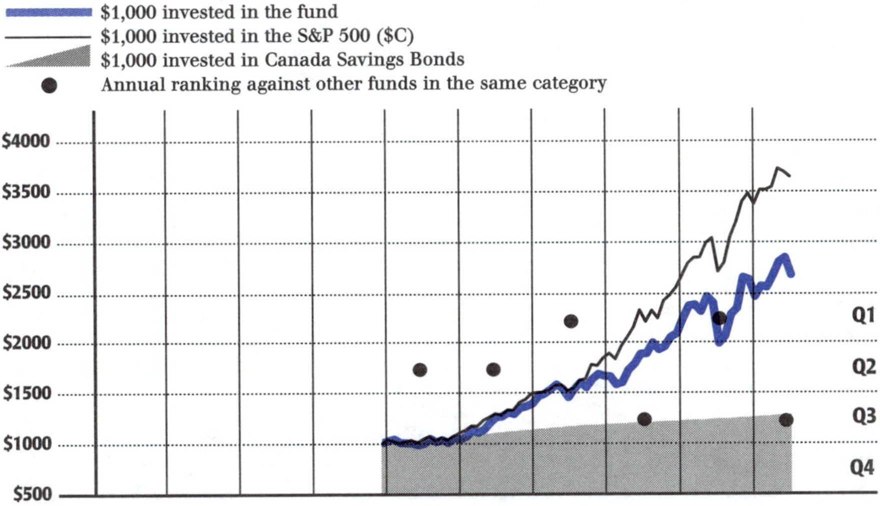

Annual Return (%)	1990		1992		1994		1996		1998	8/31/99
	-4.2	27.7	5.8	8.4	0.5	35.3	21.8	32.3	27.7	7.6

Compound Return (%)	10 yr	9 yr	8 yr	7 yr	6 yr	5 yr	4 yr	3 yr	2 yr	1 yr
	15.6	18.3	17.6	19.3	20.4	23.8	24.9	27.5	22.0	38.5

U.S. EQUITY

GREEN LINE U.S. MID-CAP GROWTH NO LOAD

Primary Objective:	Growth
Sponsor:	TD Asset Management
Fund Manager:	Brian Berghuis, T. Rowe Price Assoc.
Style:	Bottom-up, Growth
Size (MMs):	$273.604
RRSP:	20%
Expense Ratio:	2.33%

COMMENTS

Managed by the venerable T. Rowe Price & Associates. Brian Berghuis is highly recognized in the U.S. business media and is ranked 5-star by Morningstar. He returns to Smart Funds this year after being wrongly dropped last year. A great way to play the U.S. market away from the highly valued large-cap name and get additional diversification in your portfolio. No denying the performance, 20.6% five-year CAGR and a first quartile performer for the five-, three- and two year periods. **Smart Funds History: 1998, 1997, 1996.**

RISK

How Often Money was Lost:.......23 of 68 Months
....14 of 66 Quarters
....0 of 57 Years
Worst 3 Months: ....-15.95% (1998)
Best 3 Months: 28.25% (1998)

ASSET ALLOCATION

Technology 27.3
Consumer products—cyclical ...18.5
Health care 12.5
Financial services 9.0
Consumer products—staples.......8.9
Other 23.8

COMPARISON OF FUND TO INDEXES

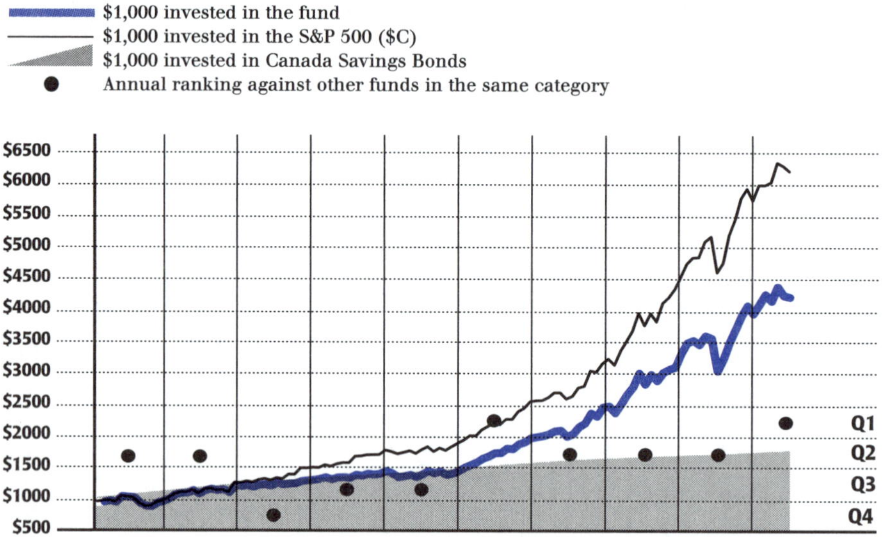

	1990		1992		1994		1996		1998	8/31/99
Annual Return (%)					4.4	30.1	23.6	21.7	28.9	0.9

	10 yr	9 yr	8 yr	7 yr	6 yr	5 yr	4 yr	3 yr	2 yr	1 yr
Compound Return (%)						20.6	20.5	20.2	18.8	34.1

GUARDIAN AMERICAN EQUITY CLASSIC **LOAD**

Primary Objective:	Growth
Sponsor:	Guardian Mutual Funds
Fund Manager:	Michael Rome, Lazard since 2/98
Style:	Bottom-up, Growth
Size (MMs):	$49.354
RRSP:	20%
Expense Ratio:	2.04%

COMMENTS

Michael Rome, the highly respected money manager from Lazard, just keeps driving top performance. The BPI American Small Companies fund was a Smart Fund in 1996 and 1997 when he was the subadvisor. Rome runs a concentrated portfolio of about 60 stocks selected based on value criteria. You will find that this fund generates consistent performance, with less volatility and is a great style complement to the high-flying Maxxum American equity or AGF American Growth funds. Since taking over the fund, Rome has steered it to first quartile. **Smart Fund History: 1999, 1996.**

RISK

How Often Money was Lost:.....37 of 116 Months
....27 of 114 Quarters
....3 of 105 Years
Worst 3 Months:..............................-20.13% (1990)
Best 3 Months:..................................27.40% (1998)

ASSET ALLOCATION

Financial services 13.7
Technology 11.2
Communications.........................11.2
Entertainment.............................10.9
Consumer products 6.4
Other 46.6

COMPARISON OF FUND TO INDEXES

$1,000 invested in the fund
$1,000 invested in the S&P 500 ($C)
$1,000 invested in Canada Savings Bonds
● Annual ranking against other funds in the same category

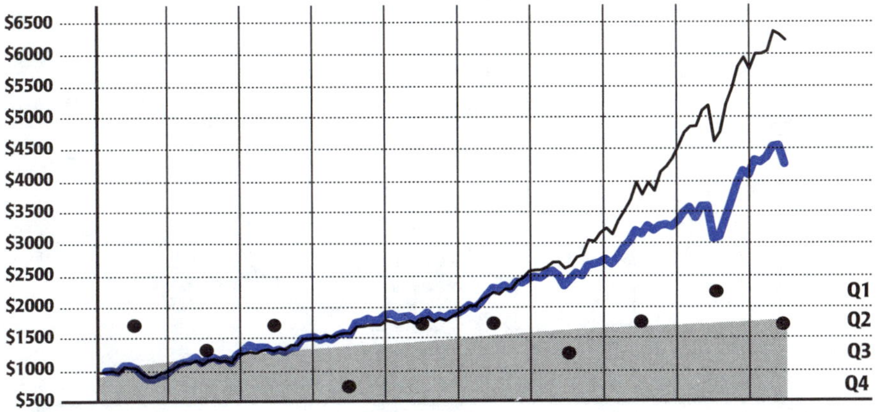

Annual Return (%)	1990		1992		1994		1996		1998	8/31/99
	-8.0	35.0	22.2	18.2	5.0	26.1	12.4	23.4	19.9	7.6

Compound Return (%)	10 yr	9 yr	8 yr	7 yr	6 yr	5 yr	4 yr	3 yr	2 yr	1 yr
	15.1	18.4	17.1	18.6	16.0	17.4	16.9	20.5	16.3	38.6

HSBC U.S. EQUITY

NO LOAD

Primary Objective: Growth
Sponsor: HSBC Investment Funds
Fund Manager: Frederic Lutcher III, HSBC Asset Mgmt
Style: Top-down, Growth
Size (MMs): $74.124
RRSP: 20%
Expense Ratio: 2.08%

COMMENTS

Hard to deny this top performer. With consistent strong performance, this bank no-load has squeezed out some other previous Smart Funds. Riding the top names in its portfolio, IBM, Cisco, Microsoft, Intel, AOL, Sun Microsystems, and MCI Worldcomm, gives you an idea on why this one has been first quartile for the three-, two-, and one-year periods. The manager buys dominant growth companies. This one also gives you a reasonable MER of 2.09%. **New Smart Fund.**

RISK

How Often Money was Lost: ....14 of 57 Months
.......8 of 55 Quarters
.......0 of 46 Years
Worst 3 Months: ....-10.81% (1998)
Best 3 Months: 23.87% (1998)

ASSET ALLOCATION

Consumer products 25.5
Industrial products 22.0
Financial services 15.0
Communications 11.1
Health care 7.3
Other 19.1

COMPARISON OF FUND TO INDEXES

$1,000 invested in the fund
$1,000 invested in the S&P 500 ($C)
$1,000 invested in Canada Savings Bonds
Annual ranking against other funds in the same category

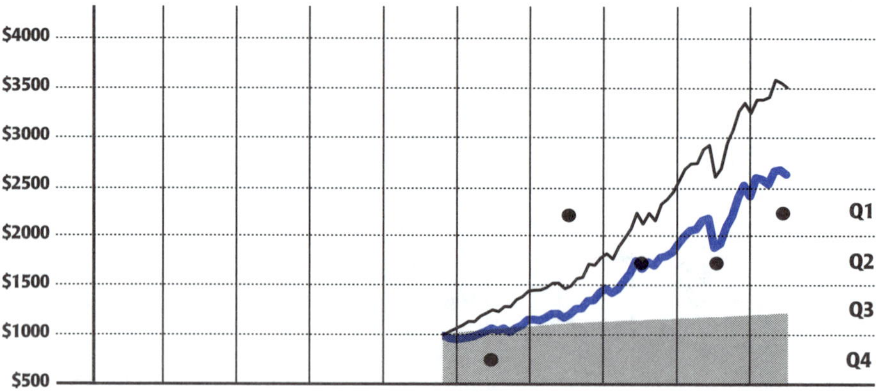

Annual Return (%)	**1990**		**1992**		**1994**		**1996**		**1998**	**8/31/99**
						13.5	23.4	33.0	32.5	9.9
Compound Return (%)	**10 yr**	**9 yr**	**8 yr**	**7 yr**	**6 yr**	**5 yr**	**4 yr**	**3 yr**	**2 yr**	**1 yr**
							25.8	29.4	25.3	39.0

LONDON LIFE AMERICAN EQUITY

LOAD

Primary Objective:	Growth
Sponsor:	London Fund Management
Fund Manager:	Warren Lammert, Janus Capital Corp.
Style:	Bottom-up, Growth
Size (MMs):	$33.127
RRSP:	20%
Expense Ratio:	2.58%

COMMENTS

A great "guaranteed" way of buying the top-performing Janus team. This seg fund buys units of the two-time Smart Fund Maxxum American Equity, which is up 70% for the year ended August 31. See additional comments on the underlying fund in the Scudder Maxxum entry. This one's guarantee comes with an MER of 2.58%. Remember that this one is available only through life-licensed sales reps and generally those affiliated with London Life. This is a good choice for nervous investors desiring the extra seg protection. **New Smart Fund.**

RISK

How Often Money was Lost: ....4 of 13 Months
....1 of 11 Quarters
....0 of 2 Years
Worst 3 Months: ....-1.00% (1998)
Best 3 Months:..................................36.72% (1999)

ASSET ALLOCATION

Technology 35.2
Consumer products—non cyclical.....17.1
Consumer products—cyclical....15.1
Health care 6.4
Financial services 6.3
Other 19.9

U.S. EQUITY

COMPARISON OF FUND TO INDEXES

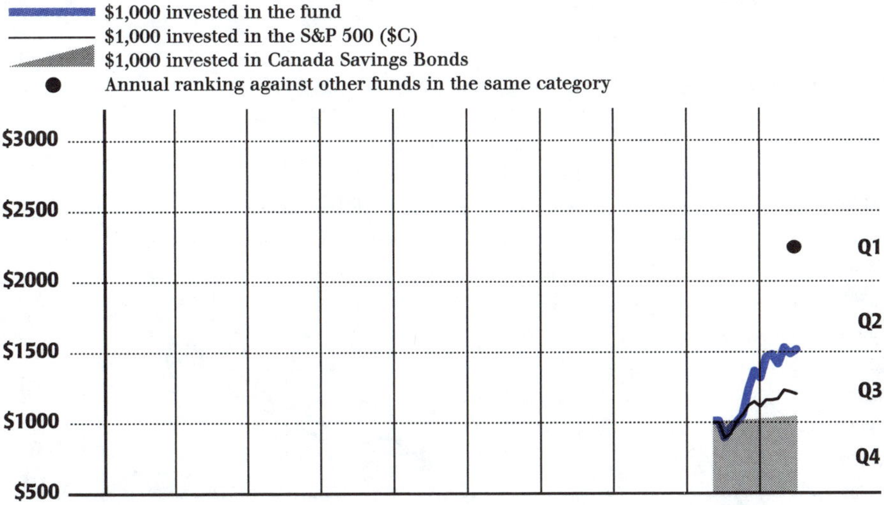

Annual Return (%)	1990		1992		1994		1996		1998	8/31/99
										23.0%

Compound Return (%)	10 yr	9 yr	8 yr	7 yr	6 yr	5 yr	4 yr	3 yr	2 yr	1 yr
										71.2%

MAXXUM AMERICAN EQUITY

LOAD

Primary Objective: Growth
Sponsor: Scudder Maxxum Co.
Fund Manager: Warren Lammert, Janus Capital
Style: Bottom-up, Growth
Size (MMs): $121.025
RRSP: 20%
Expense Ratio: 2.90%

COMMENTS

Available in RSP version

New to Smart Funds last year when it rocketed to a 67.8% return in 1998 and now sports a lofty 40.5% CAGR over three years. One of two Maxxum funds managed by highly regarded Denver-based Janus Capital Corp. Manager Warren Lammert, who manages the Janus Mercury Fund, can invest up to 30% outside the U.S.. Fund continues to ride its 30% technology weighting to the top of the class. All stocks are picked, after detailed bottom-up research, for their growth aspects regardless of industry. The fund is first quartile over the one-, two-, three-, and four-year return periods ending August 31. You may have to ask around for Maxxum funds because they are not well known, but watch the two managed by Janus. Since Janus took over managing this fund in October 1997, the NAV has gone from $8.82 to $13.10. **Smart Fund History: 1999.**

RISK

How Often Money was Lost:.......18 of 55 Months
....10 of 53 Quarters
....0 of 44 Years
Worst 3 Months: ....-6.16% (1996)
Best 3 Months: 37.52% (1999)

ASSET ALLOCATION

Technology 35.2
Consumer products non cyclical.....17.1
Consumer products cyclical ...15.1
Health care 6.4
Financial services 6.3
Other 19.9

COMPARISON OF FUND TO INDEXES

$1,000 invested in the fund
$1,000 invested in the S&P 500 ($C)
$1,000 invested in Canada Savings Bonds
Annual ranking against other funds in the same category

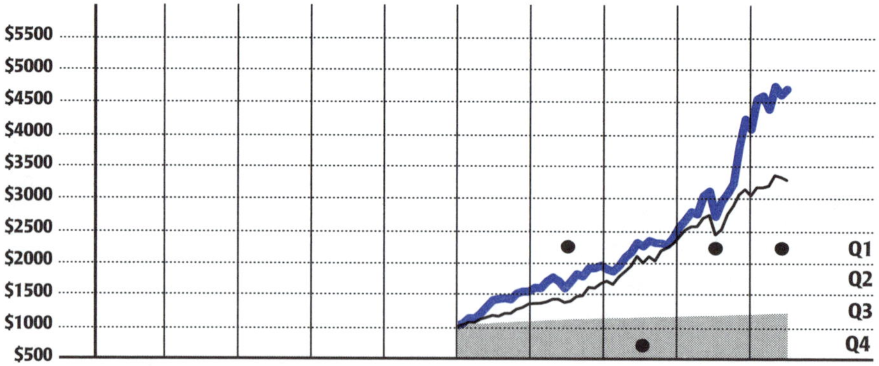

Annual Return (%)	**1990**		**1992**		**1994**		**1996**		**1998**	**8/31/99**
							23.9	19.1	67.8	23.4
Compound Return (%)	**10 yr**	**9 yr**	**8 yr**	**7 yr**	**6 yr**	**5 yr**	**4 yr**	**3 yr**	**2 yr**	**1 yr**
							34.9	40.5	44.7	73.0

U.S. EQUITY

MD U.S. EQUITY

NO LOAD

Primary Objective:	Growth
Sponsor:	MD Management
Fund Manager:	Alliance Capital Mgmt
Style:	Bottom-up, Growth
Size (MMs):	$548.239
RRSP:	20%
Expense Ratio:	1.27%

COMMENTS

Alliance Capital is one of the top U.S. growth managers around. Just look at the performance on this fund and on Ethical North American. This fund is restricted to members of the medical establishment. A top-quartile performer over the five-, three-, two-, and one-year periods and a regular on the Smart Funds list, this is a great long-term hold if you're eligible. This fund clones manager Alfred Harrison's Alliance Premier Growth B (ranked 5-star by Morningstar) fund available to American investors. Fund continues to hold Dell Computer, Cisco, and other great growth stocks. This fund split its units 5 for 1 in July 1999. **Smart Fund History: 1999, 1998, 1996.**

RISK

How Often Money was Lost:	24 of 83 Months
	15 of 81 Quarters
	1 of 72 Years
Worst 3 Months:	-9.61% (1998)
Best 3 Months:	30.12% (1998)

ASSET ALLOCATION

Consumer products	27.6
Technology	23.4
Financial services	21.0
Health care	13.0
Industrial products	5.0
Other	10.0

COMPARISON OF FUND TO INDEXES

$1,000 invested in the fund
$1,000 invested in the S&P 500 ($C)
$1,000 invested in Canada Savings Bonds
● Annual ranking against other funds in the same category

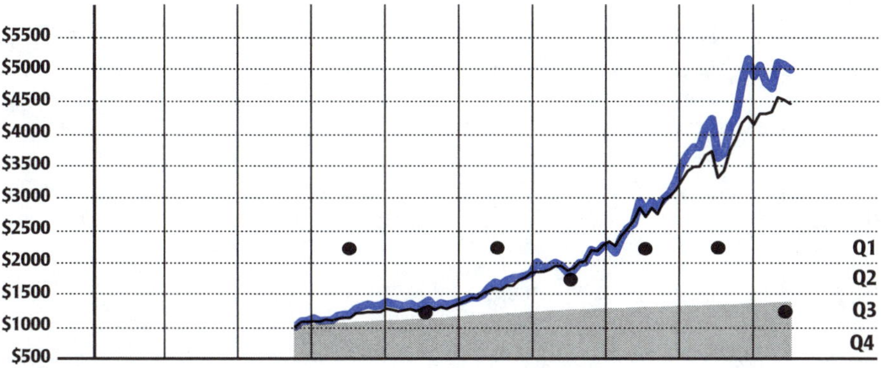

	1990		1992		1994		1996		1998	8/31/99
Annual Return (%)				21.7	2.0	31.6	20.5	42.4	56.3	3.8

	10 yr	9 yr	8 yr	7 yr	6 yr	5 yr	4 yr	3 yr	2 yr	1 yr
Compound Return (%)					25.4	28.7	31.7	38.6	34.0	37.9

ROYAL U.S. RSP INDEX FUND **NO LOAD**

Primary Objective:	Index
Sponsor:	Royal Mutual Funds Inc.
Fund Manager:	State Street Global Advisors
Style:	Passive
Size (MMs):	$165.456
RRSP:	20%
Expense Ratio:	0.50%

COMMENTS

Do not hold this one outside an RRSP or in a taxable account. All distributions in this and other RSP-eligible foreign funds are taxed as income. Still, this is a great way to gain foreign exposure without going offside on your foreign content. Since managers don't often beat the highly efficient S&P 500 index, the 0.50% MER makes it a deal over the previous Smart Funds for this type Canada Trust's AmeriGrowth and CIBC's U.S. Index RSP. For this we just look for the lowest MER in an index fund run by a renowned index manager, like State Street Global Advisors. **New Smart Fund.**

RISK

How Often Money was Lost:	4 of 10 Months
	1 of 8 Quarters
	0 of 0 Years
Worst 3 Months:	-0.33% (1999)
Best 3 Months:	15.53% (1999)

ASSET ALLOCATION

Consumer	34.1
Capital goods	30.6
Financial services	14.5
Utilities	7.7
Energy	6.2
Other	6.9

COMPARISON OF FUND TO INDEXES

$1,000 invested in the fund
$1,000 invested in the S&P 500 ($C)
$1,000 invested in Canada Savings Bonds
Annual ranking against other funds in the same category

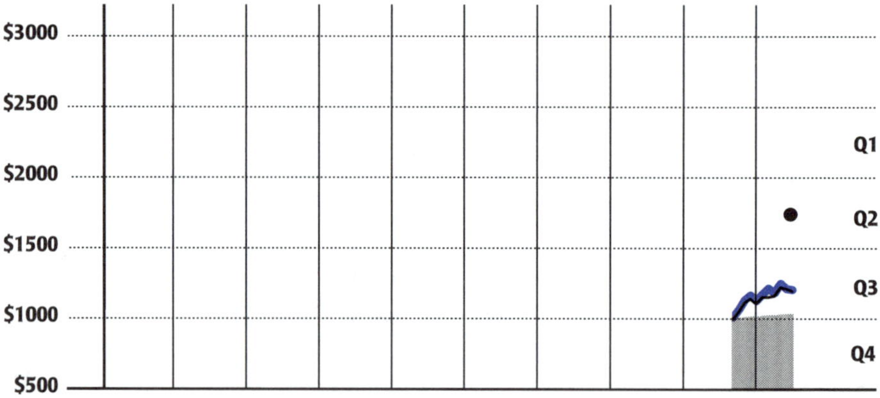

	1990		1992		1994		1996		1998	8/31/99
Annual Return (%)										6.4

	10 yr	9 yr	8 yr	7 yr	6 yr	5 yr	4 yr	3 yr	2 yr	1 yr
Compound Return (%)										

SPECTRUM UNITED AMERICAN GROWTH LOAD

Primary Objective:	Growth
Sponsor:	Spectrum United Mutual Funds
Fund Manager:	John Ballen & Toni Shimura, MFS Institutional (12/95)
Style:	Bottom-up, small-and mid-cap growth
Size (MMs):	$774.945
RRSP:	20%
Expense Ratio:	2.41%

COMMENTS

This fund has expanded its mandate to buy anything it wants and is now more of a large-cap fund. Top holdings include Cisco, MCI, Microsoft, Oracle, and AT&T. Manager John Ballen is highly acclaimed with stellar long-term numbers. Once the handicap of playing only in the small- and mid-cap arena was removed, Ballen steered this to first-quartile returns in the three-year period. This one is clearly a bottom-up, growth portfolio with a 25.8% five-year CAGR. **Smart Fund History: 1999.**

RISK

How Often Money was Lost:.....46 of 116 Months
..........28 of 114 Quarters
..........2 of 105 Years
Worst 3 Months:..........-17.59% (1990)
Best 3 Months:..........32.13% (1999)

ASSET ALLOCATION

Communications..........35.1
Technology..........22.3
Leisure..........8.9
Cash & equivalents..........8.2
Global equities..........6.1
Other..........19.4

COMPARISON OF FUND TO INDEXES

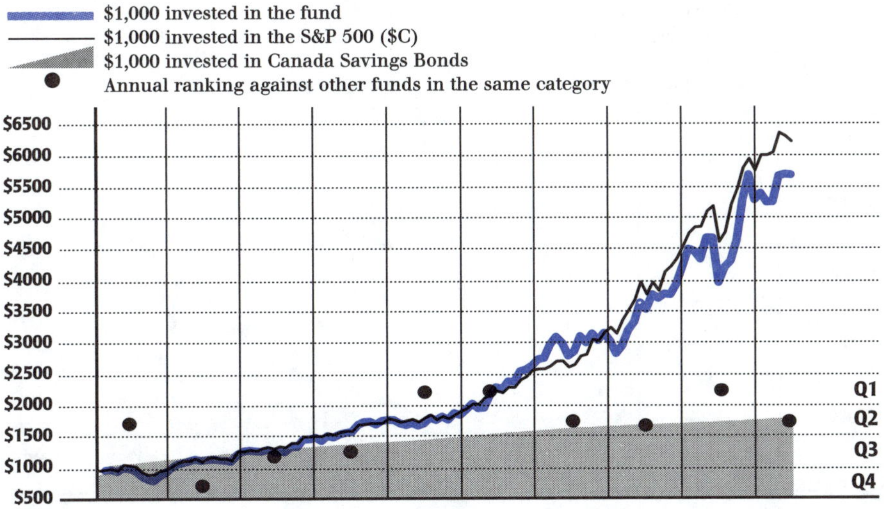

Annual	1990		1992		1994		1996		1998	8/31/99
Return (%)	-6.5	31.3	20.0	20.0	6.7	37.2	18.1	23.9	40.2	7.5

Compound	10 yr	9 yr	8 yr	7 yr	6 yr	5 yr	4 yr	3 yr	2 yr	1 yr
Return (%)	18.3	22.9	22.1	24.0	22.4	25.8	26.0	25.7	26.8	43.5

U.S. EQUITY

AGF INTERNATIONAL VALUE

LOAD

Primary Objective:	Growth
Sponsor:	AGF Funds Inc.
Fund Manager:	Charles Brandes & Jeff Busby, Brandes Partners
Style:	Bottom-up, Value
Size (MMs):	$3,407.100
RRSP:	20%
Expense Ratio:	2.77%

COMMENTS

Available in RSP version

This global fund's three-year CAGR of 24.3% is nothing to sneeze at. Charles Brandes and Jeff Busby's value-investing approach has been even more successful than Templeton. This is a top-quartile performer, with modest volatility. Investors have finally noticed this five-time Smart Fund. It had assets of $106 million when we first recommended it in our 1996 edition. It is now at $3.4 billion, having increased by over $1 billion in the last 12 months. Buy this one for your RSP and hold it as long as you can! AGF has got to lower the MER from its outrageous 2.77% and get closer to its competitors. With those kind of fees, we should recommend the AGF stock. **Smart Fund History: 1999, 1998, 1997, 1996.**

RISK

How Often Money was Lost: ....19 of 57 Months
....10 of 55 Quarters
....1 of 46 Years
Worst 3 Months: ....-10.88% (1998)
Best 3 Months: 20.03% (1998)

ASSET ALLOCATION

USA...36.3
Japan...10.7
UK...10.3
Hong Kong.......................................9.9
Brazil..6.7
Other..26.1

COMPARISON OF FUND TO INDEXES

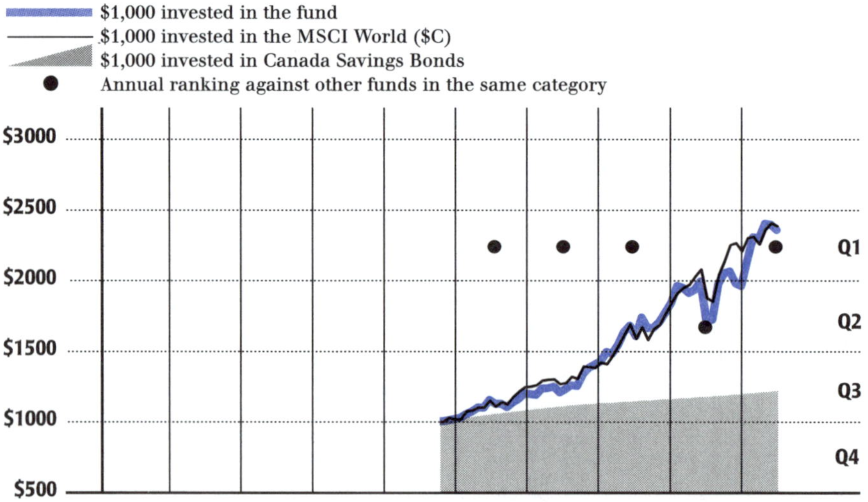

Annual Return (%)	**1990**		**1992**		**1994**	15.0	**1996** 19.0	23.6	**1998** 20.9	**8/31/99** 14.3
Compound Return (%)	**10 yr**	**9 yr**	**8 yr**	**7 yr**	**6 yr**	**5 yr** 16.6	**4 yr** 20.3	**3 yr** 24.3	**2 yr** 21.2	**1 yr** 38.0

BPI GLOBAL EQUITY VALUE

LOAD

Primary Objective:	Growth
Sponsor:	BPI Mutual Funds
Fund Manager:	Dan Jaworski, BPI Global Asset Management
Style:	Bottom-up, Growth
Size (MMs):	$941.000
RRSP:	20%
Expense Ratio:	2.44%

COMMENTS

Available in RSP version

Solid performance has pulled this fund into the top quartile across all compound periods through 10 years. Big weighting of 54% in U.S. large-cap stocks like GE, Microsoft, and Wal-Mart continues to pay off. Don't be confused by the name, it is not a value fund and would make a great complement to the AGF International Value fund. **Smart Fund History: 1999.**

RISK

How Often Money was Lost:.....39 of 116 Months
.....24 of 114 Quarters
.....6 of 105 Years
Worst 3 Months: .....-11.11% (1998)
Best 3 Months: 20.49% (1998)

ASSET ALLOCATION

North America 58.4
Europe 24.6
Japan 12.0
Far East.....3.9
Australia 1.0
Other.....0.1

COMPARISON OF FUND TO INDEXES

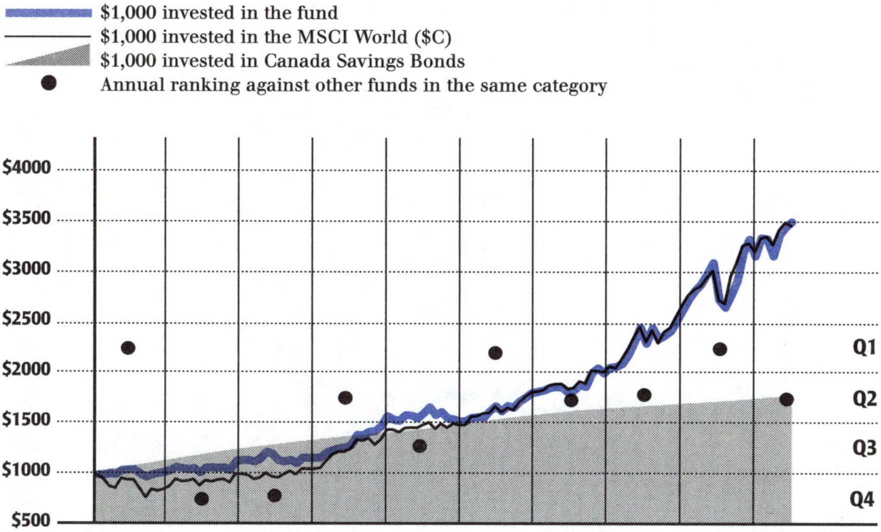

Annual Return (%)	1990		1992		1994		1996		1998	8/31/99
	1.0	11.2	2.9	27.4	4.5	14.3	16.6	18.0	32.2	9.6

Compound Return (%)	10 yr	9 yr	8 yr	7 yr	6 yr	5 yr	4 yr	3 yr	2 yr	1 yr
	13.7	15.0	16.1	17.7	16.8	16.1	21.3	24.2	23.5	28.4

GLOBAL EQUITY

CI GLOBAL

LOAD

Primary Objective:	Growth
Sponsor:	CI Mutual Funds
Fund Manager:	Bill Sterling
Style:	Top-down, Blend
Size (MMs):	$1,845.254
RRSP:	20%
Expense Ratio:	2.49%

COMMENTS

Available in RSP version

Top-down strategist Dr. Bill Sterling of C.I. Global Advisors is a keen student of demographics with the release of his new book *Boomernomics*. Many of his themes will play out in the direction of the fund and its positioning going forward, including technology, financial services, and biotechnology. Well diversified, its biggest holding, Microsoft, makes up just 1.6% of the fund. Almost 80% of the fund is split between Europe and the U.S. Since Sterling took over, it has risen from back-to-back fourth-quartile years in 1994 and 1995 to a first-quartile ranking in 1997 and 1998, raising it to a first-quartile 19.7% CAGR over the three-year compound period to August 31, 1999. **Smart Fund History: 1999.**

RISK

How Often Money was Lost:.....40 of 116 Months
.....30 of 114 Quarters
.....13 of 105 Years
Worst 3 Months:.....-12.66% (1990)
Best 3 Months:.....18.09% (1998)

ASSET ALLOCATION

USA.....45.9
Europe.....30.2
Japan.....11.7
Cash & equivalents.....3.8
Asia (ex-Japan).....3.3
Other.....5.1

COMPARISON OF FUND TO INDEXES

$1,000 invested in the fund
$1,000 invested in the MSCI World ($C)
$1,000 invested in Canada Savings Bonds
Annual ranking against other funds in the same category

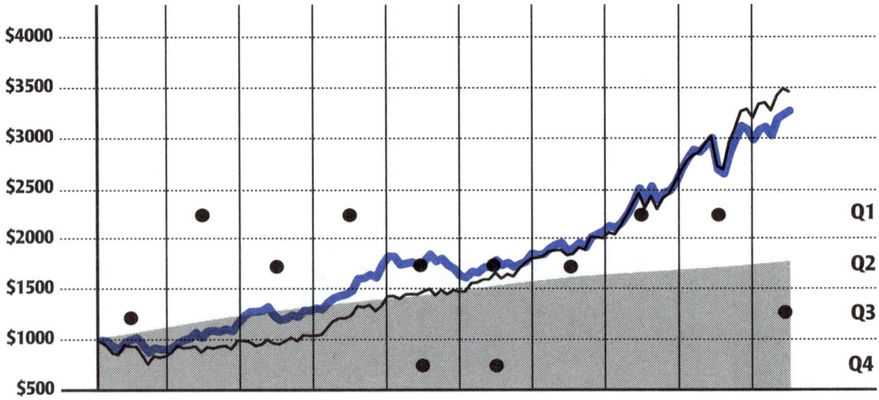

Annual	1990		1992		1994		1996		1998	8/31/99
Return (%)	-11.2	29.8	10.5	35.7	-2.1	4.0	15.4	21.1	26.2	4.8

Compound	10 yr	9 yr	8 yr	7 yr	6 yr	5 yr	4 yr	3 yr	2 yr	1 yr
Return (%)	13.0	14.8	14.8	15.4	12.6	12.2	17.2	19.7	17.3	21.8

GLOBAL EQUITY

FIDELITY INTERNATIONAL PORTFOLIO LOAD

Primary Objective: Growth
Sponsor: Fidelity Investments Canada
Fund Manager: Richard Habermann
Style: Bottom-up, Growth
Size (MMs): $5,925.177
RRSP: 20%
Expense Ratio: 2.58%

COMMENTS

Available in RSP version

Steady, consistent performers can appear boring in comparison with the high flyers. This fund proves slow and steady wins the race. With first- or second-quartile performance every calendar year since 1992, it is first quartile across ten-, five-, and three-year compound periods, with modest volatility. Habermann makes the country-allocation calls and then Fidelity's regional managers pick the stocks. For those in the Fidelity family, this fund could easily provide the only foreign content you need. It has certainly proven popular, growing by over $1.5 billion since December 1998. **Smart Fund History: 1999, 1998, 1997.**

RISK

How Often Money was Lost:.....39 of 116 Months
.....31 of 114 Quarters
.....10 of 105 Years
Worst 3 Months:.....-17.86% (1990)
Best 3 Months: 19.43% (1998)

ASSET ALLOCATION

USA.....49.8
Japan.....14.1
UK.....10.1
France.....4.6
Canada.....4.4
Other.....17.0

COMPARISON OF FUND TO INDEXES

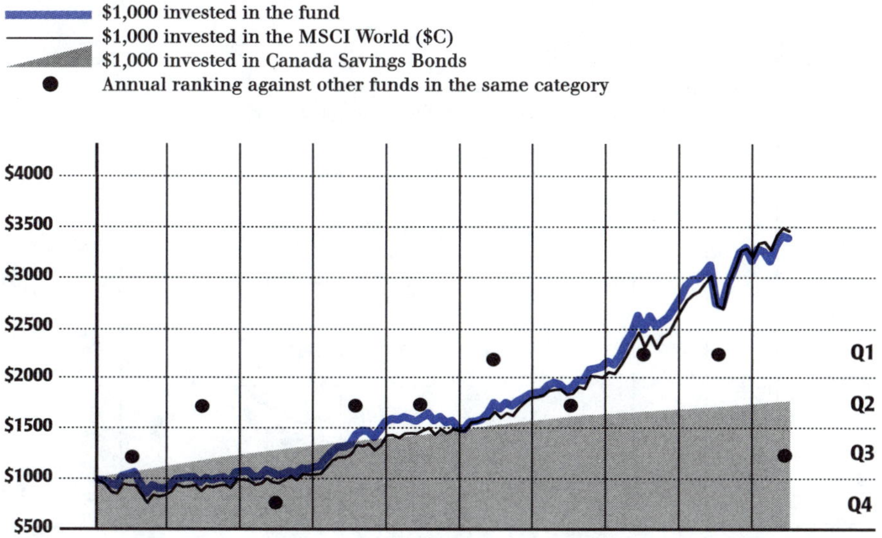

Annual Return (%)	1990		1992		1994		1996		1998	8/31/99
	-8.8	17.7	2.9	35.1	6.4	14.4	16.0	24.1	24.6	4.4

Compound Return (%)	10 yr	9 yr	8 yr	7 yr	6 yr	5 yr	4 yr	3 yr	2 yr	1 yr
	13.7	15.1	16.6	18.2	15.3	15.4	18.8	21.0	16.8	23.7

GLOBAL EQUITY

GWL INTERNATIONAL EQUITY B **LOAD**

Primary Objective:	Growth
Sponsor:	GWL Investment Management
Fund Manager:	Putnam Investments
Style:	Bottom-up, Growth
Size (MMs):	$103.734
RRSP:	20%
Expense Ratio:	2.60%

COMMENTS

Our only seg fund last year. Expense ratios are high on others and we are not sure being locked in for 10 years is worth the price. Y2K-wary investors may feel the guarantee is worth it. This is the only way for Canadians to get the benefits of Putnam's asset management expertise. This fund does not invest in the United States and is now properly compared with funds that are ex-U.S. It will normally hold around 100 stocks from at least 10 countries. It is first quartile over the three- and two-year periods, even after the 2.60% MER, which is down from 2.93% in last year's edition. This fund is similar to the 5-star rated Putnam International Growth A Fund managed by a team led by Justin Scott. **Smart Fund History: 1999.**

RISK

How Often Money was Lost:.......15 of 58 Months
....12 of 56 Quarters
....1 of 47 Years
Worst 3 Months:.............................-14.65% (1998)
Best 3 Months:..................................18.67% (1998)

ASSET ALLOCATION

Japan 20.1
UK 18.2
France 11.3
Germany 7.4
Netherlands 6.1
Other 36.9

COMPARISON OF FUND TO INDEXES

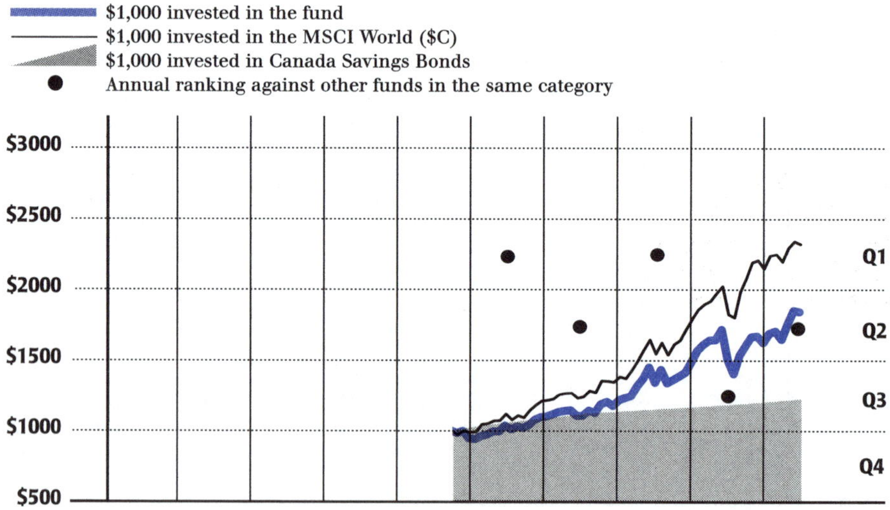

Annual Return (%)	1990		1992		1994		1996		1998	8/31/99
						8.1	12.1	15.6	20.3	10.8

Compound Return (%)	10 yr	9 yr	8 yr	7 yr	6 yr	5 yr	4 yr	3 yr	2 yr	1 yr
							16.5	18.9	17.5	22.8

GLOBAL EQUITY

GLOBAL STRATEGY WORLD COMPANIES **LOAD**

Primary Objective: Growth
Sponsor: Global Strategy Financial
Fund Manager: Rothschild, Montgomery Asset Management
Style: Multi-Manager
Size (MMs): $264.565
RRSP: 20%
Expense Ratio: 2.65%

COMMENTS

The portfolio is split between Montgomery Asset Management and Rothschild, who are free to invest anywhere. Each has its relative strengths and offers diversification for unitholders. A first-quartile performer in 1995, 1996, 1998, and so far in 1999 and has a CAGR of 24.7% since its inception in late 1994. This fund is highly diversified, so no single position or industry weighting can torpedo the net asset value. Despite being a five-time Smart Fund, it still has only $260 million in it. **Smart Fund History: 1999, 1998, 1997, 1996.**

RISK

How Often Money was Lost:.......14 of 56 Months
....10 of 54 Quarters
....1 of 45 Years
Worst 3 Months:..............................-14.55% (1998)
Best 3 Months: 30.66% (1998)

ASSET ALLOCATION

USA...30.5
UK...14.5
France...10.0
Japan...8.0
Netherlands.....................................6.1
Other..30.9

COMPARISON OF FUND TO INDEXES

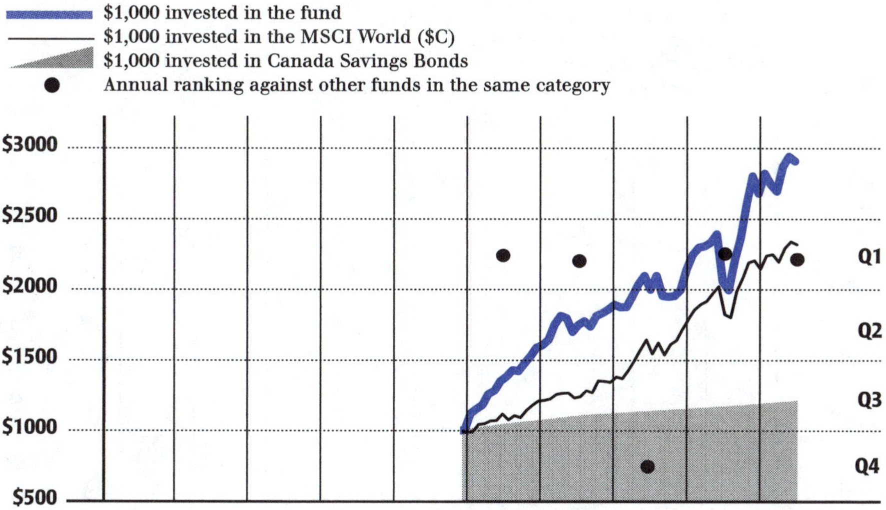

Annual Return (%)	**1990**		**1992**		**1994**	52.8	**1996** 19.9	6.7	**1998** 33.4	**8/31/99** 11.5
Compound Return (%)	**10 yr**	**9 yr**	**8 yr**	**7 yr**	**6 yr**	**5 yr**	**4 yr** 20.4	**3 yr** 18.4	**2 yr** 20.6	**1 yr** 41.5

GLOBAL EQUITY

LONDON LIFE GLOBAL EQUITY (MAXXUM) LOAD

Primary Objective:	Growth
Sponsor:	London Life Insurance Co.
Fund Manager:	Helen Young Hayes, Janus Capital Corp.
Style:	Bottom-up, Growth
Size (MMs):	$11.570
RRSP:	20%
Expense Ratio:	2.58%

COMMENTS

The seg fund version of Maxxum Global Equity. Take the guarantee on this one because you need the protection and desire some creditor proofing. The fund buys units in the Maxxum Global Equity, a Smart Fund managed by venerable Janus Capital. MER of 2.58% is actually below some international funds. Helen Young Hayes continues to collect accolades from the U.S. media for her stellar performance on Janus Worldwide, the clone for the Maxxum fund. Fund is up 22.5% for the year ended August 31. **New Smart Fund.**

RISK

How Often Money was Lost:.........6 of 13 Months
....3 of 11 Quarters
....0 of 2 Years
Worst 3 Months: ....-9.38% (1998)
Best 3 Months: 19.83% (1998)

ASSET ALLOCATION

USA...35.2
Netherlands 9.5
Japan 9.4
France...7.0
UK 6.9
Other 32.0

COMPARISON OF FUND TO INDEXES

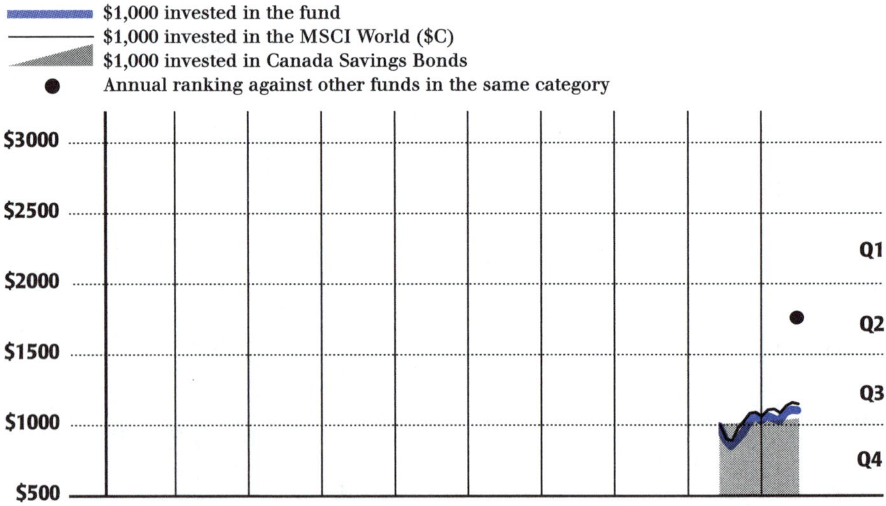

Annual Return (%)	1990		1992		1994		1996		1998	8/31/99
										8.0

Compound Return (%)	10 yr	9 yr	8 yr	7 yr	6 yr	5 yr	4 yr	3 yr	2 yr	1 yr
										22.5

GLOBAL EQUITY

MAXXUM GLOBAL EQUITY

LOAD

Primary Objective:	Growth
Sponsor:	London Life Insurance Co.
Fund Manager:	Helen Young Hayes, Janus Capital
Style:	Bottom-up, Growth
Size (MMs):	$47.307
RRSP:	20%
Expense Ratio:	2.90%

COMMENTS

Here's one we missed last year. Managed by the sizzling Janus Capital's Helen Young Hayes. Ms. Hayes manages the spectacular Janus Worldwide, which has consistently beaten the MSCI World Index. She was named Morningstar's International Manager of the Year for 1997. Fund is first quartile for three and two years ended August 31, 1999. This one follows the growth style of Janus, by selecting great companies from around the world such as Cisco (U.S.), Mannesmann (Germany), and Nokia (Finland). Hayes tends to be a higher turnover manager so this would be a good one to hold in your RRSP. **New Smart Fund.**

RISK

How Often Money was Lost:.......15 of 55 Months
....14 of 53 Quarters
....0 of 44 Years
Worst 3 Months:..............................-12.54% (1998)
Best 3 Months: 22.44% (1995)

ASSET ALLOCATION

USA..35.2
Netherlands 9.5
Japan 9.4
France..7.0
UK...6.9
Other 32.0

COMPARISON OF FUND TO INDEXES

$1,000 invested in the fund
$1,000 invested in the MSCI World ($C)
$1,000 invested in Canada Savings Bonds
Annual ranking against other funds in the same category

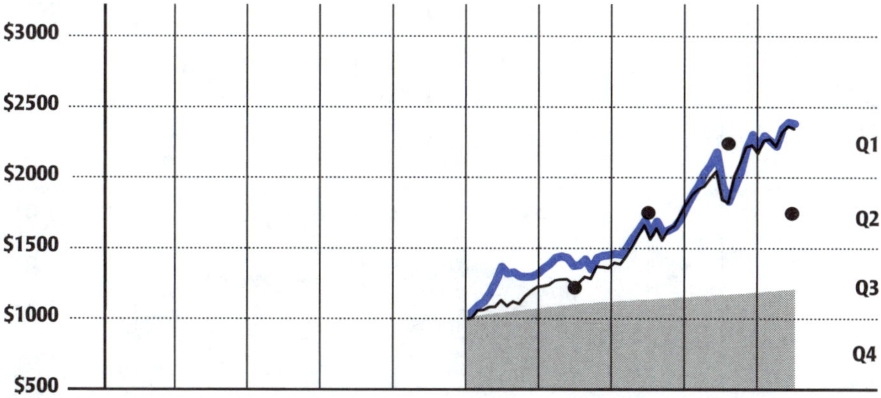

Annual Return (%)	1990		1992		1994		1996		1998	8/31/99
							11.5	14.2	33.7	8.1

Compound Return (%)	10 yr	9 yr	8 yr	7 yr	6 yr	5 yr	4 yr	3 yr	2 yr	1 yr
							16.2	20.1	22.1	23.0

MD GROWTH

NO LOAD

Primary Objective:	Growth
Sponsor:	MD Management
Fund Manager:	Templeton Global Advisors
Style:	Bottom-up, Value
Size (MMs):	$3,897.646
RRSP:	20%
Expense Ratio:	1.28%

COMMENTS

Everything said about Templeton Growth Fund applies equally to this fund since it is managed by the Templeton team. The bottom-up, Value-oriented stock picks from around the world. A great fund for those in the medical establishment, who can get it at no-load with a 1.28% MER, low volatility, and consistent top-quartile returns. Templeton has struggled a bit recently, but don't count them out. This fund was first quartile in each of 1995, 1996, and 1997, and has slipped into the second quartile for the three years ended August 31, 1999. **Smart Fund History: 1999, 1998, 1997, 1996.**

RISK

How Often Money was Lost:.....41 of 116 Months
.....30 of 114 Quarters
.....12 of 105 Years
Worst 3 Months: .....-4.32% (1995)
Best 3 Months:.....14.92% (1998)

ASSET ALLOCATION

USA.....25.8
UK.....13.6
Hong Kong.....6.7
Netherlands.....6.4
France.....5.8
Other.....41.7

COMPARISON OF FUND TO INDEXES

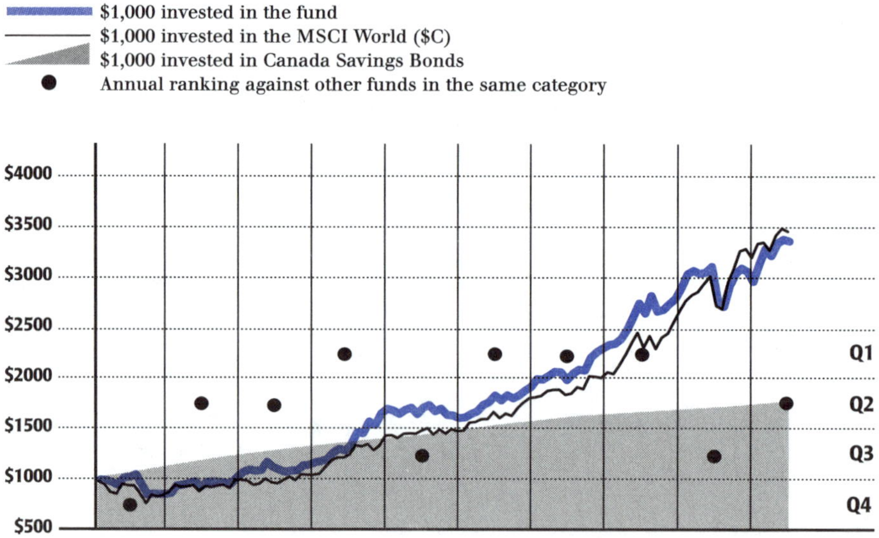

Annual Return (%)	1990		1992		1994		1996		1998	8/31/99
	-15.9	20.3	12.2	44.9	-1.1	15.3	20.4	21.1	13.0	18.7

Compound Return (%)	10 yr	9 yr	8 yr	7 yr	6 yr	5 yr	4 yr	3 yr	2 yr	1 yr
	12.9	15.2	16.8	17.8	15.0	14.2	17.2	18.0	12.8	21.5

GLOBAL EQUITY

SCUDDER GLOBAL

NO LOAD

Primary Objective: Growth
Sponsor: Scudder Canada
Fund Manager: Nicolas Bratt & William Holzer
Style: Bottom-up, Value
Size (MMs): $74.344
RRSP: 20%
Expense Ratio: 1.75%

COMMENTS

Fund has been a first-quartile performer since its inception in Canada in 1995 with a 17.9% CAGR. Holzer is the manager of the same fund in the U.S. This fund has a 10-year record of outperforming the MSCI World Index by a considerable margin. The U.S. fund is ranked 5-star by Morningstar. In this fund, country and stock selection is value based and is theme driven with particular emphasis on the impact of aging populations. Holzer will move to bonds if he cannot find value. He hates to overpay for any stock. Fund is carrying a 41% weighting in the U.S., but the single largest holding, IBM, is only 2.3% of the fund. **Smart Fund History: 1999, 1997.**

RISK

How Often Money was Lost:.......11 of 46 Months
..........9 of 44 Quarters
..........0 of 35 Years
Worst 3 Months: ....-8.25% (1998)
Best 3 Months:..........13.38% (1998)

ASSET ALLOCATION

USA..........41.0
UK..........16.0
Japan..........11.0
Germany..........10.0
Switzerland..........8.0
Other..........14.0

COMPARISON OF FUND TO INDEXES

$1,000 invested in the fund
$1,000 invested in the MSCI World ($C)
$1,000 invested in Canada Savings Bonds
Annual ranking against other funds in the same category

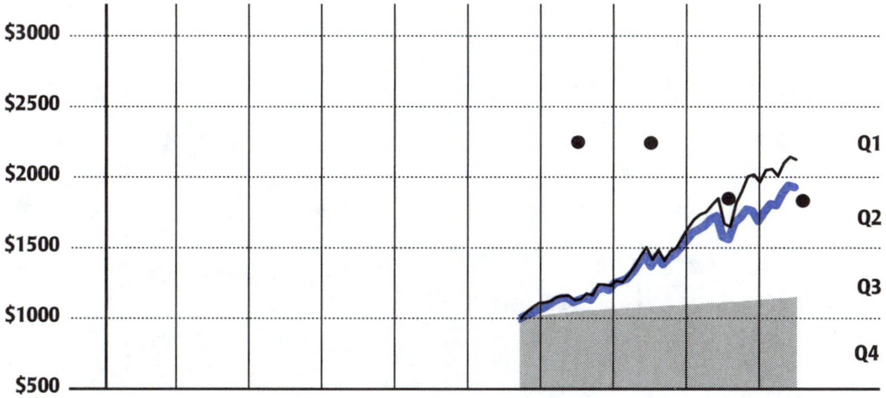

Annual Return (%)	1990		1992		1994		1996		1998	8/31/99
							17.6	19.6	21.6	8.8

Compound Return (%)	10 yr	9 yr	8 yr	7 yr	6 yr	5 yr	4 yr	3 yr	2 yr	1 yr
								19.5	18.6	22.1

GLOBAL EQUITY

TEMPLETON GROWTH

LOAD

Primary Objective:	Growth
Sponsor:	Templeton Management
Fund Manager:	Mark Holowesko
Style:	Bottom-up, Value
Size (MMs):	$11,065.505
RRSP:	20%
Expense Ratio:	1.97%

COMMENTS

Available in RSP version

A consistent top-quartile performer with a reasonable 1.97% MER and good risk-adjusted performance. Manager Mark Holowesko has stood up well under the pressure from short-term thinkers as the fund suffered, in 1998, its first fourth-quartile calendar year since 1990. It has returned to first quartile for the year to date. The fund's $11 billion size tells us that just about every Canadian knows about it by now. It is the single largest mutual fund in Canada and has grown by $4.8 billion since the end of 1996. If you are worried about Y2K, buy the segregated version, Templeton Growth GIF. **Smart Fund History: 1999, 1998, 1997, 1996.**

RISK

How Often Money was Lost:.....38 of 116 Months
..........28 of 114 Quarters
..........9 of 105 Years
Worst 3 Months:..........-20.23% (1990)
Best 3 Months:..........15.69% (1992)

ASSET ALLOCATION

USA	28.5
UK	11.8
Hong Kong	9.8
Netherlands	4.2
Japan	4.0
Other	41.7

COMPARISON OF FUND TO INDEXES

$1,000 invested in the fund
$1,000 invested in the MSCI World ($C)
$1,000 invested in Canada Savings Bonds
Annual ranking against other funds in the same category

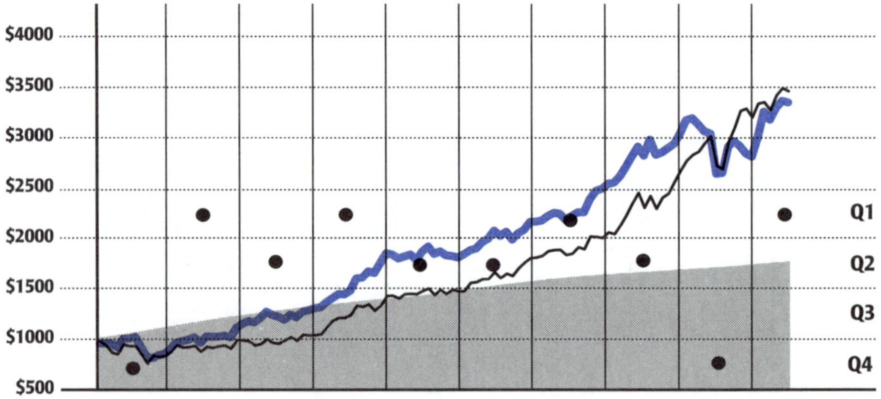

Annual	**1990**		**1992**		**1994**		**1996**		**1998**	**8/31/99**
Return (%)	-13.6	30.3	15.2	36.3	3.8	14.1	18.4	17.1	0.7	14.9
Compound	**10 yr**	**9 yr**	**8 yr**	**7 yr**	**6 yr**	**5 yr**	**4 yr**	**3 yr**	**2 yr**	**1 yr**
Return (%)	12.9	15.3	15.8	15.8	13.0	11.7	13.3	14.6	8.9	26.7

TEMPLETON INTERNATIONAL STOCK **LOAD**

Primary Objective:	Growth
Sponsor:	Templeton Management
Fund Manager:	Don Reed
Style:	Bottom-up, Value
Size (MMs):	$6,322.258
RRSP:	20%
Expense Ratio:	2.46%

COMMENTS

Available in RSP version

Another mainstay from Templeton, this fund is redundant if you already have the Templeton Growth Fund. However, it adds excellent diversification for those who already have significant holdings in North American securities. Manager Don Reed has used the Templeton buy list to achieve first-quartile performance. MER of 2.46% is a bit much for a $6.3 billion fund. Makes you want to own the Franklin Resources stock instead. This one has lagged the other international funds in 1998, but has rebounded nicely in 1999. Prior to that it was first quartile in six of the last seven years. **Smart Fund History: 1999, 1998, 1997.**

RISK

How Often Money was Lost:.....38 of 116 Months
.....27 of 114 Quarters
.....12 of 105 Years
Worst 3 Months:.....-15.34% (1990)
Best 3 Months:.....23.43% (1992)

ASSET ALLOCATION

UK	19.6
France	9.6
Hong Kong	6.6
Netherlands	6.3
Japan	6.1
Other	51.8

COMPARISON OF FUND TO INDEXES

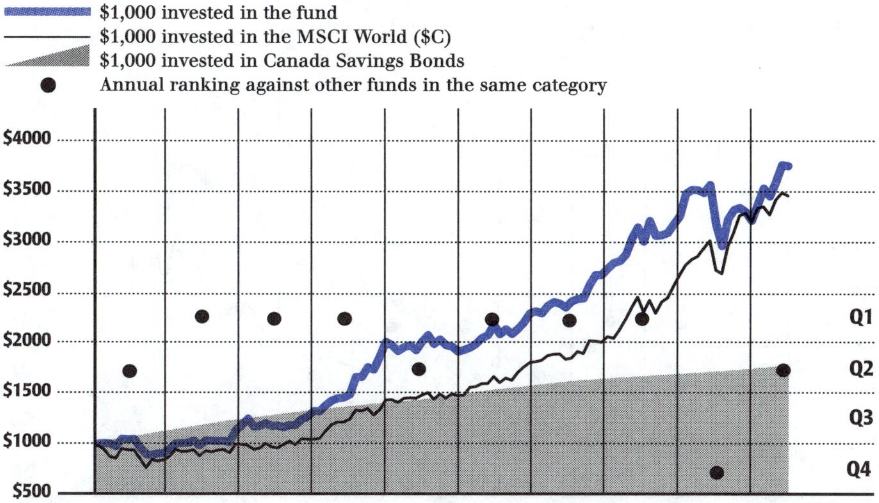

Annual Return (%)	**1990**		**1992**		**1994**		**1996**		**1998**	**8/31/99**
	-11.5	25.7	12.2	48.1	5.2	12.2	21.5	15.9	8.1	12.4

Compound Return (%)	**10 yr**	**9 yr**	**8 yr**	**7 yr**	**6 yr**	**5 yr**	**4 yr**	**3 yr**	**2 yr**	**1 yr**
	14.0	16.5	17.8	18.4	14.7	12.7	15.9	16.0	11.8	18.4

TRIMARK FUND

LOAD

Primary Objective: Growth
Sponsor: Trimark Investment Management
Fund Manager: Bill Kanko & Judith Adams
Style: Bottom-up, Growth
Size (MMs): 2,764.411
RRSP: 20%
Expense Ratio: 1.52%

COMMENTS

Available in RSP version

Trimark has been consistent in its investment philosophy of buying great businesses and holding them for five years. The team is led by Bob Krembil and the returning Bill Kanko, manager of former Smart Fund Ivy Foreign Equity, Judith Adams from Sceptre, and Jim Young from Royal Bank. Its high exposure to the U.S. market was not in the high tech growth stocks. It would be premature to demote this fund, given its outstanding long-term track record dating back to 1981. **Smart Fund History: 1999, 1998, 1997, 1996.**

RISK

How Often Money was Lost:.....39 of 116 Months
.....26 of 114 Quarters
.....5 of 105 Years
Worst 3 Months:.....-23.14% (1990)
Best 3 Months:.....24.22% (1992)

ASSET ALLOCATION

USA.....52.9
Japan.....17.4
Germany.....8.5
UK.....2.3
Mexico.....1.3
Other.....17.6

COMPARISON OF FUND TO INDEXES

$1,000 invested in the fund
$1,000 invested in the MSCI World ($C)
$1,000 invested in Canada Savings Bonds
Annual ranking against other funds in the same category

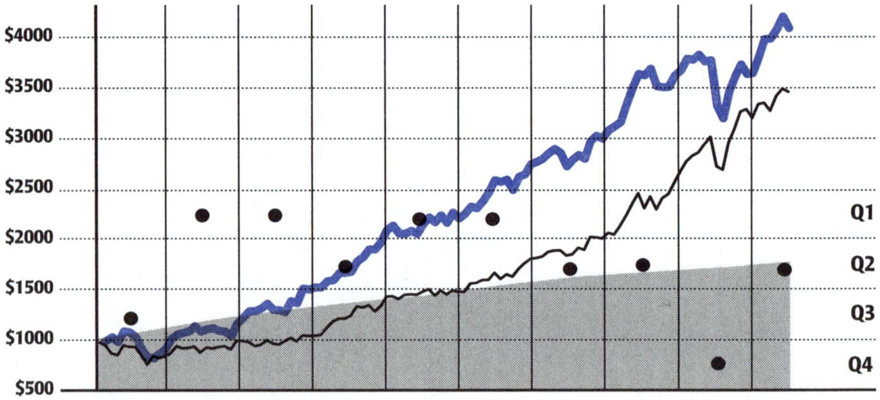

Annual Return (%)	1990		1992		1994		1996		1998	8/31/99
	-9.9	28.3	29.0	31.6	14.9	16.7	14.7	16.0	6.4	9.6

Compound Return (%)	10 yr	9 yr	8 yr	7 yr	6 yr	5 yr	4 yr	3 yr	2 yr	1 yr
	14.4	18.3	17.7	18.2	14.9	13.1	12.4	13.7	6.3	23.1

GLOBAL EQUITY

AGF DIVIDEND FUND

LOAD

Primary Objective:	Conservative Growth
Sponsor:	AGF Funds Inc.
Fund Manager:	Gordon MacDougall & Martin Gerber
Style:	Bottom-up, Blend
Size (MMs):	$2,317.580
RRSP:	100%
Expense Ratio:	1.87%

COMMENTS

After riding high for a couple of years, dividend funds have come back to earth. Martin Gerber and the Connor Clark Lunn team continue their steady performance of first- or second-quartile years. Over the ten-, five-, and three-year periods, this fund is in the top quartile in the category. It invests more in solid common stocks that pay dividends, so its volatility will be higher than other funds in the category. For nervous types, this could be a core RRSP holding, despite the loss of the dividend tax credit in registered plans. In fact, distributions have been minor of the fund for the past two years. **Smart Fund History: 1999, 1998, 1997.**

RISK

How Often Money was Lost:.....45 of 116 Months
....32 of 114 Quarters
....11 of 105 Years
Worst 3 Months:.....................-18.60% (1998)
Best 3 Months:.......................19.77% (1996)

ASSET ALLOCATION

Financial services 19.5
Oil & Gas 13.4
Industrial products 11.1
Environment 9.6
Consumer 6.7
Other 39.7

COMPARISON OF FUND TO INDEXES

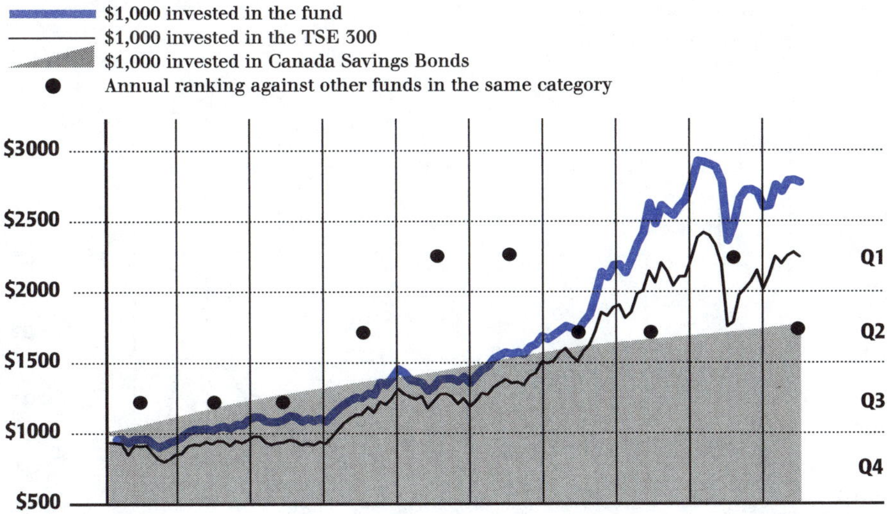

Annual Return (%)	1990		1992		1994		1996		1998	8/31/99
	-5.1	15.1	1.0	26.3	0.4	16.3	29.1	24.1	4.4	1.9

Compound Return (%)	10 yr	9 yr	8 yr	7 yr	6 yr	5 yr	4 yr	3 yr	2 yr	1 yr
	11.0	13.0	13.0	13.9	13.7	15.0	15.5	15.8	5.7	17.5

AIM GT GLOBAL CANADA INCOME CLASS LOAD

Primary Objective:	Income
Sponsor:	AIM Funds Management Inc.
Fund Manager:	Derek Webb, AIM Capital Management
Style:	Bottom-up, Blend
Size (MMs):	$934.260
RRSP:	100%
Expense Ratio:	2.09%

COMMENTS

Returns as a Smart Fund primarily for its yield focus. It is the emphasis on yield that lowers its relative ranking against the likes of AGF Dividend or PH&N. The fund invests in blue-chip, high-yielding common stocks, REITs, and Royalty Trust Units, and is committed to returning a fixed payout of 3.8 cents per unit per month, roughly a 7% yield. Manager Derek Webb writes covered calls against these stocks to generate more income for the unitholders. MER of 2.09% erodes yield a bit but still fund has a three-year CAGR of 10.7%. **Smart Fund History: 1999, 1998, 1997.**

RISK

How Often Money was Lost:.......13 of 39 Months
.......9 of 37 Quarters
.......12 of 2 8 Years
Worst 3 Months:.......-20.36% (1998)
Best 3 Months:.......18.26% (1996)

ASSET ALLOCATION

Energy	18.4
Real estate	12.8
Multi industry	9.6
Financial services	8.6
Other	50.6

COMPARISON OF FUND TO INDEXES

$1,000 invested in the fund
$1,000 invested in the TSE 300
$1,000 invested in Canada Savings Bonds
Annual ranking against other funds in the same category

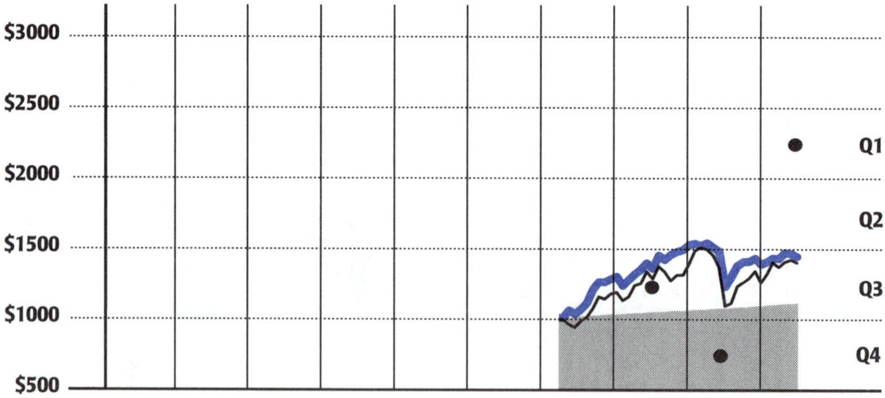

Annual Return (%)	1990		1992		1994		1996		1998	8/31/99
								17.4	-4.7	2.5
Compound Return (%)	10 yr	9 yr	8 yr	7 yr	6 yr	5 yr	4 yr	3 yr	2 yr	1 yr
								10.7	3.1	17.7

BPI DIVIDEND INCOME

LOAD

Primary Objective:	Income
Sponsor:	BPI Mutual Funds
Fund Manager:	Eric Bushell, since 1/95
Style:	Bottom-up, Value
Size (MMs):	$741.700
RRSP:	100%
Expense Ratio:	1.50%

COMMENTS

The least volatile pick of the bunch. Manager Eric Bushell's focus is more on yield and low volatility than on trying to capture capital gains from common equity holdings. Bushell will hold royalty trust units and preferred shares in high-yielding common stocks. He also tries to manage after-tax returns by minimizing the amount of interest income distributed. The MER has increased each of the last two years and is now 1.50%, as BPI removed the expense cap and began charging the fund's expenses back to unitholders. The fund is committed to making monthly distributions of about 4.5 cents per unit, for a pre-tax yield of 4%. C.I. is committed to keeping Eric Bushell around after the merger. **Smart Fund History: 1999, 1998, 1997, 1996.**

RISK

How Often Money was Lost:.....31 of 116 Months
.....23 of 114 Quarters
.....14 of 105 Years
Worst 3 Months:.....-11.41% (1998)
Best 3 Months:.....11.23% (1996)

ASSET ALLOCATION

Preferreds.....53.0
common.....35.0
Cash.....3.0
REITs.....9.0

COMPARISON OF FUND TO INDEXES

$1,000 invested in the fund
$1,000 invested in the TSE 300
$1,000 invested in Canada Savings Bonds
Annual ranking against other funds in the same category

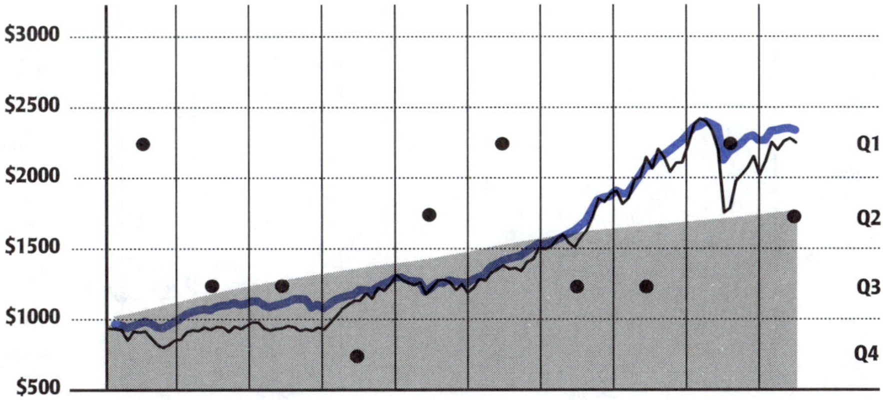

Annual Return (%)	1990		1992		1994		1996		1998	8/31/99
	-0.9	12.6	-0.4	15.0	-0.6	19.4	23.3	19.5	2.7	2.3

Compound Return (%)	10 yr	9 yr	8 yr	7 yr	6 yr	5 yr	4 yr	3 yr	2 yr	1 yr
	9.0	10.2	9.9	10.7	11.6	13.1	13.1	12.1	5.8	10.0

BPI HIGH INCOME

LOAD

Primary Objective:	Income
Sponsor:	BPI Mutual Funds
Fund Manager:	Eric Bushell & Ben Chen
Style:	Value
Size (MMs):	$280.400
RRSP:	100%
Expense Ratio:	1.77%

COMMENTS

Recognizing the market's demand for yield, Bushell and co-manager Ben Cheng seek high yield by investing in royalty trust units, high-yield corporate bonds, and real estate investment trusts. All of this in a portfolio with an MER of 1.48%. The fund distributes 6.5 cents per unit per month for those looking for a pre-tax yield of 7.5%. All funds holding royalty trust units suffered big in 1998 as the market clobbered their NAVs. Still, they yield good after-tax cash flows. **Smart Fund History: 1999, 1998.**

RISK

How Often Money was Lost:.........9 of 32 Months
....8 of 30 Quarters
....10 of 21 Years
Worst 3 Months:...............................-17.83% (1998)
Best 3 Months:...................................10.75% (1997)

ASSET ALLOCATION

Royal inco 42.0
Corporate bonds..........................29.0
REITs 26.0
Cash & equivalent.........................2.0
Preferreds 1.0

COMPARISON OF FUND TO INDEXES

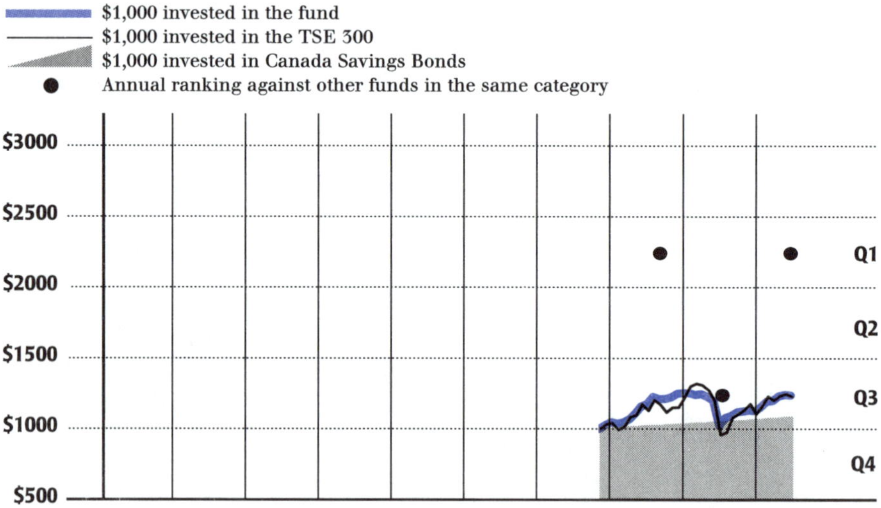

Annual Return (%)	1990		1992		1994		1996		1998	8/31/99
								22.4	-8.1	10.1

Compound Return (%)	10 yr	9 yr	8 yr	7 yr	6 yr	5 yr	4 yr	3 yr	2 yr	1 yr
									2.6	20.9

BISSETT DIVIDEND INCOME FUND NO LOAD

Primary Objective: Total Return
Sponsor: Bissett & Associates
Fund Manager: Fred Pynn since 12/91
Style: Bottom-up
Size (MMs): $46.378
RRSP: 100%
Expense Ratio: 1.31%

COMMENTS

Last year's Smart Fund Manager of the Year, Fred Pynn delivers solid first- and second-quartile performance in an asset class that is increasingly sought by yield-hungry Canadians. It invests in high-yielding common equities, preferred stocks, and some U.S. stocks. The modest MER of 1.31% and the reasonable volatility make this a solid conservative fund for many investors. Solid double-digit returns have been generated with a standard deviation (measure of volatility) 30% less than most equity funds. The fund pays its modest 10-cent distribution only quarterly, so it is less attractive for those dependent on the yield. **Smart Fund History: 1999, 1998.**

RISK

How Often Money was Lost:.....37 of 116 Months
.....27 of 114 Quarters
.....12 of 105 Years
Worst 3 Months:.....-14.50% (1998)
Best 3 Months:.....16.72% (1996)

ASSET ALLOCATION

Canadian equities.....48.3
Preferred shares.....26.7
U.S. equities.....15.2
Fixed income.....9.0
Other.....0.8

COMPARISON OF FUND TO INDEXES

$1,000 invested in the fund
$1,000 invested in the TSE 300
$1,000 invested in Canada Savings Bonds
Annual ranking against other funds in the same category

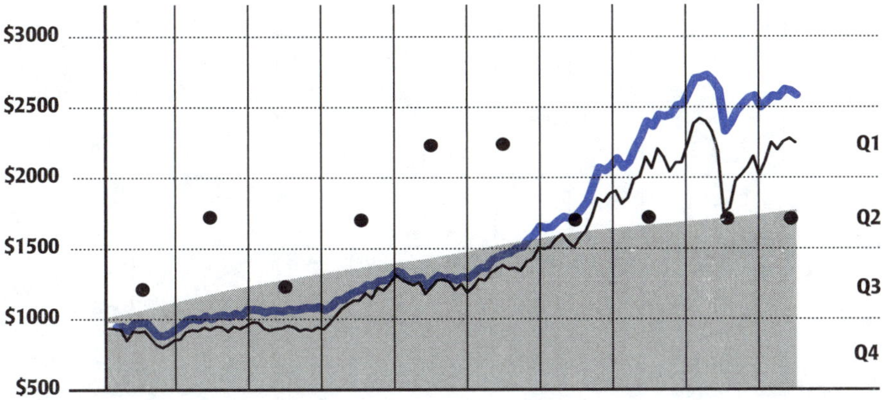

Annual Return (%)	1990		1992		1994		1996		1998	8/31/99
	-7.2	15.1	1.8	18.7	0.7	22.9	28.5	22.5	2.1	0.8

Compound Return (%)	10 yr	9 yr	8 yr	7 yr	6 yr	5 yr	4 yr	3 yr	2 yr	1 yr
	9.8	12.1	12.2	13.5	13.0	14.6	15.2	13.4	4.5	10.9

DYNAMIC PROTECTED DIVIDEND GROWTH FUND LOAD

Primary Objective: Growth
Sponsor: Dynamic Mutual Funds Ltd.
Fund Manager: David Goodman
Style: Bottom-up, Value
Size (MMs): $12.029
RRSP: 100%
Expense Ratio: 4.33%

COMMENTS

This one is almost tailor-made for Y2K-fearful investors. A conservative equity fund wrapped with a guarantee and available at all fund distributors and discount brokers. Hefty 4.33% MER, which clearly detracts from the yield, is steep to pay for a guarantee. So after we have certainty around Y2K, you may wish to switch to the regular Dynamic fund. TD, CIBC, BCE, and TCPL make up the core of this fund's holdings. **New Smart Fund.**

RISK

How Often Money was Lost: ....3 of 8 Months
..........2 of 6 Quarters
..........0 of 0 Years
Worst 3 Months: ....-1.01% (1999)
Best 3 Months: 5.10% (1999)

ASSET ALLOCATION

N/A 100.0

COMPARISON OF FUND TO INDEXES

$1,000 invested in the fund
$1,000 invested in the TSE 300
$1,000 invested in Canada Savings Bonds
Annual ranking against other funds in the same category

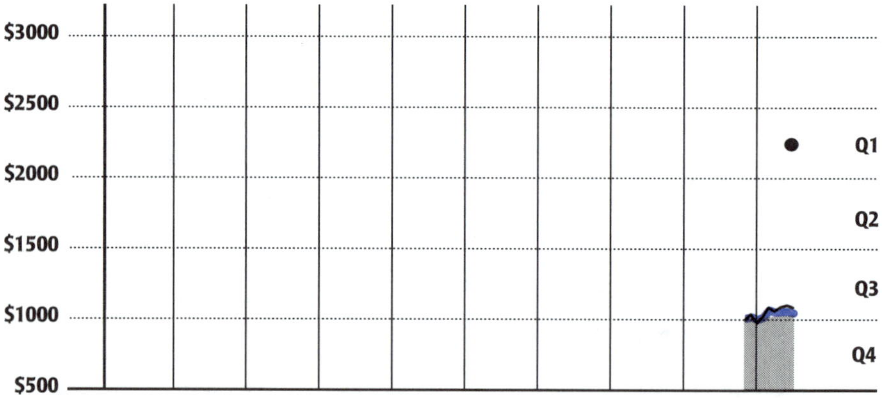

Annual Return (%)	1990		1992		1994		1996		1998	8/31/99
										3.8

Compound Return (%)	10 yr	9 yr	8 yr	7 yr	6 yr	5 yr	4 yr	3 yr	2 yr	1 yr

FIRST CANADIAN DIVIDEND FUND NO LOAD

Primary Objective: Conservative Growth
Sponsor: First Canadian Funds
Fund Manager: Michael Stanley, Jones Heward Investment Counsel
Style: Bottom-up, Value
Size (MMs): $997.177
RRSP: 100%
Expense Ratio: 1.67%

COMMENTS

Another conservatively managed blue-chip equity fund that generates a yield and still gives the investor an opportunity for capital gains. The reasonable 1.67% MER, no-load status, the convenience of Bank of Montreal, and the first-quartile performance add up to a compelling story. This could be your primary RRSP holding in the First Canadian family. Michael Stanley has the fund loaded with bank stocks and utilities, which has fuelled the 18.9% three-year CAGR and made it number three in its category. Smart Fund 1999, 1998.

RISK

How Often Money was Lost:.......15 of 58 Months
....8 of 56 Quarters
....5 of 47 Years
Worst 3 Months:................................-22.13% (1998)
Best 3 Months:..................................19.83% (1996)

ASSET ALLOCATION

Interest sensitives.........................54.0
Consumer products.....................13.8
Resources.......................................12.7
Cash...9.1
Industrial products........................4.4
Other...6.0

COMPARISON OF FUND TO INDEXES

$1,000 invested in the fund
$1,000 invested in the TSE 300
$1,000 invested in Canada Savings Bonds
● Annual ranking against other funds in the same category

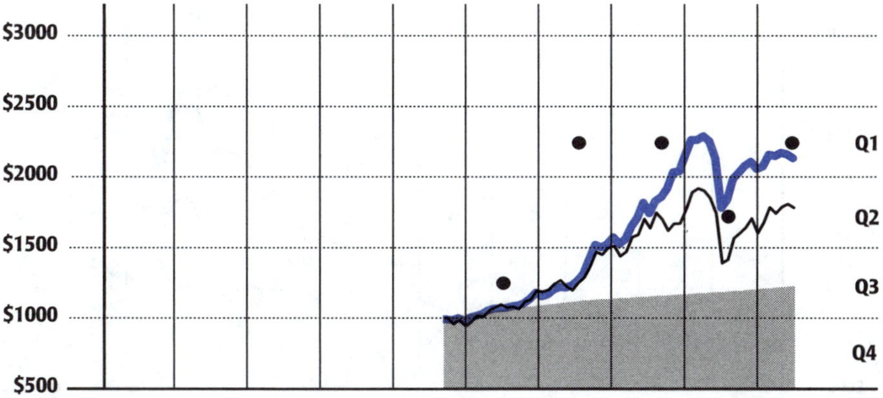

Annual Return (%)	1990		1992		1994		1996		1998	8/31/99
						13.2	32.3	35.2	2.3	2.6

Compound Return (%)	10 yr	9 yr	8 yr	7 yr	6 yr	5 yr	4 yr	3 yr	2 yr	1 yr
							18.7	18.9	10.6	19.6

SCUDDER MAXXUM DIVIDEND FUND OF CANADA LOAD

Primary Objective: Conservative Growth
Sponsor: Scudder Maxxum Co.
Fund Manager: Jacqueline Pratt
Style: Bottom-up, Blend
Size (MMs): $229.799
RRSP: 100%
Expense Ratio: 2.40%

COMMENTS

Ms. Pratt has led the fund to first- or second-quartile performance every year since 1995. It has a lower three-year standard deviation than PH&N, AGF, First Canadian, and Royal, all Smart Funds. Fund holds big weightings in the banks, BCE, Nortel, and TCPL, and carries a 1.75% MER. **Smart Fund History: 1999, 1998, 1997.**

RISK

How Often Money was Lost:.....44 of 116 Months
.....28 of 114 Quarters
.....11 of 105 Years
Worst 3 Months: .....-21.77% (1998)
Best 3 Months:.....16.30% (1996)

ASSET ALLOCATION

Financial services 22.5
Utilities 22.0
Industrial products 12.3
Pipelines.....7.5
Oil & Gas.....7.0
Other 28.7

COMPARISON OF FUND TO INDEXES

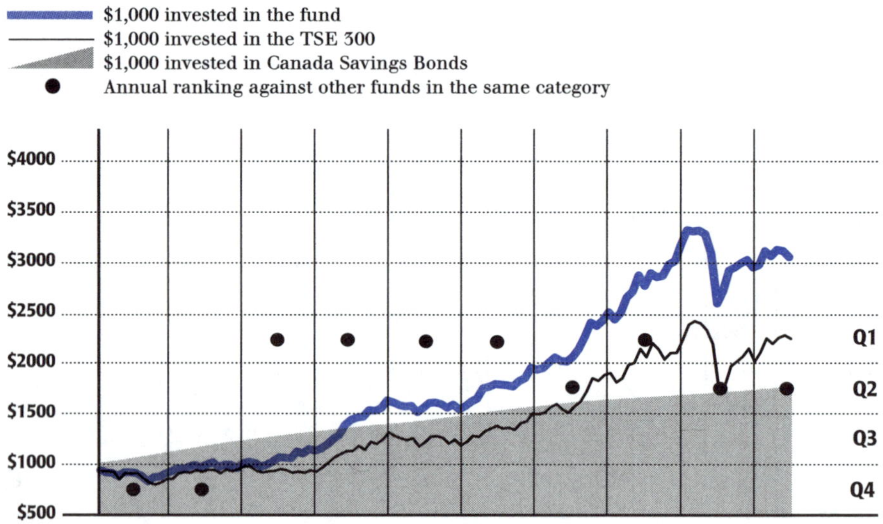

Annual Return (%)	1990		1992		1994		1996		1998	8/31/99
	-9.3	5.9	19.7	35.1	2.9	16.6	27.7	25.8	0.5	1.9

Compound Return (%)	10 yr	9 yr	8 yr	7 yr	6 yr	5 yr	4 yr	3 yr	2 yr	1 yr
	11.2	14.8	14.8	16.3	13.1	13.7	14.3	13.9	5.0	17.7

PH&N DIVIDEND INCOME

NO LOAD

Primary Objective:	Conservative Growth
Sponsor:	Phillips, Hager & North Investment Management
Fund Manager:	Team
Style:	Bottom-up, Blend
Size (MMs):	$654.234
RRSP:	100%
Expense Ratio:	1.21%

COMMENTS

Always near the top of the class, this is another solid PH&N low-MER, top-quartile performer. If we sound like a broken record on PH&N, forgive us. This is the number one fund in the category for the ten-, five-, three-year compounded returns ending August 31, 1999. You have to buy this on your own, directly from the Vancouver-based firm and pony up the $25,000 minimum (less inside an RRSP). In exchange you get no-loads and a 1.21% MER. This provides some uniqueness, as it is 33% weighted to the pipelines and utilities. BCE and three of the big five banks are there. **Smart Fund History: 1999, 1998, 1997, 1996.**

RISK

How Often Money was Lost:.....35 of 116 Months
..........28 of 114 Quarters
..........11 of 105 Years
Worst 3 Months:..........-21.56% (1998)
Best 3 Months:..........20.33% (1996)

ASSET ALLOCATION

Financial services 28.3
Pipelines..........17.5
Utilities 16.6
Oil & Gas..........12.0
Industrial products 8.7
Other 16.9

COMPARISON OF FUND TO INDEXES

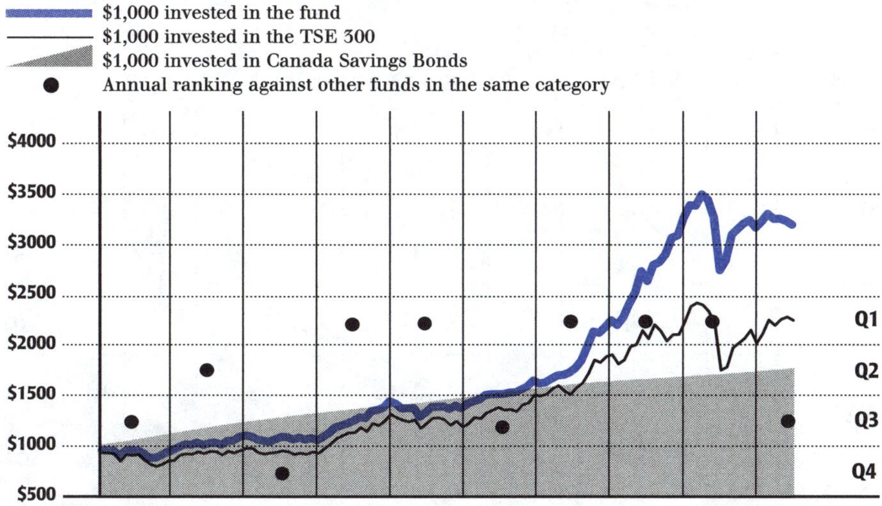

Annual Return (%)	1990		1992		1994		1996		1998	8/31/99
	-6.0	15.6	-0.9	28.0	1.3	13.9	33.3	44.5	4.7	-0.4

Compound Return (%)	10 yr	9 yr	8 yr	7 yr	6 yr	5 yr	4 yr	3 yr	2 yr	1 yr
	12.7	14.8	15.2	16.7	16.4	18.2	20.5	21.7	10.1	16.5

ROYAL DIVIDEND

NO LOAD

Primary Objective:	Conservative Growth
Sponsor:	Royal Mutual Funds
Fund Manager:	John Kellett
Style:	Bottom-up, Value
Size (MMs):	$1,897.873
RRSP:	100%
Expense Ratio:	1.75%

COMMENTS

Most dividend funds have been on a roll since 1996, but this merged survivor of RoyFund Dividend and Royal Trust Growth and Income Fund did better than most with back-to-back 30+% returns in 1996 and 1997. Manager John Kellett has rewarded bank clients with more than just a top-quartile fund. It is the number two fund over the five-year period ended August 31. This may be the best choice for many Royal Bank "GIC refugees" outside their RRSPs, where dividends receive preferential tax treatment. This is a blue-chip equity fund comprising mostly good dividend-paying common stocks like the banks, BCE, and the pipelines. The fund's MER of 1.75% could be lowered, now that it is near $2 billion in assets. **Smart Fund History: 1999, 1998, 1996.**

RISK

How Often Money was Lost:.......24 of 79 Months
....13 of 77 Quarters
....10 of 68 Years
Worst 3 Months:...............................-20.29% (1998)
Best 3 Months: 22.32% (1996)

ASSET ALLOCATION

Common.......................................76.0
Bonds 16.7
Preferred.......................................4.9
Cash 2.4

COMPARISON OF FUND TO INDEXES

$1,000 invested in the fund
$1,000 invested in the TSE 300
$1,000 invested in Canada Savings Bonds
Annual ranking against other funds in the same category

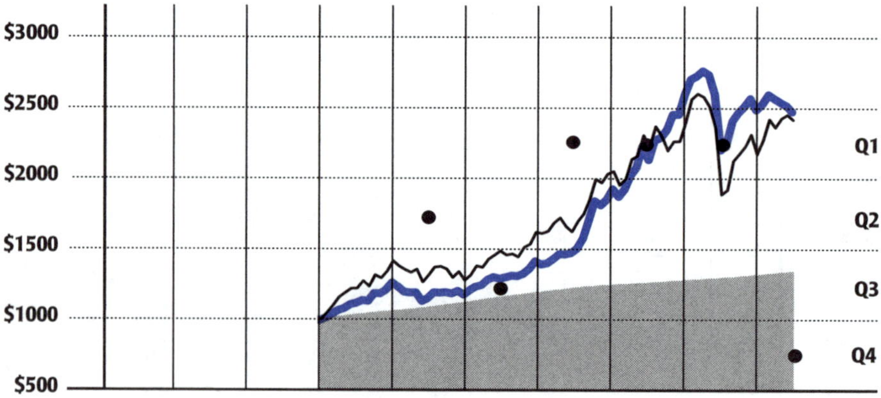

Annual Return (%)	1990		1992		1994		1996		1998	8/31/99
					-0.7	13.1	3.1	35.4	2.3	-1.5

Compound Return (%)	10 yr	9 yr	8 yr	7 yr	6 yr	5 yr	4 yr	3 yr	2 yr	1 yr
					13.8	15.7	17.4	18.0	7.7	12.3

FIDELITY EUROPEAN GROWTH **LOAD**

Primary Objective: Growth
Sponsor: Fidelity Investments Canada
Fund Manager: Thierry Serero
Style: Bottom-up, Growth
Size (MMs): $2,255.123
RRSP: 20%
Expense Ratio: 2.60%

COMMENTS

Fidelity supports this fund with the largest buy-side research team in Europe. A solid fund, with outstanding risk-adjusted returns that put it near the head of the class. This could serve as everyone's foreign content if there is enough room to diversify into regional funds. It has never returned less than 10% or been ranked less than second quartile since it opened in 1993. With a five-year CAGR of 16.7%, why consider emerging markets or Asia? Poor 1999 puts the spotlight clearly on Mr. Serero after Sally Walden's spectacular run. **Smart Fund History: 1999, 1998, 1997, 1996.**

RISK

How Often Money was Lost: ....27 of 87 Months
....20 of 85 Quarters
....4 of 76 Years
Worst 3 Months: ....-13.49% (1998)
Best 3 Months: 18.52% (1998)

ASSET ALLOCATION

UK 30.3
Germany 19.5
France 16.6
Switzerland 8.6
Netherlands 6.0
Other 19.0

COMPARISON OF FUND TO INDEXES

$1,000 invested in the fund
$1,000 invested in the MSCI Europe ($C)
$1,000 invested in Canada Savings Bonds
● Annual ranking against other funds in the same category

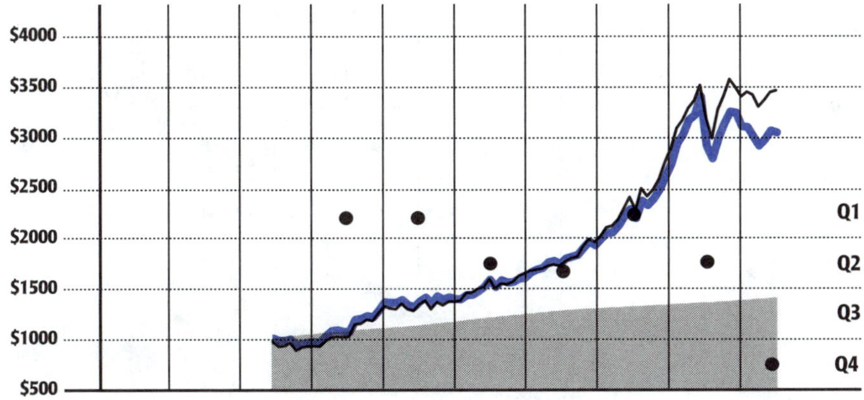

Annual Return (%)	1990		1992		1994		1996		1998	8/31/99
				33.0	10.1	13.3	22.9	26.2	31.3	-6.3

Compound Return (%)	10 yr	9 yr	8 yr	7 yr	6 yr	5 yr	4 yr	3 yr	2 yr	1 yr
				17.5	17.0	16.7	19.1	19.2	17.8	4.5

UNIVERSAL EUROPEAN OPPORTUNITIES LOAD

Primary Objective:	Growth
Sponsor:	Mackenzie Financial
Fund Manager:	Stephen Peak, Henderson Administration
Style:	Bottom-up, Growth with small-caps
Size (MMs):	$966.505
RRSP:	20%
Expense Ratio:	2.40%

COMMENTS

Available in RSP version

First quartile for four, three, two, and one year ending August 31, 1999 and a three-year CAGR of 23.3%. Stephen Peak managed the fund to the top of the category in both 1995 and 1996 and it has not finished a year with less than 20% return. Peak is a recognized authority in European small-cap investing and has more than 20 years of experience. Henderson Administration, based in London, England, is a fundamental, research-driven organization that has been in business since. 1934. **Smart Fund History: 1999, 1998, 1997, 1996.**

EUROPEAN EQUITY

RISK

How Often Money was Lost:.......11 of 59 Months
.......5 of 57 Quarters
.......3 of 48 Years
Worst 3 Months:.......-15.48% (1998)
Best 3 Months:.......23.03% (1998)

ASSET ALLOCATION

UK	36.0
Germany	15.0
France	10.0
Netherlands	8.0
Emerging Europe	7.0
Other	24.0

COMPARISON OF FUND TO INDEXES

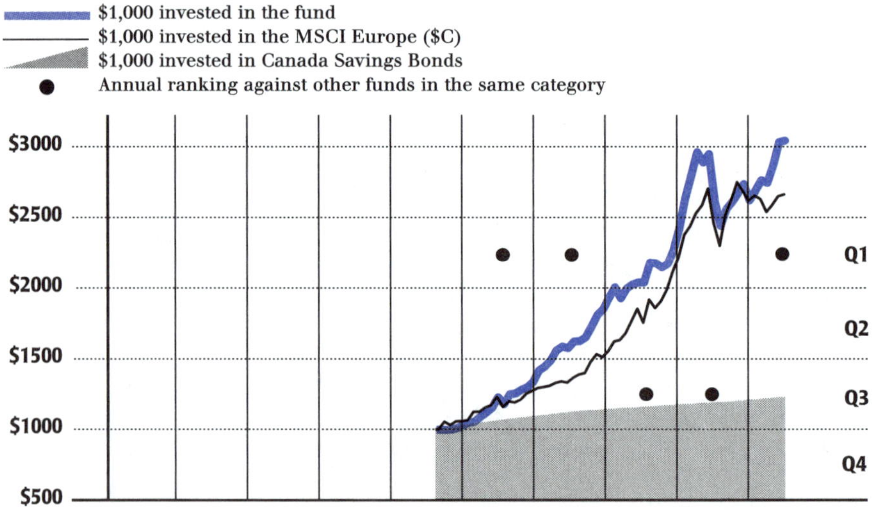

Annual Return (%)	1990		1992		1994		1996		1998	8/31/99
						28.8	39.2	20.0	22.9	13.9

Compound Return (%)	10 yr	9 yr	8 yr	7 yr	6 yr	5 yr	4 yr	3 yr	2 yr	1 yr
							26.7	23.3	22.1	16.5

AIC ADVANTAGE

LOAD

Primary Objective:	Growth
Sponsor:	AIC Limited
Fund Manager:	Michael Lee-Chin
Style:	Bottom-up, Blend
Size (MMs):	$2,298.255
RRSP:	100%
Expense Ratio:	2.26%

COMMENTS

Jonathan Wellum, has relinquished the reins to his partner, Michael Lee-Chin. The fund still focuses on the financial services sector in Canada. TD Bank, Berkshire Hathaway, Mackenzie, Trimark, Fairfax Financial, and Newcourt Credit make up 47.4% of the fund; making it highly correlated to the success of the stock market and vulnerable to interest rate increases. Our advice has always been to ride out the interim dips on this potentially volatile fund. We are currently going through one of those periods like 1994 when the fund lost 13% and fell to fourth quartile. This fund is a financial services sector fund that has a 17.3% 10-year CAGR. **Smart Fund History: 1999, 1998, 1997, 1996.**

RISK

How Often Money was Lost:.....40 of 116 Months
..........38 of 114 Quarters
..........22 of 105 Years
Worst 3 Months:..........-25.09% (1998)
Best 3 Months:..........28.88% (1997)

ASSET ALLOCATION

Financial services..........31.9
Banks & trusts..........13.0
Communications..........12.3
Conglomerates..........10.7
Insurance..........8.0
Other..........24.1

COMPARISON OF FUND TO INDEXES

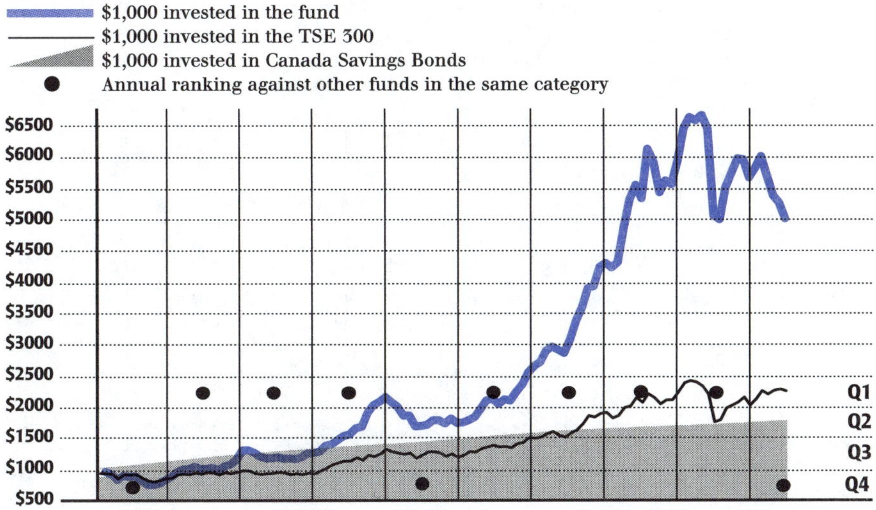

Annual Return (%)	**1990**		**1992**		**1994**		**1996**		**1998**	**8/31/99**
	-18.0	39.8	8.9	65.9	-12.9	30.7	66.5	43.3	6.3	-16.1

Compound Return (%)	**10 yr**	**9 yr**	**8 yr**	**7 yr**	**6 yr**	**5 yr**	**4 yr**	**3 yr**	**2 yr**	**1 yr**
	17.3	22.5	22.1	23.2	20.3	24.1	25.3	17.8	-3.1	-0.9

SPECIAL EQUITY

AIM GLOBAL HEALTH SCIENCES

LOAD

Primary Objective:	Aggressive Growth
Sponsor:	AIM Funds Management Inc.
Fund Manager:	John Schroer, INVESCO
Style:	Bottom-up, Growth
Size (MMs):	$625.417
RRSP:	20%
Expense Ratio:	2.64%

COMMENTS

This is the number seven fund in the Canadian industry for the five years ended August 31, 1999, with a 27% CAGR (five of the other six are Smart Funds). Finally, investors and advisors are waking up to this five-time Smart Fund; it has more than tripled to over $600 million since January 1998. The fund's parent, Invesco Health Sciences, has assets over US$1.6 billion and is rated 4-star by Morningstar. John Schroer has been moved heavily into the large blue-chip pharmaceuticals, with a 47% weighting, and this has hurt the fund in the short term; however, he is rewarded with a performance bonus if the results exceed a recognized benchmark. This has always been our top health care pick. **Smart Fund History: 1999, 1998, 1997, 1996.**

RISK

How Often Money was Lost:.......27 of 82 Months
....17 of 80 Quarters
....2 of 71 Years
Worst 3 Months: ....-12.66% (1993)
Best 3 Months:..................................29.77% (1993)

ASSET ALLOCATION

Pharmaceuticals..........................45.1
Medical equipment......................21.7
Cash & equivalent.......................15.9
Biotechnology 14.4
Health care......................................2.9

COMPARISON OF FUND TO INDEXES

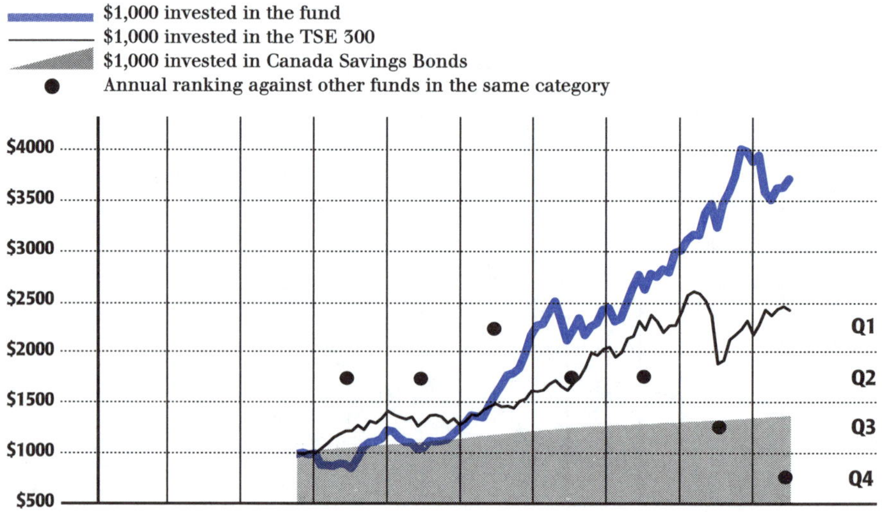

Annual Return (%)	1990		1992		1994		1996		1998	8/31/99
				15.7	4.2	66.3	15.3	21.9	43.7	-7.3

Compound Return (%)	10 yr	9 yr	8 yr	7 yr	6 yr	5 yr	4 yr	3 yr	2 yr	1 yr
					25.6	27.0	22.1	18.8	19.1	14.8

SPECIAL EQUITY

AIM GLOBAL TECHNOLOGY

LOAD

Primary Objective: Aggressive Growth
Sponsor: AIM Funds Management Inc.
Fund Manager: Bill Keithler, Invesco
Style: Bottom-up, Sector Growth
Size (MMs): $146.293
RRSP: 20%
Expense Ratio: 2.93%

COMMENTS

Manager Bill Keithler took over for Dan Leonard and keeps the top returns coming. This clone of U.S. fund, Invesco Technology burst out of the gates with a two-year CAGR is 48.6% as at August 31, 1999. This fund could be bought in combination with AIM's Global Health Sciences fund, to give an investor exposure to the biggest growth areas in North America. Intel, Microsoft, Cisco, Nokia, and IBM are all in the top 10 holdings, driving this to a one-year return of 140.4% to August 31. Fund's since inception return is 48.7%, meaning Smart Fund readers could have tripled their money before its third birthday on November 28, when other guide books will finally recognize it! **Smart Fund History: 1999, 1998.**

RISK

How Often Money was Lost:.........9 of 33 Months
....7 of 31 Quarters
....2 of 22 Years
Worst 3 Months:...............................-14.83% (1998)
Best 3 Months: 43.21% (1999)

ASSET ALLOCATION

Computer software.......................29.7
Computer hardware.....................16.9
Electronics.....................................12.8
Communications...........................10.5
Other...30.1

COMPARISON OF FUND TO INDEXES

$1,000 invested in the fund
$1,000 invested in the TSE 300
$1,000 invested in Canada Savings Bonds
● Annual ranking against other funds in the same category

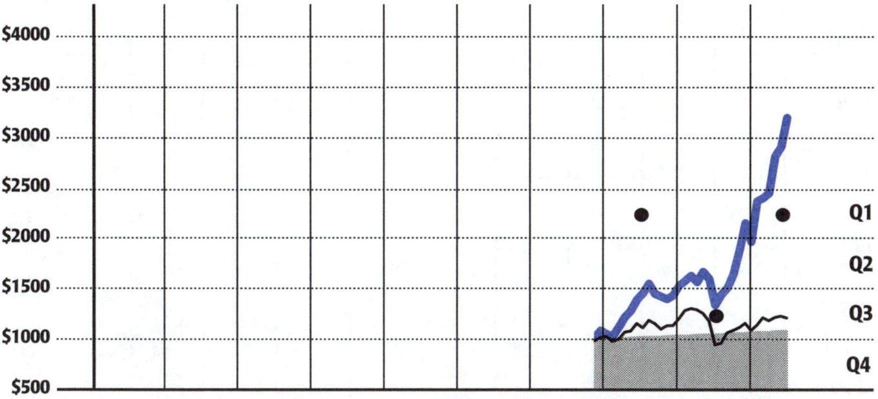

	1990		1992		1994		1996		1998	8/31/99
Annual Return (%)								37.9	34.5	71.2
Compound Return (%)	**10 yr**	**9 yr**	**8 yr**	**7 yr**	**6 yr**	**5 yr**	**4 yr**	**3 yr**	**2 yr**	**1 yr**
									48.6	140.4

@RGENTUM MARKET NEUTRAL PORTFOLIO LOAD

Primary Objective:	Growth
Sponsor:	@rgentum Management & Research
Fund Manager:	Chris Guthrie, Hillsdale Investment Mgmt
Style:	Bottom-up, Blend
Size (MMs):	$35.462
RRSP:	20%
Expense Ratio:	2.50%

COMMENTS

One of a few hedge funds in Canada, it will go long and short in U.S. equities. With this combination of long and short stocks, you can get whacked coming and going if you pick the long and shorts poorly. T his alternative investment vehicle also thrives on leverage. Managed by Chris Guthrie and Arun Kaul of Hillsdale Investment Management, it is not for the faint of heart since investors must have $150,000 to enter. This one uses quantitative models to select stocks. It has settled down to a 5.7% one-year return after its NAV went from $11.34 to $13.16 and back down to $10.80. **New Smart Fund.**

RISK

How Often Money was Lost: ....7 of 15 Months
.........5 of 13 Quarters
.........0 of 4 Years
Worst 3 Months: ....-14.35% (1999)
Best 3 Months: 15.84% (1999)

ASSET ALLOCATION

Foreign equity 36.3
Cdn equities 32.4
Cash & equivalents 17.8
Cdn Income trusts 6.9
Cdn bonds 4.9
Other 1.7

COMPARISON OF FUND TO INDEXES

$1,000 invested in the fund
$1,000 invested in the TSE 300
$1,000 invested in Canada Savings Bonds
Annual ranking against other funds in the same category

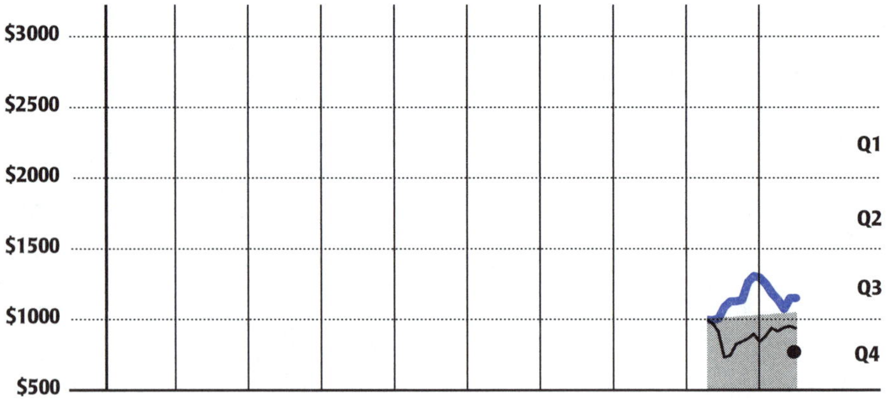

Annual Return (%)	1990	1992	1994	1996	1998	8/31/99
						-9.0

Compound Return (%)	10 yr	9 yr	8 yr	7 yr	6 yr	5 yr	4 yr	3 yr	2 yr	1 yr
										5.7

ALTAMIRA SCIENCE & TECHNOLOGY **NO LOAD**

Primary Objective:	Aggressive Growth
Sponsor:	Altamira Investment Services
Fund Manager:	Ian Ainsworth
Style:	Bottom-up, Sector Growth
Size (MMs):	$222.337
RRSP:	20%
Expense Ratio:	2.36%

COMMENTS

We feared that Ian Ainsworth might become too stretched with all his duties at Altamira. So far it hasn't impacted the performance of this one. Investments in Cisco, Microsoft, Intel, Nortel Networks, AOL, and JDS Uniphase have driven returns on this fund to near the absolute top of the specialty category with a four-year CAGR of 39.5% after a monster year in 1998 when the fund gained 65.6%. It is now up 131.4% for the year ended August 31. MER is 2.36%, but then Altamira was never the bargain many people thought it was, despite its no-load status. **Smart Fund History: 1999.**

RISK

How Often Money was Lost:.......16 of 48 Months
..........10 of 46 Quarters
..........2 of 37 Years
Worst 3 Months:..........-16.03% (1996)
Best 3 Months:..........49.07% (1999)

ASSET ALLOCATION

Electronics semiconductors....32.8
Computer software services......18.7
Communications equipment.....17.1
Health care & biotech..........8.9
Content..........5.7
Other..........16.8

COMPARISON OF FUND TO INDEXES

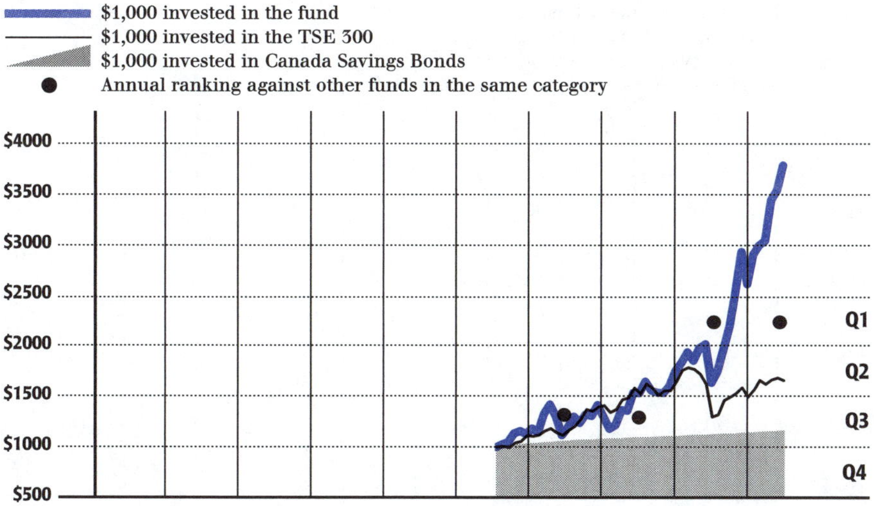

Annual Return (%)	**1990**		**1992**		**1994**		**1996** 13.0	17.3	**1998** 65.6	**8/31/99** 49.2
Compound Return (%)	**10 yr**	**9 yr**	**8 yr**	**7 yr**	**6 yr**	**5 yr**	**4 yr** 39.5	**3 yr** 47.0	**2 yr** 57.3	**1 yr** 131.4

SPECIAL EQUITY

ALTAMIRA E-BUSINESS

NO LOAD

Primary Objective:	Aggressive Growth
Sponsor:	Altamira Investment Services
Fund Manager:	Ian Ainsworth & David Cooke
Style:	Growth
Size (MMs):	$140.224
RRSP:	20%
Expense Ratio:	2.79%

COMMENTS

Again, run by Ian Ainsworth. This is like Sci Tech with a different spin to it. Investments are in emerging Internet companies and also more established companies that are adopting e-business strategies. Fund debuted with a $10 NAV on November 12, 1998, and hit $18.66 on August 31, a spectacular rise; up 55% so far in 1999. Top holdings include IBM, Time Warner, MCI, Cisco, Microsoft, Schwab, FedEx, and Ford Motor. We are relying on Mr. Ainsworth to ride this hot area of the stock market. Think of this one as another early find by Smart Funds. It won't have a three-year number until November 2001 when it might start appearing in other guides. **New Smart Fund.**

RISK

How Often Money was Lost: ....3 of 9 Months
..........1 of 7 Quarters
..........0 of 0 Years
Worst 3 Months: ....-6.34% (1999)
Best 3 Months: 46.09% (1999)

ASSET ALLOCATION

Technology 28.8
Commercial services..........20.9
Consumer services 12.2
Financial services 6.2
Consumer products 5.9
Other 26.0

COMPARISON OF FUND TO INDEXES

$1,000 invested in the fund
$1,000 invested in the TSE 300
$1,000 invested in Canada Savings Bonds
● Annual ranking against other funds in the same category

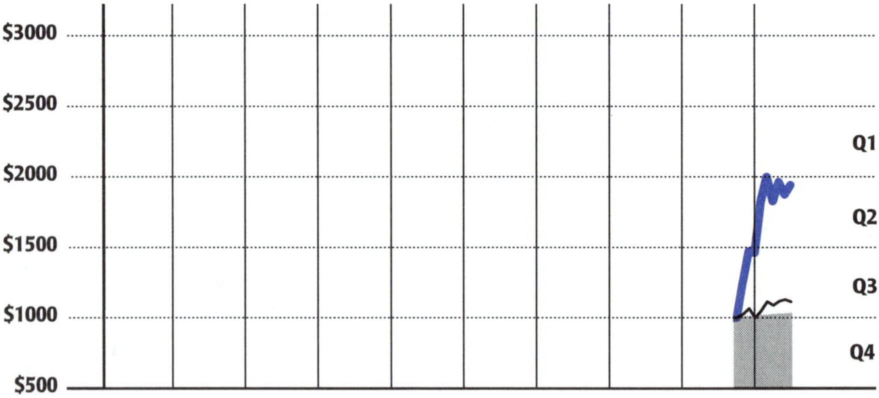

Annual Return (%)	1990	1992	1994	1996	1998	8/31/99
						55.1

Compound Return (%)	10 yr	9 yr	8 yr	7 yr	6 yr	5 yr	4 yr	3 yr	2 yr	1 yr

SPECIAL EQUITY

CLARINGTON GLOBAL COMMUNICATIONS **LOAD**

Primary Objective:	Aggressive Growth
Sponsor:	Clarington Capital Management
Fund Manager:	Oscar Castro, Montgomery Asset Management
Style:	Bottom-up, Blend
Size (MMs):	$75.790
RRSP:	20%
Expense Ratio:	2.90%

COMMENTS

Clarington hired former GT Telecom manager Oscar Castro of Montgomery Asset Management to run their fund. The authors believe this sector will be a growth area for many years, benefiting from the laying of the information highway, as well as the installation of telecommunications systems, in emerging countries. Castro, who is often featured in *Barron's* financial newsweekly, has not disappointed, with a 36.2% two-year CAGR. This is the backbone to the Net and we view this as a beter bet than an emerging markets fund. **Smart Fund History: 1999, 1998.**

RISK

How Often Money was Lost:.........7 of 32 Months
....7 of 30 Quarters
....0 of 21 Years
Worst 3 Months: ....-15.13% (1998)
Best 3 Months: 28.95% (1998)

ASSET ALLOCATION

USA...26.6
UK...11.5
Netherlands...7.9
Japan..6.2
France...4.5
Other...43.3

COMPARISON OF FUND TO INDEXES

$1,000 invested in the fund
$1,000 invested in the TSE 300
$1,000 invested in Canada Savings Bonds
Annual ranking against other funds in the same category

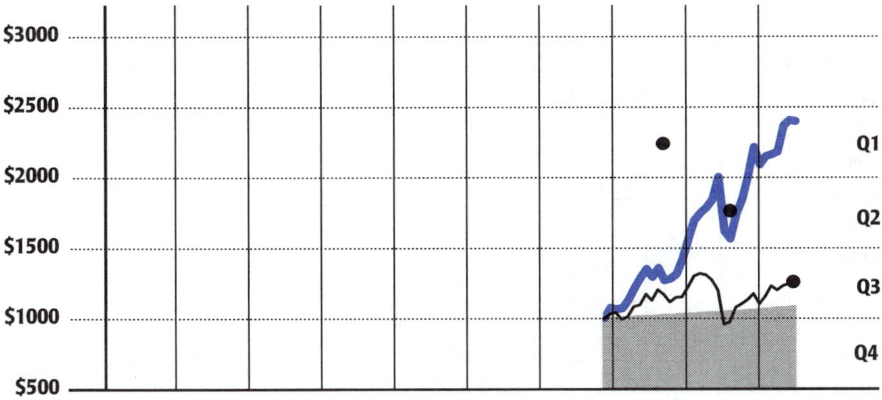

Annual Return (%)	**1990**		**1992**		**1994**		**1996**	31.3	**1998** 52.8	**8/31/99** 19.5
Compound Return (%)	**10 yr**	**9 yr**	**8 yr**	**7 yr**	**6 yr**	**5 yr**	**4 yr**	**3 yr**	**2 yr** 36.2	**1 yr** 48.4

SPECIAL EQUITY

GREEN LINE SCIENCE & TECHNOLOGY **NO LOAD**

Primary Objective: Aggressive Growth
Sponsor: TD Asset Management
Fund Manager: Chip Morris, T. Rowe Price Associates
Style: Bottom-up, Growth
Size (MMs): $360.055
RRSP: 20%
Expense Ratio: 2.58%

COMMENTS

We identified this one early and it is a five-time Smart Fund. Manager Charles (Chip) Morris runs one of the largest technology funds in the world, the US$6.9 billion T. Rowe Price Science & Technology Fund. That fund is rated 4-star by Morningstar. Technology may be volatile, but it is pervasive in our lives. This is a great way to invest in a diversified portfolio of stocks that most investors cannot understand. Fund has the top five-year CAGR in Canada at 33.1%. Microsoft, Lucent, and Cisco are in the top holdings, but Chip doesn't own the same names as the rest of the crowd. There are some other tech funds, but this one seems to keep on getting it right, including a 115.5% return for the year ended August 31. **Smart Fund History: 1999, 1998, 1997, 1996.**

RISK

How Often Money was Lost:.......25 of 68 Months
.......20 of 66 Quarters
.......4 of 57 Years
Worst 3 Months: ....-16.73% (1998)
Best 3 Months: 48.24% (1998)

ASSET ALLOCATION

US equities.......91.3
Global equities.......7.5
Cash & equivalents 1.2

COMPARISON OF FUND TO INDEXES

$1,000 invested in the fund
$1,000 invested in the TSE 300
$1,000 invested in Canada Savings Bonds
Annual ranking against other funds in the same category

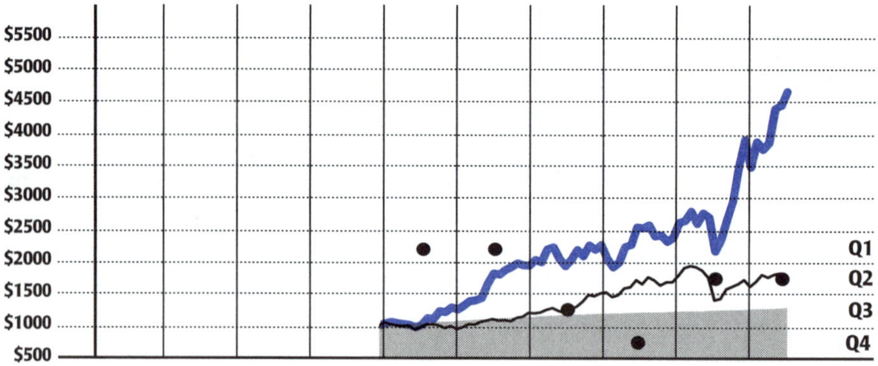

Annual Return (%)	1990		1992		1994		1996		1998	8/31/99
					28.3	51.2	12.7	5.9	51.1	33.1

Compound Return (%)	10 yr	9 yr	8 yr	7 yr	6 yr	5 yr	4 yr	3 yr	2 yr	1 yr
						33.1	26.9	32.0	35.8	115.5

ALTAMIRA BOND

NO LOAD

Primary Objective:	Income
Sponsor:	Altamira Investment Services
Fund Manager:	Robert Marcus
Style:	Interest Rate Anticipator
Size (MMs):	$553.291
RRSP:	100%
Expense Ratio:	1.36%

COMMENTS

An aggressive interest rate anticipator, manager Robert Marcus has managed this to be the number one bond fund over the ten- and five-year periods and number two for the three- and two-year periods ending August 31, 1999. Fund only invests in AAA credits. This one has also been recognized at the Mutual Funds Awards. Marcus firmly believes that we are in a long-term secular trend where interest rates will continue to decline. Therefore, he holds long duration bonds, meaning his fund will suffer when short-term interest rates rise. **Smart Fund History: 1999, 1998.**

RISK

How Often Money was Lost:.....39 of 116 Months
.....25 of 114 Quarters
.....8 of 105 Years
Worst 3 Months:.....-10.82% (1994)
Best 3 Months:.....13.77% (1992)

ASSET ALLOCATION

Long-term.....69.6
Medium-term.....15.0
Short-term.....14.2
Cash.....1.2

COMPARISON OF FUND TO INDEXES

$1,000 invested in the fund
$1,000 invested in the SCMU Bond Total Return
$1,000 invested in Canada Savings Bonds
Annual ranking against other funds in the same category

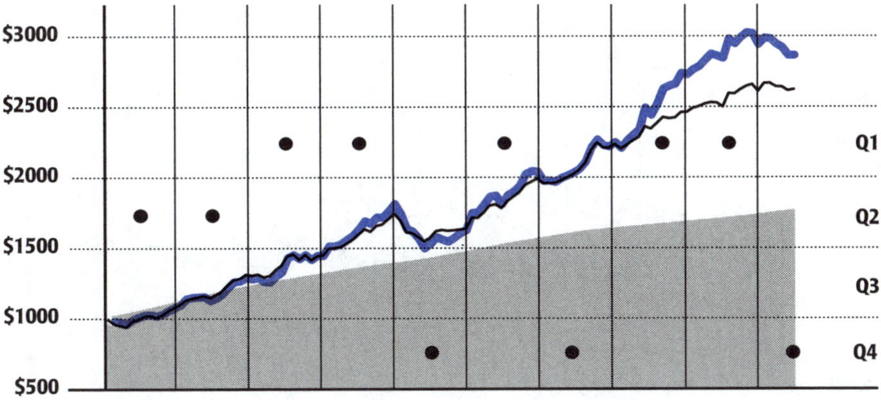

Annual Return (%)	1990		1992		1994		1996		1998	8/31/99
	7.4	19.7	12.4	21.6	-8.8	27.4	9.0	19.6	13.6	-5.3

Compound Return (%)	10 yr	9 yr	8 yr	7 yr	6 yr	5 yr	4 yr	3 yr	2 yr	1 yr
	11.3	12.1	11.8	10.2	9.2	12.7	11.2	11.7	8.3	0.7

CANADIAN BOND

BISSETT CANADIAN BOND

NO LOAD

Primary Objective:	Income
Sponsor:	Bissett & Associates
Fund Manager:	Michael Quinn
Style:	Interest Rate Anticipator
Size (MMs):	$270.000
RRSP:	100%
Expense Ratio:	0.75%

COMMENTS

Bissett & Associates proves they are not just an equity house with this top-performing bond fund. This one is no-load, low 0.75% MER, and available through most brokers. Manager Michael Quinn and co-manager Guy LeBlanc can invest in A-rated bonds and have almost 40% of fund in corporates. The payback: first quartile over five, three, and one year. **Smart Fund History: 1999, 1998.**

RISK

How Often Money was Lost:.....34 of 116 Months
..........22 of 114 Quarters
..........5 of 105 Years
Worst 3 Months:..........-7.34% (1994)
Best 3 Months:..........9.82% (1996)

ASSET ALLOCATION

Corporates..........38.5
Provincials..........25.5
Canadas..........33.5
Other..........2.5

COMPARISON OF FUND TO INDEXES

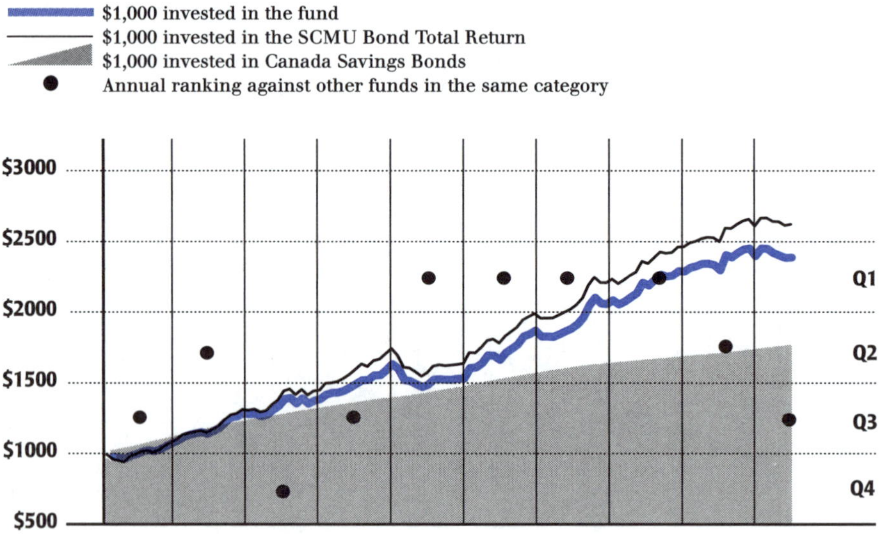

Annual Return (%)	1990		1992		1994		1996		1998	8/31/99
	6.9	20.0	7.0	15.6	-3.8	20.6	11.8	9.6	8.2	-2.3

Compound Return (%)	10 yr	9 yr	8 yr	7 yr	6 yr	5 yr	4 yr	3 yr	2 yr	1 yr
	9.3	9.9	9.2	8.0	7.8	9.4	8.7	7.7	4.5	4.0

CANADIAN BOND

CANADA TRUST BOND INDEX — NO LOAD

Primary Objective: Total Return
Sponsor: CT Investment Management Group
Fund Manager: Team
Style: Passive
Size (MMs): $40.837
RRSP: 100%
Expense Ratio: 0.75%

COMMENTS

One of the only bond index funds we know. Most bond fund managers have difficulty, adding value against the Scotia Capital Markets Bond Universe. When fees are tacked on, it becomes nearly impossible. This one tries to match the index, net of its 0.74% MER. So far, it seems to be tracking the index and has produced first-quartile results for the two years ended August 31. **New Smart Fund.**

RISK

How Often Money was Lost: 10 of 23 Months
5 of 21 Quarters
0 of 12 Years
Worst 3 Months: -2.02% (1999)
Best 3 Months: 4.68% (1998)

ASSET ALLOCATION

Corporates	17.2
Provincials	20.4
Canadas	51.3
Mortgages	3.5
Cash	5.4
Other	2.2

COMPARISON OF FUND TO INDEXES

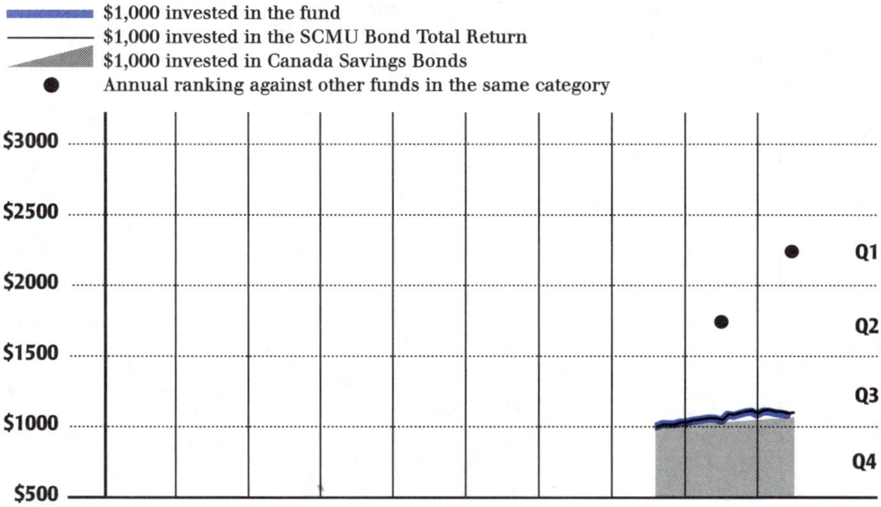

Annual Return (%)	1990		1992		1994		1996		1998	8/31/99
									8.3	-1.6

Compound Return (%)	10 yr	9 yr	8 yr	7 yr	6 yr	5 yr	4 yr	3 yr	2 yr	1 yr
									4.8	4.2

CANADIAN BOND

CI CANADIAN BOND

LOAD

Primary Objective:	Total Return
Sponsor:	CI Mutual Funds
Fund Manager:	Jeff Herold, J. Zechner Associates
Style:	Interest Rate Anticipator
Size (MMs):	$363.950
RRSP:	100%
Expense Ratio:	1.68%

COMMENTS

Managed by former Elliott & Page manager Jeff Herod. Fund invests mainly in Triple "A" Government of Canada bonds of varying maturities with about 20% in corporates. Amazingly, this fund has performed despite its MER of 1.67%, but then your dealer gets 0.50% of that. First-quartile performer over the five-, three-, and one-year periods ending August 31, 1999, and pays out monthly income for those who need it. **New Smart Fund.**

RISK

How Often Money was Lost:.......23 of 79 Months
....15 of 77 Quarters
....8 of 68 Years
Worst 3 Months: ....-5.89% (1994)
Best 3 Months:.................................10.38% (1996)

ASSET ALLOCATION

Corporates.......................................17.4
Provincials.......................................7.0
Canadas...60.2
Cash..15.4

COMPARISON OF FUND TO INDEXES

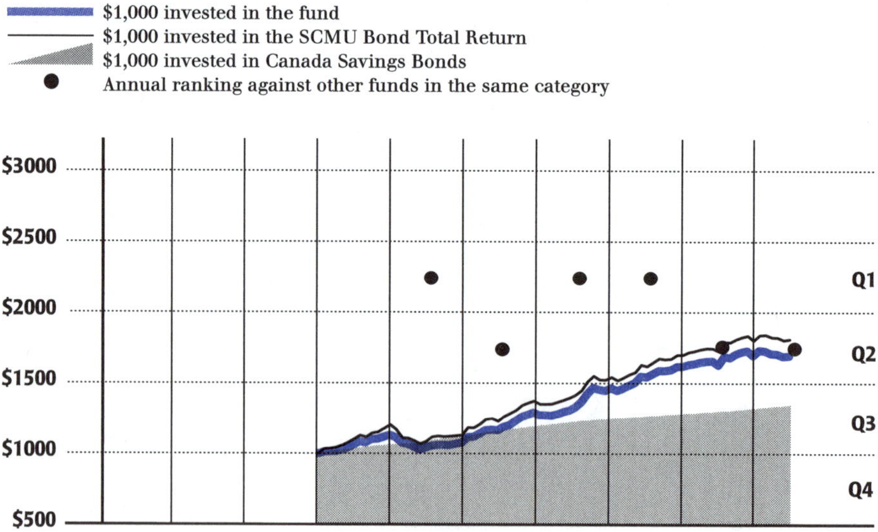

Annual Return (%)	**1990**		**1992**		**1994**		**1996**		**1998**	**8/31/99**
					-4.3	19.2	14.0	9.5	8.0	-1.7
Compound Return (%)	**10 yr**	**9 yr**	**8 yr**	**7 yr**	**6 yr**	**5 yr**	**4 yr**	**3 yr**	**2 yr**	**1 yr**
					7.7	9.9	9.2	8.4	4.8	4.0

CANADIAN BOND

GREEN LINE CANADIAN BOND **NO LOAD**

Primary Objective: Total Return
Sponsor: TD Asset Management
Fund Manager: Satish Rai and Paul Gardner
Style: Interest Rate Anticipator
Size (MMs): $1,171.660
RRSP: 100%
Expense Ratio: 0.94%

COMMENTS

A good fund from the best group of bank funds. Paul Gardner and Satish Rai have been able to find good returns in some corporates. Fund had 66% in corporate bonds as of August 31. First quartile every year from 1995 on. Top-quartile performer with a 0.94% MER, this will be more volatile than some of the others in the category. The highly sought-after Satish Rai cannot hide anymore; the fund has doubled to $1.2 billion since December 1997. **Smart Fund History: 1999, 1998, 1997.**

RISK

How Often Money was Lost:.....33 of 116 Months
....24 of 114 Quarters
....9 of 105 Years
Worst 3 Months: ....-8.84% (1994)
Best 3 Months:...........................10.84% (1992)

ASSET ALLOCATION

Corporates..........................65.7
Provincials 3.6
Canadas 19.3
Strips...................................7.3
Cash 2.6
Other....................................1.5

COMPARISON OF FUND TO INDEXES

$1,000 invested in the fund
$1,000 invested in the SCMU Bond Total Return
$1,000 invested in Canada Savings Bonds
● Annual ranking against other funds in the same category

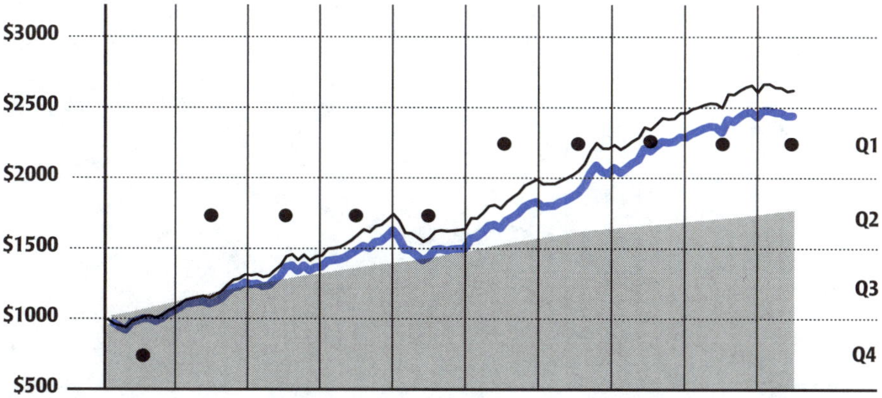

Annual Return (%)	1990		1992		1994		1996		1998	8/31/99
	4.8	19.3	8.9	16.2	-5.6	21.4	12.4	10.6	9.1	-0.8

Compound Return (%)	10 yr	9 yr	8 yr	7 yr	6 yr	5 yr	4 yr	3 yr	2 yr	1 yr
	9.7	10.5	10.0	8.5	8.3	10.4	9.5	8.8	5.6	5.1

LONDON LIFE MORTGAGE

LOAD

Primary Objective:	Income
Sponsor:	London Life Investment Mgmt
Fund Manager:	Team
Style:	Bottom-up
Size (MMs):	$554.745
RRSP:	100%
Expense Ratio:	2.00%

COMMENTS

MER of 2.00% is tough for a mortgage fund, but you get the guarantee of a seg fund. Steady positive returns every year. Could be a good place to hide during the Y2K storm. No distributions, so not exactly geared for income-oriented investors. Think of this as a safe haven during these volatile times. Choose a date now when to redeploy this investment into London Life American Equity or London Life Global Equity, both Smart Funds and managed by Janus Capital. Reasonable first-quartile performance for three and two years ended August 31, 1999. **New Smart Fund.**

RISK

How Often Money was Lost:.....18 of 116 Months
.....12 of 114 Quarters
.....1 of 105 Years
Worst 3 Months: .....-4.73% (1994)
Best 3 Months:.....5.41% (1991)

ASSET ALLOCATION

Residential 61.6
Commercial.....27.2
Other 11.2

COMPARISON OF FUND TO INDEXES

$1,000 invested in the fund
$1,000 invested in the SCMU Bond Total Return
$1,000 invested in Canada Savings Bonds
Annual ranking against other funds in the same category

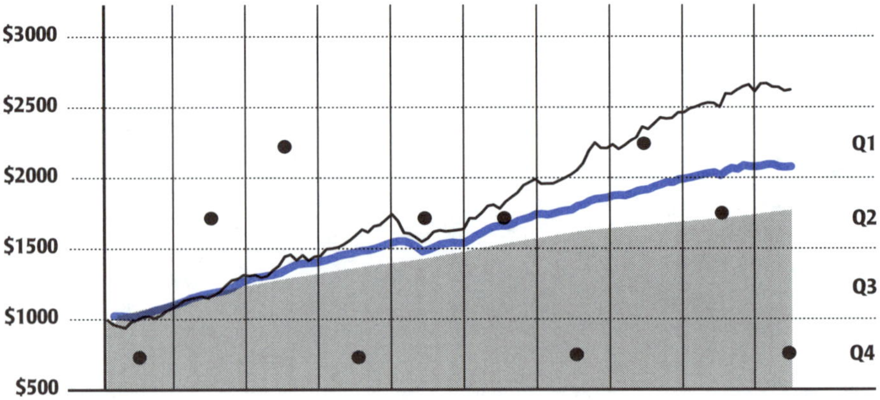

Annual Return (%)	1990		1992		1994		1996		1998	8/31/99
	8.3	15.9	10.5	9.4	0.6	11.9	7.8	6.2	6.0	-0.4

Compound Return (%)	10 yr	9 yr	8 yr	7 yr	6 yr	5 yr	4 yr	3 yr	2 yr	1 yr
	7.9	8.0	7.2	6.2	5.8	6.7	5.8	4.9	4.1	3.2

CANADIAN BOND

PH&N BOND

NO LOAD

Primary Objective:	Total Return
Sponsor:	Phillips, Hager & North Investment Mgmt
Fund Manager:	Team
Style:	Spread Traders
Size (MMs):	$2,399.750
RRSP:	100%
Expense Ratio:	0.57%

COMMENTS

One of the best bond funds in the country: no-load, low MER, and consistent performance. Fund was first quartile in seven of the last nine years. The 0.57% MER gives this one a big head start in the performance game. Holds about 25% in corporate bonds. This fund's 10-year CAGR of 10.2% would rank it in the top 10 of all Canadian equity funds in Canada. Now that is a scary thought; no wonder Canadian investors are flocking to the 100 percent eligible foreign-content funds. **Smart Fund History: 1999, 1998, 1997, 1996.**

RISK

How Often Money was Lost:.....31 of 116 Months
....20 of 114 Quarters
....7 of 105 Years
Worst 3 Months:........................-7.77% (1994)
Best 3 Months:........................10.50% (1992)

ASSET ALLOCATION

Corporates........................26.1
Provincials........................17.2
Canadas........................46.1
Mortgages........................1.7
Foreign 7.6
Other........................1.3

COMPARISON OF FUND TO INDEXES

$1,000 invested in the fund
$1,000 invested in the SCMU Bond Total Return
$1,000 invested in Canada Savings Bonds
Annual ranking against other funds in the same category

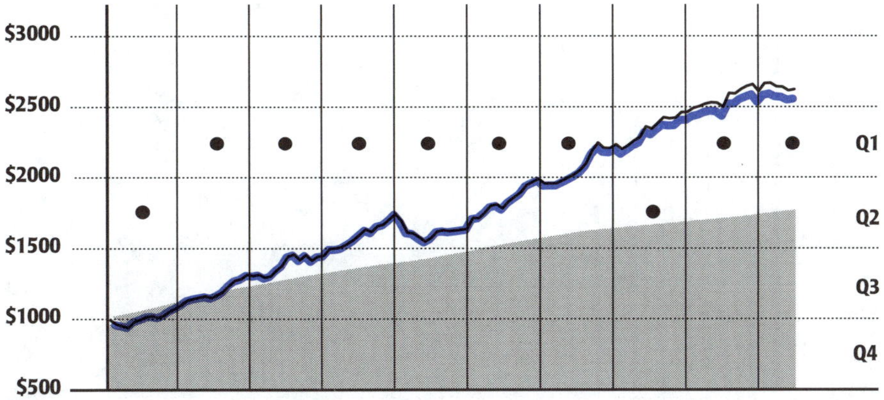

Annual Return (%)	1990		1992		1994		1996		1998	8/31/99
	8.1	21.7	9.9	17.8	-4.1	20.4	11.2	8.7	8.5	-0.6

Compound Return (%)	10 yr	9 yr	8 yr	7 yr	6 yr	5 yr	4 yr	3 yr	2 yr	1 yr
	10.2	10.7	10.0	8.4	7.8	9.6	8.8	7.9	5.3	5.0

CANADIAN BOND

SCEPTRE BOND

NO LOAD

Primary Objective:	Total Return
Sponsor:	Sceptre Investment Counsel
Fund Manager:	Ian Lee
Style:	Interest Rate Anticipator
Size (MMs):	$76.058
RRSP:	100%
Expense Ratio:	0.94%

COMMENTS

At least their bond department is performing. Ian Lee has been at Sceptre since 1996 and pulled this to the top first decile since. This one is now first quartile over the ten-, five-, three-, and two-year periods. MER is 0.94%, which is competitive. **Smart Fund History: 1999.**

RISK

How Often Money was Lost:.....33 of 116 Months
22 of 114 Quarters ....8 of 105 Years
Worst 3 Months: ....-6.40% (1994)
Best 3 Months:..................................10.01% (1996)

ASSET ALLOCATION

Canadas...99.1
Cash..0.2
Other...0.7

COMPARISON OF FUND TO INDEXES

$1,000 invested in the fund
$1,000 invested in the SCMU Bond Total Return
$1,000 invested in Canada Savings Bonds
Annual ranking against other funds in the same category

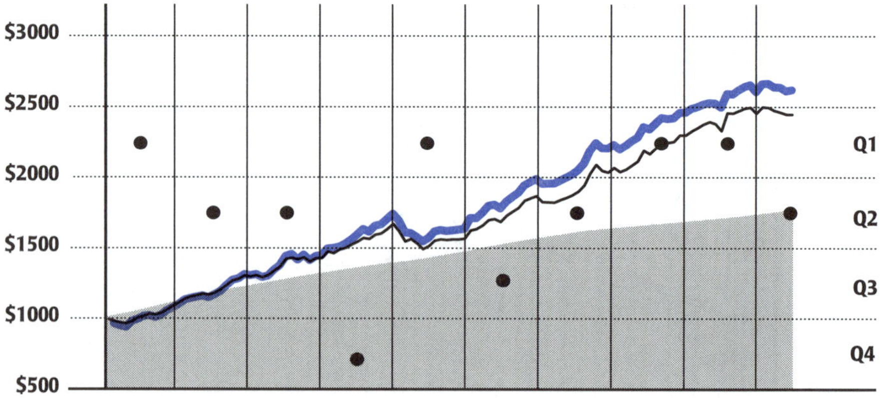

Annual Return (%)	1990		1992		1994		1996		1998	8/31/99
	8.9	19.8	9.4	14.4	-4.4	18.6	10.5	10.2	10.4	-1.7

Compound Return (%)	10 yr	9 yr	8 yr	7 yr	6 yr	5 yr	4 yr	3 yr	2 yr	1 yr
	9.8	10.1	9.3	8.0	7.7	9.5	9.1	8.8	6.3	5.0

CANADIAN BOND

SCUDDER CDN SHORT-TERM

NO LOAD

Primary Objective:	Income
Sponsor:	Scudder Maxxum
Fund Manager:	Adam Greshin, Scudder Kemper Investments
Style:	Spread Traders
Size (MMs):	$17.007
RRSP:	100%
Expense Ratio:	0.85%

COMMENTS

Many investors are starved for income-generating ideas and with rates so low the alternatives tend to have too much volatility. This one has a top-quartile ranking in the short-term category and has a reasonable 0.85% MER. For income-needy investors, it has been paying a steady 5+ cents per month. **Smart Fund History: 1999.**

RISK

How Often Money was Lost:.........8 of 46 Months
....5 of 44 Quarters
....0 of 35 Years
Worst 3 Months:................................-0.66% (1997)
Best 3 Months:...................................4.93% (1996)

ASSET ALLOCATION

Corporates......................................59.0
Provincials 6.0
Canadas 34.0
Mortgages..1.0

COMPARISON OF FUND TO INDEXES

$1,000 invested in the fund
$1,000 invested in the SCMU Bond Total Return
$1,000 invested in Canada Savings Bonds
● Annual ranking against other funds in the same category

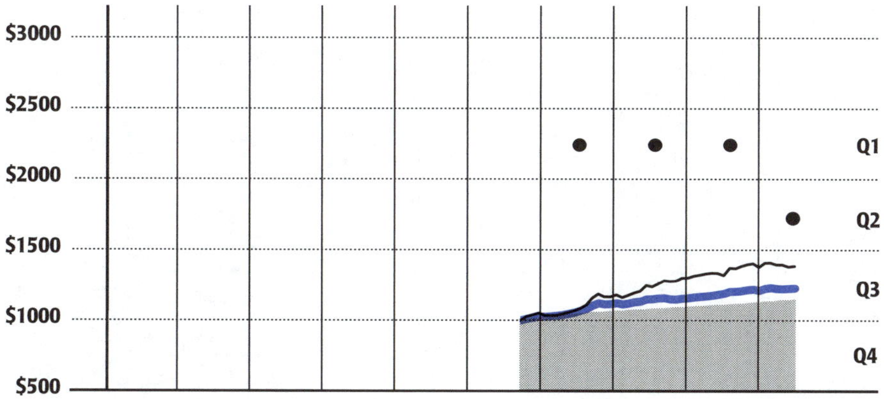

Annual Return (%)	1990		1992		1994		1996		1998	8/31/99
							9.4	4.0	5.8	1.0

Compound Return (%)	10 yr	9 yr	8 yr	7 yr	6 yr	5 yr	4 yr	3 yr	2 yr	1 yr
								5.1	3.8	3.2

CANADIAN BOND

TALVEST HIGH YIELD

LOAD

Primary Objective:	Total Return
Sponsor:	TAL Fund Management
Fund Manager:	Chris Currie
Style:	High Yield
Size (MMs):	$106.204
RRSP:	100%
Expense Ratio:	2.12%

COMMENTS

If you take on more risks, you can enhance your yield. One way to do that is to move from government guaranteed bonds to higher-yielding corporates. This is not for amateurs and we recommend owning corporates through a fund with a professional manager. TAL is one of the top fixed-income managers in Canada, and with the addition of top high-yield analyst Christopher Currie, this should be a good one. MER of 2.12% is as high as an equity fund and needs to be addressed. You will get some volatility in this one so be prepared. It does pay monthly income for unitholders. **Smart Fund History: 1999.**

RISK

How Often Money was Lost:.......12 of 34 Months
....6 of 32 Quarters
....11 of 23 Years
Worst 3 Months:...................................-7.18% (1998)
Best 3 Months:......................................6.62% (1997)

ASSET ALLOCATION

Corporates.......................................25.7
Foreign Pay.....................................39.5
Other...15.0
Foreign..19.8

COMPARISON OF FUND TO INDEXES

$1,000 invested in the fund
$1,000 invested in the SCMU Bond Total Return
$1,000 invested in Canada Savings Bonds
● Annual ranking against other funds in the same category

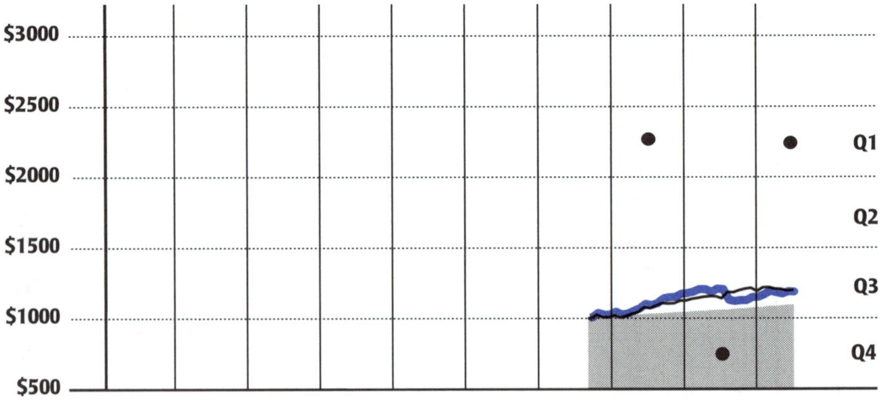

Annual Return (%)	**1990**		**1992**		**1994**		**1996**		**1998**	**8/31/99**
								12.4	-2.2	5.5
Compound Return (%)	**10 yr**	**9 yr**	**8 yr**	**7 yr**	**6 yr**	**5 yr**	**4 yr**	**3 yr**	**2 yr**	**1 yr**
									4.3	-1.5

TRIMARK ADVANTAGE BOND

LOAD

Primary Objective: Total Return
Sponsor: Trimark
Fund Manager: Patrick Farmer & Rex Chong
Style: High Yield
Size (MMs): $814.192
RRSP: 100%
Expense Ratio: 1.24%

COMMENTS

A high-yield fund that invests in corporate as well as government bonds. This solid performer with its low 1.24% MER makes it very competitive. That MER should be the benchmark for others in the category. Consistent performer that pays out a monthly income and is one of the most popular funds at Trimark. Pat Farmer has made money for his unitholders every full calendar since inception in December 1994 and has achieved a 10.5% CAGR over that period. **Smart Fund History: 1998.**

RISK

How Often Money was Lost:.......13 of 56 Months
..............................8 of 54 Quarters
..............................0 of 45 Years
Worst 3 Months: ....-2.96% (1998)
Best 3 Months:................9.08% (1996)

ASSET ALLOCATION

Corporates........41.7
Foreign........27.1
Canadas........19.2
Equities........5.7
Cash........3.5
Other........2.8

COMPARISON OF FUND TO INDEXES

$1,000 invested in the fund
$1,000 invested in the SCMU Bond Total Return
$1,000 invested in Canada Savings Bonds
Annual ranking against other funds in the same category

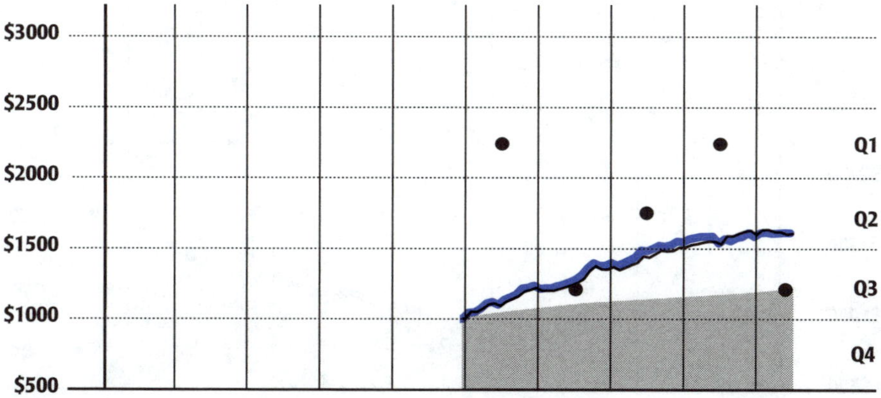

Annual Return (%)	**1990**		**1992**		**1994**		**1996**		**1998**	**8/31/99**
						22.7	12.9	10.5	3.9	1.7
Compound Return (%)	**10 yr**	**9 yr**	**8 yr**	**7 yr**	**6 yr**	**5 yr**	**4 yr**	**3 yr**	**2 yr**	**1 yr**
							9.2	7.9	4.3	4.8

GUARDIAN FOREIGN INCOME A **LOAD**

Primary Objective:	Income
Sponsor:	Guardian Mutual Funds
Fund Manager:	Laurence Linklater, Kleinwort Guardian
Style:	Bottom-up
Size (MMs):	$14.227
RRSP:	100%
Expense Ratio:	2.04%

COMMENTS

An RRSP-eligible fund that is a solid, if unspectacular, performer. Small size leaves this one vulnerable to being shut down by Guardian and probably keeps the MER high. Guardian International Income, also managed by Laurence Linklater, was a Smart Fund in 1997. Asset class has been out of favour for some time, but with increased volatility in world markets, some may find comfort in fixed-income products, even with lower yields. **Smart Fund History: 1999, 1998.**

RISK

How Often Money was Lost:.......20 of 61 Months
...............15 of 59 Quarters
...............1 of 50 Years
Worst 3 Months: ....-6.00% (1999)
Best 3 Months:...............10.43% (1998)

ASSET ALLOCATION

USA	42.7
Germany	22.3
Japan	15.7
UK	9.2
Italy	4.9
Other	5.2

COMPARISON OF FUND TO INDEXES

$1,000 invested in the fund
$1,000 invested in the LB Government Bond Index
$1,000 invested in Canada Savings Bonds
● Annual ranking against other funds in the same category

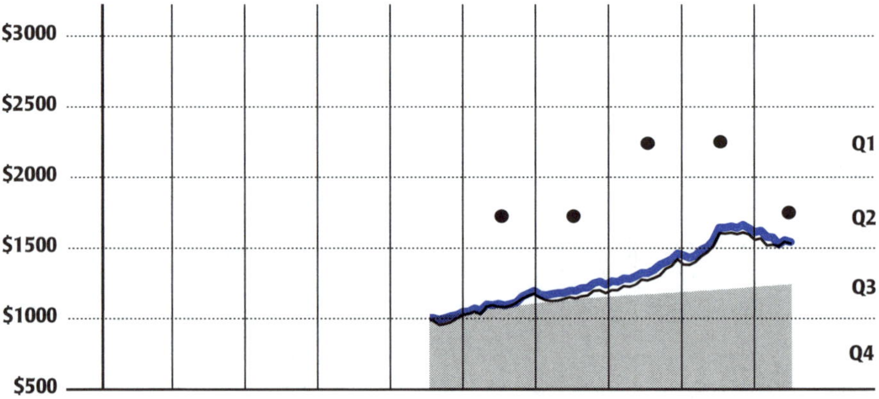

Annual	**1990**		**1992**		**1994**		**1996**		**1998**	**8/31/99**
Return (%)						14.8	7.4	12.6	17.2	-7.3

Compound	**10 yr**	**9 yr**	**8 yr**	**7 yr**	**6 yr**	**5 yr**	**4 yr**	**3 yr**	**2 yr**	**1 yr**
Return (%)						9.0	9.1	8.9	8.0	-6.3

UNIVERSAL WORLD INCOME RRSP **LOAD**

Primary Objective: Growth & Income
Sponsor: Mackenzie Financial Corp.
Fund Manager: Richard Gluck
Style: Interest Rate Anticipator
Size (MMs): $645.556
RRSP: 100%
Expense Ratio: 2.06%

COMMENTS

Fully eligible as Canadian content for an RSP. This one is a conservative way to prepare for potential Y2K concerns. You can weather the storm and volatility that may show up in equity funds. This global bond fund will provide diversification without impacting your foreign-content limits. **New Smart Fund.**

RISK

How Often Money was Lost:.......19 of 59 Months
....12 of 57 Quarters
....4 of 48 Years
Worst 3 Months: ....-5.17% (1999)
Best 3 Months:...................................6.38% (1996)

ASSET ALLOCATION

USA..28.0
Europe 23.0
Canada......................................16.0
Cash & equivalents 5.0
Japan 4.0
Other 24.0

COMPARISON OF FUND TO INDEXES

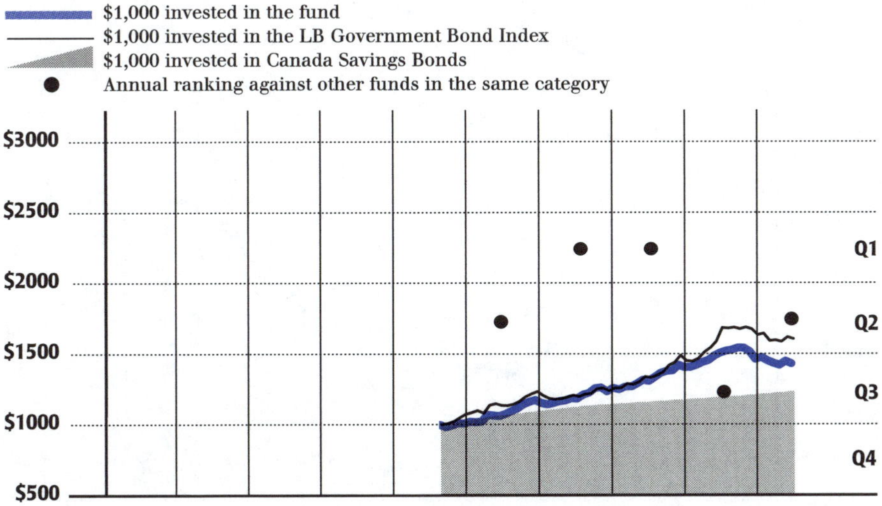

Annual Return (%)	**1990**		**1992**		**1994**		**1996**		**1998**	**8/31/99**
						14.9	8.8	9.6	11.4	-7.2

Compound Return (%)	**10 yr**	**9 yr**	**8 yr**	**7 yr**	**6 yr**	**5 yr**	**4 yr**	**3 yr**	**2 yr**	**1 yr**
							7.4	6.6	4.5	-5.1

BISSETT RETIREMENT FUND

NO LOAD

Primary Objective:	Growth & Income
Sponsor:	Bissett & Associates
Fund Manager:	Michael Quinn
Style:	Fund of Funds
Size (MMs):	$264.045
RRSP:	100%
Expense Ratio:	0.23% plus MER on the funds

CANADIAN BALANCED

COMMENTS

This fund of funds has been one of the top-performing balanced funds over the last five years. It has a solid track record of first-quartile and second-quartile performance over each calendar year back to 1992. The fund has a superior risk-reward profile, and manager Michael Quinn decides on the most optimum asset mix. The asset mix comes at a cost of 0.23% MER (a decrease from 0.44% last year), but there are expenses in the underlying Bissett funds. We have the Bissett Canadian Equity, Multi-National Equity, and Bond Funds already as Smart Funds. With this fund of funds you get it all in one place at a great price. **Smart Fund History: 1999, 1998.**

RISK

How Often Money was Lost: ....29 of 97 Months
....19 of 95 Quarters
....10 of 86 Years
Worst 3 Months: ....-12.08% (1998)
Best 3 Months: 13.41% (1997)

ASSET ALLOCATION

Canadian equities 59.0
Fixed income.................................40.6
Cash 0.4

COMPARISON OF FUND TO INDEXES

$1,000 invested in the fund
$1,000 invested in the 60% TSE 300 – 40% SCMU Bond Index
$1,000 invested in Canada Savings Bonds
● Annual ranking against other funds in the same category

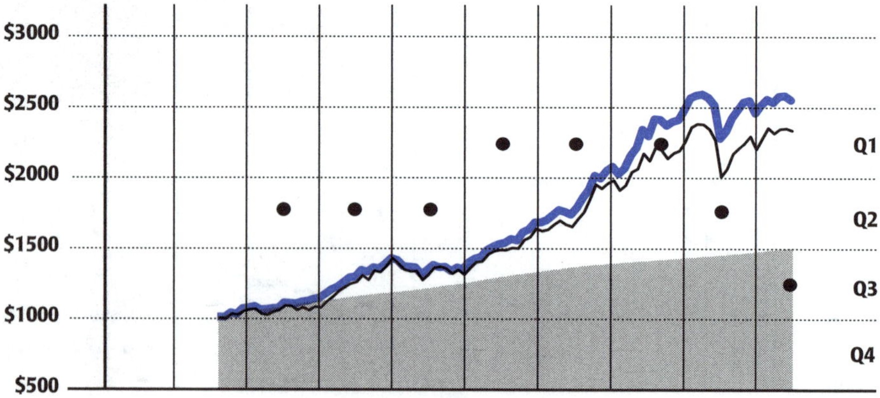

Annual	1990		1992		1994		1996		1998	8/31/99
Return (%)			6.3	22.2	-1.8	19.8	22.2	20.2	5.8	0.6
Compound	10 yr	9 yr	8 yr	7 yr	6 yr	5 yr	4 yr	3 yr	2 yr	1 yr
Return (%)			12.3	12.7	11.3	13.1	13.5	12.6	5.4	11.9

CL GENERATIONS CONTINUUM CONSERVATIVE MODEL LOAD

Primary Objective:	Growth & Income
Sponsor:	Canada Life Assurance Co.
Fund Manager:	The Continuum Advisory Team
Style:	Fund of Funds
Size (MMs):	$7.920
RRSP:	100%
Expense Ratio:	n/a

COMMENTS

Another fund of funds. This one owns seven pools of funds managed by managers: TAL, McLean Budden, Bissett, Laketon, Knight Bain Seath & Holbrook, and TD Quantitative Capital. This fund is about 60/40 fixed income/equity. It is a great way to get asset and manager diversification in one stop from your Canada Life representative. All of this comes with a seg fund guarantee to boot. Not bad protection for those nervous in these volatile times. Management fee is about 2.75%. **New Smart Fund.**

RISK

How Often Money was Lost: ....5 of 9 Months
..........2 of 7 Quarters
Worst 3 Months: ....-1.21% (1999)
Best 3 Months: 1.56% (1999)

ASSET ALLOCATION

Canada bonds 56.1
U.S. equities 14.4
Global equities 4.9
Cash & equivalents 4.8
Other 19.8

CANADIAN BALANCED

COMPARISON OF FUND TO INDEXES

$1,000 invested in the fund
$1,000 invested in the 60% TSE 300 – 40% SCMU Bond Index
$1,000 invested in Canada Savings Bonds
Annual ranking against other funds in the same category

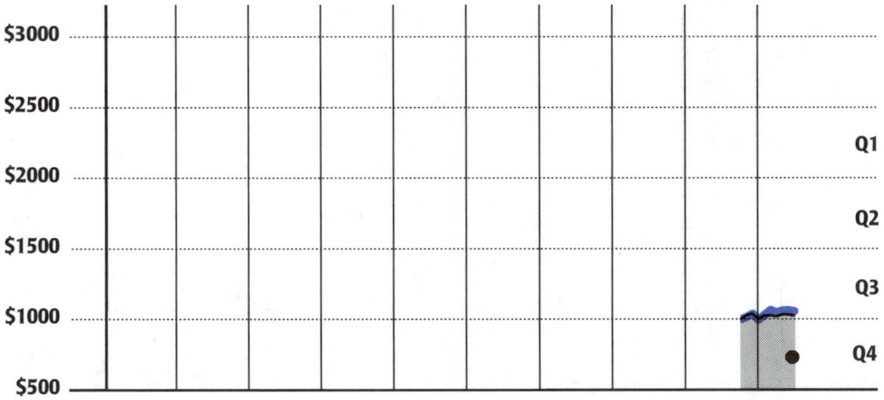

Annual Return (%)	1990		1992		1994		1996		1998	8/31/99
										-3.2

Compound Return (%)	10 yr	9 yr	8 yr	7 yr	6 yr	5 yr	4 yr	3 yr	2 yr	1 yr

CLARINGTON CANADIAN BALANCED LOAD

Primary Objective:	Growth & Income
Sponsor:	Clarington Funds
Fund Manager:	Peter Marshall, Seamark
Style:	Bottom-up
Size (MMs):	$52.816
RRSP:	100%
Expense Ratio:	2.70%

COMMENTS

Terry Stone has quietly built a solid little fund company. His advisors, Seamark, have put up steady performance. This fund passed its three-year mark in September 1999 and might now begin to get recognized by other guides. This one was first quartile in 1998 and so far in 1999. Even its third quartile in 1997 was an 11% return. It is first quartile over the two- and one-year period ended August 31, 1999. **New Smart Fund.**

RISK

How Often Money was Lost:.......12 of 35 Months
..........9 of 33 Quarters
..........2 of 24 Years
Worst 3 Months:..........-12.88% (1998)
Best 3 Months:..........11.30% (1997)

ASSET ALLOCATION

Bonds..........34.7
Equities..........30.5
Foreign equities..........23.7
Cash..........11.1

COMPARISON OF FUND TO INDEXES

$1,000 invested in the fund
$1,000 invested in the 60% TSE 300 – 40% SCMU Bond Index
$1,000 invested in Canada Savings Bonds
Annual ranking against other funds in the same category

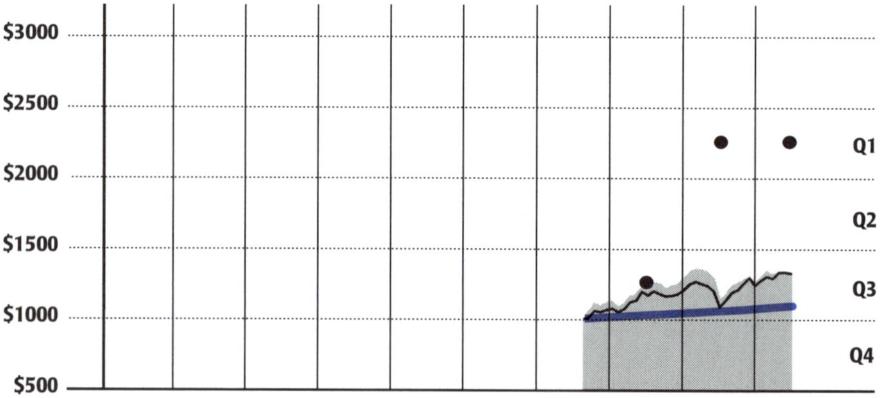

Annual Return (%)	**1990**		**1992**		**1994**		**1996**		**1998**	**8/31/99**
								11.0	7.3	6.0
Compound Return (%)	**10 yr**	**9 yr**	**8 yr**	**7 yr**	**6 yr**	**5 yr**	**4 yr**	**3 yr**	**2 yr**	**1 yr**
									6.6	21.9

CT BALANCED INDEX

NO LOAD

Primary Objective: Growth & Income
Sponsor: Canada Trust Mutual Funds
Fund Manager: CT Investment Management Group
Style: Passive, Fund of Funds
Size (MMs): $24.774
RRSP: 100
Expense Ratio: 0.85%

COMMENTS

The only balanced index fund in Canada. This fund of five CT index funds has about a 50/50 bond to equity weighting. The MER of 0.10% on top of the underlying index funds makes this one of the best deals in Canada. It is still early to judge performance, but with index investing you know what you're getting a fully invested fund that will match the market. This balanced fund pays out a distribution each quarter, if you need the income. New Smart Fund

RISK

How Often Money was Lost: ....5 of 14 Months
..........2 of 12 Quarters
..........0 of 3 Years
Worst 3 Months: ....-8.13% (1998)
Best 3 Months: 9.51% (1998)

ASSET ALLOCATION

Equities 49.6
Canada bonds 37.2
Corporate bonds 8.3
Cash 4.9

COMPARISON OF FUND TO INDEXES

$1,000 invested in the fund
$1,000 invested in the 60% TSE 300 – 40% SCMU Bond Index
$1,000 invested in Canada Savings Bonds
Annual ranking against other funds in the same category

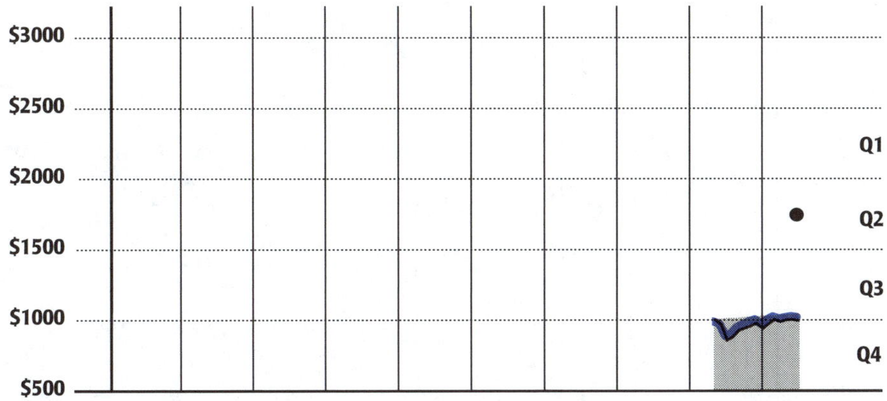

Annual Return (%)	1990		1992		1994		1996		1998	8/31/99
										15.1

Compound Return (%)	10 yr	9 yr	8 yr	7 yr	6 yr	5 yr	4 yr	3 yr	2 yr	1 yr
										2.8

FIDELITY CANADIAN ASSET ALLOCATION **LOAD**

Primary Objective:	Total Return
Sponsor:	Fidelity Investments Canada
Fund Manager:	Dick Habermann, Alan Radlo, Ford O'Neil
Style:	Top-down
Size (MMs):	$5,208.024
RRSP:	100%
Expense Ratio:	2.41%

COMMENTS

This is a top-decile performing balanced fund over the one-, two-, and three-year periods ending August 31. Dick Habermann makes the asset allocation decision. Alan Radlo, picks stocks, and Ford O'Neil, the bonds. This has been one of the most popular funds at Fidelity, growing by $1.3 billion in eight months in 1999. It has higher volatility than most balanced funds but with a standard deviation about 20% lower than most equity funds, and still has a 15.7% compound return for the three years ended August 31. **Smart Fund History: 1999, 1998.**

RISK

How Often Money was Lost:	16 of 56 Months
	6 of 54 Quarters
	1 of 45 Years
Worst 3 Months:	-11.77% (1998)
Best 3 Months:	16.51% (1997)

ASSET ALLOCATION

Cdn equities	48.2
Corporate bonds	11.5
Foreign equities	13.2
Provincials	8.7
Canada bonds	10.8
Other	7.6

COMPARISON OF FUND TO INDEXES

$1,000 invested in the fund
$1,000 invested in the 60% TSE 300 – 40% SCMU Bond Index
$1,000 invested in Canada Savings Bonds
Annual ranking against other funds in the same category

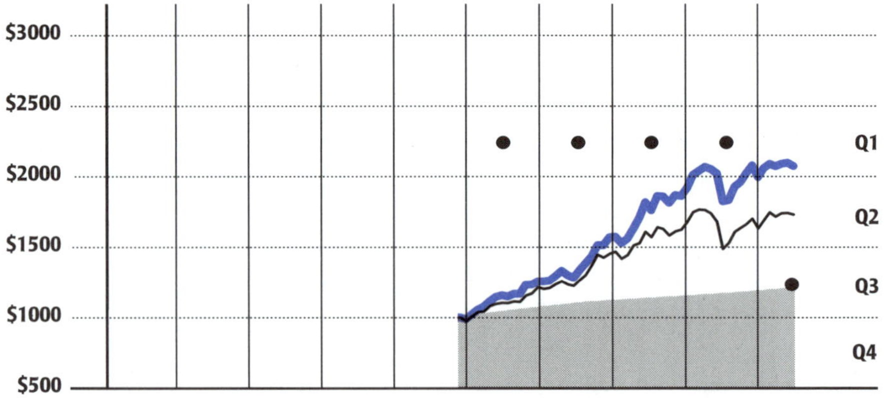

Annual Return (%)	1990		1992		1994		1996		1998	8/31/99
						23.4	22.6	23.4	8.4	2.4

Compound Return (%)	10 yr	9 yr	8 yr	7 yr	6 yr	5 yr	4 yr	3 yr	2 yr	1 yr
							15.9	15.7	8.5	13.6

GLOBAL STRATEGY INCOME PLUS LOAD

Primary Objective:	Growth & Income
Sponsor:	Global Strategy Financial
Fund Manager:	Tony Massie
Style:	Bottom-up
Size (MMs):	$2,078.701
RRSP:	100%
Expense Ratio:	2.37%

COMMENTS

No longer the little-known Global Strategy balanced fund. This $2 billion fund has slipped a bit in the past 18 months after stringing together several first-quartile years while paying out its 35-cent distribution every quarter. This fund is loaded with bank and utility stocks that will come back when the interest rate environment stabilizes. **Smart Fund History: 1999, 1998, 1997.**

RISK

How Often Money was Lost:.......28 of 88 Months
....18 of 86 Quarters
....14 of 77 Years
Worst 3 Months: ....-13.46% (1998)
Best 3 Months:...................................13.04% (1996)

ASSET ALLOCATION

Cdn equities..................................58.6
Preferreds 2
Cash..6.8
Fixed Income 32.6

CANADIAN BALANCED

COMPARISON OF FUND TO INDEXES

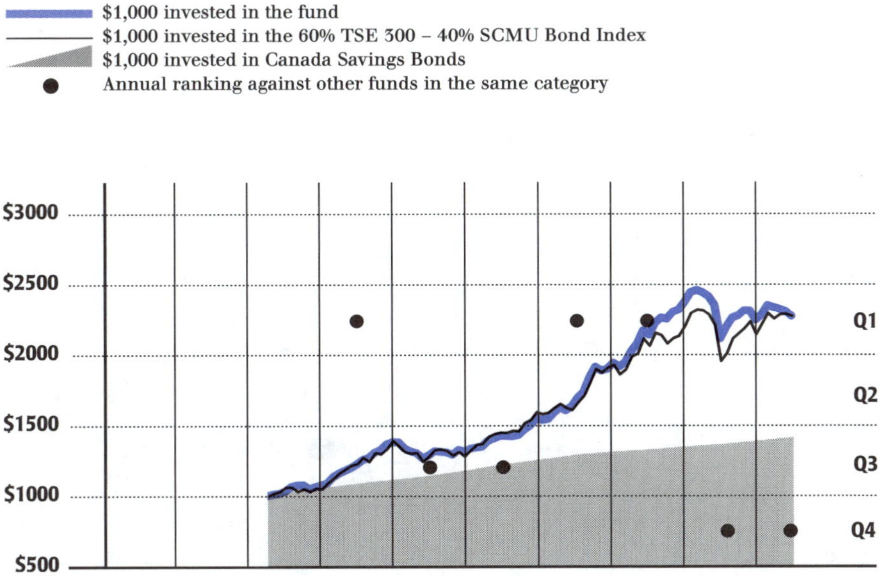

Annual	**1990**		**1992**		**1994**		**1996**		**1998**	**8/31/99**
Return (%)				28.7	-3.0	13.1	25.8	22.1	0.4	-1.7
Compound	**10 yr**	**9 yr**	**8 yr**	**7 yr**	**6 yr**	**5 yr**	**4 yr**	**3 yr**	**2 yr**	**1 yr**
Return (%)				11.4	10.4	11.5	12.4	10.3	3.0	7.5

INDUSTRIAL PENSION

LOAD

Primary Objective:	Growth & Income
Sponsor:	Mackenzie Financial
Fund Manager:	Bill Procter
Style:	Bottom-up
Size (MMs):	$273.567
RRSP:	100%
Expense Ratio:	2.31%

COMMENTS

This is a top-performing balanced fund from the Industrial family of Mackenzie from a family that can give you two other very good balanced funds. Ivy Growth & Income and Universal Canadian Balanced both deserve Smart Fund recognition, but we went with Industrial Pension for its uniqueness. Manager Bill Procter revitalized this former chronic fourth-quartile performer. The fund has one of the higher volatilities, as measured by standard deviation, in the balanced class. This one is more equity oriented, with about 70 to 75% of the fund in equities. There have been very few distributions for the last three years. **Smart Fund History: 1999, 1998.**

RISK

How Often Money was Lost:.....50 of 116 Months
.....42 of 114 Quarters
.....35 of 105 Years
Worst 3 Months:.....-16.06% (1998)
Best 3 Months:.....21.73% (1993)

ASSET ALLOCATION

Industrial products 20
Financial services 16
Natural resources.....12
Cash 8
Fixed income.....24
Other 20

COMPARISON OF FUND TO INDEXES

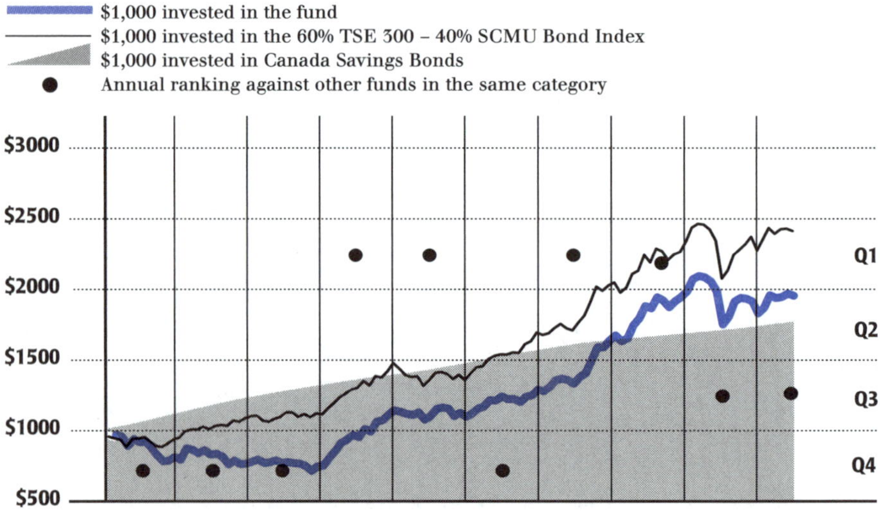

Annual	1990		1992		1994		1996		1998	8/31/99
Return (%)	-20.5	-5.7	-2.7	50.5	1.0	11.4	27.6	20.7	1.0	1.1

Compound	10 yr	9 yr	8 yr	7 yr	6 yr	5 yr	4 yr	3 yr	2 yr	1 yr
Return (%)	6.3	9.5	11.7	14.5	11.8	11.3	12.6	12.4	2.4	11.7

CANADIAN BALANCED

INVESTORS MUTUAL OF CANADA LOAD

Primary Objective:	Growth & Income
Sponsor:	Investors Group
Fund Manager:	Geoff Barth
Style:	Bottom-up
Size (MMs):	$1,121.200
RRSP:	100%
Expense Ratio:	2.38%

COMMENTS

With the high MERs on the IG Sceptre Canadian Balanced and the GS Rothschild Balanced, we are suggesting this one from Investors Group and buy the others directly from Sceptre and Global Strategy. So far this one is having a solid 1999 and its three-year CAGR is about 10%. **New Smart Fund.**

RISK

How Often Money was Lost:.....44 of 116 Months
.....31 of 114 Quarters
.....14 of 105 Years
Worst 3 Months:.....-17.15% (1998)
Best 3 Months:.....12.34% (1997)

ASSET ALLOCATION

Cdn equities.....40.1
Foreign equities.....20.5
Preferreds.....7.8
Cash.....6.3
Fixed income.....25.3

COMPARISON OF FUND TO INDEXES

$1,000 invested in the fund
$1,000 invested in the 60% TSE 300 – 40% SCMU Bond Index
$1,000 invested in Canada Savings Bonds
Annual ranking against other funds in the same category

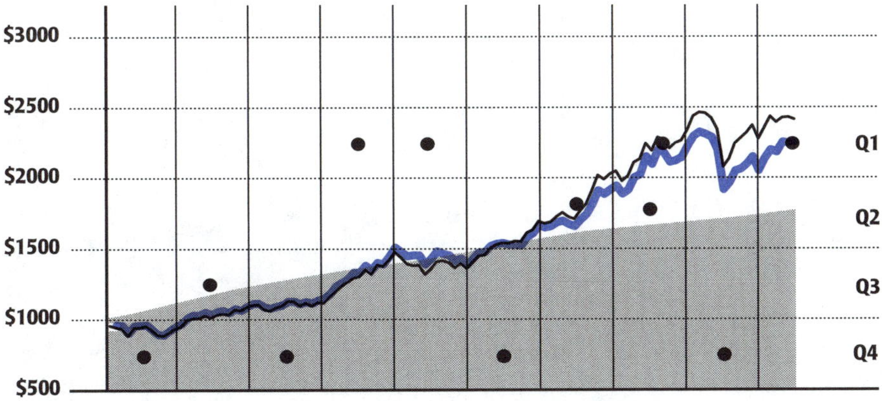

Annual Return (%)	1990		1992		1994		1996		1998	8/31/99
	-6.3	15.1	3.9	27.8	-0.8	12.5	17.3	12.6	-1.1	7.6

Compound Return (%)	10 yr	9 yr	8 yr	7 yr	6 yr	5 yr	4 yr	3 yr	2 yr	1 yr
	8.5	10.5	10.0	10.5	8.6	8.9	10.3	9.9	3.8	17.9

LEITH WHEELER CANADIAN BALANCED FUND **NO LOAD**

Primary Objective:	Growth & Income
Sponsor:	Leith Wheeler Investment Counsel
Fund Manager:	Team
Style:	Bottom-up
Size (MMs):	$198.742
RRSP:	100%
Expense Ratio:	1.10%

CANADIAN BALANCED

COMMENTS

The MER of 1.1% is roughly between the 1.4% of the pure Canadian equity fund and the 0.75% of the fixed-income fund. Of the Smart Funds in this category, only PH&N has a lower MER. From 1987 until 1994, this was the only retail-level fund in the Leith Wheeler family. Its 10-year CAGR to August was a first-quartile return of 9.6%. It carries a hefty $50,000 minimum investment, but the performance is there. In only one year (1995) in the last seven was the fund below second quartile. Over that same time span its worst calendar return was 1.7%. You may have difficulty getting this one other than dealing directly with Leith Wheeler. **Smart Fund History: 1999.**

RISK

How Often Money was Lost:.....42 of 116 Months
....25 of 114 Quarters
....11 of 105 Years
Worst 3 Months:..............................-12.69% (1998)
Best 3 Months:..................................11.96% (1996)

ASSET ALLOCATION

Cdn equities..................................39.4
US equities...................................16.8
Cdn bonds.....................................36.8
Cash 7.0

COMPARISON OF FUND TO INDEXES

$1,000 invested in the fund
$1,000 invested in the 60% TSE 300 – 40% SCMU Bond Index
$1,000 invested in Canada Savings Bonds
● Annual ranking against other funds in the same category

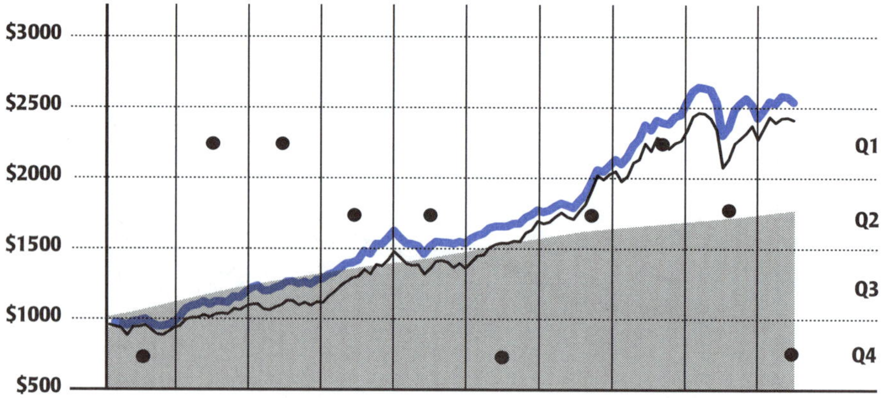

Annual Return (%)	**1990**		**1992**		**1994**		**1996**		**1998**	**8/31/99**
	-3.1	21.8	7.7	23.5	-1.7	12.5	17.6	19.1	5.4	-1.1

Compound Return (%)	**10 yr**	**9 yr**	**8 yr**	**7 yr**	**6 yr**	**5 yr**	**4 yr**	**3 yr**	**2 yr**	**1 yr**
	9.6	11.3	10.8	10.5	9.4	10.5	11.3	11.4	4.1	10.2

PH&N BALANCED FUND

NO LOAD

Primary Objective: Growth & Income
Sponsor: Phillips, Hager & North Investment Counsel
Fund Manager: Team
Style: Bottom-up
Size (MMs): $614.862
RRSP: 100%
Expense Ratio: 0.91%

COMMENTS

For conservative investors, this is as close as it gets to being a one-stop Canadian RRSP holding. This low-MER balanced fund could be the holding for anyone who can reach their minimum threshold. The fund ranges from 45 to 65% equities, 30 to 50% fixed income, and 0 to 30% cash. This five-time Smart Fund might be the best in the category. Consistently good performance, low volatility, add one of the lowest MERs in the category, at 0.91%. Fund has been first or second quartile every year since its inception in 1992. **Smart fund History: 1999, 1998, 1997, 1996.**

RISK

How Often Money was Lost:.......29 of 95 Months
.......23 of 93 Quarters
.......3 of 84 Years
Worst 3 Months: ....-12.10% (1998)
Best 3 Months:.......12.42% (1996)

ASSET ALLOCATION

Cdn equities.......54.8
Cash.......6.2
Fixed Income 39.0

COMPARISON OF FUND TO INDEXES

$1,000 invested in the fund
$1,000 invested in the 60% TSE 300 – 40% SCMU Bond Index
$1,000 invested in Canada Savings Bonds
Annual ranking against other funds in the same category

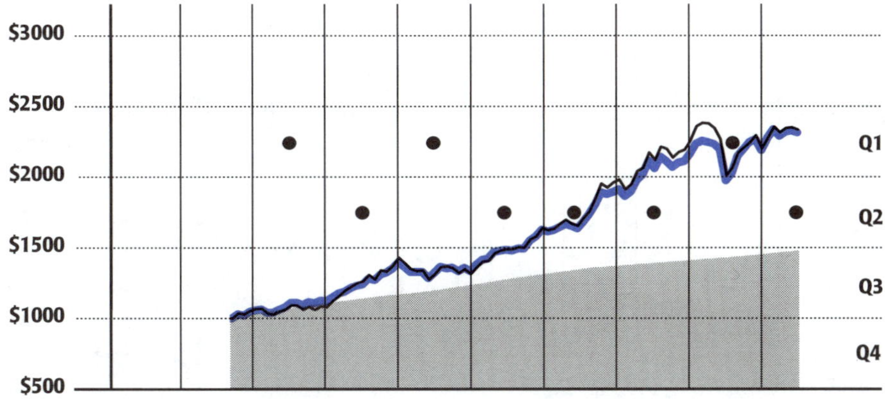

Annual Return (%)	1990		1992		1994		1996		1998	8/31/99
			7.4	20.2	0.4	16.4	18.8	11.8	7.1	3.0

Compound Return (%)	10 yr	9 yr	8 yr	7 yr	6 yr	5 yr	4 yr	3 yr	2 yr	1 yr
				11.1	10.4	11.1	11.8	11.2	6.0	17.2

SCEPTRE BALANCED GROWTH **NO LOAD**

Primary Objective: Growth & Income
Sponsor: Sceptre Investment Counsel
Fund Manager: Lyle Stein
Style: Top-down
Size (MMs): $185.108
RRSP: 100%
Expense Ratio: 1.46%

CANADIAN BALANCED

COMMENTS

Lyle Stein won the 1996 and 1997 Mutual Funds Awards for the top balanced fund after generating top-quartile performance in 1995, 1996, and 1997. It took a big dip in 1998 when Stein turned bearish and went to fixed income. The top holding in Sceptre International Equity has really hurt the fund and must be removed. There are no restraints on asset mix, giving Stein the freedom to go with whatever asset class will outperform. We will stick with Stein for another year to see if the magic comes back. Like all of the Sceptre funds, this one is in the lowest quartile for its MER. **Smart Fund History: 1999, 1998, 1997.**

RISK

How Often Money was Lost:.....39 of 116 Months
.....31 of 114 Quarters
.....14 of 105 Years
Worst 3 Months: .....-12.35% (1998)
Best 3 Months:.....13.72% (1996)

ASSET ALLOCATION

Cdn bonds	42.2
Cdn equities	38.4
Mutual funds	5.8
US equities	5.2
Cash	4.1
Other	4.3

COMPARISON OF FUND TO INDEXES

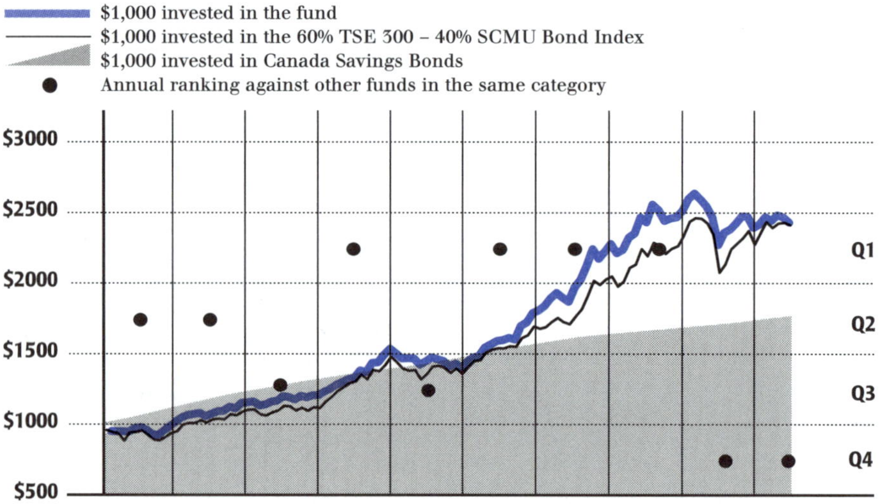

Annual Return (%)	1990		1992		1994		1996		1998	8/31/99
	-0.6	16.5	4.7	23.9	-4.2	20.4	26.0	14.1	0.5	-1.8

Compound Return (%)	10 yr	9 yr	8 yr	7 yr	6 yr	5 yr	4 yr	3 yr	2 yr	1 yr
	9.4	10.9	10.6	10.8	10.0	10.6	11.2	7.5	0.0	6.9

SCOTIA CANADIAN BALANCED **NO LOAD**

Primary Objective: Growth & Income
Sponsor: Scotia Funds
Fund Manager: Scotia Cassels
Style: Bottom-up
Size (MMs): $1,032.874
RRSP: 100%
Expense Ratio: 1.64%

COMMENTS

A solid balanced from this low-profile bank fund family. This had a 50% weighting in equities and has been generating solid first- and second-quartile performance since 1995. Arguably, the best fund in the Scotia fund line-up, reasonable 1.64% MER combined with first-quartile, five-year performance makes this a core RRSP holding for many Scotia bank clients. **New Smart Fund.**

RISK

How Often Money was Lost:.....35 of 110 Months
.....21 of 108 Quarters
.....8 of 99 Years
Worst 3 Months: .....-10.72% (1998)
Best 3 Months:.....14.00% (1996)

ASSET ALLOCATION

Common equities.....50.5
Canada bonds.....30.0
Corporate bonds.....16.4
Cash.....3.1

COMPARISON OF FUND TO INDEXES

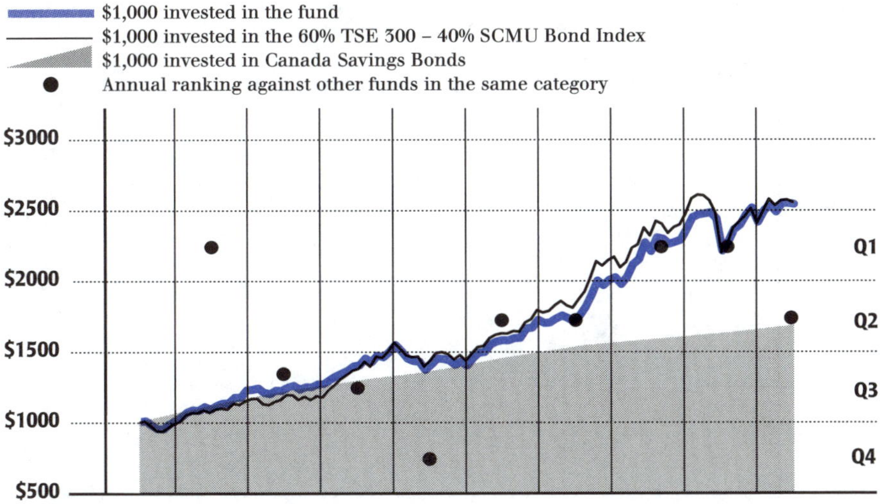

Annual Return (%)	1990		1992		1994		1996		1998	8/31/99
		21.4	4.3	18.0	-4.5	16.8	17.9	15.6	8.5	3.0

Compound Return (%)	10 yr	9 yr	8 yr	7 yr	6 yr	5 yr	4 yr	3 yr	2 yr	1 yr
		11.3	10.8	10.7	9.8	11.9	12.7	13.2	7.3	15.1

SYNCHRONY CONSERVATIVE RRSP PORTFOLIO LOAD

Objective	Growth & Income
Sponsor:	Talvest
Fund Manager:	TAL Investment Counsel
Style:	Fund of Funds
Size (MMs):	$52.787
RRSP:	100%
Expense Ratio:	3.00%

COMMENTS

Another seg fund product. This one from Talvest. You pay 3% MER to sleep at night with a guaranteed mutual fund. This one offers daily resets to lock in gains as they happen. The fund is a fund of funds offered by Talvest and Maritime Life. **New Smart Fund.**

CANADIAN BALANCED

RISK

How Often Money was Lost:.........3 of 10 Months
.........1 of 8 Quarters
.........0 of 0 Years
Worst 3 Months: ....-0.16% (1999)
Best 3 Months:.........5.38% (1999)

ASSET ALLOCATION

Talvest Foreign Pay.........15.0
Maritime Bond Fund.........22.0
Maritime Diversified Equity.........12.0
Talvest Cdn. Equity Growth.........41.0
Talvest Global Equity.........10.0

COMPARISON OF FUND TO INDEXES

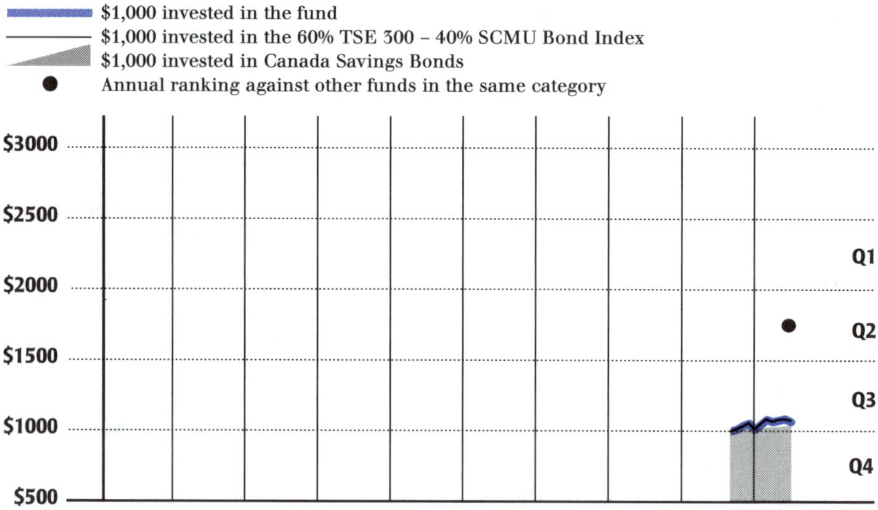

Annual Return (%)	1990		1992		1994		1996		1998	8/31/99
										2.6

Compound Return (%)	10 yr	9 yr	8 yr	7 yr	6 yr	5 yr	4 yr	3 yr	2 yr	1 yr

TEMPLETON BALANCED GIF

LOAD

Primary Objective:	Growth & Income
Sponsor:	Templeton Investment
Fund Manager:	George Morgan
Style:	Bottom-up, Value
Size (MMs):	$10.935
RRSP:	100%
Expense Ratio:	2.82%

COMMENTS

Use the conservative Templeton management and then wrap a guarantee on it may seem like wearing a belt and suspenders, but for those Y2K-sensitive RSP investors, this might be the single best fund. The underlying Templeton Balanced fund has returned an average of 10.4% for the five years ended August 31. Fund was about 65% weighted in equities at June 30. **New Smart Fund.**

RISK

How Often Money was Lost:.........3 of 11 Months
....2 of 9 Quarters
....0 of 0 Years
Worst 3 Months: ....-4.00% (1999)
Best 3 Months:....................................9.31% (1999)

ASSET ALLOCATION

Cdn equities..................................64.4
Bonds 32.1
Cash..3.2
Preferreds 0.3

COMPARISON OF FUND TO INDEXES

$1,000 invested in the fund
$1,000 invested in the 60% TSE 300 – 40% SCMU Bond Index
$1,000 invested in Canada Savings Bonds
Annual ranking against other funds in the same category

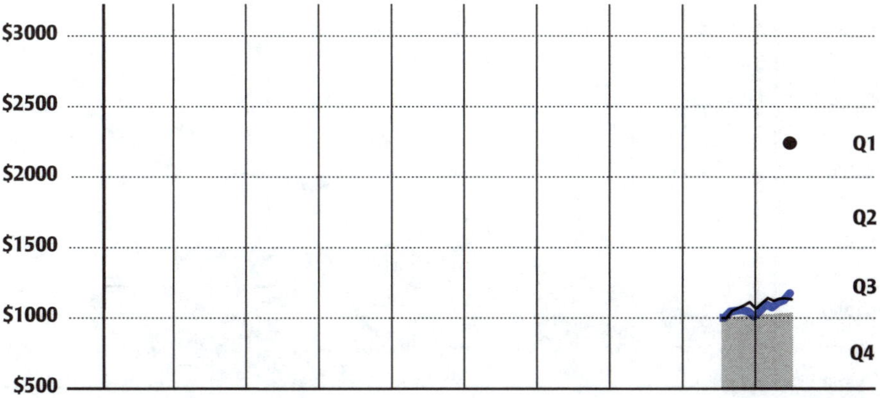

Annual Return (%)	1990		1992		1994		1996		1998	8/31/99
										11.4

Compound Return (%)	10 yr	9 yr	8 yr	7 yr	6 yr	5 yr	4 yr	3 yr	2 yr	1 yr

TRIMARK INCOME GROWTH

LOAD

Primary Objective: Growth & Income
Sponsor: Trimark Investment Management
Fund Manager: Pat Farmer, Keith Graham, & Geoff McDonald
Style: Bottom-up
Size (MMs): $842.365
RRSP: 100%
Expense Ratio: 1.56%

COMMENTS

Formerly, the automatic broker and dealer's choice for a balanced fund. From 1991 through 1996 the fund was either first or second quartile and then suffered back-to-back fourth-quartile years. Equity manager Vito Maida was replaced, and the fund, thanks to its overweighting in resource stocks, has climbed back to first quartile in 1999. Patrick Farmer's fixed-income picks have added stability to the fund. It has a low MER of 1.52% and is one of the least volatile in the category. **Smart Fund History: 1999, 1998, 1997, 1996.**

RISK

How Often Money was Lost:.....39 of 116 Months
.....28 of 114 Quarters
.....14 of 105 Years
Worst 3 Months:.....-13.20% (1998)
Best 3 Months:.....12.26% (1991)

ASSET ALLOCATION

Cdn equities.....33.7
Corporate bonds.....14.8
US equities.....14.8
Foreign equities.....6.4
Canada bonds.....23.5
Other.....6.8

COMPARISON OF FUND TO INDEXES

$1,000 invested in the fund
$1,000 invested in the 60% TSE 300 – 40% SCMU Bond Index
$1,000 invested in Canada Savings Bonds
● Annual ranking against other funds in the same category

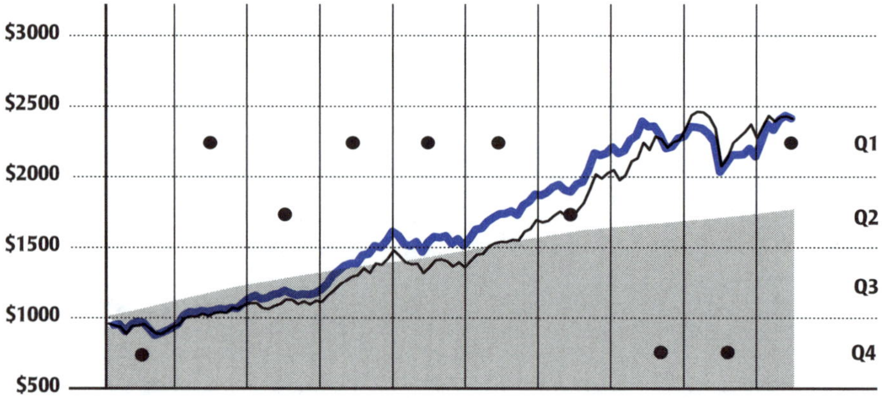

Annual Return (%)	1990		1992		1994		1996		1998	8/31/99
	-7.2	19.2	6.0	31.9	0.9	17.0	17.8	3.0	-2.5	11.9

Compound Return (%)	10 yr	9 yr	8 yr	7 yr	6 yr	5 yr	4 yr	3 yr	2 yr	1 yr
	9.3	11.3	10.8	10.9	8.9	8.9	8.6	7.5	1.3	18.7

AGF AMERICAN TACTICAL ASSET ALLOCATION **LOAD**

Primary Objective:	Growth & Income
Sponsor:	AGF Funds Inc.
Fund Manager:	Kathy Taylor, Barclays Global Investors
Style:	Value
Size (MMs):	$681.248
RRSP:	20%
Expense Ratio:	2.56%

COMMENTS

Available in RSP version

This would be a solid addition to any portfolio. It is focused only on the U.S. market, so it is not quite as diversified as others in the category. This fund has shown positive returns in each year back to 1989. First-quartile performer for ten-, five-, three-, two-, and one-year CAGR to August 31, 1999. This one has an outstanding risk-adjusted return (10-year CAGR of 14.2%) as Barclays actively manages the asset mix. Fund was 60% S&P 500 and 40% bonds at mid-year down from 80% equities early in 1999. **New Smart Fund.**

RISK

How Often Money was Lost:.....35 of 116 Months
....27 of 114 Quarters
....3 of 105 Years
Worst 3 Months: ....-3.99% (1994)
Best 3 Months:..................16.26% (1998)

ASSET ALLOCATION

S&P 500 Index 60.0
Lehman Brothers
long bond index 40.0

COMPARISON OF FUND TO INDEXES

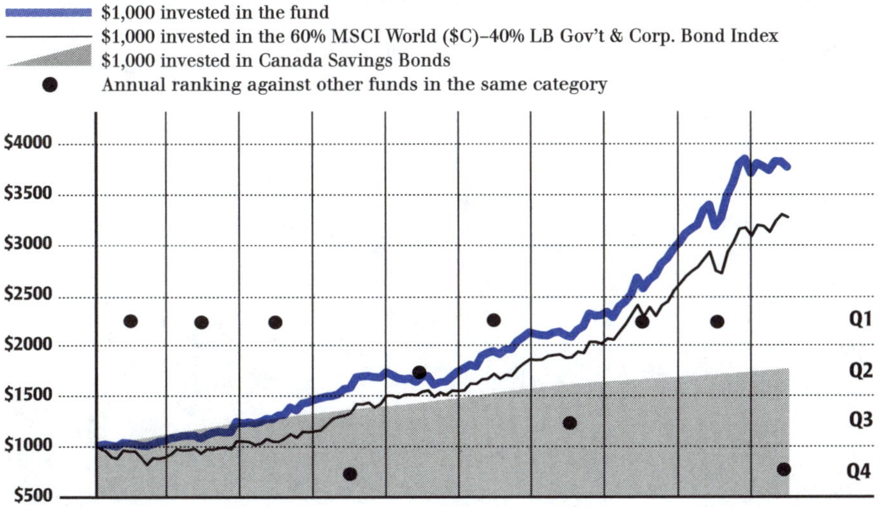

Annual Return (%)	**1990**		**1992**		**1994**		**1996**		**1998**	**8/31/99**
	5.3	18.2	15.3	17.3	0.6	22.9	10.0	24.9	32.6	-0.8

Compound Return (%)	**10 yr**	**9 yr**	**8 yr**	**7 yr**	**6 yr**	**5 yr**	**4 yr**	**3 yr**	**2 yr**	**1 yr**
	14.2	15.8	16.2	16.2	14.3	17.3	18.4	21.8	21.3	18.3

C.I. INTERNATIONAL BALANCED RSP LOAD

Primary Objective:	Growth & Income
Sponsor:	CI Mutual Funds
Fund Manager:	Bill Sterling, BEA Associates
Style:	Top-Down
Size (MMs):	$633.734
RRSP:	100%
Expense Ratio:	2.46%

COMMENTS

The major strength of this fund is the asset allocation decisions made by Bill Sterling. This has previously been a top-quartile performer, which has slipped a bit. Still it has had steady double-digit returns each of the last four years. Fund has 58% in equities, mostly large-cap U.S. growth stocks with GE, Intel, Microsoft, Cisco, AT&T, and Merck all in the top ten holdings. Steady performer that does not tie up your foreign content and could be considered a core holding in your RRSP. This one should pick up as the fund will now better track the performance of the first-quartile parent fund, CI International Balanced. **Smart Fund History: 1999, 1998, 1997.**

RISK

How Often Money was Lost:.......14 of 57 Months
....11 of 55 Quarters
....0 of 46 Years
Worst 3 Months: ....-3.89% (1998)
Best 3 Months:...................................10.36% (1997)

ASSET ALLOCATION

Equities...57.5
Cash & equivalents......................22.5
Bonds 20.0

COMPARISON OF FUND TO INDEXES

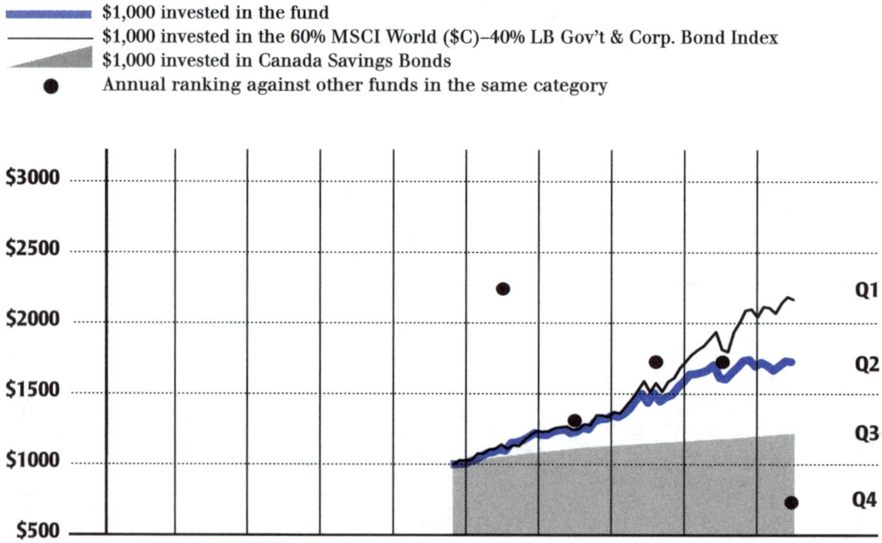

Annual	**1990**		**1992**		**1994**		**1996**		**1998**	**8/31/99**
Return (%)						19.6	10.5	13.2	16.2	-0.5
Compound	**10 yr**	**9 yr**	**8 yr**	**7 yr**	**6 yr**	**5 yr**	**4 yr**	**3 yr**	**2 yr**	**1 yr**
Return (%)							12.1	12.0	9.6	7.1

FIDELITY GLOBAL ASSET ALLOCATION **LOAD**

Primary Objective:	Growth & Income
Sponsor:	Fidelity Investments Canada
Fund Manager:	Richard Habermann
Style:	Top-down, Growth
Size (MMs):	$837.399
RRSP:	20%
Expense Ratio:	2.59%

COMMENTS

Available in RSP version

This is a solid holding for foreign diversification but more conservative than an all-equity fund. Smart Fund readers should consider the RSP-version of this fund, which does not tie up foreign content. Manager Dick Habermann and Bill Eigen determine the asset mix, then use the picks from the equity managers representing the regions. The fund does not sway too far from index country weightings but will move the equity/fixed-income mix. This one has more than tripled in size since the end of 1997 to $840 million at August 31. The fund was first quartile for 1996, 1997, and 1998, and has a three-year CAGR of almost 20%, which has been fuelled by the 70% weighting in U.S. equities. **Smart Fund History: 1999.**

RISK

How Often Money was Lost:.......26 of 79 Months
....18 of 77 Quarters
....7 of 68 Years
Worst 3 Months: ....-6.48% (1998)
Best 3 Months:..................................14.49% (1998)

ASSET ALLOCATION

Foreign equities 72.9
Foreign bonds..............................17.1
Cash & equivalents........................7.9
Canadian equities..........................1.4
Canada bonds................................0.7

COMPARISON OF FUND TO INDEXES

$1,000 invested in the fund
$1,000 invested in the 60% MSCI World ($C)–40% LB Gov't & Corp. Bond Index
$1,000 invested in Canada Savings Bonds
Annual ranking against other funds in the same category

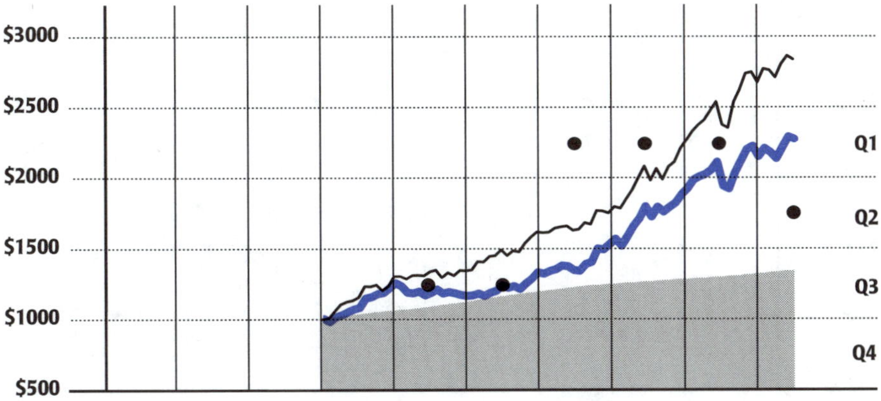

Annual Return (%)	**1990**		**1992**		**1994**		**1996**		**1998**	**8/31/99**
					-4.1	10.0	16.0	22.1	20.7	3.4

Compound Return (%)	**10 yr**	**9 yr**	**8 yr**	**7 yr**	**6 yr**	**5 yr**	**4 yr**	**3 yr**	**2 yr**	**1 yr**
					12.1	13.5	16.8	19.2	14.8	17.1

UNIVERSAL WORLD BALANCED RRSP

LOAD

Primary Objective: Growth & Income
Sponsor: Mackenzie Financial
Fund Manager: Richard Gluck & Barbara Trebbi
Style: Top-down
Size (MMs): $495.477
RRSP: 100%
Expense Ratio: 2.31%

COMMENTS

A Smart Fund regular that generates second-quartile returns in a fund that doesn't tie up your foreign content. Only hold this one in your RRSP. By using futures to buy indexes in the major markets, managers Barbara Trebbi and Michael Landry can concentrate on the individual selections in the emerging markets. Fund has decreased its weighting in emerging markets to 11%. This might be just the right amount of emerging market exposure for investors. This one has been more volatile than other funds in the category because of its emerging markets exposure. **Smart Fund History: 1999, 1998, 1997.**

RISK

How Often Money was Lost:.......24 of 66 Months
.......19 of 64 Quarters
.......4 of 55 Years
Worst 3 Months:.......-8.41% (1997)
Best 3 Months:.......15.00% (1998)

ASSET ALLOCATION

Developed markets 45
Federal & corporate bonds.......33
Emerging markets 11
Cash & equivalents 11

INTERNATIONAL BALANCED

COMPARISON OF FUND TO INDEXES

$1,000 invested in the fund
$1,000 invested in the 60% MSCI World ($C)–40% LB Gov't & Corp. Bond Index
$1,000 invested in Canada Savings Bonds
Annual ranking against other funds in the same category

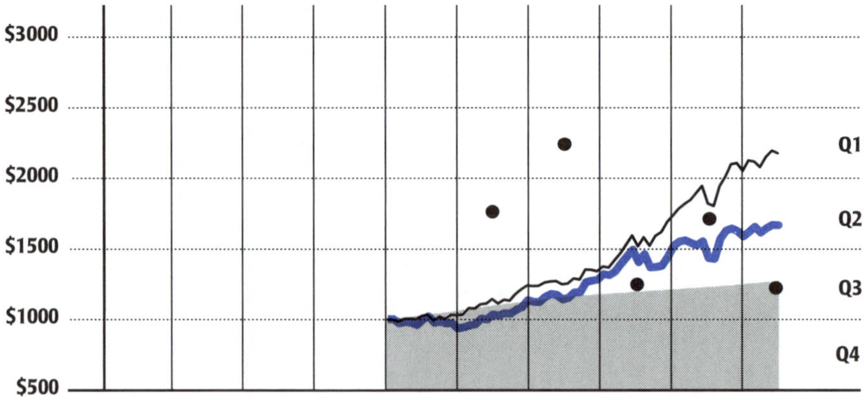

	1990		1992		1994		1996		1998	8/31/99
Annual Return (%)						11.6	17.3	8.4	19.1	0.8

Compound Return (%)	10 yr	9 yr	8 yr	7 yr	6 yr	5 yr	4 yr	3 yr	2 yr	1 yr
						10.2	12.8	12.9	8.6	15.5

Index of Smart Funds